Lev Razgon in 1991. Photo: A. Volodin.

LEV
RAZGON

TRUE
STORIES

TRANSLATED BY JOHN CROWFOOT

ARDIS

Ardis Publishers
24721 El Camino Capistrano
Dana Point, California 92629

Library of Congress Cataloging-in-Publication Data

Razgon, Lev Emmanuilovich.
[Nepridumannoe. English]
True Stories : the memoirs of Lev Razgon / translated by John Crowfoot.
p.   cm.
ISBN 0-87501-108-X (Cloth, alk. paper)
1. Razgon, Lev Emmanuilovich–Friends and associates.
2. Political prisoners–Soviet Union–Biography.
3. Political persecution–Soviet Union.   4. Soviet Union–Politics and
government–1936-1953.   I. Title.
DK268.R39A3   1996
365'.45'092247—dc20   94-9229
[B]   CIP

CONTENTS

BIOGRAPHICAL NOTE

LEV EMMANUILOVICH RAZGON was born in 1908 in the small Belorussian town of Gorky. In the early 1920s his family moved to Moscow. His father, Emmanuel, remained an unassuming factory worker (in a memoir of their pre-revolutionary life, Razgon describes him as preferring to play the flute to regularly attending synagogue). Emmanuel's sons, however, made rapid and successful careers for themselves and none more so than the third son, Lev, who became a journalist and then married into one of the leading families of the new Soviet elite.

In 1938 this new life abruptly ended. For the next eighteen years Lev Razgon would either be held in labor camps or would lead a precarious existence, exiled to various provincial towns. In 1956 he was rehabilitated and re-admitted to the Party. He resumed his literary activities. At the same time he privately began to record the vanished world and names of the pre-war years, before the revolution finally turned on its own children.

With the coming of perestroika, Razgon was able to publish his memoirs in Russia, to great acclaim. He left the Communist Party and was among the founding members of Memorial, the organization that commemorates the the countless victims of the Bolshevik regime.

Today Lev Razgon lives in Moscow, where, together with other notable public figures, he sits on the Presidential Clemency Commission which weekly examines appeals by convicted criminal offenders and, especially, those sentenced to capital punishment.

J. C.

A CHRONOLOGY OF THE LIFE OF LEV RAZGON

1908 LEV RAZGON BORN IN SHTETL IN GORKI, WESTERN BELORUSSIA, TO A FAMILY WHOSE MEMBERS GOT IN TROUBLE WITH THE GOVERNMENT FOR GENERATIONS

1922 THE RAZGON FAMILY MOVES TO MOSCOW

1927-28 RAZGON STUDIES HISTORY AT MOSCOW UNIVERSITY

1929-30 RAZGON GRADUATES, BECOMES PARTY MEMBER. BEGINS WORK AS A JOURNALIST AND AS A WRITER OF BOOKS FOR YOUNG ADULTS

1932-33 MARRIES OKSANA BOKY, DAUGHTER OF GLEB BOKY, A HIGH-RANKING SECRET POLICEMAN IN LENINGRAD. SUBSEQUENTLY OKSANA BECOMES STEP-DAUGHTER OF IVAN MOSKVIN, A MEMBER OF THE CENTRAL COMMITTEE

1934 RAZGON ATTENDS THE 17TH PARTY CONGRESS

1936 ARRESTS OF LEADING POLITICAL FIGURES, GREAT SHOW TRIALS BEGIN

1937 RAZGON'S FATHER-IN-LAW ARRESTED, ALONG WITH MANY FRIENDS AND ACQUAINTANCES OF THE FAMILY

1938 RAZGON AND HIS WIFE OKSANA ARRESTED; SHE DIES IN THE TRANSIT PRISON ON THE WAY TO A NORTHERN CAMP

1941 CONDITIONS IN ALL CAMPS RAPIDLY DETERIORATE AFTER HITLER ATTACKS THE SOVIET UNION

1945 END OF WAR; RAZGON GETS CONDITIONAL RELEASE—BUT HE IS FORBIDDEN TO RETURN TO MOSCOW, LIVES PRECARIOUSLY IN VARIOUS PROVINCIAL TOWNS

1949-50 REARREST OF RAZGON AND HIS SECOND WIFE, RIKA (REBECCA) BERG, THE DAUGHTER OF A LEADING FIGURE WHO OPPOSED THE BOLSHEVIK PARTY, A MAN WHO WAS IMPRISONED IN THE 1920S

1953-56 STALIN DIES. RAZGON AND HIS WIFE RETURN FROM CAMPS. RAZGON RETURNS TO WRITING CHILDREN'S LITERATURE

1988-97 FIRST INSTALLMENTS OF RAZGON'S MEMOIR, *NEPRIDUMANNOE* PUBLISHED; WITH BOOK PUBLICATION A YEAR LATER, RAZGON BECOMES ONE OF RUSSIA'S MOST POPULAR AUTHORS. HIS MEMOIRS ARE TRANSLATED INTO ALL MAJOR EUROPEAN LANGUAGES; A DOCUMENTARY FILM OF HIS LIFE IS MADE IN RUSSIA.

PREFACE

"What can my name mean to you?" This line from Pushkin comes to mind when I imagine my Western readers. They have already read so much about mass executions, terror, wrecked lives and decimated families that it will probably strike them as absurd to offer yet another book on the subject. But do you remember how *Anna Karenina* begins? "Each unhappy family is unhappy in its own way." The last four words indeed constitute the interest and value, both for the reader and the author himself.

The tales in this book evoke my own story, that of my family and friends, and of the numerous people I met during seventeen years in prison, on transports and in exile. I still cannot understand, even today, by what miracle I remained alive, and why I did not share the fate of those millions who lie in unmarked graves and are now among the principal fossil remains beneath the earth of my vast native land. I cannot explain why I survived, just as the soldier who returns from the war, safe and sound, cannot explain why the bullet missed him. In part, though, I attribute this happy outcome to my insatiable curiosity, to a genuine interest in those who slept, like me, on the plank beds of the camp barracks, with whom I was marched across the Northern forests and with whom I chatted when we were felling trees. Whether it was the President's wife, a village teacher or blacksmith, I found them all interesting. For each of them possessed that quality which makes human beings unique, and permits us to say, there is no one else like this person... When it became possible to write about such matters our magazines took a great interest in the famous and notable victims of the Soviet terror—from generals and other such dignitaries, to aristocrats, royal princes and the last Tsar himself. That enthusiasm was quite legitimate. I am simply of the opinion that the life of a peasant is no less valuable than that of an emperor. At times, indeed, it proves to be more intriguing.

But curiosity is not everything. I did not intend to deliver a "brief and moving lecture" to my reader. My publishers, I am sure, have many reasons for wishing to translate this book. Wherever we live, whoever we are, we are all members of the same human race. It is customary, at such moments, to recall the words of John Donne: "...Any Man's death diminishes me, because I am involved in Mankinde; And therefore never send to know for whom the bell tolls, It tolls for thee."

Violent death ended not one but millions of lives in our country. The steam roller of Stalin's terror crushed an incalculable number of victims. The cracking of their bones still rings in the ears of all humanity, prompting numerous memoirs, books, stories and academic studies. This book is an inseparable part of that reaction.

The reader should not be astounded to meet executioners in my book as well as their victims. The jailers stood side by side with their prisoners. Our life was a surreal existence in which all were either victim or perpetrator. And if there were innumerable victims, the numbers of jailers and butchers were also legion. To shoot a million people requires a great many executioners. Thousands, tens of thousands, were engaged in killing others, washing away the blood, carting off the corpses, digging the trenches and burying or burning the bodies. How many were there in the "Gulag Archipelago" who guarded the prisoners, sent them out to labor in murderous conditions and shot them, on orders or without reason, if it was necessary? That still leaves out the most awful figures of all. They never killed or tortured anyone with their own hands, and never saw a dead body. They were content to remain in their handsome comfortable carpeted offices, with shaded lamps on large desks, at which they drafted and signed documents. Absentmindedly they added signatures of approval or beside some surname, they wrote in the coded letters, EM, "extreme measure" (i.e. death penalty), or, more simply S, to be shot. I have never had the opportunity to visit such curious persons, and I hope that others, who know them better, will be able to describe them. For one cannot draw the line at Stalin and the dozen psychopaths who gravitated around him! The most notorious and odious were shot or retired as soon as the Leader died. In this way it was hoped one could stop up the vast and hungry mouth of justice. Yet there are several hundred thousand others who are still alive today, some much younger than myself. They live among us, the people of my fate, and visit the same theaters and cinemas; on occasion we even find ourselves sitting side by side, in a mutual friend's house, exchanging smiles and sharing a convivial glass or two of vodka. After all, you cannot read a person's past in his face ...

In the past we spent decades, side by side. The jailers, to me, were also human beings and I tried eagerly to discover what we shared in common, and what divided us. The Gulag is a very special system and, undoubtedly, has no equal in history. It was distinguished, above all, by its extent and continuity in time and space. If the prisoner did not quickly die, then he or she spent not one, and not two decades in the Gulag but remained its captive for years on end. Whether you like it or not, it is life of a kind. It has its own customs, joys and sorrows, its loves and partings, friendships and betrayals. No matter how perverse and anomalous that universe was, it was nevertheless peopled by ordinary human beings. All of this is more or less represented here. I do not know how well I have been able to reflect that life in my book. I think, though, for such was my intention, that the reader will find no hatred in what I have written. I may detest and despise or feel many other emotions—but not the blind hatred that prevents us from telling the truth. I can also assure the reader, on my word of honor, that nothing here has been invented. Not a date, a name or an episode.

I would like to end with a word about my readers, whether in Russia or abroad. When an author pretends that he is writing for "no one," and that he puts pen to paper "for himself alone," then he is lying, consciously or not. However much he may be carried away by his creative impulse, this does not prevent the writer from engaging with readers and talking to them. I am no exception. I was convinced, however, that these stories would never be published and that neither its author nor my contemporaries, even those many years younger, would live to see this book appear. I wrote for a small group of my immediate family and friends. There remained a secret hope, I confess, that perhaps in the distant future the truth would become known and everyone would hear about those I have described.

I knew then that no one else would summon back to life or even remember these numerous individuals who disappeared in the Gulag. And if I left this life without recording things which only I remembered then I would have in some sense committed a sin. Thus, over twenty years, in moments of leisure and with frequent interruptions, I wrote these memoirs.

Lev Razgon

Lev Razgon, right, with his brother Israel, 1925.

First row, third from left: Gleb Boky, the highly-placed member of the Cheka and
then the OGPU (who became Razgon's father-in-law), sailing with his
OGPU colleagues in 1928.

THE PRESIDENT'S WIFE

A Saturday evening in summer. It would remain light all night through, but we had finished work long ago and I should have been on my way by now. I usually spent my brief weekends at Ustvymlag headquarters in Vozhael, and was used to covering the thirty kilometers from our camp on foot, and making the same journey back twenty-four hours later. In winter the road was packed down hard and smooth as asphalt, the cold air was exhilarating, and I had little difficulty putting the distance, almost a full marathon, briskly behind me. In summer the surface was churned up into fine, shifting sand by the wheels of lorries and the going was much tougher. I would seize any opportunity of a lift.

A likely-looking vehicle was standing outside the camp gates. It was a small, cross-country "Kozlik," a Soviet version of the jeep. For all its toy-like appearance it was capable of speeding me to Vozhael in just over an hour. Some top brass from the medical section had arrived in it a few hours earlier: the head of our medical department had brought over a colonel who was deputy Chief Medical Officer for the whole Gulag. Why not try getting a lift with them? After all, I was a free man now and, in theory at least, the equal of any of them.

The brass came out of the camp and moved towards their jeep. I went over to our doctor. "Comrade Major! If you have a spare seat in your vehicle may I ask you to take me to Vozhael?"

I was counting on the major's reputation as a fair-minded, even sympathetic man, and I was not disappointed. The tall colonel, with green tabs on his collar and the medical serpent emblazoned on his uniform, treated me with studied politeness. I got in the back beside him and the jeep set off, bumping along the sandy road. The two officers continued a conversation evidently begun back in the camp. Unlike our major, whose entire medical career since graduation had been spent in the camps, the colonel was a newcomer to our particular branch of the state. After studying at the Academy of Military Medicine he had served exclusively in the Army. Needless to say, nothing in their conversation gave me any clue as to why the colonel now found himself working for the Gulag.

Of the two, the colonel was the more talkative, describing life at the front and the interesting people he had met. One of his subordinates had made a particularly strong impression. The colonel had been commanding officer of an army medical corps where the senior surgeon was the son-in-law of Mikhail Kalinin, the "President" of the Soviet Union. This circumstance produced a number of very tangible benefits for his medical personnel, and also resulted in my travelling companion being introduced to Kalinin himself. While on official business with his senior surgeon in Moscow, he was invited out to Kalinin's dacha, where he chatted and dined with our Head of State without the slightest formality.

The colonel's voice trembled with emotion as he described how charming Kalinin had been, how unassuming and steadfast in his beliefs, and he spoke of the high regard in which he was held throughout the country. Then he went on to sing the praises of the son-in-law: how much he regretted their ways had parted. His former subordinate was now working as army surgeon in such-and-such a place, he told the major.

It was then I most unwisely interrupted. In fact Kalinin's son-in-law was currently the chief surgeon at one of the fronts, I told them, and working in quite a different town. The colonel said nothing for a moment. Then he turned to enquire with icy politeness, "Forgive my asking, but how do you know that?"

His tone was so cutting that I calmly replied,

"His wife, Lydia Mikhailovna, told me."

The colonel was silent for quite some time, evidently digesting an unexpected nugget of information obtained from a man with a manifestly murky past. Finally he could contain himself no longer.

"Forgive me again, but when did Lydia Mikhailovna tell you this?"

I had all but burnt my bridges.

"A couple of weeks ago... "

The colonel was now silent for even longer. His face registered hectic, but evidently fruitless, mental activity. Perplexed, but consumed with curiosity, he turned to me again.

"Do forgive me if I seem to be prying... But where did Lydia Mikhailovna tell you this?"

O Lord! Why had I ever got myself involved in this? And our major sitting in the front seat... God only knew what might come of this idiotic conversation. It was too late to think about that now, however.

"We were talking in Vozhael."

This time the colonel reacted instantly.

"No, this really is quite beyond me! What on earth could Lydia Mikhailovna be doing in Vozhael? What could possibly have brought her here?"

I was silent as the tomb. What could I say? For all I knew, the colonel wasn't supposed to be told things that were common knowledge in Ustvymlag.

"Major, perhaps you can enlighten me. What could Lydia Mikhailovna be doing in Vozhael?"

The major answered very coolly,

"She came on a visit to one of the prisoners."

"What do you mean, man? What prisoner could she possibly have been visiting?!"

"Her mother. Kalinin's wife is one of our prisoners here at the

Ustvymlag base camp in Vozhael."

I've seen plenty in my time, but seldom anyone as shocked as the colonel. He clasped his head in his hands and with a groan buried his face between his knees. Rocking from side to side as if he were having a fit, he babbled hysterically and incoherently, the words pouring uncontrollably out of him, "For heaven's sake! This is beyond comprehension. It's beyond belief! The wife of Kalinin? The wife of our president?! No matter what she did or what crime she committed... to put the wife of Kalinin in a common prison, an ordinary labor camp?! Lord above, this is scandalous! Terrible! When was this done? How could it happen? Is it possible? What did the president have to say about it? No, I don't believe it! It can't be true!"

The colonel drew himself up as if about to rise from his seat.

"I wish to pay my respects to her, Major! You must introduce me!"

I was angry with myself for ever getting involved. I found neither the cause of the colonel's hysterics nor his hysteria itself any laughing matter; still it was hard to keep a straight face at the idiotic mouthings of a man who was, after all, deputy Chief Medical Officer of the entire Gulag. I had a fleeting vision of the ever-meticulous president's wife. There she was, sitting in her tiny room in the washhouse at the base camp, carefully scraping nits from the gray, newly-washed, prison-issue long johns with a piece of glass just as the colonel arrived to pay his respects...

* * *

To give the colonel his due, such a violent reaction was a natural response. Even the most hardened found it difficult to accept that Yekaterina Ivanovna, the wife of a leading and much respected figure in the Communist Party, the President, was an ordinary prisoner in a most ordinary labor camp. The intelligence had the potential to shock people a good deal more conversant with the ways of our world than this newcomer to the Gulag.

Even Rika had reacted similarly. It was through her I had first discovered that Yakaterina Kalinin was in our camp.

When Rika was staying over with me one time at Camp No. 1 she told me she had become great friends with an old woman who had recently arrived from another part of the Gulag. Her form stated that she was to be employed only on escorted gang labor, but the doctors at base camp had recategorized her as unfit for heavy labor. They managed to fix her up with a job at the washhouse, picking nits out of the underwear before it was issued to the prisoners who were washing there. Yekaterina Ivanovna lived in the linen room, able at last to rest from the many years she had spent at hard labor. Rika would go to see her every day after finishing work in the office, tak-

ing her some of the better food supplied to the camp's free employees. She enjoyed just sitting and talking to a charming intelligent old
lady. Rika told me she wasn't Russian. She evidently came from one
of the Baltic states but had become totally Russified years ago. She
didn't look like an ordinary working woman, although she had once
mentioned working in a factory a long while back. Her surname was
wholly Russian...

"What is it?" I asked.

"Kalinin."

"She can only be Mikhail Kalinin's wife."

Rika did not throw a fit like the colonel, but she categorically refused to believe me. It was out of the question! And anyway the two
of them were so close that Yekaterina Ivanovna could never have
kept something like that from her. Besides, everybody would be just
bound to know.

For my part I was almost certain I was right. I did not know
Yekaterina Ivanovna personally, but she had been on friendly terms
with my in-laws. In the summer of 1937, we began to find a void
forming around us as our numerous friends and acquaintances vanished and the telephone stopped ringing. Yekaterina Ivanovna was
one of the very few people to continue enquiring after the health of
my wife Oksana, getting her supplies of medicines—unavailable to ordinary mortals—from the Kremlin dispensary. Towards the end of
1937 this source of help dried up, and we learned that Yekaterina
Ivanovna had been arrested.

* * *

To be honest, neither the colonel nor Rika should have been so
thrown by the knowledge that the wife of a Politburo member was in
jail. If members of the Politburo were themselves liable to be arrested
and shot without more ado, why should their wives enjoy special immunity?

We already knew that Stalin, despite his enthusiasm for modern
technology, found it hard to part with the old ways. He saw to it that
many of his henchmen had close relatives arrested and indeed, as I
recall, that applied to every member of his inner circle. One of
Kaganovich's brothers was executed, while another chose to shoot
himself; Stakh Ganetsky, who was married to Shvernik's only daughter and actually lived with them, was arrested and shot; the parents
of Voroshilov's daughter-in-law were arrested, and they also attempted to arrest Yekaterina Davydovna, Voroshilov's own wife;
Paulina Zhemchuzhina, as well as being married to Molotov, was a
People's Commissar—she too was arrested... And the list could go on.

It was not really so surprising, then, that Kalinin's wife should also have been taken away. Especially when Stalin, as it seemed to me, might have old scores to settle with Kalinin. His elderly colleague was an idealist of sorts.

Kalinin himself had long since ceased to be a force to be reckoned with. I was still a free man when they came for his oldest and closest friend, Alexander Shotman. The two of them had been workers and revolutionaries together at the Putilov factory in St. Petersburg before the revolution. I was a friend of Shotman's son and he filled me in on some of the details. It was a fairly typical story for those days. Not only was Shotman a friend of Kalinin's, and a Bolshevik from the earliest days who had also been close to Lenin: as a member of the Central Executive Committee he theoretically enjoyed parliamentary immunity. At the very least, his arrest should have been sanctioned formally by Kalinin, as Chairman of the Executive Committee.

However, they simply arrived at the Shotmans' apartment during the night, put to him the same question they asked of all the Old Bolsheviks: "Do you have weapons or documents relating to Lenin?" and took the old man away. Shotman's wife could hardly bring herself to wait until morning before ringing Kalinin. He was delighted to hear from her, and began to croon down the telephone, "How wonderful to hear from you at last, even if Alexander hasn't found time to phone an old friend for the best part of a week. Imagine abandoning me at a time like this. Tell me, how is his rheumatism? How are the children?"

Shotman's wife interrupted the cheerful banter, "Misha! Surely you know they took Alexander away last night?!"

A protracted silence was disrupted by the old man's despairing cry, "I had no idea! I swear to you, I had no idea!"

That evening Shotman's wife was herself arrested. How many such calls must Kalinin have received!

* * *

Rika remained unconvinced by my arguments. Next time she saw Yekaterina Ivanovna, I suggested, she should give her my regards and ask whether she had any news of the Shotmans. The very next day there was a telephone call for me from the base camp, and I heard Rika's voice crack with emotion, "You were right! It's just as you said!"

Later she described her dramatic conversation with Yekaterina Ivanovna in the washhouse. Hesitantly Rika had passed on my message as instructed. For all her Estonian restraint, Yekaterina Ivanovna turned pale. Rika burst into tears and asked her straight out, "Can this be happening?! Are you really...?"

Yekaterina Kalinin flung her arms around Rika's neck, and they both wept the tears women weep the whole world over, even women as self-possessed and experienced as the wife of the Soviet president.

The arrangements for her arrest had been banal rather than theatrical. She had simply been phoned from the Kremlin couturier's, where she was having a dress made, and asked to come in for a fitting. When she arrived they were already waiting for her.

I have mentioned Yekaterina Ivanovna's typical Estonian taciturnity and her years in the underground as the wife of a professional revolutionary. She was a long-standing revolutionary in her own right and did not readily talk about the things that had happened since that phone call from her dressmaker, but we knew she had had a hard time of it. They threw half the Soviet Criminal Code at her, including the dreaded Article 58:8, Terrorism. Her form was crossed through, which meant that she was to be given hard labor and kept under guard at all times. For the greater part of her ten-year sentence Yekaterina Ivanovna was given the most gruelling work women could be forced to do in the camps. Fortunately, she was a robust woman accustomed to hard work from an early age and she survived. It was only when her previous camp was disbanded during the war and she came to us that a way was found of fixing her up with one of the cushier jobs.

During the last year of the war things began to change for the better. Evidently Kalinin, unlike some of Stalin's other close comrades-in-arms, kept interceding on behalf of his wife. Molotov, on the contrary, uttered never a squeak about Zhemchuzhina and when his daughter first joined the Party she stated that her father was Molotov and that she had no mother. At all events, during that last year of the war Yekaterina Ivanovna began to receive regular visits from her daughters, Yulia and Lydia. When one of them came to the settlement they would be allocated a room which was stylishly furnished and even had carpets. They were, after all, the president's daughters, and the president's criminal wife was allowed to live with one or other of them for a whole three days without the supervision of the camp guards.

The first time Lydia came to visit, Yekaterina Ivanovna invited me, through Rika, to pay a social call. I had never met her before. There I sat, drinking fine wine all the way from Moscow, a taste I had long forgotten, dining on improbable delicacies, and listening to the tales of someone freshly arrived from the capital.

Even I quailed to hear how often Kalinin had begged Stalin to have mercy and release his wife so that they could at least be together for a time before he died. Eventually, when victory over Germany was assured, he caught Stalin in a sentimental mood and, weary of his aged colleague's tears, the Leader decided to kick over the traces and let the old bat go free, just as soon as the war was over! Now Kalinin and his family were waiting for the war to end with perhaps even greater trepidation and impatience than the rest of the country. It was during one of these visits that I learned the whereabouts of Kalinin's son-in-law, the information which so disturbed the mental equilibrium of the deputy Chief Medical Officer of the Gulag.

After the three-day visit from her daughter prisoner Kalinin was returned to the camp, where she again took up her tools: one piece of glass for the removal of nits.

When some future novelist is immortalizing the acts of Stalin and comes to describe the great man's exalted feelings at his successful prosecution of the war, let him not forget to mention that in this moment of glory Stalin did not overlook even so insignificant a detail as his promise to Kalinin. Almost exactly one month after the end of the war a telegram arrived ordering the release of Yekaterina Ivanovna. Admittedly the telegram omitted to mention the grounds for her release, so that there was no reason for the camp administration not to issue her with one of their customary poisoned passports for ex-convicts which would have deprived her of the right to live in Moscow and 270 other towns. An urgent request for clarification was sent to Moscow and the camp commandant, wreathed in smiles and overflowing with the milk of human kindness, invited Yekaterina Ivanovna to come and stay with him in the interim. She chose, however, to spend those last days with Rika. A short time later a limousine laden with the camp's top brass drew up outside Rika's humble hut. They proceeded to lug out the suitcases of their former ward and, with Rika to see her off, the president's wife departed for the railway station.

In autumn 1945 I was in Moscow and went to visit Yekaterina Ivanovna on several occasions. It was a trying experience for a number of reasons. She was living with her daughter in the apartment block where my wife Oksana had spent most of her short life and where I too had lived. Indeed, Lydia Kalinin lived directly below what had once been our apartment, and to cross the courtyard and out of habit glance up at those windows again caused me great pain.

Yekaterina Ivanovna was always glad when I visited her. She couldn't bring herself to go and live with her husband in the Kremlin, and Mikhail Ivanovich himself recognized that this would be inadvisable. It was obvious that by this time he himself no longer had any illusions. When Rika was in Moscow she saw a great deal of Yekaterina Ivanovna and they would go to the theater together. Back in Vozhael she received many pleasant letters from her.

It is not hard to understand why Yekaterina Ivanovna was reluctant to live in the Kremlin. She was frightened of bumping into Stalin by chance, unlikely though that was. In any event, she was unable to avoid it.

Kalinin was already terminally ill when he was permitted to see his wife again. He died only a year later, in the summer of 1946. At that time Rika and I were still living in Ustvymlag. We reacted with very mixed feelings to the rhetoric gushing from the radio and the press about how deeply the deceased had been loved by the Party, the Soviet people and Comrade Stalin himself. Even more bizarre was to read in the papers a telegram of condolence from the Queen of England to a woman who only a year earlier had been picking nits out of underwear in a prison camp. But most terrible of all was to see the newspaper and magazine photographs of Kalinin's funeral, with Yekaterina Ivanovna following the coffin, and Stalin and his entire retinue walking beside her.

So she did bump into Stalin again, forced to act out a charade so diabolically improbable that it would seem out of place in one of Shakespeare's plays. It would have been heartless to enquire what she was feeling during that encounter. Yet I would have done so, had I ever met her again. Rika and I had only a brief interval of freedom, however, and when we returned to Moscow in the 1950s Yekaterina Ivanovna was no longer living there. After the suicide of her son, she stayed constantly at the dacha and we did not try to see her.

* * *

I once bumped into Yulia Kalinin, some years after, at DETGIZ, the publishing house for children's literature. She had written a book for the young about her father. I told her we had met before.

"Of course. I thought your face was familiar. We probably met on vacation at some sanatorium or other. At Barvikha, was it, or the Pines?"

"No, we weren't on vacation. It was at a place called Vozhael."

I saw her eyes glisten with compassion and dismay, just as they had when we first met in Ustvymlag.

Translated by Rachel Osorio and Arch Tait

Niyazov

It was November 1977. I was at the Cardiology Institute in Petroverigsky Street. During the night, they moved me out of the intensive care unit (someone else needed the bed) and into the ward opposite. There was no hope of getting to sleep again. I waited impatiently for the cleaners to begin shuffling in the corridor outside, for the squeaking of doors opening and shutting, and the brisk footsteps of the nurses. There was something terribly familiar about these sounds and about my own impatient eagerness to examine my new surroundings. They didn't just remind me of the Botkin Hospital from the previous year. They took me back to much earlier events: to the Inner Prison at the Lubyanka and to Butyrki, to Stavropol prison, the Georgievsk transit prison, and to numerous transit prisons and camps in Ustvymlag and Usolag.

The resemblance between prison and hospital does not stop with a certain external similarity. They both keep you in constant expectation of something new, and of changes that will decide your fate. You meet new and unfamiliar people and you all find yourselves in the same position. Conversations in a hospital ward are very like those in a prison cell: what is going on, we forever ask ourselves and each other, what will happen to us next?

At first every daily event is of interest: mealtimes, when the nurses bring you your food, the appearance of the sisters and their aides with their hypodermic syringes and specimen jars, and the daily rounds of the doctor. Our doctor was a young, pretty Georgian intern who tried to compensate for her youth and semi-student status by being exaggeratedly grave, strict and meticulous. With time, though, this all becomes familiar and attention shifts to one's neighbors.

There were four of us in ward 114. One, a massive and unhealthily bloated official from the Ministry of Power Engineering, was dissatisfied with everything. Morning, evening and, sometimes, even at night he was forever munching on the large quantities of rich food they brought him: caviar, chicken and real cheese—quite literally the Soviet bureaucrat's diet which Alexander Galich satirized ("for them the caviar, the wine and cheese, while I must eat this hospital garbage").[1] Opposite me lay a geology professor. Youthful in appearance, he was stoical, ironic, and well-spoken. We were recovering from run-of-the-mill heart attacks. He was suffering from something that even the most experienced staff at the institute could not understand. A monitor constantly displayed his cardiogram, and measured the pulse, rhythm and other indicators of how that small but essential part inside us was performing.

The fourth patient was Niyazov. He was a Tatar but did not come from the Crimea or from Kazan on the Volga—he was from Omsk. It was the first time I had seen a Siberian Tatar. To look at, he was no different from the classic portrayal in Gorky's *The Lower Depths* which I had seen staged at the Moscow Art Theater. He even sat the same way, with his legs folded under him on the bed. His Russian was peculiar. It was not just a problem of accent but of the way he used the words, and sometimes it was impossible to understand what he was saying. Very quick on his feet, he was always moving around and talking to everyone. His eyes missed nothing and his hearing was so acute that he could distinguish what people were saying in the continuous hum in the corridor outside.

I found myself attracted to him. Though of much more modest social origins than his fellow patients, he did not let that inhibit him at all, and he showed no signs of an inferiority complex. He was the only one who could move around, and so, without any fuss or awkwardness, he looked after the rest of us. He would pass us our food and check whether we had taken all the tablets the nurses had left. Niyazov did not like the plump bureaucrat. The professor, however, he treated with a tender care. It deeply impressed him, for some reason, that the monitor to which the professor was wired up had cost $60,000 and was so well constructed. Niyazov learned to distinguish all the complex flickering lights and read the cardiogram that constantly jumped across the oscillograph screen. All the time he checked the readings on the instrument. "Volodya," he would announce with concern, "those bad jagged lines have started up again..." He talked to us all without any formality. He called the professor by his first name, even using the familiar "Volodya." He also respected me. It pleased him that I was a writer and could give copies of my books to the doctors with my name in large letters on the cover. He addressed me by my first name and patronymic but since he found the latter difficult to pronounce he would call me "Lev Naumovich" (or, more often, simply "Naum'ich") instead. In turn I also addressed him as Grigory Ivanovich. This thoroughly un-Russian man had a thoroughly Russian name and patronymic.

He was an interesting companion. Both the unpleasant bureaucrat and the attractive professor were already familiar types. Niyazov was something new. And he was quite out of the ordinary. Without the slightest embarrassment, he declared he did not like reading books and that in all his sixty-two years he had never read one from beginning to end. Yet he was clever and quickly grasped the point of anything. He played chess superbly and could have easily become a professional. He spoke of himself and his life with a frankness that was by turns touching and repellent. The tale of how he married was moving. It happened during the war, when he was on his way back home to Siberia from the front. He was in Moscow with his ticket already in his pocket. At the station he went into the wooden bar to down a large glass of vodka. The woman behind the counter gave him a curious and affectionate look as she handed him a battered sandwich to eat with his drink, "Don't you disappear now," she said. "Come back again."

"What for?"

"You look like my husband," she answered quietly. "He was killed right at the beginning of the war, in summer 1941..."

Niyazov left the bar and walked about the streets for an hour or two. Then he threw away his ticket and went back to the barmaid. And that was how he came to live in Moscow. She bore him three daughters and they brought him little but sorrow. Often he would reflect aloud on this, becoming angry with fate and human ingratitude. He supported the oldest daughter while she was training to become an engineer and she made a good marriage. Niyazov bought her a two-room apartment and fitted it out with expensive Hungarian furniture. Now that he was sick and a pensioner, however, she could not care less and not once had she come to visit him in the hospital. The youngest daughter was eighteen and had gone astray several years before. She drank, smoked and ran around in all kinds of dubious company. "The sooner you die the better, you miserable old man!" she would tell him, with a mixture of hatred and hopeful expectation.

Only the middle daughter gave him any satisfaction. She had graduated from the institute and become an accountant. She often came to visit her father in the hospital, bringing him a great variety and quantity of rich food. His wife, the former barmaid, also came. Plump and now running to fat, it was clear that she still loved her Tatar who so strangely resembled the first and, evidently, one great love of her life.

At the same time there was something intangible and troubling about him that irked me. For one thing, he was extraordinarily obsessed with himself, his body and his health. He was forever listening to his insides, to his inner organs. Before he had not been aware of their existence, but now they restricted his every move. He drove the doctors to distraction, demanding that they cure him "once and for all," and he constantly suspected they had not done everything they could for him. The institute was full of complicated and incomprehensible machines. Who had been taken where? He eagerly questioned those he met in the corridor. What apparatus had they been tested on? Then he would ensure that he was also taken to all those intricate and highly expensive devices. It was the last consideration, that of cost, which was of especial, if not the greatest, importance to him.

Until he became ill he had evidently been a very fit man. He could shift an upright piano single-handed and cross himself with a thirty kilo weight. He could not accept that his body was no longer as strong as before. Greedily he devoured the large quantities of meat that his family brought him, almost totally convinced that this would restore his former strength.

* * *

Why have I described this stranger, this chance hospital acquaintance, at such length? We were not together for long and then we returned to our own different parts of Moscow. It was clear we would never meet again. Yet I shall never forget that round face with its high cheekbones and tiny attentive eyes. I could never have imagined that there, in ward 114 of the city's cardiology institute, I would at last find someone I had waited several decades to meet. I had been waiting to find out something that no one but he could tell me.

By then I had met hundreds of people who had been through our prisons and camps. I had read dozens of books, both memoirs and historical studies. But not one of those people and not a single one of the books could tell me exactly how so many people had been murdered.

How did they actually do it? We know, down to the smallest detail, how the Nazis carried out their killings. Everything is known—how they rounded people up, took them away, dug the mass graves, gassed or shot people and then destroyed the bodies.

But how did our killers do their work? How did they shoot people in 1937, in 1938, and thereafter? We know the classic scenario: a garage with a car engine running to drown out the sound of the bullets; shots in the back of the head; and a truck loaded up with bodies and driven somewhere out of town. However, this amateurish method only remained in use until 1937. After that, thousands and tens of thousands were being murdered. The number of those condemned to "ten years in distant camps without the right to correspondence" reached colossal figures. In some cases it might be possible to resort to such exotic forms of mass murder as the sinking of a barge loaded with prisoners. But they couldn't take everyone to Vladivostok to dispose of them in this way. Evidently, there were much simpler methods, closer to home.

For years I wondered constantly about this. The further that accursed time receded into the past, the less hope I had of ever solving this mystery. Yet all it required was a single meeting with one of the "executioners," or whatever the official term was for such people. We had to meet, and then I could learn from him how exactly it had been done.

Niyazov, it turned out, was the person I had been looking for all those years.

So now we had met. Why he decided to reveal such a thing to me

I cannot explain. He never mentioned it to anyone else in the hospital and I was the first person, he said, he had ever told. This ailing murderer took a liking to me. Indeed, he became quite genuinely attached to me and was disappointed, it seems, that I did not give him my telephone or take down his address when I left the hospital...

They allowed us both to start going out for walks in the courtyard at almost the same time. I was very pleased. I wanted to clear up something that had been nagging me ever since the day he accused our doctor of not giving him a full examination: "You can't hide anything from me, you know!" he told her proudly. "I have a Chekist's eye!"

* * *

The exercise yard at the Cardiology Institute was much like that in a prison. It was surrounded by tall buildings and a high wall, and there was no exit to the street, to the world outside. Actually, two courtyards had been joined together and during the exercise period solitary individuals and couples would slowly move around them in a circle, just as in prison.

The very first time we went out together I asked Niyazov, "You were a Cheka man, were you, Grigory Ivanovich? Where?"

"Yes, I most certainly was! In Omsk."

"A prison warder?"

"That's right, in Omsk Prison. First in the ordinary prison and then in the NKVD prison."

"And how did you get that job?"

I then heard the story of how the Omsk Tatar Niyazov began to work for the Cheka, or NKVD as it was already called by that time.

His mother, a laundress, had a family of eleven children and they lived in indescribable poverty. His father was a janitor, a traditional urban occupation for a Tatar, but one that did not bring him much money. My fellow patient grew up a sturdy and embittered boy. He did not want to study and his mother had great difficulty in getting him to stay in school until the seventh class.[2] It was not his mother's tears or the cuffs his father gave him that got him through, moreover, so much as the fear the teachers had of this savage little beast. He was quite capable of attacking them at night, breaking their windows and, perhaps, even murdering them. He was capable of anything! Still only a young boy, he carried a steel ramrod in the hem of his quilt jacket and used it against those he hated. And he hated all the teachers' favorite pupils, and all those who were well-off and smartly dressed. Nor did he only attack his personal enemies. If he was paid, he would attack anyone.

"They would give me a large meat pie or twenty kopecks and say: beat him up," Niyazov frankly explained. "So I'd come up to him after school, pull out my rod and give him a hard punch..."

After leaving school he became one of the "waifs" on the streets—"the family needed my help." By "waif" he meant a petty thief, and he worked the markets and shops. He kept clear of professional gangs, though. He preferred to work on his own, it was quieter and safer that way. Even the experienced criminals were scared of him: he was strong, fearless and calculating.

He knew, for instance, that he would have to stop stealing as soon as he officially ceased to be a teenager. For at that moment it was no longer the juvenile section at the local police station but another more serious organization that would begin to take an interest in him. So when the police found him a job he went off to work at the factory. Standing by a lathe all day bored him. First he lugged heavy items around; then he began to work as a watchman, and won the trust of the chief security guard. Niyazov's moment came in 1935 when some sharp-eyed person spotted and recruited him. He was made a junior warder at the Omsk city prison. Something about him evidently inspired the confidence of his superiors, because only six months later he was offered the chance to join the Party and became a senior warder. Then he was moved to the NKVD's own detention center, a sign of especial trust and favor. He remained there until 1937. In that year, without even being consulted, he was transferred to a "special installation." This was located fifteen kilometers from Bikin station on the railway from Khabarovsk to Vladivostok. Convicted prisoners from Voroshilovsk, Khabarovsk, Vladivostok and other large cities and small administrative towns in the area were brought here to be shot. Just as a vacuum cleaner sucks up the dust, so the "punitive organs," as they were openly and officially termed, gathered their victims from everywhere around and sent them to their deaths.

I do not know how best to convey everything Niyazov told me. It will be better, probably, to give my questions and his answers exactly as though someone else had noted them down. This is not for artistic effect. Not at all. I memorized each word he spoke in reply then and shall never forget a single one of them. So let my recollection take the following form. I am willing to defend its accuracy to anyone and before my own conscience.

"What was Bikin? And where was it?"
"It's a railway station. Quite a big one."
"Where was the camp?"
"Fifteen kilometers from the station. There was once a military base there, and the barracks and other buildings were still standing. So they cordoned off the whole place with barbed wire, built watchtowers, and set up a barrier and a checkpoint on the road. There was only one road leading to it. No one could drive or walk up to the

camp."

"Was it supposed to hold many people?"

"No, the camp wasn't very big, only for about 200-250 people. But sometimes they'd bring a lot of people all at once and then it held up to 300. They even turned the old canteen into a barrack and put up board beds there. But it never became especially crowded, they were only bringing in people for two to three days, after all. And Bikin wasn't the only operation of its kind. There was another at Rozengartovka, sixty kilometers down the line towards Khabarovsk. And there were operations like that in other places too."

Niyazov pronounced the word "operation" firmly and with a certain dignity, as though it meant something important to him.

"You were a warder there?"

"That's right."

"What work did you do?"

"The usual. Twenty-four hours on duty, twenty-four off. During the day you drove to the station to meet a train. You collected the prisoners and took them back. Then you put them in their cells. You would accompany the trusties when they carried the soup canister and you'd stand by the food hatch while they handed out the rations—like I said, the usual."

"But who shot them, then? Were there other people who did it? Did they live at the camp?"

"There were never any other people! It was us who shot them."

"How?"

"It was like this. In the morning we'd hand everything over to the new shift and go into the guardhouse. We'd collect our weapons, and then and there they'd give us each a shot glass of vodka. After that we'd take the list and go round with the senior warder to pick them up from the cells and take them out to the truck."

"What kind of truck?"

"A closed van. Six of them and four of us in each one."

"How many trucks would leave at the same time?"

"Three or four."

"Did they know where they were going? Did someone read them their death sentence before, or what?"

"No, no sentences were announced. No one even spoke, just, 'Come out, then straight ahead, into the van—fast!'"

"Were they in handcuffs?"

"No, we didn't have any."

"How did they behave, once they were in the van?"

"The men, well, they kept quiet. But the women would start crying, they'd say: 'What are you doing, we're not guilty of anything, comrades, what are you doing?' and things like that."

"They used to take men and women together?"

"No, always separately."

"Were the women young? Were there a lot of them?"

"Not so many, about two vanloads a week. No very young ones but there were some about twenty-five or thirty. Most were older, and some even elderly."

"Did you drive them far?"

"Twelve kilometers or so, to the hill. The Distant Hill, it was called. There were hills all around and that's where we unloaded them."

"So you would unload them, and then tell them their sentence?"

"What was there to tell them?! No, we yelled, 'Out! Stand still!' They scrambled down and there was already a trench dug in front of them. They clambered down, clung together and right away we got to work..."

"They didn't make any noise?"

"Some didn't, others began shouting, 'We're Communists, we are being wrongly executed,' that type of thing. But the women would only cry and cling to each other. So we just got on with it..."

"Did you have a doctor with you?"

"What for? We would shoot them, and those still wriggling got another bullet and then we were off back to the van. The work team from the Dalag camps was already nearby, waiting."

"What work team was that?"

"There was a team of criminal inmates from Dalag who lived in a separate compound. They were the trusties at Bikin and they also had to dig and fill in the pits. As soon as we left they would fill in that pit and dig a new one for the next day. When they finished their work, they went back to the compound. They got time off their sentence for it and were well fed. It was easy work, not like felling timber."

"And what about you?"

"We would arrive back at the camp, hand in our weapons at the guardhouse and then we could have as much to drink as we wanted. The others used to lap it up—it didn't cost them a kopeck. I always had my shot, went off to the canteen for a hot meal, and then back to sleep in the barracks."

"And did you sleep well? Didn't you feel bad or anything?"

"Why should I?"

"Well, that you had just killed other people. Didn't you feel sorry for them?"

"No, not at all. I didn't give it a thought. No, I slept well and then I'd go for a walk outside the camp. There's some beautiful places around there. Boring, though, with no women."

"Were any of you married?"

"No, they didn't take married men. Of course, the bosses made out all right. There were some real lookers on the Dalag work team! Your head would spin! Cooks, dishwashers, floor cleaners—the bosses had them all. We went without. It was better not to even think about it..."

"Grigory Ivanovich, did you know that the people you were shooting were not guilty at all, that they hadn't done anything wrong?"

"Well, we didn't think about that then. Later, yes. We were summoned to the procurators and they asked us questions. They explained that those had been innocent people. There had been mistakes, they said, and—what was the word?—excesses. But they told us that it was nothing to do with us, we were not guilty of anything."

"Well, I understand, then you were under orders and you shot people. But when you learned that you had been killing men and women who were not guilty at all, didn't your conscience begin to bother you?"

"Conscience? No, Naum'ich, it didn't bother me. I never think about all that now, and when I do remember something... no, nothing at all, as if nothing had happened. You know, I've become so soft-hearted that one look at an old man suffering today and I feel so much pity that I even cry sometimes. But those ones, no, I'm not sorry for them. Not at all, it's just like they never existed..."

Naturally, Grigory Ivanovich was just as frank with me about the rest of his life, when he was not engaged in mass murder. I listened very closely. I wanted so much to find proof that he was not, in fact, just like me or anyone else.

He proved to be little or no different. That is, if one ignores his refusal to keep up a pretense that there were some things he would never agree to do.

At the end of 1939 the "operation" at Bikin began to work at only half-capacity. In 1940 it was shut down altogether. Niyazov was transferred back to his old job, as prison warder in Omsk.

"But I got fed up with the work there, Naum'ich. All the former guards had gone. And the young ones were always whispering behind my back—you made a lot, shooting innocent people.... It was envy, of course. The pay at Bikin was much better. I got so mad that I left the job."

"Where did you go?"

"Nowhere, I decided to take a rest. But it didn't work out. The war started."

So he went off to fight and, evidently, Niyazov was a good soldier. He served as a private on the Leningrad front. He was wounded and awarded two Orders of the Red Star and several medals. He survived to march all over defeated Germany and returned a rich and healthy man.

"You can't imagine how rich I was after the war, Naum'ich!"

"Where did it all come from?"

"It was right at the beginning of the war. We were marching through a small Soviet town on our retreat. There were three of us, a sergeant and two privates. The town was empty, everything was wide open and suddenly we saw the sign "Bank." We went in and there lay large canvas bags full of money. We took three of the bags and decided to hide them until the war was over. And we hid them so well, you know, that when the war ended I came back to the town and no one else had found them. All three bags were lying there. I took mine and off I went."

"Why only one?"

"I'm not stupid, am I? I was one of the first to be demobilized. What if that sergeant, and the other soldier, were still alive? They knew my surname and where I came from. No, I didn't grab other people's things. But I took my share. I'm a sharp fellow, Naum'ich. Others dragged back clothes and dinner services from Germany— filled a sack so full they could hardly move it. Me, I only took a motor- cycle and some little 'stones,' in a three-liter can."

"What kind of stones?"

"Flints for cigarette lighters. The black marketeers were selling them for twenty-five rubles each in Russia. I sold them straight off for ten. Do you know how many you can fit in a three-liter can? A mil- lion! So much money you could go crazy!"

Life continued to treat Niyazov well. The military wanted to pack him off somewhere, but he went over their heads. They're trying to make a Cheka-man go and dig ditches, he complained. Immediately he was transferred to security for government communications. Later when he was fully demobilized he found himself the best job of all: he was put in charge of security at the central warehouse supplying goods to the officers in Anti-Aircraft Defenses. For the next thirty years, he worked there.

He told me at length, sometimes stuttering with excitement, how advantageous and profitable his new position was. Of course, he creamed off the best of everything around.

"You've never seen so much gold! And silver! Rings, bracelets, fancy tea-glass holders, that kind of thing. Well, it never actually reached the warehouse. We only saw the invoices and the receipts: the bosses had already taken the stuff and paid for it themselves.

"And the furs, you wouldn't believe! When they were delivered the big bosses would drive over themselves, even Batitsky, and pick out some of the best bits, the foreign materials and the others. Then we would go into action."

"How do you mean?"

"There's a trick in every trade, Naum'ich. We had an 'agreement' with certain places. We would send out a container, for instance, full of the most expensive things to some way-out anti-aircraft garrison right next to the frontier. The container would stand idle there for as long as the law required, and then be sent back to us: 'We are re- turning these goods, because they have not been sold.' So then, quite legally, as soon as we got them back, we set up a commission and repriced them, as goods 'not in demand that had lost their commercial value.' Then we'd take our pick! You see this coat, Naum'ich? Just feel the material. It'll last forever, the purest and most expensive wool. Twenty-eight rubles!! The very best shirts we bought up for three rubles. A musquash or deerskin fur hat went for eight rubles. Of course, the warehouse chief and the managing officers would have first choice. But I wasn't small fry either: I was head of security and had 47 men under my command."

Then a new man was put in charge of the warehouse who unjustly and meanly deprived Niyazov of his job. The new boss sacked all the old established staff and brought in his own people. He waited until Grigory Ivanovich reached sixty and then organized an extravagant celebration to mark his well-deserved retirement ("the bastard"). That was the cause of his first heart attack. The second, the reason he was in his hospital with me, was because of that little tramp, his youngest daughter. He gave her such a beating that he thought she'd never recover. But she survived, and he had another heart attack...

Why am I writing all this down? Why should the life, character and moral horizons of this person be of any importance to me?

The "special operation" at Bikin existed for almost three years. Well, two and a half, to be more exact. It also probably had its holidays and weekends—perhaps no one was shot on Sundays, May Day, Revolution Day and the Day of the Soviet Constitution. Even so, that means that it functioned for a total of 770 days. Every morning on each of those days four trucks set out from Bikin compound for the Distant Hill. Six people in each truck, a total of 24. It took 25-30 minutes for them to reach the waiting pit. The "special operation" thus disposed of 15,000 to 18,000 people during its existence. Yet it was of a standard design, just like any transit camp. The well-tried, well-planned machinery operated without interruption, functioning regularly and efficiently, filling the ready-made pits with bodies—in the hills of the Far East, in the Siberian forests, and in the glades of the Tambov woods or the Meshchera nature reserve. They existed everywhere, yet nothing remains of them now. There are no terrible museums as there are today at Auschwitz, or at Mauthausen in Austria. There are no solemn and funereal memorials like those that testify to the Nazi atrocities at Khatyn,[3] Salaspils or Lidice. Thousands of unnamed graves, in which there lie mingled the bones of hundreds of thousands of victims, have now been overgrown by bushes, thick luxuriant grass and young new forest. Not exactly the same as the Germans, it must be admitted. The men and women were buried separately here. Our regime made sure that even at that point no moral laxity might occur.

And the murderers? They are still alive. Not all of them have had such disappointments (comparatively speaking) as Niyazov. There were a great many, of course, who took part in these shootings. There were yet more, however, who never made the regular journey to the Distant Hill or the other killing grounds. Only in bourgeois society are the procurator and others obliged to attend an execution. Under our regime, thank God, that was not necessary. There were many, many more involved in these murders than those who simply pulled the trigger. For them a university degree, often in the "humanities," was more common than the rudimentary education of the Niyazovs. They drafted the instructions and decisions; they signed beneath the words "agreed," "confirmed," "to be sentenced to..." Today they are all retired and most of them receive large individual pensions. They sit in the squares and enjoy watching the children play. They go to concerts and are moved by the music. We meet them when we attend a meeting, visit friends, or find ourselves sitting at the same table, celebrating with our common acquaintances. They are alive, and there are many of them. They're my age and younger. I am over the shock I experienced in the hospital after listening to the stories of that elderly murderer. To my horror, I discover that I feel no hatred whatsoever towards him. He is no better or worse than the others. The murderers are among us. And there is nothing we can do about it. All I can do is to powerlessly recall the words of Yury Dombrovsky:

And I cannot bring back the dead
Or cross out the living from the list.[4]

IVAN MOSKVIN

I am not going to write about the famous actor here. There are books and films about that Moskvin, and his puggish face has been reproduced in countless paintings, photographs, caricatures and statuettes. I knew the actor, too; and he will be part of the story that follows, if only because he was friendly with his namesake, my Moskvin. Both were named Ivan Mikhailovich. Yet the other has been wiped from the historical record and erased from people's memories. Only the rare handbooks and publications that list all the members of the Bolshevik administrative elite still retain a reference to him. Only there is he not concealed by an eloquent "et al."

It still seems extraordinary to me that Ivan Moskvin could disappear so completely. He was in the upper ranks of the elite that controlled Party and state. For many years he was a member of the Central Committee, of its Orgburo and its Secretariat, and headed "Orgraspred," the Central Committee's crucial personnel department.[1] He also played a significant role in the history of the Party. Moskvin was one of the leaders of the Party's Petrograd organization before the First World War. On 16 October 1917 he took part in the celebrated meeting on Bolotnaya Street at which the Bolsheviks decided to organize the armed uprising that became the October Revolution. He never fell into disfavor as a member of the various inner-Party oppositions. And yet... it is as though he never existed! People several ranks lower than Moskvin were awarded a modest but respectable mention in the post-Stalin Soviet encyclopedias, and were respectfully recalled on special anniversaries by admiring articles in *Pravda*: "Deceased 1937. We shall never forget this loyal son of the Party," they invariably concluded.

No such memory of Ivan Moskvin remains. Perhaps the reason is that no family or relatives survived him. His sister, who was a middle-ranking Party official, died in Petrograd when she was still young, in 1923 if I remember rightly. A street there is named after her to this day. Usually it was only the surviving relatives, and not any official body like the Institute of Marxism-Leninism, who tried to ensure that articles were written and entries were added to encyclopedias, and even that memoirs appeared in one of the magazines. On her own return from the camps Moskvin's stepdaughter, Yelena Boky, managed to obtain a rehabilitation certificate for Moskvin from the Military Procurator's Office, and ones for her own father, mother and sister, as well. She was the only one of them to come back. Either Yelena was unable to do more, or she simply did not want to. Soon she died too. So the duty to remind people who Ivan Moskvin was has fallen to me.

No one else alive now remembers him. But I was a member of his family for several years and I owe much of what I know to him. Particularly that knowledge which, as they say, brings sorrow. I could not force myself to petition the "authorities" to restore his name and reputation. I could not bring myself to plead with those who had erased not only Moskvin from their own memories (they knew nothing whatsoever about him) but the entire time in which he lived. So as I sit here writing these memoirs—for whom, it is not clear!—I want to remember Ivan Moskvin. Then, at least, my anonymous reader will know that he once existed.

Not a single photograph of him has survived. His face was quite ordinary and not at all distinctive. Only the deep-set eyes and tiny toothbrush mustache set it apart. And his skull was completely shaved. Moskvin was proud of his "ordinary" appearance. He said it was this that explained why between 1911 when he joined the Party and 1917 he was never once arrested, although by then he was an important figure. "A revolutionary should not boast that he has often been imprisoned and for long periods of time," he used to say. "There's no credit in that, only years lost for Party work." At the end of 1936 people came to take a photograph of Moskvin for the next volume of the *Shorter Soviet Encyclopedia*. We family members were all highly amused at the prospect of seeing his "unremarkable" face there. As it turned out, we didn't.

I never inquired of Ivan Mikhailovich where he came from, where he had studied or what he had done before. In casual conversation I learned that he had graduated from a *gymnasium* in Tver. Whether he continued his studies further I don't know. Probably he was quite a capable person. Otherwise his excellent knowledge of Latin would be hard to explain. He not only enjoyed reading his favorite Latin verse but also conversed freely in that language. When he met Winter, an equally passionate enthusiast, at sessions of the Soviet government, the Council of People's Commissars, they would chat together in Latin, disconcerting and embarrassing those around them. Moskvin was also good at mathematics and in his spare time liked to solve complicated mathematical puzzles.

His profession, though, was as a Party functionary, and he devoted his whole life to the Bolshevik cause after leaving the Tver gymnasium. In Petersburg he began work in the local Party organization. Just before the outbreak of the First World War he was made a member of the Central Committee's Russian Bureau and after the 1917 Revolution he held leading posts in the Petrograd organization. When the Northwestern Bureau was established he was put in charge, placing him second only to Zinoviev in the Leningrad hierarchy.

He did not like Zinoviev at all. It was not simple dislike, so much as an active contempt. Zinoviev was cowardly and cruel, he would say.

When Yudenich and the White forces were on the outskirts of Petrograd in 1919 and the city's Party organization was preparing to go underground again, Zinoviev was overcome by a hysterical fear. He demanded that he immediately be smuggled out of Petrograd. He had good reason for feeling afraid: shortly before, he and the newly-arrived Stalin had given orders to shoot all the Tsarist army officers who had registered, as instructed, with the new authorities... Many hundreds of former political leaders, lawyers and capitalists who had not managed to hide were executed at the same time.

Meanwhile Ivan Mikhailovich was busy organizing underground printing presses. Some of them were so thoroughly camouflaged that they could not be found even after Yudenich and the Civil War itself had become no more than a part of history. Several years later Moskvin would put one of these presses into use at a time that would mark a fatal turning point for him, and for many others.

When Zinoviev became the focus of the Leningrad or "New" opposition in the mid 1920s, Moskvin was one of the three leading Party functionaries in the city who did not join him and his followers. But whereas Lobov and Kodatsky simply did not join the others, Moskvin very actively confronted the Zinovievites.

This was not at all a simple matter, it turned out. Only by listening to Ivan Mikhailovich did I gain some idea of the nature of the struggle within the Party then. It seems quite inconceivable today—especially the role played by the GPU, the Secret Police. The Resolutions of the Fourteenth Party Congress, at which the Zinovievites were outvoted, were banned in Leningrad. Newspapers that had published them were not on sale at the kiosks and were impounded at the post office. The Leningrad branch of the GPU was a submissive tool in the hands of Zinoviev and seized people who distributed the papers of the congress. It was then that Moskvin activated all his ties and connections dating back almost to the pre-1917 Bolshevik underground. The documents of the Congress were printed on one of the printing presses that had remained undiscovered since 1919. They were sent to specially organized secret addresses and taken at night by hand to the factories where they were distributed in the workers' toolboxes. Only after all the leading officers of the Leningrad GPU had been replaced was it possible to organize the famous "raid" on the city in 1927 that was led by Kalinin, Voroshilov, Chaplin and other Party leaders. At that point the "purging" of the city's Party organization began. New policies were adopted which no one at the time referred to as Stalinist, although that is, of course, what they were.

I don't believe that Ivan Mikhailovich had any idea of advancing his career during this affair. But afterwards he shot to the pinnacle of power. From the second rank he was promoted to the top of the Party oligarchy. At the next plenum of the Central Committee he was elected to the Orgburo and made a candidate member of its

Secretariat. He moved to Moscow and was put in charge of the Central Committee's personnel department, the "all-powerful Orgraspred" to which Bezymensky composed his odes of praise. It was indeed the most powerful body within the all-powerful Central Committee. At the time there were no separate sections covering different parts of the economy and administration, as was the case later, so Moskvin was in charge of every type of appointment—within the Party and the Soviets, in industry, research and education... This gave him enormous power within the Party.

Moskvin rose so high because of Stalin's affection for him. If one can use the term "affection," that is, when talking of Stalin. He assessed people only in terms of the strength of their personal loyalty. Probably, Stalin thought that Moskvin's behavior in rebellious Leningrad was an expression of such loyalty. In any case, Stalin did everything to make Moskvin one of "his circle." He invited him to go hunting and to join in his Georgian feasts; he paid friendly calls on him when Moskvin went south on vacation. It would have been hard to find a less suitable object for such ploys than Moskvin. He was a strict character and not very amenable. In all his life Moskvin never drank one glass of wine or beer. He never smoked a single cigarette. He did not enjoy "ribald" stories or crude expressions. He did not attach value to good food and was not interested in entertainment. Neither did he want to change his habits.

Therefore, Moskvin turned down all Stalin's invitations: to banquets, to drive off to some southern resort or spend all night around the table carousing with Stalin and his cronies. He was quite unsuited to be one of the Leader's "close comrades-in-arms," and his downfall was inevitable. An event of apparently very private character, a purely family tragedy, would herald his fall.

On 5 November 1932 Nadezhda Alliluyeva, Stalin's wife, committed suicide. She was, by all accounts, a modest, kindly and deeply unhappy woman. Several times when I went to visit the Sverdlov family at their apartment in the Kremlin I found a tear-stained Alliluyeva there. After she had left, Klavdia Timofeyevna, Sverdlov's widow, would clutch her head in her hands and exclaim, "Oh, that poor, poor woman!" I did not enquire why Stalin's wife had been crying. Yet all who inhabited the tiny provincial town that was the Kremlin until 1936 knew the answer. As in any small community, all who lived there eagerly discussed each other's personal affairs: Demyan Bedny's mistress, the forthcoming marriage of Vladimirsky's son Sergei and Avel Yenukidze's late-night parties. Of course, they also talked about "poor Nadezhda Sergeyevna" who was forced to put up with the difficult character of her rather terrifying husband. How Stalin would beat his children, Svetlana and Vasya, and mistreat his retiring young wife. And how, of late, "Koba" (Stalin) had begun to join in Yenukidze's revels...

There are several versions as to why Alliluyeva killed herself. Some said that she could not stand Stalin's persecution of old Party members, including her own friends. I don't believe this was the reason. I think people have taken their wishes for reality. In the circles close to the highest reaches of the Party there was more precise information as to why Stalin's wife committed suicide. It was at this time that Stalin made his announcement, "life has become merrier." Evidently, he presumed that not only his subjects but he himself ought to be leading a merrier life now. He began to join in the carefree existence pursued by Avel Yenukidze, his closest friend since boyhood. Rumors began to circulate that the grim, unbending Koba had started to unwind...

The contents of the letter Alliluyeva left behind her were known to the "upper circles" and avidly discussed in the Kremlin families. She wrote that she could not watch while the Leader of the Party sank lower and lower, and stained a reputation which was not his personal possession but belonged to the Party as a whole. She was taking an extreme measure because she could see no other way to halt the Leader's moral decline.

The legend that Stalin himself shot Alliluyeva has become very widespread. It is quite untrue. Stalin himself never killed anyone and, in all probability, was simply incapable of doing so. But he was well aware that such a rumor might arise. When Stalin and Yenukidze were summoned from their debauch the latter suggested that a postmortem report be issued attributing death to a heart attack. "No," responded the wily Stalin, "then they'll say that I killed her. Call in the forensic experts and issue a statement that it was suicide, which, actually, is the case."

The oldest, strait-laced Party functionaries were disturbed and even outraged by the entire story. Poor Stalin! He still had to take heed of this crowd of elderly people who did not understand the first thing about him. He would have to appease them somehow... So he sacrificed his closest friend. At the plenum which assembled soon after, Yenukidze was accused of moral turpitude. Excluded from the Central Committee, dismissed as Secretary of the Central Executive Committee and driven out of Moscow, he was put in charge of the health resorts of Mineralnye Vody in the North Caucasus. Stalin covered his head with ashes and demonstrated the most profound repentance. A sculptor erected an excellent monument of white marble over Alliluyeva's grave, and a marble bench was placed opposite her bust for the inconsolable husband to come and mourn her. A lamp was specially set up to illuminate the attractive features of the deceased, and security men stood concealed behind the neighboring tombstones. All of the Novodevichy cemetery was sealed off and thoroughly searched so that no one could distract Stalin from his grief. Or from thoughts of what to do with those who had dared to show their "outrage." I think it was then that he began to draw up the lists of the condemned in his excellent memory. But that all came later. For the time being the death and funeral of his wife became for Stalin a test of loyalty. He demanded compassion and protestations of affection. Not for Alliluyeva, of course, but for himself. The body of the deceased lay in what is today the GUM department store. At that time it housed the administration and supply department of the Central Executive Committee. A stream of people flowed past the coffin, all his faithful comrades-in-arms stood in the guard of honor, and the newspapers carried declarations of boundless compassion for Stalin.

All this time Stalin sat by the coffin, noting with his sharp, yellow, all-seeing eyes who had come, how they behaved and what expression they wore on their faces... It was second nature to him. Without knowing a thing about the Alliluyeva funeral, the poet Boris Slutsky captured this perfectly in the lines, "And when he would force me to weep, he thought that my tears were false."

Moskvin was not good at putting on a face. I think that was why he did not go to pay his last respects or stand in the guard of honor, and did not approach the devastated husband wearing a mournful expression. He stayed at home. Stalin quickly discovered that the man whom he had promoted and advanced, whom he had depended on, was not among the crowd of "chicken-necked leaders" who surrounded him.

Kuibyshev, then a friend of Moskvin's, rang him up from GUM, "Ivan! He's asking where you are, whether you came."

"No, I did not come. I'm not coming. If he asks again, tell him I'm probably ill."

"Ivan, don't be foolish! Drive over here at once. The procession is just setting out."

Still Moskvin did not go. Kuibyshev evidently was a genuine friend. On the way to the cemetery he rang again, "Ivan! He's already asked about you twice. Don't do something stupid you won't be able to put right. Order your car and come to the cemetery."

Sophia Alexandrovna understood Stalin better than her husband. Afterwards she described to me in great detail how she had clung to Moskvin and, weeping uncontrollably, demanded that he have pity on her and her daughter Oksana. He must go straightaway. Moskvin never turned down any request that Sophia Alexandrovna made of him, as I knew from experience. He drove to the cemetery.

Stalin stood by the open grave. He lowered his head or covered his face with his hands but in such a way that he could still see if everyone was there.

"Is Moskvin here?" he asked.

Ivan Mikhailovich was standing behind a group of other leaders. Kuibyshev pushed him forward. His hand stretched out, Stalin walked towards Moskvin—"Ivan, what a loss!"

Moskvin expressed all the ritual condolences. But Stalin did not forgive him. I don't think that this episode influenced Moskvin's ultimate fate. His end would be exactly the same as that of the "comrades-in-arms" who wept by the coffin and earnestly expressed their boundless love and loyalty. It did have an effect on his immediate career, though. Some time afterwards he was transferred from the Central Committee apparatus to the People's Commissariat of Heavy Industry. There he was again put in charge of personnel and the post was a very important one: as one of the minister Ordzhonikidze's deputies, he not only was responsible for appointments throughout industry but also the training of such personnel since all the technical colleges and polytechnical institutes were then under the ministry's direct control. Still, this was a step down... At the Seventeenth Party Congress in 1934 Moskvin was made a member of the bureau in the Soviet Control Commission that monitored heavy industry. This was already a very insignificant post. The name of Moskvin would briefly appear once more in the upper reaches of the Party. At the last congress of the Comintern in 1939 a Moskvin was elected member of the Presidium. His initials were not indicated, however, and this was not Ivan Mikhailovich but Trilisser, deputy head of the NKVD, who had been transferred to work in the Comintern and adopted the popular Party surname of Moskvin.

* * *

Ivan Mikhailovich nevertheless formally continued to be a member of the highest ranks of the nomenklatura. He had a red government telephone in his apartment, and government couriers brought him confidential dispatches... The number of colleagues and comrades who came to visit him when he was unwell, though, or who simply dropped by for a chat, decreased. Ordzhonikidze came just as often as before. But one person who had formerly been a very frequent visitor, due to the fact that Moskvin was the one who had helped bring him out of nowhere, now disappeared altogether.

It was Ivan Moskvin who first found and then encouraged and promoted Nikolai Yezhov. For some reason he took a liking to this quiet, modest and efficient secretary of a distant Party regional committee. He summoned Yezhov to Moscow and brought him in at the lowest level in his own department. Then he made him one of his assistants and, later on, one of his deputies. A couple of times during that period I found myself sitting at the same table, drinking vodka with the future "iron commissar." Soon his name alone would be used to terrify children and adults but Yezhov did not at all resemble a vampire. A small slender man, he was always dressed in a crumpled cheap suit and a blue satin collarless peasant shirt. He sat at the table, quiet, not very talkative and slightly shy; he drank little, did not take much part in the conversation but merely listened, with his head slightly bowed. Now I can understand how attractive such a person, with his shy smile and taciturn manner, must have been to Moskvin. At one time Yezhov had had tuberculosis and Sophia Alexandrovna was very concerned about his health.

"Come on, my little sparrow," she would fuss encouragingly around him, "try some of this. You must eat more."

She called that monster "little sparrow"!

What had drawn Ivan Moskvin to the "little sparrow"? Yezhov became a favorite of Stalin's and in the space of a few years made the most incredible career: he became a secretary of the Central Committee, then chairman of the Central Control Commission and, finally, in 1936 Commissar General of State Security. "Who is this Yezhov?" I once asked Moskvin. He thought for a moment and then said, "I know of no more ideal administrator than Nikolai Yezhov. To be more exact, I should say not administrator but subordinate. Entrust him with some task and you have no need to check up—you can rest assured he will do as he is told. Yezhov has only one, admittedly substantial, shortcoming. He does not know where to stop. In certain situations it's impossible to achieve any results and you must call a halt. Yezhov never gives up. Sometimes you have to check and make sure that he stops in time..."

Yezhov ceased coming to visit the family on Spiridonov Street when Ivan Mikhailovich left the Central Committee and he took Moskvin's place as head of personnel. Still, Yezhov continued to regard his former chief with some apprehension. It was thanks to the rather strained relations between Moskvin and his former protege that I attended every session of the Seventeenth Party Congress.

Would it be difficult, I asked Moskvin, to obtain a guest ticket for the Congress? I would have a ticket, he said. Some time later a courier from the Central Committee brought an envelope containing a complete set of daily guest tickets in my name. Moskvin for some reason became very annoyed. He had requested a more prestigious type of invitation. I was there when he rang Malenkov, then Yezhov's deputy, and began to assert his rights... Evidently, Malenkov replied that Yezhov had sent ordinary daily tickets instead of a pass for the whole Congress because he did not know who Razgon was. Ivan Mikhailovich yelled into the telephone, "I am sending these tickets straight back and you can throw them on his desk! It's not enough, it seems, that I recommend a member of the Party whom I not only know but who is a close friend of mine! What next?!"

I don't know what Malenkov said to Yezhov. A few hours later, however, a courier brought the kind of guest ticket only issued to very senior Party officials who had not been selected as delegates.

This entitled me to sit in the main hall and not in the gallery with all the other guests.

For almost a week I sat in that now so-familiar hall. It was the first time I had ever been there. The old Kremlin Palace, which I had been shown around in 1929 during the All-Union Young Pioneers Conference, no longer existed. Stalin had been "tidying up" the Kremlin. The Chudov and Ascension Monasteries had been demolished and so had the Chudov Palace. Once upon a time, in autumn 1826, Nicholas I summoned Alexander Pushkin from his exile in Mikhailovskoe and received him there. Now a large and ugly barracks had been erected for the Central Executive Committee college on the site of these buildings ("No longer extant" the guidebooks briefly inform us). Today the Presidium of the Supreme Soviet is located there.

The Congress was held in the Great Kremlin Palace which had also undergone alteration. The separate Andrei and Alexander halls[2] with their twisting columns, unbelievable swirls of fretwork, gilded decorations and priceless parquet had been made into one long and very capacious hall. A gallery had been added for guests, with its own separate foyer, and an extension had been built on to provide space for the presidium to take exercise, rest and be fed. The oldest church in the Kremlin, the Saviour in the Grove, had been knocked down to make way for these outbuildings. The encyclopedias tell us that it, too, is "not extant." It is astonishing, on reflection, that any of the cathedrals in the Kremlin survived. Our great Soviet architects would have pulled them down without batting an eyelid. I suspect that they simply did not yet need room for new buildings.

I would go into this austere, chilly and uncomfortable hall and listen to everything being said. I heard Stalin's report, the speeches of other Party leaders, and the repentant and reconciliatory words of those who had formerly headed the various inner-Party oppositions. I was young, naive and very much wanted to believe that all the battles within the Party were a thing of the past, that a period of unity and fraternal peace had begun. Only a few trifles disturbed this harmony. Once I came late and the hall was already full. Standing by the doors I looked around for an empty place. There it was! a chair in one row that no one had occupied. I squeezed my way forward, sat down and looked around me. To my right was Zinoviev and to my left, Karl Radek. It took me a moment to realize that they did not want—or feared—to sit next to each other.

In one of the intervals Alexei Rykov spotted me and happily strolled with me round the enormous George hall. I respected Rykov and was deeply attracted to him, and he made a pleasant and interesting companion. It never occurred to me to ask why a political figure of his stature should want to spend his time strolling about with a young friend of his daughter.

Only the very last session unsettled my still almost pristine innocence. The results of the elections to the Central Committee were announced. The list was not read out in alphabetical order, as printed in the newspapers, but according to the number of votes cast. The first name was not Stalin's. Neither was the second, the third nor the fourth... The names of Kalinin, Kirov, Voroshilov and some others were read out—but no Stalin! He came, I believe, either ninth or tenth. The list was read without any breaks and rather nervously. I had the impression that not just for me, but for all those sitting there as well, it seemed a terribly long time between the beginning of the list and the moment when, at last, the name of Stalin was pronounced. Old-fashioned writers would have described our sensation at the time as being "brushed by the wing of Death." In fact, that is just what it proved to be: but how many of those in the hall then understood it? The overwhelming majority sitting downstairs (and upstairs as well) had only three or four years left to live. Did any of them understand? Apart, that is, from Stalin, of course. I don't know. And now I shall never find out.

Moskvin was undoubtedly a loyal "comrade in arms" who always followed Stalin. Yet I believe that he did not feel a normal human attraction to the man, let alone love. Probably, everyone felt the same, including those closest to Stalin. Once I asked Moskvin why the Twelfth Party Congress in 1924 had decided not to carry out Lenin's recommendation and choose someone else to be General Secretary. Moskvin answered that it had cost the Party such irreplaceable losses to confirm Stalin as its leader that they could not consider going through the same thing again. "We lost almost a third of the most gifted and experienced members of the Party then. If we try to follow Lenin's advice now, we shall lose another third..." The near future would show that, for once, Ivan Mikhailovich's mathematical gifts had failed him. Neither his calculation nor his prediction proved correct.

It might be easy from my account to imagine Moskvin a cold and dull man, a person who would not be at ease on social occasions. This was not the case. Though he did not smoke or drink Moskvin enjoyed large cheerful gatherings, noisy family celebrations and amusing games. I cannot say whether this came naturally or was instead the influence of his wife, Sophia. She was not only an interesting person but in many ways a striking character.

Her biography was unusual. Her father Alexandre Doller was a Frenchman, born in Russia and employed as a skilled worker at a factory in Vilno. Thoroughly russified, he joined one of the radical populist organizations (either Land and Liberty or the People's Will), was arrested, spent time in prison, served a period of hard labor in Siberia and then lived in exile for a while in Yakutia. It was there that he met his future wife, Shekhter, a member of the People's Will organization. Korolenko, Felix Kon and other memoirists of the time all mention them. Doller and Shekhter were quite different in temperament. He was a cheerful, exuberant and carefree character, as we Russians expect a Frenchman to be. She was an unbending fanatic who served a much longer and harsher sentence in prison than others because she refused to recognize the authority of the Tsarist government—she would not take an oath of allegiance to the new Tsar Nicholas II, and refused on principle to obey any orders of the prison administration. Nevertheless the two of them met and married in exile and Sophie was their one and only child. Soon after she was born, Doller drowned while swimming in a dangerous fast-flowing Siberian river. The young exile Shekhter was left alone with a small child who accompanied her into all her subsequent prisons and terms of exile.

Sophia Doller was already grown-up and she had managed to spend time in European Russia and even attend the Women's Higher Courses when she met the young Bolshevik, Gleb Boky. At the time she was once again in exile, as was he. They married. As a couple they presented almost as much of a contrast as her parents. I know because I was well acquainted with both of them during an important period in my life.

When I knew her Sophia Alexandrovna Boky was a plump and rather short woman, very active, cheerful and incredibly energetic. It was she alone who ran the household and, despite a childhood spent in exile, did so with all the style and taste of a turn-of-the-century member of the intelligentsia. Apart from the cook and the housemaid there were always various distant female relations or "companions" living in the apartment—a great many people, in a word, who helped looked after this ebullient family.

Gleb Boky and Sophia Alexandrovna evidently parted at the beginning of the 1920s. It was probably by then rather difficult for him to have such a mother-in-law as Shekhter and a wife such as Sophia Alexandrovna: it was Boky who succeeded Uritsky as head of the Petrograd Cheka when the latter was assassinated in 1918, and he was later a member of the Cheka and OGPU directorates. Shekhter, like all former members of the People's Will, had gone on to join the Socialist Revolutionaries, or SRs, and if she was not by then very active, I am sure she remained quite unshakeable in her allegiance to the party. In her youth Sophia Alexandrovna was also evidently an SR. She joined the Bolshevik party in the spring of 1917, but even to such an inexperienced person as myself it was noticeable that she did not radiate any recognizably "Bolshevik spirit." When the Right SRs were being tried in 1922 the names of Shekhter and Sophia Alexandrovna were still mentioned as people from whom the armed wing of the party tried to obtain certain information. Admittedly, it was of a rather comic nature: they were asked to supply the address... of Gleb Boky.

Once in the magazine *Illustrated Russia*, published by White emigres in Paris, I came across a story by the wife of one of the grand dukes, describing how she had saved him from being shot during the Red Terror of autumn 1918. Her husband was being held in prison together with the other grand dukes and his fate was sealed: by that time the Tsar's family had already been shot in Yekaterinburg. Someone mentioned to the duke's wife that Boky was supposedly married to a rather decent woman. So she went in search of the apartment where the intimidating head of the Petrograd Cheka lived, and when a young and attractive woman opened the door she began to weep uncontrollably and implore her help... Sophia Alexandrovna said that she could not influence her husband. Any request on her part might only accelerate the fatal outcome. There was, nevertheless, one person to whom Boky owed his life, a certain Dr. Manukhin. I later read a good deal about this admirable man. But he is not the subject of the present story.

The duchess had only one request: that her husband, as a sick man, be transferred from the prison to a hospital (the only place from which his escape could then be organized). Sophia Alexandrovna told her visitor how Gleb Boky was already suffering from advanced tuberculosis when he was sent to prison. There the disease worsened and Boky stood almost no chance of surviving. However, Sophia Alexandrovna appealed to Dr. Manukhin and, through some very powerful connections, he managed to secure Boky's transfer to his own hospital. There he cured him—once and for all!—of consumption. The only person who could influence Boky, therefore, Sophia Alexandrovna considered, was Manukhin. What followed was like a conventional heart-warming Christmas tale. The doctor demanded that the Cheka chairman move his patient from the prison to the hospital. "All patients are equal to me," he told him. "I treated you, a Bolshevik, and now I shall treat a different patient, who is a grand duke. If you are a decent man then you must move the duke to my hospital." Boky transferred the grand duke and his escape abroad was soon organized.

The entire story was told in great detail. With interest I brought the magazine to Sophia Alexandrovna on Spiridonov Street. The account of her kind deeds apparently did not cheer her. Yet the description of her by this emigre author as a "charming, kind person" was correct. Sophia Alexandrovna was not merely kind and generous but indeed charming as well. These qualities ensured that Moskvin's apartment was always filled with noisy activity and many guests. For the constant friends of the house were not Moskvin's colleagues from work or their dull families, but a bohemian and largely theatrical company. I do not remember how and under exactly what circumstances such incongruous people as our Moskvin and Ivan Moskvin the actor became acquainted and friendly. Nor do I recall why the famous bass Nikolai Ozerov was so close to both our Moskvin and Sophia Alexandrovna. But of all the many people who were always visiting the family on Spiridonov Street, they are the two I recall more than anyone else.

* * *

The family of the actor Moskvin were, perhaps, the closest of their friends. Often Moskvin himself would visit Spiridonov Street after a performance. He enjoyed eating and drinking, and was a dashing card player; he took part in all the games of the younger generation, directed and took the main role in theatrical charades, was a great storyteller and felt himself thoroughly at ease there. His wife Lyubov Vasilievna usually dropped by during the day and would take Sophia Alexandrovna aside, evidently to confide in her the sorrows of her family life. We young ones, for our part, were very friendly with Volodya, their son. A rather gloomy, heavy-drinking young man, Volodya took a poor view of his famous father's conformism: he himself was a gifted actor with the Vakhtangov Theater. In such a theatrical family the other son, Fedya, was hardly noticed. We often visited the Moskvin family apartment on Bryusov (now Nezhdanova) Street. The walls were covered with paintings by famous Russian artists: Repin, Levitan, Korovin, Somov... There were even more pictures in the apartment of Lyubov Vasilievna's sister, on the top floor of the same building. Yekaterina Geltser lived alone in an enormous apartment filled with paintings. I was always staggered by the rehearsal room there, complete with exercise bar and an ever-present young accompanist at the piano. A famous ballerina of the day, Geltser was a somewhat arrogant person. Whenever she came to visit us, either on Spiridonov Street or even out at our dacha on the grounds of the Central Committee sanatorium at Volynskoe, she would invariably wear a black semi-transparent dress with the Order of Lenin pinned to the breast. It was a most bizarre combination.

When Nikolai Ozerov invited us to visit him we would often find A. V. Nezhdanova, of the Bolshoi, and the director N. S. Golovanov there. Although the latter had the reputation of being a vindictive anti-semite and supporter of the Black Hundreds, he struck me as a cheerful old fellow who was partial to family singing parties and jokes that were most inappropriate for a family gathering. That, evidently, was why Ozerov's younger son was so rarely allowed to stay up with us. A very neat, slender and well-brought-up boy, he was the spitting image of his father. When I now frequently see the overblown figure and swollen features of the younger Ozerov on television, it is rather awful to realize that my own appearance has undergone a similar transformation.

How merry those evenings at Spiridonov Street were! The two Ivan Moskvins would appear late: one came from the theater, the other from his office. By that time the younger and less inhibited members of the company were already at their most uproarious. Both Moskvins immediately joined in the noisy conversations. Well into the night, until two or three in the morning, Ozerov would sing folk songs while the actor Moskvin organized a choir to sing military songs and told funny but barely decent stories that, he insisted, had been written by Gorbunov or even Chekhov. Only at that late hour would our Ivan Mikhailovich call up a car to take our guests home.

Apart from these actors and singers, however, a quite different type of visitor would also often gather in Moskvin's apartment. These were the doctors. They came not to treat anyone but as friends, whose scientific ideas found support there. Several were in charge of the All-Union Institute of Experimental Medicine, which had only just been set up and was at the time extremely fashionable. The encyclopedias and medical histories today provide only a mysteriously vague and uninformative account of this peculiar institution.

There was something, as I now recall, of the later charlatan Lysenko about it. Those who had organized the institute and then become its directors supposed that they would very quickly be able to locate "a certain something" in the human organism that provided the key to overcoming illnesses, of which the most virulent was old age. Apart from being extremely attractive in itself, such a goal was very much in the spirit of the day: it was barely enough to "conquer space and time"—all that was still unknown and beyond human control should also be conquered and subjugated. This coincided entirely with the wishes of Stalin, who could not tolerate the existence of anything that was not subject to his power. It was this and not just an opportunist attempt to rapidly benefit humanity that explains why Lysenko, Olga Lepeshinskaya, Boshyan and the other holy fools and lesser frauds all flourished then.

Those who had organized the institute were, of course, not frauds. But their scientific ideas were so in tune with the aims and wishes of the bosses that they were swept impetuously upward by a powerful force. Their theories enraptured first Gorky and then Stalin. Almost every week the Institute's researchers would gather in Gorky's mansion at the end of Spiridonov Street and there expound —before Stalin, Gorky and the handful of others admitted to this select company—their ideas about the extraordinary prospects for bringing the human organism under control. After these informal get-togethers they would come round to Moskvin's apartment nearby, and these conversations would continue in an atmosphere much less inhibited by the presence of such august persons.

Why Moskvin? Because Ivan Mikhailovich himself shared a faith in the unlimited capacities of science. He had also been close to Lev Nikolayevich Fyodorov, the organizer and director of the institute, and helped him in all kinds of ways when they were both still in Petrograd. Undoubtedly, Fyodorov was a very interesting character. He went to fight in the Civil War when still a student and returned a Communist. Then he approached Pavlov and asked to be taken on at the latter's famous laboratory. Evidently, Fyodorov was not only cheekily self-assured but also possessed a certain charm, for Pavlov gave him a job and soon Fyodorov was effectively in charge of the whole laboratory. I can pass no judgment on Fyodorov as a scientist. In all probability he was no genius. As an organizer, though, he was superb. The flourishing of Pavlov's laboratory and the strengthening of the monopoly his ideas exercised in Soviet physiology were due, so far as I now recall, more to Fyodorov's organizational abilities than to Pavlov.

Fyodorov was also behind the creation of the Institute of Experimental Medicine. He managed, not without the aid of Moskvin, perhaps, to attract the attention of Gorky and arouse Stalin's passionate interest. In an extraordinarily short period of time an enormous institute with a vast staff and unheard-of privileges came into being... An entire complex of buildings was erected on the outskirts of Moscow and public lecturers, journalists and writers rushed to publicize the unprecedented flowering of Soviet medicine that was just around the corner.

I do not now remember Grashchenkov or any of the others in charge of the institute very well. I do not retain any remotely vivid memories of Fyodorov himself. I was totally enchanted, on the other hand, by Alexei Speransky, who was the most brilliant and interesting figure among them. When I recall those years on Spiridonov Street I realize that of all the many people I met there, each striking in their own way, no one made such an impression on me as Speransky.

He had almost reached the status of Academician, and the press already referred to him as a god among scientists. Yet there was nothing that could be termed imposing or Olympian about him. Speransky adopted an emphatically simple manner, moved about rapidly, expressed himself in rough and often crude language, and liked to drink. At the same time, he had a profound understanding and knowledge of music. An excellent cellist, he had earned extra money in difficult years, he would tell us, by playing in movie houses. It was his knowledge of poetry, however, that most astounded me. He knew almost all of twentieth-century Russian poetry by heart and, after a bottle of brandy, could recite for hours. These were not the approved authors, moreover, but Kuzmin, Annensky, Solovyov, Blok and Gumilyov. He very much loved Mayakovsky and gave brilliant recitals of his work.

It was not this alone, though, that I found so attractive in

Speransky. He also exuded an air of independence—from his superiors, and from the dominant views in science and politics. In company his behavior was not just independent—it was rude. He thought nothing of interrupting some important fellow guest and telling him he was talking nonsense. "You keep out of this, you silly woman!" he might say to Sophia Alexandrovna, when she became involved in an argument about science, "What do you know about it!" At one of the gatherings at Gorky's house, he told Molotov that even though the latter was only just learning how to run the state, he already wanted to philosophize about the human organism. Since everything and everyone was already imbued with the same universal conformism, these qualities made Speransky irresistibly attractive. He understood this himself and of all the vast company who gathered at Spiridonov Street he singled me out, a young man with no official position, for his special attention. Not only that, he treated me as a friend and in various ways emphasized the equality of our relations. To me he seemed the ideal scientist, a man whose independence and friendship were not affected by changing circumstances.

So I was very irritated, simply furious, when my new friend Shura Vishnevsky, who was a real medical doctor, would say, "You don't understand the first thing about people. I've known Alexei Speransky since childhood, he's a close family friend. Mark my words: when put to the test, he will prove less reliable than anyone else. He'll betray you, lock, stock and barrel. It's amazing the way you fall for all his theatrical stunts and somersaults..."

That conversation took place at the very beginning of 1937. Not one of us then imagined how soon such qualities as human dignity, independence and courage would be put to the test.

Less than six months passed and we found ourselves left with only two rooms: the door leading into the rest of the apartment was officially sealed. Of all the telephones there before, only the ordinary telephone remained and it stood silent. Everyone who lived through that period, staying behind in a half sealed-up apartment, knows that of the many shocks they then experienced, one of the greatest was the way the telephone ceased to ring. It was still in perfect working order and we could call others, but it almost never rang itself... The numerous friends of the Moskvin family stopped calling, my own close friends almost all fell silent, and there were days when our recently installed new Czech telephone did not once emit its silvery ring.

In this repugnant and cowardly silence the failure of Alexei Speransky to call was particularly bitter to me. Only a week or two before he had said that he looked on me as a friend and on Oksana, my wife, as something like a daughter... What was such a bold and independent man afraid of? During those days and months I crossed off the names of many friends and acquaintances. The hardest of all, though, was to break with Speransky. But I did so. I was terribly afraid of meeting him somewhere else, however, not for myself, but for his sake. How would he be able to look me in the eye? And yet he did.

By then we had already been evicted from the government apartments on Spiridonov Street and were living in two rooms of a vast communal apartment on Grenade Alley. The terrible autumn of 1937 had passed, as had the no less terrible winter, and it was already spring 1938. During this time I had been expelled from the Children's Publishing House and for a while was unemployed. Then I found work with an exotic organization known as the Society for the Friends of a Green Moscow, planting flowers and trees in courtyards. After February 1938 I was allowed back at the publishers, though in a less important position, as a "victim of excesses": in that month Stalin, giving one of his regular theatrical performances, had raised the issue of "certain excesses" at the Central Committee plenum. Again I plunged into publishing work. Then came a day I shall never forget. It was my last day of freedom.

The date was 18 April 1938. It was a very busy day for me. The famous children's writer Marshak had come to visit Moscow from Leningrad and was staying outside the city in the sanatorium at Uskoe. I went there that morning to discuss a series of popular scientific books for children with him. Samuil Marshak never rushed things. He interspersed his ideas about the subjects for these educational texts with reminiscences about Gorky; he recited Pushkin's verse and his own; he gave me lunch; in the end, it was time for him to make the trip into Moscow and we had still not finished our business.

"Come in the car with me," Marshak said decisively. "We'll spend a little more time together where I'm staying and finish our work there."

When we were already in Moscow I wanted to ask him which hotel he was staying at but then I saw that we were stopping outside a very familiar building on Novinsky Boulevard. It was then that I guessed. His son had married Speransky's daughter and we would soon be in Alexei Speransky's apartment which I knew so well.

I was in luck: the loud voice of its master was not to be heard, he was not home.

Marshak made himself comfortable in Speransky's study and immediately began to pull books, manuscripts and pages of paper covered with his wonderfully legible hand out of his large briefcase. We had almost finished our work when the door opened and in walked Alexei Speransky.

"Ah, Lyova, hello," he greeted me, as though we had seen each other only the evening before. He made some witty remarks about the sanatorium, asked me if I had seen the Blok volume which had just been published, and left the room. He had looked me in the eye and, as always, laughed and joked. There had not been the slightest hint of embarrassment on his plain and expressive face.

I thought to myself, What shall I say to Shura Vishnevsky when he comes round to Grenade Alley this evening, as he did almost every day? But Shura did not drop by and after that I had no more evenings for conversation with him.

* * *

Here I should probably say something about Vishnevsky. Many tales have now been told and written about him, and a great many memoirs. During our short but intense friendship, however, he was neither Academician nor lieutenant-general nor a deputy of the Supreme Soviet. He did not yet wear a single medal and there were no legends about him yet. He was more often called Shura than Alexander Alexandrovich. Even then, however, he had already gotten his doctorate and was the man he would remain: the student of his father and a good surgeon.

We became acquainted thanks to Speransky. Oksana was seriously, almost fatally, ill. With his customary determination, Speransky drove all the famous Kremlin doctors to her bedside and himself brought Alexander Vishnevsky the elder to our apartment. There was something reassuring and comforting about this massive and taciturn doctor; he seemed so very like the old experienced pre-revolutionary doctors in the provinces who could cure any complaint. He began to treat Oksana and after several days brought his son along to continue looking after her. When Oksana rapidly recovered, the elder Vishnevsky disappeared and Shura remained. By then he was not a doctor so much as a close friend.

In no way, either physically or in character, was he like his famous father. Small, puny, reminiscent of a chicken, he was always very upset that no one would acknowledge his importance. Without the slightest trace of humor, rather sorrowfully, he told us how the doorman had severely pointed him towards the students' cloakroom when he came to give a lecture at some scientific society. Indeed, he did not give an impression of professorial gravitas. One day, I remember, we were eating at the dacha when Tarasova rang us up in a panic, and said that Moskvin the actor (who had left his wife to live with her) had been taken seriously ill. Sophia Alexandrovna said that Professor Vishnevsky was with us and that I would immediately drive him there.

I climbed up the staircase to the actress's apartment on Strastnaya (now Pushkin) Square with Vishnevsky, who was very tipsy. We rang the doorbell. Tarasova herself, most informally dressed, opened the door. Little Shura stood on tiptoe, patted her on the cheek, and demanded imperiously: "Where is the master, my dear?" Tarasova grabbed my arm, and pulled me to one side: "For God's sake, where is Professor Vishnevsky?"

Nevertheless, Shura was a genuinely good surgeon who loved medicine above all. He was one of the first to operate successfully on the digestive tract. He was totally wrapped up in his work and could describe it for hours on end. Once he persuaded me to attend one of his operations. I was horrified by the sight of the disembowelled human body and the conversation that Vishnevsky conducted with his patient, after cutting open his back and sawing through two ribs. As the faithful son of his father, he conducted all his operations under local anesthetic. His medical anecdotes were superb and I am surprised that his memoirs as a field surgeon during the war are so dully written. Probably, he was already a general then and those notes were written by some minor assistant.

But most of all it was Shura's contempt for titles, rank and medals that attracted me... He used to make fun of them when we met in the elite and official surroundings of Moskvin's apartment. Once we had moved to the communal apartment on Grenade Alley he abandoned all restraint in his criticism.

Shura was almost the only one of my friends who was not scared off by our misfortune. He spent almost all his free evenings with us. Oksana's sister Yelena had returned from Paris, where she worked in the Soviet embassy, and the four of us would spend every evening together. Moreover, by no means did we pass the time in tears, but in a state of merriment which, I now understand, was even euphoric. Such outbursts of gaiety, such "feasts in the time of plague" are, evidently, a common reaction. Our cell No. 29 in Butyrki prison was periodically overcome by outbursts of merriment and uncontrollable laughter, and when I later read *The Gods Are Thirsty* I was amazed at the confidence with which Anatole France described the hysterical gaiety of the inmates of the Conciergerie, almost all of whom were to face the guillotine on the Place des Grèves.

We joked, and played cards and other entertaining games. We tried every conceivable form of divination. We drank the wine that I had set aside or that Shura brought with him. If we ran short, he would make out a prescription for surgical pure spirits, add his stamp, and I would run down to the chemist's at the Nikita Gates on the Boulevard and obtain a (free!) bottle of this necessary constituent of our evening entertainments.

It was when we saw each other almost daily at Grenade Alley that Shura Vishnevsky gave free rein to his feelings about officials of every rank and type, not excluding the very highest of all. He derided the renowned doctors who pursued awards and medals and all other inflated self-important personages. He also made fun of my Party membership. I think he was quite sincere in what he said then.

Neither during the brief respite between arrests after the war nor when I finally returned to Moscow in 1955 did I feel any desire to meet my old friend. By then he had already risen to the top of the social ladder. He had all that he had so despised before: the rank of general, a mass of awards, numerous different titles, the directorship of a vast institute and an incredible amount of attention from the press. The man who had once teased me about my Party membership was now a delegate at Party congresses, large and small, a member of the Moscow city Party committee, and so on. I realized he would inevitably feel awkward if we met, and I did not want that. Especially since he knew that I was back in Moscow, since we had common acquaintances. He operated on and then became friendly with Shura Kron, who told him that I was living in Moscow again. He made no effort to find me...

I was the one to seek him out. Ill health was the cause. The year was 1968. My daughter Natasha developed symptoms that deeply alarmed us, and my wife Rika forced me to go to the Vishnevsky Institute (only a short walk away from our apartment). Beforehand I telephoned Shura's wife and he knew I was coming. He met me just as Speransky had once greeted me, as though we had only parted the evening before. He expressed his condolences, of course, about Oksana's death and asked after Yelena. But all this was conveyed in a rapid, business-like way, and interspersed between the almost obscene commands he barked at his subordinates when they appeared in his office, a room hung with various bird-cages. He preferred to tell me about these birds rather than ask about my past and present life. With Natasha he was gentle and examined her himself. He performed the minor operation, decided when she could go home, and sent his greetings.

And that was that. We did sometimes meet again, it is true, by chance, in the Writers Club where he liked to speak once in a while. Awkwardly and rapidly he would embrace me and say, indignant with whom it was not clear, "Why don't we ever see each other? We must get together sometime and have a chat!"

However, he did not call and I felt it inappropriate to do so myself. Whatever could we "chat" about now? We each lived our own quite different lives. He received the next title or award, gave the next interview and wrote his articles and books. He went abroad to congresses and met visiting foreigners; he attended government and diplomatic receptions, went to all the theatrical premieres and openings, and was invited to elite banquets. He played tennis, divorced, remarried—then suddenly died, as though he had stumbled in this ceaseless, unrelenting race.

When I remember him now I feel a lasting gratitude for the ten months of our friendship and a certain pity: he was so unlike his father and his life was spent in the pursuit of such unnatural vanities.

Describing all these actors and doctors I have neglected someone who came to the apartment on Spiridonov Street as a matter of course, and so often that it is impossible to consider him a "guest."

Almost every week, alone or with his wife, Gleb Boky would come to visit. He was quite a different character from Ivan Moskvin.

Boky would not join in the noisy parties but enjoyed being there and did not disturb anyone with his presence. He sat drinking wine or something stronger and smoked one cigarette after another—he rolled them in yellow Turkish paper himself from aromatic tobacco. Gleb Boky was not at all like the other Old Bolsheviks. He never led an ascetic life, like Moskvin. He had certain "strange" convictions of his own. He never shook hands with anyone and refused all the privileges of his rank, the dachas and sanatoria, and so forth. Instead he and a group of his subordinates leased a dacha together at Kuchino, outside Moscow, and in the summer rented a house near Batum from a Turk in the village of Makhindjauri. He shared a tiny three-room apartment in Moscow with his wife and elder daughter Yelena, and it would never have occurred to his relations and acquaintances to use his government car for their own needs. Winter and summer he wore a raincoat and crumpled cap and even in the rain and snow never put up the roof on his Packard convertible.

His judgments of others were categorical and based on certain details that were decisive for him.

"Litvinov: there's a person you can't do business with," he would say. "He's a man you can't trust. Just imagine, in 1922 I told him that the safe containing his confidential documents was in a room that was not properly guarded. If he wasn't careful, someone would filch them... Litvinov roared with laughter and so I bet him a bottle of French cognac that I would steal the documents from his safe. We shook hands on it. Then he behaved quite improperly: he put a sentry outside the door leading into the room where there had been no one before. Of course, my people got in all the same, opened the safe and took the documents. I sent them back to Litvinov with a note that he should send round the bottle he'd lost. You know what he did? The next day Lenin rang me up and said that a complaint had reached him from Litvinov that I had broken into his safe and stolen secret materials. Would you trust someone after an experience like that?"

Yet for all these quirks and oddities there was a definite charm to Boky. Of course, women felt it most. Even such formidable women as Yelena Stasova and Yekaterina Kalinin told me that they had never met a more charming man than Gleb Boky. And men also proved susceptible. One of them, amusingly enough, was none other than Fyodor Chaliapin.

We knew that Boky was not only acquainted with the singer but friendly with him as well. He had all the records that Chaliapin had

made in Russia and every new recording made abroad by the great
bass was specially sent to him. In 1936 I came across a copy of *Mask
and Soul*, Chaliapin's memoirs. In the Soviet Union only the first part,
which presents the singer's artistic credo, was published. The second
part contains memoirs of his life under the Soviet regime and there
he denigrated the authorities and all the Bolshevik bigwigs, using
every word that can decently be printed. So I was amused to find
that he referred to both Moskvin and Boky. The first he called the
"governor-general of Petrograd" and employed very strong language
about him for banning a certain poster announcing one of his concerts. But the Chekist Boky was described at length and in such terms
that it was amazing to think of Chaliapin writing such words.

Once after a concert he was handed an enormous basket full of
rare vintage wines and a large bouquet of flowers, Chaliapin wrote.
They were followed behind stage by the man who had presented
such an extraordinary gift, a small, quiet and charming fellow who
led a tiny girl by the hand. This was Gleb Boky, the chairman of the
Petrograd Cheka. Although rumors circulate to this day that the man
was a bloodthirsty sadist, continued Chaliapin, I can confirm that
they are lies: Boky is one of the most kind and charming men I have
met. I was his friend and am proud of such a friendship...

I was able then to check these memoirs against reality. How far
was this a true story, I once asked Gleb Boky. He grinned and replied,
"Well, it wasn't quite like that. A gang of sailors were roaming
around the city, looking for something to drink. One of them suddenly had a bright idea: Chaliapin was sure to have some drinks on
hand. His address was widely known and they poured into his apartment, declaring that they were Cheka agents searching for arms.
They ransacked the apartment and of course found no small number
of the necessary bottles. They seized them and triumphantly departed. Chaliapin kicked up a hell of a fuss. So in order to calm him
down I ordered that a basket of wines be collected from the various
palace cellars and delivered to him behind stage. To check that they
reached him, I went to visit him there. Well, I also wanted to make
his acquaintance—I'm very fond of him as a singer. Then we really did
become friendly..."

Contrary to what an already embittered Chaliapin wrote in his
memoirs he was not at all above hobnobbing with the Soviet leaders.
He was friendly not only with Gleb Boky but also Demyan Bedny and
when he did emigrate, he was not only restrained in his attitude to
the Soviet government but proud that his was no emigre Nansen
passport but the real thing.

One time Oksana was staying at the small government sanatorium
on the former Yusupov estate at Arkhangelskoe. While visiting her I
made the acquaintance of our ambassador to France, Christian
Rakovsky. He was a handsome, urbane, very attractive and sociable

person. It was easy and pleasant to make his acquaintance and ask him about life abroad, of which I had not the faintest conception. Chaliapin came up in conversation and Rakovsky told me how he had to inform the singer that he had been deprived of his Soviet citizenship.

Chaliapin's behavior gave no grounds whatsoever for such treatment, according to Rakovsky. He did not take part in the various emigre actions and protests, joyfully accepted invitations to receptions at the embassy, and would sing at the events organized to mark various Soviet celebrations. Neither did he give money to other emigres. This was partly because he did not like giving anyone any of his money, and partly because he was extremely careful not to get closely involved with the actively anti-Soviet part of the White emigration. However, he loved to attend the church not far from the embassy, and sometimes sang there with the famous choir directed by Afonsky. Chaliapin, incidentally, also made several wonderful records of church music.

Once the church organized a concert by Afonsky's choir to raise money to help its poor parishioners, in other words, of course, white emigres. It invited another regular member of the congregation, Chaliapin, to sing and he, naturally, did not refuse. The ambassador did not attribute any great significance to the event but there were large numbers of informers of various ranks within the embassy. And it was they who reported back... Evidently, the order to deprive Chaliapin of his Soviet passport was issued by someone whose decrees could not be questioned. Rakovsky had no alternative, and invited Chaliapin to come in and see him.

I can imagine how Rakovsky announced this cruel and unjust decision to Chaliapin, deploying all the gentleness and tact of which he was capable. Nevertheless, he told me, Chaliapin burst into tears. They had great difficulty in calming him down and he left the embassy, tear-stained and embittered, never to set foot there or in Russia again. Understandably, Rakovsky voiced no criticism of his instructions from Moscow but even his young and orthodox listeners could clearly see that this was a barbarous act of gross injustice towards the great singer and Russian art as a whole. Stalin showed his attitude to the arts quite clearly, though, when he blew up several very old churches in the Kremlin, destroyed so much of Russia's artistic heritage, and sold off paintings in our state museums by Titian and Rembrandt to American millionaires. It is surprising that today, when Chaliapin has been completely rehabilitated, his ashes returned to Russia, and a museum organized to commemorate him, that people prefer to ignore the story of how he was made an emigre and deprived of his motherland. It is amazing how a deep-seated and servile fear of Stalin continues to live on in people who never knew him as a ruler. It has become almost genetically transmitted, a confirmation of

Lysenko's theory that acquired characteristics can be passed on to the next generation...

* * *

Meanwhile, our turn was rapidly drawing closer. Oksana and I saw in the New Year of 1937 at the Osinskys' apartment in the Kremlin. I cannot recall a merrier New Year's celebration. Irakly Andronikov, then young and uninhibited, introduced us to the entire Olympus of Soviet literature and drama. Nikolai Oleinikov recited his unusual poems and sang an oratorio, the text of which consisted of a solitary word: "Gvozd" (nail). Then Valerian Osinsky conducted us in the singing of "Kolodnikov," "Noble Sea, O Blessed Baikal," "A Wagon Races along the Dusty Road" and others. Prison songs from a distant and naive past, which could never happen again. And in fact it was not repeated, since what came next was quite different.

Of that large and merry gathering at the New Year of 1937 four people survived: Osinsky's daughter Sveta, who was then only a little girl; Petya Karlik, a friend of Dima Osinsky and of mine, who served his full ten years in Norilsk; the now seriously ill Irakly Andronikov; and myself.

* * *

January was over and February had begun, but I do not have any clear memory of those months because it was then that Oksana fell seriously, almost fatally, ill. When she finally recovered and I could think of something else, it had begun. All the military leaders we worshipped were arrested, tried and shot. Rudzutak was arrested, and then the others. I don't remember any conversations about this with my father-in-law. It seems there weren't any. Life continued as before, Oksana got better and we somewhat feverishly made up for lost time, visiting friends, and attending noisy and tipsy celebrations.

On 7 June Gleb Boky was summoned by the new People's Commissar for Internal Affairs and Commissar-General of State Security, Nikolai Yezhov. He did not return. Ivan Moskvin came home late each day from work, almost always finding visitors in the apartment on his arrival, and joined them at the table, inscrutably lively as ever. There was hardly a moment during that last week when we were alone together and I could have asked him... Asked him what? I wanted him to answer certain terrible questions that had occurred to me. But I waited too long.

On 14 June there was a premiere at the Vakhtangov theater. The main role was being played by our friend Volodya Moskvin. The production was a success and we waited while he removed his make-up and then, as agreed earlier, we all went back to our apartment at

Spiridonov Street. It was a wonderful summer evening and we laughed and fooled around as we walked home, hiding behind merriment from the horror that had already firmly settled within us.

We climbed the stairs to our landing and rang the doorbell. It was not our maid Klava who opened the door but an unfamiliar soldier wearing an NKVD cap. A government courier, I thought, surprised at the politeness with which he invited us to precede him. In the hall, however, there seemed, for some reason, to be a great many "couriers"... At the double doors of the dining room the white, immobile face of Sophia Alexandrovna appeared, and I immediately understood what was going on.

The polite "couriers" led us into the dining-room and told us to behave quietly. A petrified Nikolai Ozerov sat at the table with our good friends the Voznesenskys. The master of the house was not yet back from work. The Bluecaps (as the secret policemen were known) were already swarming about his study, while others stood guarding the doors and the telephone, watching every one of us. Volodya Moskvin sat down at the table, grabbed the brandy bottle and turned to the officer in charge, "Hey, you! Is drinking allowed?"

"As long as you behave..."

Volodya grinned and poured out a glass for me and himself. The remaining guests did not say a word and showed no inclination to eat or drink. Volodya and I had managed to down only a few glasses when there was a ring at the door: Ivan Moskvin had arrived. The Bluecaps met him in the hall and escorted him into the study. As he walked past us, a calm but pale Moskvin greeted his guests. Some time after they called in Sophia Alexandrovna; ten minutes later Ivan Moskvin came out of the study and an NKVD man followed, carrying the small bag of articles that each was permitted to take with him when arrested. Moskvin said goodbye to each of us in turn, with a guilty smile as if asking our forgiveness for any unpleasantness he had caused us. A car engine revved up under the window. It was suggested that the guests go home now and so they got up and, shrinking, walked to the front door through a cordon of NKVD men (somehow there seemed to be even more of them now).

Volodya Moskvin finished off the bottle and as he left the dining room he turned to me, "Where shall we meet again? Maybe there?"

I shrugged my shoulders. Then the NKVD men very politely suggested to Sophia Alexandrovna that she accompany them to the dacha at Volynskoe to conduct a search there. When she wanted to take a summer coat with her instead of a light raincoat the man in charge said, with surprise, "What for? It's warm tonight and we'll be back within an hour, at the most."

The search in the now alien and inaccessible study continued. Oksana had gone to our daughter's room, and I sat alone at the table, not feeling any effect from the brandy. An hour later the commanding officer returned. Asked where Sophia Alexandrovna was, he raised his eyebrows in surprise, "What do you mean, where? She's been arrested."

That was my first encounter with a cruelty, the causes of which I could not understand. What was the point of sending a middle-aged woman in not very good health to prison without even the tiny bag of underclothes and washing things that an arrested person has always been allowed to take with him since the time of the Pharaohs? Nor were we allowed to deliver any parcels to the prison or the camp, or send her any letters. A year or so later, Sophia Alexandrovna died in Potma, the camp in Mordovia for family members of enemies of the people, without ever knowing what had happened to her husband, daughter, granddaughter and all her friends and relatives, from whom she had been so suddenly taken away.

Each of us tried many times to imagine how those close to us behaved before they were dragged out to be executed. I shall never know what happened during Ivan Moskvin's interrogation but I am almost certain that he was subjected to brutal torture and abuse—there was a stubbornness about him that is extremely irritating to the experts in torture and interrogation.

Almost ten years later when my first sentence had finished and my second had not yet begun, I travelled to Moscow, disdaining all the rules and restrictions with the contempt of an experienced prisoner. I went to see Lyubov Moskvina, the actor's wife. The large apartment was still filled with paintings. Ivan Moskvin had left her for the comparatively young and beautiful Tarasova. Fedya had been killed during the war and Volodya continued to drink heavily.

She wept for her sons, for Sophia Alexandrovna, Oksana and herself. Then, when she had cried her fill, she said, "What a strange fate, the two Ivan Moskvins. Yours lived like a monk and worked hard all his life. I don't know what for, or why. My Ivan only loved himself and his art. He ate and drank well under every government, he loved women and couldn't give a damn about politics... Now he has state awards, he's rich and a deputy of that Supreme Soviet of yours. He probably shakes hands with Stalin. But your Ivan... Will they ever remember him?"

No, they did not and they probably never will. And we shall never hear an answer from either Gleb Boky or Ivan Moskvin, or from all their generation, an answer to the question: when, at what moment in their life—at liberty, in prison, or when being taken out to be shot—did they understand what kind of death they had prepared for themselves, and what kind of life they were leaving for those who remained behind?

* * *

These reminiscences should not be regarded as a biography of Ivan Moskvin. They involve no research, only personal impressions. They were written at a time when nothing was known about him. It is only in the last four to five years that articles about Moskvin have appeared and I have learned many new details of his life and seen his photograph.

However, I decided I should not change anything in memoirs that were written almost twenty years ago. For they not only define the level of the author's knowledge at that time but his feelings as he wrote down these stories and his assessment of events and individuals. Neither have I made changes in any of the other stories here. The author, therefore, begs the reader's forgiveness for any inaccuracies in what he has written about the living, and about those who passed on long ago. For the genre of this collection is that of the short story. The stories are autobiographical, but are still most definitely short stories.

Razgon at Chepets camp, Usollag, November 21, 1954. Razgon's barracks are to the far right. To the left is the corner of the office where Razgon worked.

Razgon taking a break from wood-cutting. Chepets camp, Usollag, summer 1952.

MILITARY MEN

What am I writing here? A kind of testimony? That's what I thought when I began. But I soon understood this was not the case. Testimony should provide answers to clear questions. I jump from one theme to another, without concealing my sympathies and dislikes. I am not just presenting the facts but trying to interpret them as well. So are they memoirs, then? Not entirely, since what I am about to describe does not, as literary specialists would say, meet the "requirements of the genre." They are best regarded as a continuation of my reflections on "what it was all about," "how it came to happen." Every time I had a moment to myself I would ponder these questions as they marched me each day to the timber-felling area, or when in solitary confinement in the Stavropol MGB prison, and during the long journeys I made on foot as an unguarded prisoner through the silent, lifeless forests of the North. These images and questions still run through my mind today when I go out for short walks after my recent heart attack.

It would not be honest to present what follows as simply a record of my thoughts in 1939, 1950 and 1956... I have learned a great deal since then and changed my views on many things. If I am not wiser I have undoubtedly had more experience. Probably, I still have no right to claim (not even to myself) that now I know what it was all about. I am not that confident. Yet like any witness and participant, I can and should tell others about another aspect of the drama in which my generation and I found ourselves swept up.

I am not thinking about how we were killed, imprisoned or exiled. That was quite ordinary by then: it had gone on before we were arrested and went on after we were released. When I refer to the drama of my generation I have in mind what used grandly to be called the "dashing of one's ideals." Before our very eyes we saw the gods die, those gods whom (in full accordance with our materialist world view) we had ourselves created. I do not mean ideas or great historic figures from the past, but our contemporaries who were real live people.

For my generation—of course, I speak only for those of my background and position—such "living gods" were the leaders of the country and the "heroes of the Civil War." It is extraordinary, looking back, that for all our sincere democratic attitudes we never considered that the ordinary soldiers in the Civil War could be heroes. Only military leaders could be heroes for us! Any person with the Order of the Red Banner (at that time an extremely rare award) pinned to his field shirt, uniform, peasant blouse or civilian jacket naturally aroused our admiration. Today I can see quite clearly that only people of the rank of brigade commander[1] and above were elevated to the status of heroes. Our recognition of their divine status was sincere. With the politicians things were rather more complicated.

We rapidly began to understand that although politicians were gods they were even more earthbound than we simple and inadequate mortals. The books I had read, from Suetonius to Pokrovsky, convinced me that they engaged in petty deceits. The politicians would not keep their promises, they intrigued and squeezed out their rivals, and they possessed an extraordinary capacity for combining a personal battle for power with the struggle for elevated and noble ideas. I was well acquainted with many major figures in the Party. Among them were educated and clever people who were graced with such excellent qualities as selflessness, modesty and simplicity. Yet they were all still politicians, and as such their promises were worthless. They submitted to superior force without a murmur and their power was only apparent—there was nothing to back it up. Their lack of independence was obvious, even to someone as excited by politics and as young as I then was. It made little difference that they were followed everywhere by bodyguards and greeted with ovations. Before our eyes a great many of these gods were rapidly and against their will ejected from Mount Olympus and sent to join us below. They became Party organizers at factories, or were put in charge of health resorts and museums.

This did not happen to the military men. Even when they retired they continued to remain our heroes. Why speak of our attitude, indeed, when people more clever and perceptive than us admired them as well.

How Timoshenko appealed to Isaac Babel! With what pleasure he painted "the beauty of his gigantic body... the purple riding breeches, the dark red cap tilted to one side, and the medal pinned to his chest." The famed Commander of Division No. 6 dictated his orders "drenched in eau de cologne and looking like Peter the Great":

> ... I lay the responsibility for this catastrophe on Chesnokov, who is to be punished with the death penalty: I shall polish him off here and now. And after serving at the front with me for more than one month, Comrade Chesnokov, you know I mean what I say...[2]

I personally never made the acquaintance of Marshal Timoshenko. This gloomy, rather stupid and unfortunate man watched in helpless despair as the tiny detachments of Finnish sharpshooters destroyed our large units, and then saw German tank divisions cut off, destroy, or capture entire armies on the front where he was in command. An outcast from the ranks of people's commissars, supreme commanders and marshals he became a nobody, living on only in the pages of dull monographs and of dissertations that no one bothered to read. As Savitsky, on the other hand, whom Babel depicted not only with genuine interest but also an unconcealed affection, he has always remained a lively, cheerful and captivating figure in Russian literature. I knew neither the Commander of Division No. 6 nor the People's Commissar for Defense, and I cannot conceive that the hero of *Red Cavalry*, my favorite book, was a real person.

I did know the "renowned and captivating Kniga," however, the commander of the Stavropol partisans. And I knew him quite well. When I was living in Stavropol after the war his former aide de camp, Ivan Ivanovich Ivanko, who was then in charge of the territory's food industry, decided to write a book about the Civil War and hired me to ghost it for him. He introduced me to retired Major-general Vasily Kniga, and I spent many days in the mansion inhabited by this former partisan leader who later, as divisional commander, was praised by Babel.

Kniga was a fussy, short man who wore his general's epaulettes even while walking around the house in his longjohns. He had a pretty young wife, an enormous orchard, a vast vegetable garden and cows, geese, chickens, pigs and piglets. Once a month he climbed into his car and his personal chauffeur drove him around all the collective farms in the Stavropol Territory that bore his name. When he returned, his car, a Horch (a war trophy), was followed by a collective-farm truck loaded with the tribute of that abundantly fertile region.

In his present state of negligent forgetfulness, he was flattered by the attentions of someone who had been introduced to him as a "Moscow writer." After issuing his household with the orders of the day he would fill a Saxon porcelain cup with vodka infused with garlic and, stroking his strikingly handsome mustaches, would begin to tell stories. The problem was not that he did not like talking about the Civil War (or any other war for that matter): he simply did not know how. "At that moment we smashed into them!... Then we cut them to pieces.... Well, we ran away from them until the horses got too tired. Then we were forced to turn and fight..." More interesting was the account of his visit to the Tsar. During the First World War, Kniga was the first to be made a full St. George cavalier[3] on the Southwest front. Together with the famous Kozma Kryuchkov, the first George cavalier on the Western front, he spent a whole week with Nicholas II.

"How was your visit?"

"They treated us well! Every morning they washed and shaved us, gave us freshly ironed clothes, and the generals looked us over, pulling off any loose threads... Then, into the hall. We're sitting there like statues with our caps in our left hand... The doors open and in walks His Highness. We jump up and greet him in the proper fashion. The Tsar bows to us and sits down in a little armchair. Immediately a servant brings him a silver tray, and on it are a silver flask and silver tumbler. His Highness gives his mustache a little brush, downs the tumbler, and says: 'Well, my Cossack lads, and what happened next...' I wasn't much of a talker but Kozma, what a chatterer he was! He got going, and you just sat back and listened. How he thrashed the Germans with sabre and lance, stamped his boot on their ugly mugs... And the whole time the Tsar gives his mustache a little stroke and knocks back one tumbler after another... When half an hour has passed he goes like this with his hand and they bring us a silver tray with a large tumbler each, also of pure silver. We knock it back—we were supposed to drink it up all at once—then: 'Our humble thanks, Your Imperial Highness!' And the Tsar would leave."

"And the next day?"

"The next day, the same again. It went on the whole week. Then the Tsar said goodbye and shook our hands. We went back to the front. And there I was drinking for a whole month with the officers and even the generals. A guest of the Tsar, no less!"

Kniga did not retain such vivid memories of the Civil War. And he did not like to recall the Great Patriotic War at all. With good reason. During the sadly famous operation in the Crimea Kniga was put in charge of the vast numbers of cavalry that had been packed off there for some reason. The Germans, joyfully relieved, sent their tanks against our cavalry divisions. Acting as he had in the past, Kniga drew up his horsemen in a straight line, rode out in front of them, cried "Draw sabres!" and hurled them at the tanks. They managed to evacuate the lightly-wounded Kniga on a small reconnaissance plane. The rest were mown down by the tanks. After this Stalin gave orders that Kniga was to be kept away from the front. To the end of the war he remained a major-general and would roundly curse his more successful comrades. Kniga was not shot, however, or demoted. Even then this did not surprise me. I had learned from the tales of my friends at Camp No. 1 in Ustvymlag that if someone had served in the First Cavalry Army they always received special treatment.

Yet no matter how closely I examined my amusing and fussy companion, I could not catch the faintest glimpse of the man who had become a living legend—for Babel, for us and even for those who knew him best—for his love of "presents." He was not very clever, a profoundly ignorant but brave man who had one great virtue in the eyes of Stalin, his loyalty. Such a man would carry out an order, even if he was told to slit his own mother's throat.

I realize that our tastes, preferences and view of the world were, to a great extent, shaped by myths. Such myth-making is not so effective today although contemporary methods of mass deception are incredibly powerful. The myth of the "legendary military leaders" was created in the 1920s before radio and television, before newspapers and magazines began to reach millions of readers, and before books about our "great" contemporaries and busts to the living were instantly produced.

Sometimes nothing at all lay behind such myths. The most typical example, of course, was that of the "first Red officer," Voroshilov. No matter how thoroughly we studied his biography we could not discover the slightest indication that he was a great military leader. A manual worker and minor Party official, he was sent to the army during the Civil War, like so many others, to carry out political work. Moreover, he was not put in charge of a front, an army or even a division: he was entrusted with a small semi-partisan unit commanded by former dragoon sergeant-major Budyonny. His "legendary biography" began with clashes outside Tsaritsyn[4] on the Volga, a battle of marginal importance that had no decisive influence in deciding the outcome of the enormous struggle between the Reds and the Whites. But there he caught the attention of Stalin who saw in him the main human quality he valued: unquestioning loyalty.

So when Stalin needed to replace the Trotskyist head of the Moscow garrison, Muralov, with his own trusted candidate, Voroshilov was put in charge of the capital's military district—a crucial post in all ages and in every state. Following the mysterious, or perhaps not so mysterious, death of Frunze, Voroshilov became the People's Commissar for Military and Naval Affairs and chairman of the Revolutionary Military Council. Voroshilov's subsequent activities could be observed by all and did not provide any grounds for continuing the legend. He reviewed parades on Red Square, mounted on a superb black steed; Brodsky, Yar-Kravchenko and Gerasimov painted his portrait; for some reason he was considered a connoisseur of the arts and patronized various artists and actors; he put his signature to the programs for teaching history in schools; during maneuvers at sea he would change into a naval uniform—and in every photograph, on every occasion, he appeared next to the short man in the long soldier's overcoat who hid something of the Mona Lisa's enigmatic smile beneath his famous mustache.

As soon as Voroshilov was deprived of almost all the gifted commanders who had created and run the Red Army, he proved a weak, confused man, quite incapable of thinking for himself. He had no military skills. Wherever Stalin sent him he lost the battle and large numbers of soldiers, since he feared to take responsibility for any remotely decisive action. While Stalin lived, the contemptuous trust of the Leader protected him; when his master had gone, he was shielded by the legend, handed down from generation to generation, of the "first Red officer." The legend even survived the only occasion on which he attempted a political intrigue and was abruptly dismissed by Khrushchev. He waited for "better" days (and they came!). After his death the legend lived on and served him well—as legends usually do after the object of their praise is gone.

Later I got to know Voroshilov and had a long conversation with him about a subject that he did not find very congenial. I also talked to many people who knew him well. He was an untrustworthy and callous man. Apart from Molotov, no one in Stalin's entourage gloated so enthusiastically over the misfortunes of his former friends, comrades and subordinates. Not only did Voroshilov calmly accept the extermination of the Red Army's leading officers, he also actively and exultantly participated in their destruction. He never interceded to help or save anyone. He even aided the NKVD's operatives in performing their distasteful work.

During the late 1950s Boris Dyakov decided to write a book about Blyukher and energetically began to gather the necessary materials. Later, when he lost any hope of its being published, he shared some of the curious episodes he had uncovered with me (we then lived in the same building). I have never forgotten the story of Blyukher's arrest. Dyakov wrote it down from the words of Blyukher's widow whom he had met in his role as the rehabilitated marshal's biographer.

Blyukher was friends with Voroshilov. Their families were close and usually tried to spend vacations together, and the two men were hunting and drinking partners. The commander of the Special Far Eastern Army was alarmed to receive a telegram from the People's Commissar summoning him to Moscow: bring your wife as well, Klim Voroshilov proposed.

They arrived in the commander's personal railway carriage. Voroshilov suggested that Blyukher and his wife go for a holiday at his dacha in Sochi. It was there they arrested Blyukher.

* * *

Perhaps all our gods of the time were, like Voroshilov, the most ordinary frauds? And, once created, perhaps their cheap legends took on a life of their own? But no, this is not true. The real military leaders had a strong sense of self-respect, they were sure of themselves, and had firmly acquired the habit of commanding others and taking responsibility. They were also constantly prepared for an uncertain and alarming future. As it happened I was quite closely acquainted with several military leaders. This was thanks to family and personal ties linking me to one professional military man in particular.

My cousin Israel Razgon was the most outstanding member of our family. The son of a petty musician who played at Jewish weddings, he somehow managed to attend commercial college and then even went to the university. He was much older than me—he had joined the Bolshevik Party in 1908, the year I was born. His youth was quite typical for that generation. He took part in student disturbances, was expelled from the university, and worked as a journalist for the party's legal publications. He tried to persuade Tolstoy to join in the revolution, even going to Yasnaya Polyana to see him; he was imprisoned and exiled in very liberal conditions to the Russian north. Nothing exceptional thus far.

He began to stand out during the First World War. Israel volunteered to fight and within a year had St. George Crosses of all four degrees. Captured outside Peremysl, he escaped and was made an ensign... Hardly a typical career for an educated Jew from Bobruisk. When, as a grown up, I became close to him, I realized that he was a natural soldier. The world of clear distinctions and discipline, making rapid decisions and taking full responsibility for them, was the closest and most familiar life for him.

Israel's military career was as stormy and unsettled as the years that followed the 1917 Revolution. During the Civil War he was a commissar on the Western front. He graduated from the Red Army Academy and was retained there as a political officer. Then he was sent to "advise" the Bukhara People's Soviet Republic in Central Asia where they put him in charge of the army. He was despatched to China as a military adviser. General Olgin, as he was known there, directed the Military Academy at Wampu, and Chou-De, Ho-Lun and other famous Red Chinese generals were among his students. The pinnacle of his career in China came when he was appointed head of the political department of the Chinese People's Army. Sometimes I dug through the piles of photographs lying in his table drawer and examined, with understandable interest, the many photographs where my cousin and Chiang Kai-Shek were shown side by side, dining or hunting together, or with their arms around each other's shoulders. The friendship did not prove lasting. With the other Soviet advisers he fled from his former friend across the Gobi after the Shanghai massacre of 1927... I cannot recall the different posts of Israel's subsequent career. All I remember is that when I emerged from the tribulations of youth my cousin was wearing a naval uniform... He was in charge of the Hydrographical administration and then, for many years, deputy to the commanding officer, first of the Black Sea and then the Baltic fleets. In late 1936 a separate Commissariat of the Navy was formed. Israel was appointed a member of its collegium and head of the armaments directorate. He was shot not later than the end of 1937, a month or two after his arrest.

That is the formal description of my cousin's career. The informal side to his biography and personality were far more interesting. He was a charmer. Not just for me, who was captivated by his long membership in the Party, his exciting biography and military titles, but for all who knew him—including, and perhaps particularly, women. This was surprising because he bore no resemblance to Lermontov's Pechorin[5] but looked more like a lower-class Jewish travelling salesman. Short, stocky and without any neck, his quite spherical, shiny and absolutely hairless head rested directly on his shoulders. A hooked Semitic nose, dark shining eyes, and the typical family dimple in his chin... He was cultured, liked poetry and read a great deal. Though he possessed none of the highest titles and ranks, he was still familiar with many of the most interesting figures of his day. Political? I somehow doubt it. One day in 1923 when he was a commissar at the Academy I dropped by his apartment on Levshinsky Street. Israel was not home but in the larger of his two rooms there sat a small, monkey-like man whom I knew well from photographs. He was rocking Israel's three-year old daughter Galya on his knees. The guest was asking the little girl who and what she knew.

"And do you know Stalin?" he suddenly asked her.

Galya thought and thought. Then she answered, "No."

"Well, God forbid that you should ever know him," Radek commented seriously.

God, alas, did not prove that considerate to Galya. However, Israel's connections were evidently not political in nature. He was not a member of the various oppositions and was indifferent to Trotsky. His circle of friends and acquaintances was more and more restricted to fellow professionals.

I think Israel's most vivid and attractive character trait was his self-respect and lack of the slightest servility. On arriving back from a business trip to Sevastopol, he would sometimes phone my mother and ask her to prepare a "real Jewish supper." Mama was a wonderful Jewish cook—rich, spicy dishes with masses of garlic. Israel dined with gusto even when he had to go and report to Voroshilov, who had strong feelings about garlic. When I once asked Israel if he didn't eat garlic on purpose, knowing that the People's Commissar could not stand the smell, the deputy commander of the fleet replied: I dine with my aunt much less often than I have to deliver reports to the Commissar and so the choice is quite natural.

In the navy they loved him. They liked his directness and simplicity, his lack of naval foppery, and his contempt for phrase-mongering. The officers in Sevastopol loved telling me about the "seventh condition of Comrade Stalin," a term that acquired wide currency in the Black Sea fleet. The story was as follows. Israel came to inspect the construction of a major shore battery. At a meeting with the construction workers the man in charge of the site reported on how the plan was being fulfilled. Evidently work was lagging far behind. Stalin had just given a speech in which he listed six conditions that would ensure the successful completion of any plan. The construction chief's report was therefore sprinkled with variations on his remarks: "on the basis of Comrade Stalin's six conditions," "guided by the six conditions of Comrade Stalin," and so on. The deputy commander of the fleet listened, getting more furious by the minute. Suddenly he could stand it no longer: "Haven't you heard of Comrade Stalin's seventh condition?" he yelled at the speaker. "No, what is it?" "There's no need to be a Dutch prick!" roared the enraged Israel.[6]

For some reason, Israel had a liking for me. So I often visited him when he lived in Moscow and I would go to Leningrad or Sevastopol to see him. He also came to see us at home and, after I married, visited Oksana and me at Moskvin's apartment as well. Sometimes he brought friends with him. I found these people not just interesting but attractive. Ivan Kozhanov, for instance. I did not look on him as commanding officer of the fleet, his present post, but as the commander of the Caspian-Volga flotilla I had read of in Larisa Reisner's novel *The Front* and in many memoirs about the Civil War. Kozhanov was calm, confident and ironic. Another friend of Israel, Nikolai Petin, head of the Red Army engineers, was similar in character. Both Kozhanov and Petin were members of the old Tsarist officer-caste and the upbringing they had received at home and in privileged military institutions was quite evident. In Israel's apartment I also met those from very poor backgrounds who had won a position in the army through their exceptional talent, iron will and intelligence.

Why did they let themselves be killed without any attempt to resist or at least to run away and save their lives? Did they really not understand what awaited them? Of course, mass terror does have a numbing effect. On St. Bartholomew's Night court fops who normally only drew their swords during formal duels slaughtered the grim battle-hardened Huguenots, the best soldiers in the French army, like so many sheep. Our legendary military heroes were arrested in the 1930s by young thugs, used to dealing with unarmed and distraught individuals. Yet only Gai among them offered a display of temperament (and he was Armenian, of course). As he was being escorted in an ordinary carriage after his arrest, he suffocated one of his guards and leapt off the train. He was later found with a broken leg and, naturally, was shot after the usual rapid procedures. Still, he died like a soldier and not like a lamb led to the slaughter.

An elderly "goner" at Ustvymlag's Camp No. 2 told me how he witnessed the arrest of Kutyakov, the deputy of the celebrated Chapayev. In 1937 Kutyakov commanded the Volga military district. My companion was then military commandant at a tiny railway station where trains would halt for only two or three minutes. When he received a telegram that the district commander would be travelling up to Moscow on such and such a train he looked in the timetable and saw that it would reach them at 1 a.m. It would stand there for only three minutes but the commander might just look out of his window or even take a stroll along the platform. With a sigh the elderly official decided that he better stay behind in his little office.

The train arrived late that night. With relief the station commandant noted that there were no lights in the commander's semi-armored carriage at the end of the train. He was about to go home to
bed when he noticed a group of people approaching the carriage
and the linesman uncoupling it from the train.

"What's going on? The commander's going to spend the night
here, is he?" The commandant asked in amazement, coming up to
them.

"Get the f... out of here, you," they replied informatively.

The commandant understood immediately. It was summer 1937
and the purges had now worked their way past the Central
Committee and the generals and corps commanders. Quickly he ran
back to his small room and observed what followed through the window.

The carriage was uncoupled, the train gave a quiet whistle and
left. A group of uniformed people wearing shoulder straps and holsters climbed up the carriage steps and began knocking. The light
came on, the door opened and in they went. In a short while there
were shouts of rage and indignation, the door opened again and the
nocturnal visitors tumbled out of the carriage one after another, pro-
pelled by kicks from a large bare foot. After the last NKVD man fell
face down onto the tracks the military district commander appeared
in the lighted doorway in his long johns, waving a sabre in his hand.
Then the door slammed shut.

Those who had "carried out" the operation picked themselves up
and ran to the station. The now-lighted carriage stood on the main
line, blocking all other trains. After some time the small shunting engine began to approach, evidently intending to push the commander
into one of the sidings. It had not got close to the offending carriage,
however, before a machine gun opened fire. The commander's carriage had been made for visiting the front, it was semi-armored with
a fully-armored platform and its machine guns carried live ammunition. An attempt to approach the carriage from the other direction
was no more successful. The operation had now been going on for
two hours and all movement along a major railway line was halted.

The commandant observed a new attempt. Only one man approached the carriage this time. He had taken off his gun holster and
shoulder straps and carried a white handkerchief in his raised hand.
He was allowed into the carriage. Ten minutes later he came out and
almost ran back to his comrades who were waiting for him by the
station entrance. The commandant was quite unprepared for what
happened next. "They" all rushed into his office, "Come on, the commander wants you!"

"I... but..."

"Come on, do as you're told! He's asking for you!"

He could not argue. The terrified commandant straightened his shirt and his cap, put on an official face and set off for the carriage. The door opened and Kutyakov appeared. He was already dressed, wearing his sabre, with a Mauser in his hand.

"Comrade Commander! The station military commandant. At your command..."

"OK, OK, forget all that. Are you a soldier or another of these bastards?"

"Since 1918, Comrade Commander..."

"Where did you serve? Which units? What battles did you fight in? Who was commander of your army and your division?"

Once Kutyakov had satisfied himself that the commandant was not "one of them" he told him to go to the telegraph and, using the direct line, to summon Voroshilov. First he was to ask the People's Commissar for Defense three questions. Then he should report what had happened and ask for further instructions. Without letting him put any questions, Kutyakov said tiredly, "Off you go... They'll do the rest. All you have to do is to put the questions and get the answers. Bring the tape back here."

At 3 or 4 a.m. Marshal Voroshilov himself came on the line. The commandant told me the three questions but now I only remember one: "Who is Auntie's wife?" Evidently Kutyakov knew Voroshilov personally, they had friends in common, and knew the family nicknames—only Voroshilov could have replied correctly. Kutyakov's friend answered the questions and then added, "I am commanding him to give himself up and come to Moscow. Then I shall personally investigate everything and talk to him myself."

"I came back to the carriage and handed him the tape. He read it and closed his eyes... At that, I turned and ran. I could not stand to see any more," said the former commandant as he finished his story. No longer young, his face swollen with dystrophy, and overgrown with a filthy gray stubble, death was already waiting to take him. There was nothing I could do to help—just as there was nothing he could do to help his commanding officer, the legendary Kutyakov...

* * *

Did Kutyakov really trust his friend Voroshilov and believe that he would "sort things out"? How could a clever and experienced man retain such hopes after the first marshals and generals had been shot and buried in unmarked graves? I think he and the others believed they would be able to give their views, ask questions and find out what was going on... I did not know Kutyakov but I had no doubts about the intelligence, honesty and fearlessness of my cousin Israel. He spent his last months in Moscow, at the height of his military career, in a vast empty service apartment on Pokrovsky Boulevard. I had never seen him in such a state before: he was gloomy, his face clouded over at his thoughts and the knowledge of what might await him. There was one thing I did not doubt, however. I saw him for the last time two to three weeks before his arrest. I came to his office and he was sitting behind an empty desk. I began to tell him the latest terrible news and he tiredly waved his hand, to let me know that he had already heard. For a long while he said nothing. Then he raised his head and suddenly declared, "But I shall tell them exactly what I think!"

When the expected terrible event took place he thought that it would be Voroshilov who talked to him. Or if not Voroshilov then someone who was his equal in Party and army rank or, at the least, in age. They all imagined that.

* * *

One of those in our cell at Butyrki was the famous engineer Oskolkov. He designed the Kiev railway station in Moscow and the new Borodinsky bridge (I think there is now even a plaque commemorating him there). He was arrested when he was in charge of building the new Aero-Hydrodynamics institute. The "Industrial Party" trial of 1930 had not affected him. But he knew so many of those interrogated then that when he was seized and taken to the Lubyanka some years later he had a very clear idea what to expect. They would be polite, but that politeness would carry a concealed threat; both sides would engage in evasive conversations; the cigarettes would be good and the tea fresh and strong...

When they handcuffed him in the elevator, however, Oskolkov suddenly realized that something in the scenario had altered. Next he was brought into a room full of laughing, tough young men. One of them turned round and asked whom they had brought in. Without waiting for the guards to name Oskolkov he gave the prisoner a skillful and practiced punch in the face that knocked out his front teeth. Getting up off the floor with difficulty, Oskolkov understood that the old rules no longer applied here...

So no passionate arguments, or attempts to understand and convince "them," awaited Kutyakov, Kozhanov, Petin, Israel and many, many others. They would face the same brutal young men, torture, a derisory five-minute trial and a drunken team of executioners who would drag them out of their cells that night.

* * *

They placed their hope in logic, logic of the most basic kind. For even a thug can only survive when he preserves elementary reasoning and predictability.

When I was a Young Pioneer we attended a training camp for the Pioneer leaders of our Moscow district. Our military instructor was an army officer with the improbable surname Postrizhigach (we made up numerous rhymes about him). I had long forgotten those happy days when in autumn 1938 I spotted him as a duty officer in the Kotlas transit camp. That was already quite an important rank. Even more surprising, he recognized me.

Quickly and familiarly he asked: where from, sentence, article, which transport did you arrive with and do you know where they're taking you? Then he ordered me to wait and twenty minutes later brought me a full can of almost real pea soup. While I was wolfing down this aromatic and tasty meal with the aid of Postrizhigach's own spoon he quickly told me his story. After graduating from the Frunze Military Academy he was sent to the Far East. There he was appointed head of the regimental staff, regimental commander, and then he was arrested.

"Like all the rest of them. There's not one commanding officer left in the Far Eastern Army. Not a single regimental or divisional commander (not to speak of the higher ranks). We were transported in Stolypin train cars through more than ten transit camps, so we found out everything—not one of our officers was left untouched! They even took the regimental heads of staff. Well, never mind, one can live anywhere. As you see, I'm all right here as well. I'm duty officer in the compound, I keep things in order, I'm well fed and I can feed others. We must just wait. You were a bright lad, Razgon, you liked politics. Well, you learn from me!"

"What are you hoping for, then?"

"Ah! given up, have we? Listen, war is inevitable, mark my words! And if you know what's what, then you should know that. War is inevitable and they won't be able to fight without us!"

"Are you so sure?"

"You don't know the first thing about it! You can appoint an assistant accountant to be accountant and a deputy head of department to be head. But you can't put a platoon commander in charge of a regiment! You understand? You can't! I'm speaking as a professional. Even during the Civil War it was hard to do, and now it's quite impossible. Without us, without the regimental commanders or the heads of regimental staff, they cannot fight. That's why they won't shoot us!"

"But they arrested you all."

"That was just over-reaction. Perhaps there were some ideas and schemes up top. Well, they went too far, they made a mess of it. But there's such a thing as logic. No one can get away from it..."

It was, it seems, the last resort. They all believed as zealously in logic as a religious person believes in the existence of God. And if they did not believe, then they nevertheless sought passionately for the reason, because if no logic could be found then what was left?

There were many interesting people in cell No. 29 at Butyrki but one of them was particularly intriguing to me. To begin with, there was his own life story. Gustav Deutsch was the son of a famous figure in the Second International, Julius Deutsch, the leader of the Austrian Left Social Democrats. Deutsch had been among the organizers of the 1934 uprising of the Schutzbund in Vienna. Together father and son had fought in the workers' apartments against the government forces, and then fled with the other surviving Schutzbund members to Czechoslovakia. From there they had made their way to the Soviet Union. Julius Deutsch had come briefly to see Stalin and other Party leaders; Gustav was here for good. He decided to stay at least until the proletariat became master of his country as well. A locomotive engineer, Gustav had no wish to work for the capitalists. He was not a communist but he respected the first workers' state and preferred to use his training to serve the working class. They sent Gustav to Voronezh where he lived with his family and worked at the railway depot.

He was by now perfectly capable of conversing in Russian and he spent his time in the cell in discussions with one expert consultant after another, tirelessly seeking for the logic of it all. Why had he been arrested? He was not suspected of ties with his former comrades in the Second International or of anything political. The accusation was simply that he had poured sand into the axle-box of the repaired locomotives so that they would break down again. Why should he pour sand into the axle-box when he was responsible for the repair and reliability of the engines? Where was the elementary logic in this? The investigators in Voronezh had knocked out all his teeth. Then they had brought him to Moscow and at the prison hospital provided him with an excellent set of false teeth as good as any he could have acquired in Vienna. A very expensive set, he knew about such things. At the first interrogation in Moscow the new teeth were smashed to pieces. Where was the logic in that? He was in prison while his father was a general in the Republican army in Spain, in charge of the entire shore artillery. Julius Deutsch stood on the extreme left-wing of world social-democracy and of all Social Democrats was the most passionate supporter of the Soviet Union. Where was the logic in keeping the son of such a man in prison and knocking out his teeth? There must have been a mistake somewhere. There was some misunderstanding, and he would certainly be released. It couldn't be otherwise, in the very nature of things.

When I was transferred to the Butyrki transit block Gustav stayed behind in cell No. 29. Only twenty years later did I learn that Gustav had never found the logic he was seeking. They shot him instead. I don't know what happened to that other seeker of logic, Colonel

Postrizhigach. All I know is that I stopped trying to find the logic behind what was happening and only in that way did I survive. There was no point in seeking the logic of actions in the events themselves, only within and for oneself.

Valerian Osinsky's daughter Svetlana told me how in the late 1950s she managed to find someone who had been in the same cell as her father. By then Osinsky had testified as a "witness" during Bukharin's trial. He been beaten unconscious by young thugs during further interrogations after the trial, and was suffering from broken ribs and internal ruptures. His cellmates asked this wise and highly educated man what was the logical way to behave in their circumstances. Await your death with dignity, he replied. In the *Gulag Archipelago* Solzhenitsyn offered the formula, "Do not ask for anything or nurture any hope." This is not particularly original: at the time anyone who had his eyes open reached the same conclusion.

* * *

In his memoirs General Gorbatov laid the blame for false testimony on those who "confessed." I believe this is both arrogant and immoral. It is wrong to shift the blame from the torturers to their victims. Gorbatov was lucky, that's all. Either his interrogator was lazy or had not been given a firm instruction to "put pressure" on his charge. Doctors, psychologists and psychiatrists have now done enough research to say whether an individual can be tortured into giving false testimony against himself. This century has provided a vast amount of evidence on the subject, far more than the Middle Ages. Of course it can be done. So I am not going to discuss whether the bravest men, who were professional soldiers and military leaders during the Civil War, did or did not "confess." Much more interesting and revealing was their behavior in prison or in the camps.

My first cell "elder" in prison was Divisional Commander I.A. Onufriev. He displayed a courageous tranquillity, humor and kindness in dealing with our cellmates. In Ustvymlag I came in close contact with several high-ranking army officers. This provided food for thought as to how well such people could withstand the ordeal of prison and the camps.

Only one of them remains alive today. I don't want to name him, although he never did anything reprehensible. Yet observing how he behaved in the camp I could not make myself believe that people like him were able to command military units, give orders during a battle, and take the responsibility for the fate of so many other individuals. Before his arrest he had commanded a division and his transport arrived when our camp was no longer controlled by the criminals but by us. So he hardly spent a day on gang labor. Yet it was amazing—any task was beyond him! When he was appointed work-team leader even the most despicable camp "jackal" would not obey him; any zek could get his way when they made him works inspector; and when he was supposed to register timber at the stores he failed to record several hundred cubic meters... In despair he would say that he had been a good divisional commander as a free man, and was confident that he could have coped with an army corps as well, but here in the camp he was incapable of dealing with a ragged work team. Towards the end he was given the most cushy job of all, as head of the washhouse. At the first routine inventory twenty-two pairs of underwear were missing. It only took one look at that "underwear" to realize that there was no problem in concealing such a shortfall. The torn-off leg of a pair of long johns or a shirt-collar could easily be passed off as a set of "underwear" during inventory. But the commander could not even cope with that! As in any Soviet institution it was quite possible to sell off a locomotive, a goods car full of timber or some tools with impunity and get drunk on the proceeds. And people did so. However, a shortfall was a shortfall. My commander was tried and had another five years added to his ten-year sentence.

His despair is hard to convey. He would not hear any words of comfort: five more years seemed the end of all his hopes, the end of his life. Then he was released. At the same time as Marshal Rokossovsky was freed, a small group of military men were also let out of the camps. This was almost at the very beginning of the war and we sadly shrugged our shoulders: how could this man, whom we considered totally broken and quite incapable, be put in charge of anything? From the few letters that he nevertheless sent to the camp we learned he had been made a colonel and given a regiment to command. Then he stopped writing, but some time later we started to hear about him again, from the orders of the Supreme Commander published in the newspapers. In brief, he ended the war as a lieutenant-general and Hero of the Soviet Union. Somehow neither I nor my comrades had any doubt that he had earned his awards and promotion.

At Camp No. 2 I got to know Yakov Pokus, the tally clerk at the stables. This tiny, silent dried-up old man who walked around without a guard, a folder tucked under his arm, would shudder not only at the stormy abuse of the camp bosses but also at the casual disrespect of the guards. His quietness, refusal to answer back, and deeply engrained prisoner's melancholy made him an attractive character. Compared to others he was privileged and did not go hungry because he could eat as much oat gruel as he wanted in the stables and roasted liver from dead horses.

But as we looked on, Pokus faded away and was dying as quietly and resignedly as he lived. When he died we felt genuinely sorry for this good man who had never done any harm to anyone. The camp director was Yepanichnikov and, against the rules, he allowed several of the trusties to accompany Pokus's body to the camp cemetery. They made a proper coffin in the carpenter's shop and dressed him in his own clothes—military breeches and a field shirt with holes where the medals used to hang. Then we took him to the cemetery where the other burial mounds had already sunk level with the ground. We buried him, covered his grave with a layer of turf and marked it with a barked and roughly shaped stake. Of course, it did not carry his name but only his camp number, the same as was written on the wooden board fixed to his leg.

Now I often find my dead comrade's name in books, articles and memoirs. It even crops up in film scripts and other highly artistic productions. For Pokus was the hero of the "bold nights of Spassk, the courageous days at Volochayevsk" and commanded the partisan division that stormed Volochayevsk during the Civil War in a series of famous and horrifically stubborn battles. Without the slightest amazement, I read of the courage, steel nerves and valor of the stable tally clerk in Camp No. 2. These qualities can appear during battle and disappear or fade in other circumstances. When all's said and done, the fearsome general or government official who is terrified of his stupid and quarrelsome wife has always been a boring standby in third-rate novels.

And yet there were officers who remained striking and interesting figures even in the degrading and demeaning conditions of the camps. I knew two of them at Camp No. 1 at Ustvymlag and I always think that my cousin Israel, and Kozhanov and Petin, and indeed many other Red Army officers, must have been like them, if they were not killed immediately but hidden away in remote camps in the northern forests.

The first was Stepan Bogomyagkov, a former head of staff with the Special Far Eastern Army. Like my cousin, Bogomyagkov became a soldier quite suddenly under the pressure of war. Before the First World War he had finished a teacher-training institute and began teaching zoology and biology in the gymnasium, subjects for which he would retain a passion long after he had ceased to teach. In 1914 he went to fight, attended the hastily organized military training courses, and became a gifted and successful officer. By 1917 he was already a lieutenant-colonel and in charge of a regiment. When the new Red Army leaders drafted former Tsarist officers, Bogomyagkov did not evade the invitation and fought just as successfully as he had for Nicholas II. At the end of the Civil War he was a divisional commander, a Communist and had been awarded the Red Banner twice. He studied at the Academy, worked on the staff and rose to become second in command of the Far Eastern army, one of the largest and most important military districts in the Soviet Union. He was an educated and cultured man who knew languages, loved poetry and music, and could spend hours enthusiastically arguing about the place of Tyutchev in Russian poetry or the accuracy of predictions in the natural sciences. It was easy to imagine him in his former post and rank. He remained true to himself in the camp, well-mannered, ironic and dignified. All the bosses, the most desperate criminals and the stupid escort guards there revered him. Whether he was sharpening saws or axes, or serving as economist in the planning section, he worked easily and without zeal but also without any slacking. By fair means and foul, he managed to get copies of the newspapers so as to find out about the fighting in Europe and, gazing at a map cut from the papers, he would speculate with his military colleague Nikolai Lisovsky on the future development of events.

I knew Lisovsky well for many years. He was a norm-setter and my assistant at Camp No. 1. We spent long hours together in the office where we worked and in the barracks where we lived together. Lisovsky was a man of a different type altogether. I suspect that in his heart of hearts he considered Bogomyagkov to be an amateur soldier and a dilettante. He could not think or even talk of anything but military matters and war. He was the oldest of us—to me he was simply an old man. Probably this was not far from the truth: long before the 1914 War he had graduated from the cadets school and the Junker college, become an officer, graduated from the General Staff Academy, and been head of regimental staff and then commander of a regiment. From the first, he had sided with the Revolution... He had been in the Red Army since it was organized and in 1930 he joined the Party. After the Civil War ended he spent almost all his time as a staff officer. For a long time he worked as head of operations on the Red Army staff and then as deputy head of the General Staff. In 1937 he was appointed commander of the Central Asian military district and two months later he was arrested.

Why they did not shoot him is unclear. Perhaps because his narrow professional interests were so unmistakably obvious. A tall, bony, stiff-backed man, the height of a Guards officer, Lisovsky had a yellow unkind face which became animated only during conversation with Bogomyagkov. During the best time of the day—after the work teams had already returned, after the evening meal, when everyone was waiting for roll call but no work reports were yet ready—the two of them would spread out their little maps of the Balkan peninsula on the table and begin to discuss the Italian invasion of Greece and the fighting in Western Europe. The war was proceeding rapidly and it was easy to verify the military ability of the two corps commanders.

Bogomyagkov was basically a Far East soldier, but Lisovsky had spent almost all his life studying our Western frontier and the potential opponents we faced there. Everything that happened in 1939 and after he regarded as of personal significance. Unshakeably convinced that we would have to fight the Germans, he considered the Soviet acquisition of territory in 1939 to be a misfortune in military terms. Lisovsky would explain this to Bogomyagkov at length and in great detail: it was fine to continue a battle on the former Polish (now Soviet) territories but very difficult to meet an attack there. The then popular theory of "little bloodshed and on foreign territory" evoked the most refined obscenities from the old Guards officer.

On 22 June 1941, the day of the German invasion, he was already on his own at Camp No. 1. Bogomyagkov had by then been transferred elsewhere. Within a matter of days Lisovsky's face became drawn and gloomy. He would talk to almost no one but me. Despite his tight-lipped restraint he predicted colossal military losses for the Red Army. When newspapers and radio reappeared after a month of total isolation we could see that Lisovsky's predictions had been confirmed with a terrifying consistency. He had given a fairly accurate picture of where the Germans would strike. In spring 1942 he sketched for me the trajectory of the coming German push to the south and south-east almost exactly as it then happened... There was something monstrous about a highly-trained military specialist, who had been preparing all his life for this war, being forced to spend it shut up in a miserable labor camp, setting spurious norms for criminal offenders. It was Vasilevsky, after all, his former pupil and subordinate, who now headed the General Staff. Apart from his numerous applications and requests to be sent to the front in any capacity, he also fired off one letter after another to Vasilevsky and Shaposhnikov, using the free workers to post them and avoid the camp censor. Some must have reached their target. However, Lisovsky continued to serve his sentence, and would not be released early.

In fact, it made no difference to the course of the war whether Lisovsky was in Ustvymlag or on the General Staff. The greatest military genius, as we now know, could not have avoided the setbacks of the first two years of the war. (Unless, that is, he had managed to shoot Stalin and take his place.)

Lisovsky had no doubt how the war would end. Even when the Germans were on the outskirts of Moscow, and later when they overran the North Caucasus and reached the Volga, he would always answer angrily (when—yet again!—I inquired about the future), "The Germans cannot win! Numbers are against them."

"Why?"

"Because they cannot win a world war, a long drawn-out war. You read history at college and even studied the First World War! Why can't you understand that the German lost that war in the very first year? They miscalculated the forces involved and did not realize it would become a world war. And this time they have also lost the war in the first year because they did not realize they would be faced by the military and other resources of the whole world. Can they fight to the Urals? They can. But that will not change a thing. They won't have the time to create industrial centers with high technology there and overtake the Americans. They don't have enough people either. No, that's all quite clear. I can't understand something else."

"What, Nikolai Vasilievich?"

"What will happen to us after the war? To each one of us? If, of course, we live that long. I hope you'll find out. I shall never know. I wish I could, though..."

*　*　*

Yet he did live to find out.

It was 1956, the end of a happy and joyful summer, full of new hope. The Twentieth Party Congress had taken place that spring and no one suspected that in six weeks time the Hungarian Uprising would begin. I was told that a Nikolai Lisovsky, who was staying at the Soviet Army's central hotel, was looking for me. I immediately went there. The hotel administrator, a senior lieutenant, said that Corps Commander Lisovsky was in a first-class room on the fourth floor. He emphasized the archaic pre-war rank, which no longer existed, and the quality of the accommodation: he wanted me to understand that although he was only a junior officer he understood and sympathized...

A wizened figure raised himself with difficulty from the enormous sarcophagus of an armchair: he seemed barely half of Lisovsky's imposing height. The old tabs of a pre-war corps commander had been untidily stitched on his new general's jacket. The jacket was baggy, and handsome riding breeches descended to new boots on his thin legs... A tiny and equally wizened woman helped me to calm down the weeping old man, in whom I could see nothing of the former deputy head of the General Staff or of my fellow norm-setter from Camp No. 1.

Lisovsky's wife quickly told me the routine tale of the corps commander's subsequent biography. After his release he went to live in the small town in Kazakhstan where his wife had served her sentence as Member of the Family of a Traitor. They had barely settled down before he was again arrested and, after many months in the revolting regional prison, sent into "eternal" exile in a remote corner of the immense Krasnoyarsk Territory. His wife joined him there and again they began to settle in. A few years later came 1953 with its joys, its hopes and its anticipation...

"How Nikolai Vasilievich waited! How sure he was! How often he used to remember you and hope to meet again. Five days ago when we arrived in Moscow he immediately told me that I should find you: if you were alive, he said, you must be in Moscow. And now you've met. Tomorrow they're going to take us to the sanatorium for a vacation while they award him his new general's rank... Perhaps he'll come round there, and then you can meet again, in better form."

I never saw Lisovsky again.

Lev Razgon with his second wife, Rika, during his first year of freedom. Peredelkino, 1963.

Usollag, Momelo, 1951. A shot of the punishment barracks.

The main section of the central hospital in Usollag. Moshevo, 1951.

Razgon in 1954 with I. Chernushin, the head of the
planning section for the free workers.

A PLAY WITH A HAPPY ENDING

I never saw Korchagina-Alexandrovskaya perform on the stage. For a Muscovite on a short visit to pre-war Leningrad it was never easy to obtain tickets for a play in which the great Russian actress was appearing. I have since read a great many memoirs about her, though. They all mention the staggering effect her performances at the Alexandrinsky Theater had on the audience, and they also describe the scenes she loved to improvise off-stage, in everyday life. I was myself a participant in two such real-life performances. One was inconsequential and amusing, and I was just a member of the cast; the other was acted out in deadly earnest and then my role was, so to speak, that of director. But to tell the whole story I must begin with the occasion when I met Yekaterina Korchagina-Alexandrovskaya for the first and last time.

It was a very long while ago, in a different and better age. I was young, a student, and sufficiently frivolous to be content enjoying my youthful successes: unlike the repentant nobleman Radishchev, I made no great effort to "look around me," or my heart, like his, might also have "been stricken with the sufferings of mankind."[1] And it was just such a youthful success that one day prompted the urge, quite abhorrent to me now, to celebrate with a strong drink. The easiest way to fulfill this slightly disreputable but guileless desire was to visit a familiar and very hospitable household.

The master of the house was the poet Demyan Bedny. It would never have occurred to me to brazen my way into his apartment for such a trifling purpose had it not been for "Mrs. Demyan," Vera Rufovna, his wife. It was she who ran the whole vast establishment. A woman of extraordinary energy and kindness, she was also a gifted organizer. She coped admirably with her rather difficult husband, with two nearly grown daughters and a pair of small sons (the most appalling little terrors!), and with an enormous household and the countless friends and acquaintances, all of whom she entertained with a hospitality of pre-Revolutionary dimensions. (Perhaps I should add that until she and her husband separated, Demyan Bedny was the only one of all the writers to actually live in the Kremlin itself.)

So I dropped by. In the enormous dining room an old woman was pottering about next to the monstrously ugly sideboard. The lady of the house tolerated any number of these elderly creatures. This one was wiping a plate and evidently was household help.

"Is Vera Rufovna home, Granny?"

"She's out, my dear. Like enough, she'll be back this evening."

"Granny! There's an unfinished bottle of brandy in the right half of this sideboard" (I was familiar with its contents, in other words, and the half-emptied bottle was some of my unfinished business). "Please, take it out and a small glass as well."

The old woman opened the sideboard, took out the bottle and laid a napkin on the edge of the vast dining-room table. Then she set out the bottle and a glass, cut some slices of cheese onto a small plate, and retreated a few paces to observe, with wonder and joy, the impudence of youth. There was something immeasurably attractive about her.

"Perhaps you'll also share a glass with me, Granny?"

"Well, my boy! perhaps I shall join you, at that... "

She took out another glass and sat down next to me. She drank the brandy in little gulps, wincing each time at the unaccustomed beverage. After each swallow she carefully wiped her mouth with a corner of her headscarf. Evidently, she was straight from the village, and she sat like elderly peasant women do. Here was a wonderful opportunity to talk to someone from that quite unfamiliar rural way of life.

Yet nothing came of this admirable plan. For at that moment the lady of the house unexpectedly entered the dining room. I felt most awkward that she had caught her old serving woman drinking the master's brandy with a young man. Instead of being outraged or indignant, however, Vera Rufovna was most polite to my boon companion, "I see that you have already made Lyova's acquaintance, Yekaterina Pavlovna. He is—" and she introduced me in the most flattering terms. I leapt to my feet. The old lady, I realized, was acting a part, and I was not just an unwitting stage extra but had made an utter fool of myself...

Korchagina-Alexandrovskaya took the train back that evening. She was civil and merry with me, and pretended not to notice my embarrassment. She wrote down her telephone number in Leningrad and invited me to attend any performance at the Alexandrinsky Theater. But I never had the chance. In no time at all I had grown up and married, and was busy working as an editor and writing my own articles and sketches. Yekaterina Pavlovna became no more than a youthful reminiscence. The next time I remembered her was to be under very different circumstances, far removed from that amusing introduction to a famous actress.

* * *

It was spring 1939 and I was at Camp No. 1 in Ustvymlag. During that first and most terrible winter most of the contingent of new prisoners, of whom I was one, died. By the spring I had already been at a semi-punitive outpost for two months, almost died of scurvy myself, and recovered again at the infirmary in the main camp. Letters had begun to reach me from family and friends and I had begun to write back. I didn't always use the camp postal system for my correspondence: it was censored and very slow, and it was impossible to ask about other friends and acquaintances in such letters, for fear of harming them as well. The drivers who went each day to the warehouse at Veslyana railroad station were allowed to move around without guards and so could take uncensored letters to mail to the world outside. They were of all kinds, the drivers. Most had been petty criminals and not all of them were willing to accept such errands from an unknown "contra" (or "counter-revolutionary"). One of the drivers, however, had himself been sentenced for a "political" offense. Pavel was from Leningrad (I have forgotten his surname), an excellent driver, and since the five years the court had given him was only for agitation (Article 58:10), a comparatively mild offense, he did not have a guard to accompany him. Moreover, it was he the camp authorities entrusted to transport the most desirable commodities, such as sugar, tinned meats and fats.

I was already doing comparatively light work, preparing feed for the horses. Working with my partner we would quickly fell a dozen of the most leafy birch trees, strip off the branches and artfully stack them so as to make the pile appear bigger. Our norm fulfilled, we calmly waited to be escorted back to the camp. We would arrive at the compound, barely tired, with a few hours to ourselves before the signal to go to bed (the white nights had already begun). We passed the time in leisurely conversation. Pavel used to join us. Evidently he was not drawn to his fellow drivers: their talk was all vodka and women, and risky schemes to dispose of the valuables that came their way. Pavel had left a wife behind in Leningrad whom he missed, and two small children. He didn't like writing—his hands were too calloused to handle a pen, he complained—and so sometimes he would dictate and I would take down his words. He liked these letters; so did his wife, who enjoyed writing the replies. Since she could send them via a free employee at the warehouse she was able to give an uninhibited and detailed description of life in Leningrad, which I also found interesting.

Once I asked Pavel a question that was considered improper in the camps, "Pavel, what ever did they give you five years for? And in a real court, at that?"

"They gave me what I deserved. Not like you and your kind. I was sent down for my own stupidity. It was late 1937, just before the elections. An old woman, an actress, was our district candidate for the Supreme Soviet. Her photo was hung up under the glass in a frame, so you could see how old she was. People said she was a good actress. I can't say, I didn't go to the theater myself. I had nothing personal against her—perhaps she was good on the stage. But this was the first time we could elect someone directly to the

Supreme Soviet. So why should we choose some actress or other, especially one who was on her last legs?... There we were, all together one day in the bar drinking beer, and I spoke my mind: Was it really so hard for them to find someone a bit more serious? I complained, Someone with a bit more life in them? One of my companions turned out to be an active and conscientious fellow. They picked me up three days later. What could I say, when everyone had heard me speaking out against the candidate of the 'bloc of Communists and non-Party members'? A month later I was in court. There were witnesses and all, and I couldn't deny the charge—well, I was guilty! So they gave me five years. And very kind with it: without 'loss of rights.' That means, the senior work distributor tells me, that I can return straight home to Leningrad as soon as I've done my time."

"Do you remember the actress's name?"

"I'd hardly forget it, would I? I'll remember it till the end of my days. A double-barrelled name, Korchagina-Alexandrovskaya."

I instantly recalled the dining room in Demyan Bedny's apartment and the old peasant woman I had magnanimously treated to the master's brandy. A plan came into my head at once: "Pavel, that old lady is going to help you. Her name is Yekaterina Pavlovna and she's a very decent sort of person. Your wife must go to the Alexandrinsky Theater, find out Korchagina's home address, and then visit her. She must tell the old woman what happened to you, and how she is struggling to bring up two small children on her own..."

And that was how the whole extraordinary performance began. There was only one professional involved, but what an actress she was! I wrote the letters to Pavel's wife for him. They were very detailed, almost like producing a play in which I conjured up each scene and gave precise stage directions. The replies Pavel's wife sent back were no less detailed. So detailed, in fact, that I could visualize each dramatic event in this most unusual production. Of course, to be on the safe side, Pavel destroyed all his wife's letters on the spot. Still, I retain a vivid memory of their contents.

In the very first letter, Pavel's wife described in full how she had found out Yekaterina Pavlovna's address, and gone to visit her. She explained the misfortune that had befallen them and said that her husband was a quiet and mild-mannered man: he was always content, never said a thing against the authorities and, if he had blurted out something unwise, then it was foolishness and the effect of a glass too many. Yekaterina Pavlovna, she wrote, heard her out, threw up her hands in horror, and they wept together. Then the old actress declared that she would free Pavel, if it killed her. She gave his wife some money to buy something nice for the children and instructed her to come back in a few days time.

In the next letter Pavel's wife repeated Yekaterina Pavlovna's account of her doings in full detail. She went to see the top boss at

Party headquarters in the Smolny. I couldn't care less about this piece of card, she told him, holding up her identity document as a deputy, but for nights on end I have not been able to sleep, for thinking how someone has suffered because of me and not just one person, but a whole family. He was probably right as well, my dear, what business does an old lady have, meddling in politics? If you don't release him, then what do I need to be a deputy for? I won't live much longer anyway, with that on my conscience...

And she said a great deal more in the same vein. They were very attentive. They tried to calm her down, gave her a glass of water, and said that, out of respect for her, they would release Pavel and he would be reunited with his family. It would only require a little time to complete all the formalities.

Yekaterina Pavlovna again gave Pavel's wife some money and told her to ring every day.

So the wife of this "anti-Soviet agitator" would ring up the actress and receive a daily report from what had become almost a battle-front. His case file had been requested. Two more weeks were needed to reach a final decision. They would then call for Yekaterina Pavlovna and everything would be in order.

Pavel was in a state of euphoria, and he could not think or talk about anything else. I was almost as excited myself. Then one day Pavel returned from the station absolutely crushed. Without changing his clothes he came into the camp compound, found me and handed over the latest letter from his wife. She was in despair. Everything had gone wrong. Korchagina-Alexandrovskaya had sent his wife a telegram, that she must come and see her immediately. Almost in tears, the old actress told her, "They summoned me and one of their procurators, or whatever they call them, was sitting there. On the table were five thick files marked 'highly confidential' and on each, the surname of your husband. What he said against me in the bar was quite trivial, they explained, and they would not have picked him up for that. They had sentenced him because he was a spy—either English or Japanese, I don't remember which—and all his crimes were recorded in those thick files. There's nothing I can do, my darling, if he's been spying. I wept out of pity for you and your poor children. If the wretch had spared no thoughts for his country he should at least have been concerned about his family!"

Yekaterina Pavlovna gave Pavel's wife some more money. She advised her to write to Pavel, encouraging him to repent for all he had done and beg forgiveness for his black treachery from the Soviet authorities. They were kind at heart, the people she had been to see, and perhaps they would have pity on the foolish man and his innocent babes...

The scoundrels! They had hoodwinked a great actress and twisted a deputy of the USSR Supreme Soviet round their little finger. But the play was not over yet!

"Pavel, if you were sentenced by a court you must have the charge sheet and the sentence with you. You weren't so stupid as to use them for cigarette paper, I hope?"

"Of course not! I've still got them."

"Go and fetch them, then. We're going to write another letter."

As I suspected, the charge sheet and sentence handed down by the special board of the Leningrad City Court left no doubt as to the crime Pavel had committed. During the investigation and the trial itself he had been proven incontrovertibly guilty. He confessed to "anti-Soviet slander and agitation against the candidate of the bloc of Communists and non-Party members" and had been given an unusually light sentence.

The letter I wrote for Pavel to his wife contained the following advice. She was to go back to Yekaterina Pavlovna, explain that she was the victim of a barefaced deception, and that all those fat files with his name on were simply stage props often used during interrogation. A deputy of the Supreme Soviet should have been officially informed that spying cases were dealt with by the Military Tribunal, not the city court. Pavel had indeed been sent to the camps for his careless remarks, as the attached documents (charge sheet and sentence) fully confirmed.

The letter was sent and impatiently we awaited the reply. It came extraordinarily quickly. His wife described in her usual garrulous way how she had rung up Yekaterina Pavlovna and gone to see her. Without saying a word, she handed her the letter from her husband and the court documents. The actress read them attentively and then "her face darkened: she looked like thunder and ordered me to ring her up each day."

I did not witness the next scene in this drama, and now I shall never know exactly what happened. I can only imagine Yekaterina Pavlovna's expression, tone of voice and the words she used when she went back to talk to those "kind people"... Pavel did not receive the reply through his wife. Three weeks later he was informed that he was being released and I received a note from him when he was already in the transit camp that he had been "totally exonerated" and was going home.

I never heard anything more of the driver from Leningrad. Neither did I ever see Korchagina-Alexandrovskaya again or hear from her about that particular real-life performance. High drama, but with a happy ending!

ROSHCHAKOVSKY

Transfers were always the same. I remember the first time. It was an hour and a half until the evening meal, and even longer before they would begin calling people out for interrogation. Unexpectedly, someone in the corridor grasped the bolt fastening the hatch in our cell door. Although we observed the ban on conversation, even in undertones, there was almost always an uninterrupted constant hum in our cell: whispered conversations, movements, belongings being rearranged—any signs of life from the seventy people crammed into a space originally intended for twenty. Yet no matter how softly the warder crept up to the door, no matter how cautiously he pushed aside the peephole-cover, the careful rustling of his movements was, by some miracle, always louder than all the noises in the cell. A piercing, anxious silence instantly descended on us.

The hatch (we called it the feedhole) opened to reveal a strange face. It wasn't one of our screws: we knew them all already. The unfamiliar warder cast a glance over the dozens of people looking attentively at him.

"Who's an 'R' here?"

I had just moved away from the slop bucket and was standing next to the door. None of the others whose surnames began with an R had managed to reply when, uncertainly, I gave my name.

"Full initials?"

Quite sure that this had nothing to do with me I gave my first name and patronymic. The warder glanced at the paper he was holding, "With your things!"

The hatch slammed shut. I stood there, stunned, unable to grasp that it had begun, that unknown, uncertain future that I had dreaded and yet waited and longed for so intensely. Suddenly I began to understand that it was almost like being taken away from my family for a second time, from those who had become close to me, who knew me and supported me; with them almost nothing was frightening because we were all together. I had spent very little time in prison compared to the others but already I was experiencing that inexplicable and indestructible attachment to my own cell and its inmates.

* * *

After my first month in prison I had been sent to the punishment cell. Actually, it was entirely the fault of a former People's Commissar. Now one of the cell elder's assistants, he had barely changed professions. Once he had worked as deputy minister for the forestry and paper industry. Now, each morning, before toilet duty, the warder gave him small and neatly-cut squares of gray paper, one for every prisoner in our cell, and then the deputy People's Commissar would hand them out. When we returned, those unfortunates whose bowels had not proved cooperative gave him back the unused scraps of paper and he returned them to the warder. Evidently our assistant elder considered me an experienced and well-informed prisoner and he did not warn me that a very strict account was kept of these papers. I held onto mine. That evening there was a sudden, extra search (a "dry wash" it was called). They found the piece of toilet paper. The warders were delighted and treated their discovery with great seriousness. A prisoner had been caught in possession of "writing equipment", they wrote in their report. I had still not forgotten my first search when I was ordered to bend down and expose my back passage. So this time I said something witty, as I thought, about their extraordinary interest in what Pushkin called the "sinful hole." The warders appreciated neither my wit nor my erudition. That evening they took me to the punishment cells.

These were of various types at Butyrki, and we had heard of damp stone holes, and of the impenetrable darkness of basements where the rats ran freely... I ended up in a "bright" cell. It was an unpleasant enough place. A small cupboard of a room, two paces long and one and a half in width, and no window. An iron frame with several cross-bars was fixed to the wall; this was the bed. It remained up all day and then, by some mechanism outside the cell, was let down for four hours during the night. Once a day they gave me 400 grams of bread and a mug of hot water. The tiny room, the floor, the walls, the ceiling, the so-called bed, and the enormous metal-lidded slop bucket were all covered in a dazzling white glossy paint. A 500-watt bulb shone from the ceiling, day and night. After an hour of this, you began to go crazy. Most of the time I stood in the corner with my eyes firmly closed. Since they stripped you to your underwear before they put you in the cell, the arms with which I tried to shield my eyes, were in a loose shirt that was also white. But nothing helped. The light penetrated the brain, it got inside you, and it was impossible to get away from it.

I was told that I was to be punished with five days "ordinary regime" and should not tap messages, talk, sit or lie on the floor, or do certain other things. Violation of any of these prohibitions would automatically lead to a further 120 hours in the punishment cell. After a few days I lost count of time. That was the most terrifying of all. I imagined that I had done something, infringed the rules and was already about to serve a second five-day term. I was sure I would not survive and if I did get out of that bright hell then I would be either blind or barely human. I recalled the dim light and friendly overcrowding of cell No. 29 where it was possible to lie on the board beds, cover your head and, protected by the compassion, help and understanding of your comrades and cellmates, hide from the peep-hole in the door.

Suddenly the door, not just the hatch, opened onto complete and total darkness. I could not even see anyone standing there. Someone took me by the elbow, led me out of the cell, and I managed to dress somehow; I took my belongings tied up in the undershirt, and walked back along the dark, quite unlit prison corridors. I did not recognize my corridor or see the number of the cell in front of which we had stopped. The door opened, I was given a push in the back, and I entered the warm dampness and stuffy air of the cell. Hands grabbed and guided me and I heard familiar voices. Something edible was shoved into my hands. "Let him have a smoke first!" a voice called out. But I could see no one. The tears suddenly began pouring and I sat with streaming eyes, drawing on the cigarette that had been put in my mouth.

"He's been in the 'bright' cell!" An experienced voice explained. "He still can't see a thing. The tears will go shortly and then he'll start seeing again..."

Perhaps that really is the physiological reaction to five days and nights of unbearable light. Probably, though, I was simply crying from self-pity and happiness that I was "home" again, with familiar people: when we were together nothing was frightening...

* * *

Now I was leaving my cellmates once again. This time, for good. They helped me gather my things and whispered from all sides, with passion and conviction: You're being freed! They're letting you out! Believe me, you're a free man. Memorize this address, and go and see my wife—don't forget! I did not know whether to believe them or not. But I repeated the address, shook hands and embraced the others and I don't know how long this went on before we heard the ring of keys outside, the clanging of the bolts and the rustle of the door as it opened. My comrades almost pushed me out into the corridor. It was clean and light. Thick strips of matting covered the floor tiles. Wide, high windows without any screens were protected by thick, opaque reinforced glass. The upper panes were of the most ordinary clear glass and the green top leaves of the poplars brushed against them.

* * *

I was taken to the very end of the corridor and led into another cell. It was more like a room. There were benches along the walls and a quite ordinary table in the corner with a chair behind it. Five men were already there. They were confused and, panting, they clutched absurd prisoner's bundles, all kinds of rags wrapped up in pillowcases, shirts or long johns. I looked just as distraught, I realized, and bewildered. I sat down on the bench and looked about me. There were two elderly men with worn-out faces and tired yet anxiously hopeful eyes which did not leave the door for a moment. A handsome young man paced up and down, like a tiger in a cage; the prison washhouse and searches had not affected the elegance of his luxurious tweed suit. Grisha Filippovsky was an artist, and he would be my companion on the transport and then in the camps.

Gradually the cell filled up. Each time the lock made a noise all glanced up hopefully. But it was only a new prisoner standing in the doorway, a bundle clutched to his stomach. At last the door swung open, confidently and wide, and in strode a young NKVD lieutenant. Two warders stood by the door. The lieutenant was neatly dressed and close-shaven, the buckles of his belt and shoulder straps shone, the folds of his field shirt were creased perfectly, and he gave off an aroma of eau de cologne, good tobacco, health, youth, home and good fortune—all the things that I had once considered quite natural. I had been just the same and, through inertia, I went on imagining that I had not changed.

No, that's not quite true. He was not the same as me or the others. Only for the first few weeks had I continued to look on the jailers and interrogators as people just like me: They might be mistaken or worthless scoundrels, I had thought, but they were human beings, nevertheless. Then, in an instant, I changed my mind. One time the warders brought someone back to cell No. 29 after interrogation. The old man had astonished us by announcing that he had been held in the same cell in 1911... He was sick, weak and, evidently, they beat him harder than the others. Two warders dragged him in. He fell to the floor like a sack and ceased moving. We could not go to him immediately because one of the warders stayed with him in the cell by the half-open door while the other left. Two minutes later the second warder returned and ahead of him, a woman in a white coat.

For a second or two, I must confess, we forgot our beaten comrade. The woman was young and very pretty. We had not seen any women for months and now here was a representative of that other, forgotten world and we could not take our eyes off her. Without bending down, the pretty woman moved the head, and then the arms and legs, of the lying man with the toe of her elegant little shoe. She turned to the warder: "There aren't any fractures, just bruises."

Without looking at us, or rather she glanced our way but did not see us, the doctor left the cell. The warders followed. It was then I understood, once and for all, that they were not like us. Not even like the people we once were, let alone those we had become and would remain in the future. It was impossible to establish any human contact with such people, or regard them as human beings; they were only pretending and we, for our part, also had to make believe that they were just like us. Yet all the while we remained totally and unshakeably convinced that they were only pretending. Some gave a better performance, others worse.

So the lieutenant entered our cell, confident that he was in command, and sat down at the table. From a handsome leather folder he took out documents, large and small. He called each of us by surname and asked our first name, patronymic, and date of birth. Then he held out a slip of paper, "Sign here. And add the date."

I was called third or fourth. Without looking up he held out a small square piece of white paper. This printed form was a "Decree of the Special Board of the NKVD, dated..." and carried the classification "Top secret." Just like the deposition at my interrogation, a vertical line divided the paper. On the left side, "Surname, name, patronymic, crime"; on the right, "Decree." The secretary of the Special Board was supposed to sign below. My form read: "Razgon Lev Emmanuilovich, member of Bolshevik Party" and, to the right, "Sentenced to five years in corrective-labor camps for Counter-Revolutionary Agitation."

I did not read it so much as glance over the entire contents. I signed, recalled and added the date (it was 21 June 1938), returned the paper and moved away. All the rest did the same in total silence. Only one older prisoner did not give back the decree immediately but, keeping it in his hand, asked the lieutenant, "Do I have the right to appeal?"

"Most certainly, you do," the lieutenant replied with exaggerated politeness.

"To whom?"

"Whomsoever you wish. To the Collective for the Disabled at the Moscow Social Security office, for instance," he answered in the same calmly polite manner.

The prisoner did not react to this witticism, which evidently had been repeated several times before, and the handing out of our sentences was rapidly completed in this humdrum workaday fashion. The lieutenant returned the documents to his folder, stood up and left the cell. Now we were alone and could ask what each had found on his paper.

A rapid, boring and bureaucratic procedure had replaced the theatrical rite of announcing the verdict and that, perhaps, explains why none of us took either the sentences or the handful of letters which denoted our offenses very seriously. Our terms of imprisonment were, we most naively believed, quite arbitrary and unreal. It did not make any difference, we supposed, whether we were to spend five, eight or ten years in the camps (the Special Board, for some reason, only gave one of those three sentences). In any case, all would be cleared up in a matter of time, and relatively quickly at that, and then we would be set free—because this unnatural, frightening process could not continue more than a month, a few months or, at the most, a year!

Years had to pass before those who survived came to realize that it had all been quite serious and intentional. They could even keep a person in after his sentence was finished (and did so, until "special instruction"). But they never let anyone out a day earlier.

The plain letters that denoted each article of the Criminal Code were also far more important than we could have supposed. Among the many wonders of our "judicial" system these letters were a striking innovation. They excluded almost any practical possibility of influencing your fate. The lieutenant was quite right when he advised us to appeal to the Collective for the Disabled. For it would have had just as much effect as a complaint to the Procurator's Office, a People's Commissar, the Presidium of the Central Executive Committee (the "President's Office"), the Central Committee or any other institution. It had nothing to do with them. The person who made the decisions was the sergeant, lieutenant or other state security officer who was "in charge" of your case and knew beforehand what to do with you. He had quite wide powers, moreover. It was he who chose the letter code which in effect determined an individual's entire subsequent life.

Small changes were of enormous significance. To be marked SVE, a Socially Harmful Element, denoted a common criminal offense and it was handed out to criminals, those who had infringed the passport regulations, prostitutes, petty thieves and rapists. These were, in the official terminology, "socially acceptable" persons. Camp instructions stated that only they should be appointed to the administration and services or as office workers and specialists. The instructions were never observed, though, because there were pathetically few doctors, economists and engineers among the thieves and rapists. It was even difficult to use them as cooks and warehousemen because of their "peculiar" attitude to state property. The camp managers, work distributors and those employed in Distribution and in Education, on the other hand, were exclusively criminal in background.

It might seem that "harmful" and "dangerous" are almost synonyms. To be classified SOE, a Socially Dangerous Element, however, meant you were a political offender. Among the long series of codes for those imprisoned under Article 58 it was, I must admit, the most innocuous. It entitled a prisoner to soon be allowed about without a guard and even to obtain a number of privileges. Next in severity came KRA and ASA, Counter-Revolutionary Agitation and Anti-Soviet Agitation. There was no logical distinction here but some instruction or other lay behind their use. Then came KRD, an entire series of

Counter-Revolutionary Activities. This broad category covered the most varied accusations. Sometimes the terrible letter T was slipped in, meaning Terrorist activities, KRTD. People with that code were, as a rule, only sent out on escorted gang labor and never allowed to work in services or the office. Sometimes an investigator with a strong imagination would add yet another T, making this not just terrorist but Trotskyist Terrorist Activities, KRTTD. Such people were held in the punitive camps under special supervision and in some places they were simply shot when orders came from Moscow to deal more firmly with the Trotskyists. It is amazing but I never met a single person with this code who had been a member of the Party or ever had the slightest contact with Trotskyism. I knew of cases when the additional T would appear in a prisoner's camp documents because of a quarrel during a general head-count with the work distributor or the head of Distribution, who were both criminals. I was acquainted with an immensely gifted smith who could mend the most complex machinery and hammer out the most complicated part. In spite of his serious offense they specially posted a guard for him so that he could go on working in the camp smithy.

Seryogin was a peasant and he had nothing to do with politics. On 2 December 1934 he was sitting in his smithy in a remote village of the Tambov Region and explaining to his fellow villagers how to make a reaping machine. Someone came to join them and announced, "You know what, Seryogin, they've killed Kirov..."

"Damned if I care," responded Seryogin. He had never heard of the man before in his life. He had died in a fight in a neighboring village, Seryogin assumed, during the saint's day celebrations. His words were passed on to the district NKVD and a file was opened on the smith. Three years later the local troika gave Seryogin 10 years, for the two dreadful T's.

One of the commonest charges, PSh, Suspicion of Espionage, was also considered a bad code. So many people were given it, however, that it almost became a common criminal offense, especially since it was used for the majority of engineers and technicians and other specialists. All those who had ever lived abroad, who had relatives or knew people in other countries, were sentenced for this offense. The very term "suspicion" excluded any obligation to provide proof, so those Suspected of Espionage often had no foreign connections whatsoever: craftsmen in small towns, teachers of foreign languages, caretakers who had annoyed their secret masters...

The "women's" category ChSIR, Member of a Traitor's Family, was clearer and more definite. Unlike all the other categories this officially legalized the arrest, conviction and imprisonment of those who were innocent even under Soviet laws. The offense derived from the institution of hostage-taking, already well established in the country. Each individual should know that if he did not return from abroad or was accused of that quite indefinable and unprovable charge of "treason" then his nearest and dearest (wife, mother, father and children) were doomed to arrest and dispossession. All of them could be sentenced as Members of a Traitor's Family. If, that is, they could not already be sentenced for failing to inform on their father or husband—an offense under Article 58:12. To begin with, all the ChSIR's were concentrated in the vast Temnikovsk camp, without the right to correspondence or to use their professional training in their work. They were kept totally in the dark as to the fate of their husbands, parents and children. The lucky ones were those who were pregnant or still breast-feeding when arrested, who could keep their babies with them. The rest were tormented by fear for their small children and a total ignorance of where or how they were. Only two to three years later did the ChSIR's begin to be moved on to ordinary camps where they could write and receive letters.

It would be wrong to imagine that the Special Boards and troikas actually met, consulted or even read the sentences they signed. In summer 1937 when a great many of my close family and friends had already been snatched away, and I myself had been sacked from my job, I once went to visit my cousin at the Moscow Criminal Investigation Department. Merik Gorokhov was a charming and kind man. For many years he had worked in the border guards. Then he was appointed deputy to the famous Vul, the scourge of the Moscow underworld, head of the city's CID, and they would eventually be shot together. Merik was a quiet Jew with light brown hair and the large blue eyes that Nesterov liked to paint. I was sitting in his office when his secretary entered, holding an enormous pile of documents (several hundred pages) in his hand. Without interrupting our conversation, Merik added his signature to others at the bottom of each sheet, with a blue pencil. He did not look at the pages but dashed off his name without a second glance. Occasionally he stopped to shake his aching hand.

"What's that you're signing?" I asked out of curiosity.

"Oh, I'm member of a troika, you see. Those are decrees ordering the isolation of criminals, Socially Harmful Elements," Merik replied. Later I saw those "elements." More than half had not committed a crime for a very long time. They had a previous conviction, served their sentence, and then given up a "life of crime," as they say; they became model citizens, married, had children and began to work in a factory or an office. Some had been in Dmitlag and thus dug the Moscow-Volga Canal, built the Gosplan building in Moscow city center, and so on; others had already been "reforged" through educational labor on the Baltic-White Sea Canal, securing early release for their shock-working, and they were decorated with orders of merit and even medals. It made no difference. They were all to be "isolated," as being sent to the camps was delicately termed.

Those sitting on the Special Board and various other troikas signed their decrees just like my cousin. Various signatures and stamps ("Agreed," "Confirmed," and so on) could be found on such papers. Yet almost all were signed in one and the same way and the only person who actually decided the fate of those convicted was the sergeant, captain or lieutenant in State Security who drew up the paper in the first place.

* * *

I have strayed a little from my story. Now convicted, we became acquainted and waited for a long time to see what they would do with us next. Next, they took us all out, first searching us, and after we were lined up two by two, they marched us along endless corridors. Prison doors opened and closed, then we passed through one more doorway and found ourselves in the almost forgotten world of greenery and vegetation. An enormous courtyard, overgrown with an extraordinary and piercingly brilliant greenness. Dandelions and buttercups were turning yellow in the grass, and poplars grew there... We had not seen anything like it since we were imprisoned. Our fifteen-minute exercise periods were in tiny yards covered with asphalt where not a blade of grass could grow. Here there seemed to be an overabundance of greenery! In the depths of the courtyard stood a gloomy, awkward round-shaped brick building. The former prison church, now the transit block. We were led in and marched up the broad staircase to the first floor. The screws unlocked the cell and eight of us were pushed towards an open door from which an uninhibited stream of voices could be heard.

Deafened, I stood next to the enormous metal slop bucket. After our cell this seemed a hall. The room was vast and bright. Although the large church windows were covered by screens outside, even they could not obstruct the rays of light. Two-tier board beds, filled with bodies pressed tightly together, ran along the walls. The space under the lower tier was also filled. Some were simply lying in the middle of the cell and the others nonchalantly stepped over them. Unlike the remand block no one whispered here. They all spoke loudly: there was no choice—otherwise no one could have heard a thing. The cell contained several hundred men. They behaved quite freely. Some slept, some did exercises or walked about the cell, while others chatted or even sang...

There was no free space on the board beds. No one met us or allocated us a place to sit or lie down, and there was not a trace here of the iron discipline and self-organization of cell No. 29! I slowly surveyed the board beds, in the hope of spotting someone I knew or recognized. Not a single one. No, over there was a very familiar face, quite unlike anyone else in here. Squatting on the lower board beds, sat a man who was extraordinarily like the famous portraits and photographs of Anatole France. A neat white, slightly parted beard, a long craftily curved nose, cream silk pyjamas and a black scholar's skullcap on a dazzlingly white head. He was reading a book, turning the pages with a graceful and extravagant gesture. Perhaps he sensed my gaze. In any case, he abandoned his book, raised his head and looked attentively at me. Then he bowed a greeting and with an equally elegant wave of his hand called me over.

"Young fellow! There is the semblance of a place here. And if you do not object to the company of a dull old man, please make yourself at home!"

He received my belongings with the same elaborate gestures, moved to one side to make space for me, and when I was seated, said, "Well, then, let us become acquainted. Mikhail Sergeevich Roshchakovsky. And whom do I have the honor of addressing?"

I spent the next month beside one of the most unusual and interesting of all the many people I got to know during my years in prison and the camps.

The surname struck me as rather familiar. Then I realized that I had come across it in Novikov-Priboi's novel, in the thick illustrated volumes on the history of the Russo-Japanese war and in some of the other countless books that I read in my youth without any stricter guide than a ferocious and insatiable curiosity. Even in our strange time Roshchakovsky's biography was extraordinary...

* * *

He had begun in a very conventional way for a member of an old gentry family, several generations of whom had been naval officers. Roshchakovsky was an excellent student at the Naval College. His only other distinction was that he studied together with several grand dukes. He was friendly with them and this, evidently, became quite important in his later life. Unlike those who requested to serve at Kronstadt, and thus near the court in Petersburg, Roshchakovsky asked to be sent to the Pacific Ocean squadron. He went to Port Arthur and thanks to his many gifts rapidly made a career for himself. By the outbreak of the Russo-Japanese war he was commanding the torpedo boat *Decisive*. The ship would enter history as a very rare example of naval success in that conflict. When the squadron attempted to break through the Japanese blockade of Port Arthur, only *Decisive* got away. Almost the entire Japanese squadron gave chase. The Japanese torpedo boats were faster and were already gaining on him when Roshchakovsky was forced to put in at the Chinese port of Chi-fu. China was neutral during the war, so the ship should have been interned by the Chinese. Even then, however, the Japanese did not give a damn about Chinese neutrality.

When the Russian ship dropped anchor in Chi-fu, the crew had barely time to take a breath before the Japanese squadron appeared on the horizon and sealed *Decisive* behind an impenetrable ring. A cutter approached and a Japanese officer climbed on board. In the most insulting terms, he suggested that Roshchakovsky immediately surrender the ship and all its crew. When Roshchakovsky replied that this was an unacceptable offer for the Russians, using the refined language of the shore-front all-night taverns (they were talking in English), the Japanese officer suddenly hurled himself at the captain of the *Decisive*, fastening his crooked but strong teeth in Roshchakovsky's hand...

"There, my boy," he extended a disfigured finger. "Because of that animal I thereafter declined to attend balls: one can hardly offer a lady such a claw!"

At their captain's orders, the sailors of the *Decisive* gave the Japanese officer a thorough and enjoyable thrashing, and threw him into the cutter. The officer sailed back to his squadron, promising the Russians that they would be feeding the fishes in thirty minutes' time. There was no reason to doubt the seriousness of this threat. Within half an hour Roshchakovsky landed all his crew on shore and remained the last on board, himself scuttling the ship. The Japanese fleet watched as *Decisive*, still flying the St. Andrew's flag, went to the bottom. Roshchakovsky reached the shore in a rowing boat and even the Japanese did not resolve to pursue him further. The sailors were interned and Roshchakovsky, not without the tacit support of the Chinese authorities, escaped to America.

From the USA he traveled back to Petersburg. Against the gloomy background of defeat and disaster the achievement of the *Decisive*'s captain appeared particularly impressive. Roshchakovsky was showered with awards and signs of favor. It was then, and perhaps not without the help of his fellow student grand dukes, that he became first acquainted, and then friendly, with the Tsar. Or as friendly as was possible, given the weak-willed and deceitfully inconstant character of Nicholas II. Roshchakovsky did not exploit this opportunity to make an instant career at court. In fact, and this struck me as strange, he was not at all interested in his own advancement. A squadron was preparing to sail and Roshchakovsky successfully pressed to join it. He survived their sadly famous journey, all the way from Petersburg to defeat in the Tsushima straits. He took part in the battle, and with the other surviving Russian sailors was picked out of the water by the Japanese, spending the rest of the war as a captive of the enemy.

During his imprisonment he drew up a very detailed report on the reasons for the Russian fleet's defeat and the necessity for its fundamental reorganization. When the war ended and he returned to Russia, he submitted this report for consideration. However, not even friendship with the Tsar helped. The report was held up in the chancery of the Naval Ministry: the Tsar's uncle, Admiral of the Fleet, was beside himself with fury. His naval career in ruins, Roshchakovsky reacted decisively and submitted his resignation. At the Tsar's request he became a diplomat, but not of the ordinary kind. He represented not Russia but the Romanov dynasty and his imperial friend, and only in those states where the Tsar had relatives: Denmark, Greece, the duchy of Darmstadt... Every summer Roshchakovsky was a guest of Nicholas at Livadia in the Crimea.

I believe Roshchakovsky was telling the truth when he said he had never been one of the court hangers-on and did not use his connections with the Tsar to advance his career or become rich. Only when the First World War began did he exploit his privileged access to the monarch. In his ill-fated report Roshchakovsky had written that a quite new fleet should now become the main force in the Russian navy. It was essential to build up a Northern fleet and use the ice-free polar ports to supply Russia by laying a railway between Murmansk and Petersburg. In 1914 Roshchakovsky abandoned diplomacy and returned to military service. In violation of every rule of promotion he was appointed rear admiral and made governor general of the Kola peninsula with almost unlimited powers.

He proved a capable colonial administrator, very like his admired colleagues in the British or Dutch colonies. Thousands of prisoners of war, together with Chinese transported from the other end of the Empire, built the Murmansk railway. Roshchakovsky did not spare men or money. While the railway was under construction he organized the transfer of shells from England to the new port of Romanov and they were then transported by reindeer to the nearest railway station. So involved did he become in his new activity, that he hardly saw his royal chum. Then, like a bolt out of the blue, came the February Revolution and the Tsar's abdication. Roshchakovsky knew that Grand Duke Mikhail, to whom Nicholas passed the tangled reins of government, was even more modestly endowed with the ability to rule...

"Our deceased monarch was a man of excellent upbringing, very tactful and well-versed in all his royal duties. He knew whom to talk to, and how to go about it—he excelled at such conversations! He possessed an extraordinary memory and understanding of the special needs and tact required in conversation. He would not converse with a Hussar and a member of the Preobrazhensky Regiment in the same way. He could talk to any professor and chat away, most simply, with a peasant. And what else, in the end, should a monarch be able to do? The Russian Tsar, however, should also be able to rule the empire. His Majesty could have done that as well, had it not been for his accursed tactfulness, diffident character and, of course, that enormous, that vast horde of idle relatives and relations! Not satisfied with all they already possessed, every one of them would thrust himself forward as an adviser, minister or director. His Majesty did not possess the force and character of his father. And then there was his family, the bitter grief of his private life!"

"You mean the Tsaritsa?"

"My good sir! Are you also going to follow those tittle-tattle journalists and say vile things to me about her? That she slept with Rasputin, I suppose? Her Majesty was a deeply unfortunate woman... Just think, one daughter after another... The Russian throne would leave the Romanov family, for the first time the line of direct descent would be broken. She thought herself to blame. She was a hysteric, moreover, running from one monastery to the next, bowing and praying, asking God for an heir. Then when he was born it turned out that he was incurably sick! She would have sold her soul not just to Rasputin but to the devil himself to save the boy! And that's how it was, my good man.

"As for Mikhail Alexandrovich, he was the most pleasant of men, but only fit for a regiment. Not even a guards regiment at that, but an ordinary army regiment, somewhere like Kaluga. And then no higher than a lieutenant-colonel. He was not even fit to command a regiment: he was shy, soft-hearted and could not stand court ceremonial. A petty lawyer would embarrass him, just like a young provincial girl with her suitor... Yet he'd been taught to be tsar! Without the slightest success. It was all quite hopeless, my dear fellow!"

Roshchakovsky had rushed to Petrograd and arrived the day after Mikhail followed his brother and also abdicated. He nurtured no more illusions.

"The empire had collapsed. Well, all those creatures—those ministers, heads of department and senators—were not worth a bent farthing! With no sense of dignity, honor or family loyalty, they fed off the state, and lived for their careers and their jobs. They'd do anything to keep them. They said and did only what would please His Highness, Her Majesty or the grand dukes. And not even just the royal family! They were ready to please any bastard if only it would help them keep their position—Rasputin, Illiodor, John of Kronstadt... No one gave a thought about Russia! The real native Russians, the Russian aristocracy, could not have cared less. They had no need to enter service, they did not lack money and they weren't used to abasing themselves. And of course, many of them had become degenerate. As for the merchants, they didn't understand the first thing! They thought they could play at parliaments for years. The blockhead had learned to drink dry sherry at lunchtime and thought he could already be Speaker!"

"But you're a real Marxist!"

"I am a monarchist, my good fellow, not a Marxist. I have not read that Marx of yours and I do not ever intend to. Everyone expects clever advice from the Jews! Each provincial governor used to keep a clever Jew beside him, and took his advice because he did not trust himself and thought other Russians were even more stupid. Of course, the Jews are a wise nation, they've been through fire and water. But if wisdom comes through suffering, then the Russians shouldn't be stupider. That Marx serves your lot like the governor's clever Jew...

"Yes, Russia was falling apart and everyone wanted to grab a piece to make sure that he would survive at least. Petrograd was like a Babylonian orgy. No one was giving any orders, and what was the point...?"

Roshchakovsky left Russia without delay. He reached Stockholm in March 1917, almost at the same time as a small group of political emigres arrived there, with the help of the Germans, travelling in a "sealed carriage" from Switzerland to Russia. With his knowledge, energy and reputation Roshchakovsky quite rapidly found himself a highly-paid job with a shipbuilding firm. He had abandoned any political activity forever, it seemed.

Until the Civil War began. The position he adopted then was so strange for a man of his convictions that Kolchak and Denikin sent delegations to see him. The technical director of the shipbuilding firm began to write to the press, to speak in public and to publish brochures and impassioned articles addressed to the officers of the White Armies. The victory of the "White Cause," he argued, would mean the total collapse of Russia as a sovereign state and great power. If the White Guard won, Russia would effectively become a foreign colony for dozens if not hundreds of years. The former ruling classes would pay a terrible price for victory in the Civil War—the empire would be dismembered and independence lost entirely. There was only one force that was capable of preserving a unified and undivided Russia, the Bolsheviks. Only a Bolshevik victory could preserve and then restore, even extend, the might of the Russian empire.

The firm sacked its director and his name was cursed as a traitor. Other emigres shot at him but Roshchakovsky stubbornly fought off all attacks and would lay bets about the outcome of the war with those members of the Swedish aristocracy who still found it amusing to keep on friendly terms with this now crazy Russian.

By the early 1930s Roshchakovsky was quite alone. His wife had died, there were no children and he was suffering appalling nostalgia. He asked for permission to return home and he was met with rare deference in Moscow. They appointed him chief consultant on warship construction and gave him almost everything they could: a high salary, a service apartment, special rations and a car. He had several talks with Stalin and often visited Voroshilov. In 1937, naturally, he was arrested and after they had held him in prison for a long time without any interrogations the Special Board gave him five years as a Socially Dangerous Element. That was when we met in Butyrki.

* * *

Roshchakovsky was infinitely fascinating to me. So much so, that I spent almost all my time talking to him. He was a revelation. To start with, I learned for the first time what a good upbringing meant. It was not just that everything this old man did was elegant and graceful (he would eat the prison soup with a wooden spoon so beautifully that it was impossible to tear your eyes away). In the primitive and revolting life of that enormous cell, crammed full of people who ate foul-tasting food, belched and broke wind, used the stinking slop bucket and poisoned the air with the stench of their unwashed sweaty bodies, Roshchakovsky did nothing that might irritate his cell-mates. He was simple and quite natural in his dealings with any of his cellmates. There was not a hint of familiarity or condescension, of any desire to ingratiate himself with his fellows or to humiliate them by displaying his greater learning and experience.

He was a convinced monarchist, nationalist and anti-semite. I was a Communist, internationalist and a Jew. We argued almost all the time. Yet, I discovered, you can argue with someone who holds quite different views without becoming irritated or embittered, and still respect one another.

It was not his impeccable behavior and upbringing, however, that distinguished him from everyone else I met in prison. He was the only one there who was happy. He was quite contented and he did not hide the fact. I knew other people in prison who also expressed their satisfaction. But in their case it took the form of the most elementary and malicious gloating.

One of them was Tsederbaum, brother of the Menshevik leader Julius Martov. He was tall and rather stupid, and not a kindly man. Many privileged and inactive years as a well-connected political exile in another, liberal era had corrupted him. Tsederbaum would remember with pleasure his period of exile in one regional town, I forget which now. Before the revolution he had held some post in the Second International and all its leading officials had known him (though probably more because of his brother than himself). On his birthday one car after another would pull up outside the villa where the celebrated exile was now living. The heads of the local GPU each brought in an enormous cake, greeted their charge and handed over a telegram from the prime minister of a "friendly" country. Almost all the European prime ministers then were socialists—in France, Belgium, Sweden, Norway and other countries... They congratulated their friend with high-flown phrases and resounding words and the shadow of their governmental majesty fell on Tsederbaum, who began to feel almost a prime minister himself...

Of course, in 1937 all that idiotic well-being collapsed. Tsederbaum was arrested and brought to Moscow. Yet he understood nothing and was convinced that he would continue to live in privileged exile and wait for better days. He did not suspect that hard labor in the camps or hunger in the prison cell awaited him and, in the end, a bullet in the back of the skull when Moscow sent out the latest lists for "liquidation." For the time being, he was filled with a joyful sense of vengeance. Demonstrating that nothing there disturbed him (he was an old experienced jailbird!) he would endlessly pace up and down the cell, stepping over those lying on the floor and warbling French songs beneath his breath. Sometimes he halted in front of a thoroughly disheartened and despondent man, gazed at him attentively, and then would ask compassionately, "What's the matter, colleague? What's happened? It's simply dreadful to look at you. Whatever is the matter? Aha! I didn't guess immediately. You're in prison! That's what amazes, astonishes, distresses and disheartens you. It can happen to others—it should happen to others!—but not, apparently, to you. Tsk, tsk! No, my dear fellow, it was all written down long ago, in the Bible and in the most basic history textbooks. It's just that you never studied. Well, start learning now, colleague, perhaps it will make you wiser..."

Roshchakovsky never took any malicious pleasure of this kind. Vengeance was not a natural feeling for him. But he was happy that he had lived to see his most passionate beliefs being put into practice.

* * *

"You're too young to understand what it means. To have undergone the pain of having all that was dearest and most important in life destroyed; to live in suffering, still believing that what was dear would be resurrected, and to survive long enough to see it happen! God has been gracious to grant me such happiness at the end of my life!"

"Which happiness?"

"This very prison, for instance. At last, I have lived long enough to see the prisons filled with Communists and those—what are they called?—Comintern people; with Jews, and all those politicians who still cannot understand a thing, or see what is happening to them. Just look at them, my dear Lev Emmanuilovich, they held the highest posts in the state. Under the old system they would have been heads of department, deputy ministers and members of the State Council. At least in our day such people did not take part in politics, while these have done nothing but play at politics all their lives. And still they do not understand the slightest thing! Neither what is happening to Russia nor to them. The idiots all imagine that some mistake has occurred! I am no politician. I am simply an ordinary thinking Russian. I have been waiting and hoping for this great man who, at last, has been sent from on high to our long-suffering motherland... "

"Well, explain to me, one of the fools, what is going on?"

"It's all starting over again, my good fellow, just as after the Time of Troubles.[1] A great Russian nation-state is being established, with its own great national tasks."

"Which tasks?"

"To transform Russia into the most powerful state, dictating its will to other nations. To restore Russia to her old borders, annex Galicia, and seize the Balkans. To resolve the Dardanelles issue and secure Russia's access to the Mediterranean. To strengthen Russia in the Near East. To penetrate to the heart of Europe—into Bohemia and Moravia, Czechia and Slovakia, gain access to the Hungarian plain... To unite and with blood and iron bind all the Slavs together in an immensely powerful state. Those are the great and immemorial tasks that the Romanovs could not manage to carry out and are destined to be fulfilled by other, greater men..."

"Now you're including the Magyars in the Slavic state. The Hungarians can't stand the Slavs! And what do the Rumanians have in common with the Slavs, apart from Orthodoxy? What about the nations of Central Asia—are they also part of the Slavic Union?"

"Well, my good man, those Sarts, Kirgiz and Bashkirs and all the rest are fated to be our colonies forever, to the end of time! When all's said and done, a state isn't a charitable enterprise. You Jews forgot your own state long ago, so you can't understand! You are engaged in noble and attractive causes—philosophy, art, those social theories and such... But a state can only be national, and it is not the poets and musicians who make a state but cold hard men... How happy I would be to live to see the day when that great man—no, that greatest of men fully understands his destiny and founds a new Russian dynasty, Joseph II!"

"But he's no Russian. He's not even Slav... "

"What of it? In all states the founders of new, stable dynasties were outsiders. The Hannovers in England, the Bernadottes in Sweden, the Holstein-Gottorps in Russia... It's not of the slightest importance! Tell me, does he have children? Sons?"

I remembered Yasha Djugashvili, with his fanatical modesty, obsessive honesty and chivalry, and his dislike for his father and the latter's treacherous nature.

"I know him well, the man you have in mind as tsarevich. You'll never make a tsar of him!"

"What of it? He'll kill the boy. Like Ivan did, like Peter did. Then he'll raise up the younger son to be monarch. If there's no younger son then he'll father one, or adopt a child. No, the man who founds a dynasty always provides his successors!"

"In one of his sketches Mikhail Koltsov wrote that such a thing was as impossible to imagine as Stalin in a tail-coat or in a uniform with general's shoulder boards."

"He's a fool, your journalist! Koltsov is probably a Jew and does not understand statesmanship. The time will come when Stalin puts on the epaulettes of a field marshal and is surrounded by a suite in general's epaulettes. People will tremble before him as they never trembled before Peter; and Nicholas I, by comparison, will seem a pathetic liberal..."

"So then, the old titles will be restored? Privy councillor, State Councillor and full-dress uniforms with braid?"

"Most certainly. Titles, though perhaps they will be slightly different, and dress coats with braid and all the other bits and pieces without which nothing works in a real state."

"And classes?"

"What classes? Oh, estates! Of course. There will be the estate of officials, of scholars, manual workers, peasants... There will be an aristocracy which will provide those who govern the state and supply the higher officials and diplomats..."

"A hereditary aristocracy?"

"My dear boy, stop playing the fool—asking me such silly questions! Of course, the elite will produce the new elite, as it should do, the officials will produce the new officials and so on... The children of the ministers will not go to work in factories, and the professors' daughters are not going to marry those collective-farm workers of yours. The divisions between the estates will be higher and firmer than in the old Russia. Because, my good fellow, they will put an end to this freedom to spit the state in the face, this intelligentsia wavering—all that Nekrasov legacy.[2] Really! The thought of it! Nekrasov's peasant will be so tightly bound that he won't dare to squeak. He'll be bound to the land and work from fear not duty. The same for the workers. There will be enough fear to go round the whole of Russia, that I guarantee! Hmph! Nicholas the Bloody... To call our late monarch that, a quiet, tactful man who could never make a real autocrat! Our new ruler will show everyone what kind of power there should be in the state! Of course, to begin with he will push too hard, yes indeed, much too hard... Because," and at this, Roshchakovsky bent to my ear, "he must do away with all his former friends and comrades! And that builds up like an avalanche. They will kill the right ones, and the wrong ones, there's always someone to kill in Russia. And someone to do the killing.

"It was very interesting coming back to Russia. Interesting and strange to begin with. I'd grown unaccustomed, you know, to Russia, the Russian spirit. When I arrived, I looked about me and saw there was a great deal of that spirit. More, in my view, than was necessary. In Scandinavia it seemed to me that if all the old ways, good and bad, were not finished in Russia, then they were almost finished. I read books about the Bolsheviks, I read a great deal—your writers, Pilnyak, Gladkov and some others. It even seemed to me that the new Russian man was becoming something like people in the West. Business-like, calculating, sizing everything up, able to turn his hands to anything... Nothing of the kind, it turns out! It's true I did meet some of that type: any major director would take them on as a manager and give them more money. But when I enquired they proved either to be Jews or old emigres who had worked for Krupps or Erikson... The Russians had remained the same, and a great deal more time will pass and much blood will be shed before the new Peter will beat the laziness, spinelessness and old Muscovite stupidity out of them...

"Your military men, your generals are gifted. Beyond doubt! No less than Napoleon's marshals. I met Tukhachevsky and Muklevich. They were clever, very able men. It's a great pity that they were shot. To raise up new ones you always need a new, great war. But war doesn't just give birth to heroes—it makes all kinds of excrement. I'm sorry that I still have not seen one important quality in the new Russians, that of self-respect. That existed in the old Russia. There was something to give people such a feeling. First, belonging to the gentry. You might be the most bedraggled and impoverished of gentlemen but still you had that title! Your honor was protected by law and imperial decree. No one could talk down to you; no one would dare use obscenities in your presence; no one could whip you as long as the court had not deprived you of your gentry title. Do you know the story about Alexander III when he was still only heir to the throne? He got overheated while he was commanding on the parade ground and cursed one ensign. The latter sent him a letter: Since I cannot challenge the future emperor to a duel I demand that he apologize to me in writing. If I do not receive those apologies by a certain hour I shall commit suicide. Well, as you know, Alexander was a wise and capable tsar but as a man he was a rough character. He did not apologize. The officer, of course, shot himself. The Tsar then forced his son to follow the coffin of the ensign, who was buried by the entire Guards regiment, across all St Petersburg on foot! Your Party does not, and could not, have such a corporate spirit; it is ruled from above, and rightly so, that's its purpose.

"Those who weren't gentry had the power and strength of money. If you're bright or rich, then no one will dare to insult you! And then service to the state, in Russia as in all the world, carried great advantages. The son of some sexton who trained to be a doctor discovered that he was good at cutting people up. After twenty-five years he became a professor, and received the full pension of a state or privy councillor. That priest's son was already His Excellency, he wore ribbons and stars, and no one could take any of it away from him. And he received them for his services, not just by being in service... So there we are. As for your lot, my good fellow, I sensed the kind of servility at the top that under the Tsar was only to be found in the local district police. A man has no title or money—today he's a minister, tomorrow they'll push him out and who is he then? So they strut about, but understand their total dependence on those above. That's all right for as long as you're undoing all the old ways, and putting an end to the habits that grew up when all were Party comrades. After that you must either restore the gentry or do as they do in the West, where the freedom to express his individuality gives a person his self-respect. That, may I say, does not work for us Russians. Russia is a country where there must be a real monarchy. Not the English or Swedish kind, but a Russian autocracy. Yes, that's right, my good man! Don't look at me as if I'm some fossil. Sometime in the next hundred or two hundred years we may be able to permit ourselves the luxury of being a free state. But now nothing but autocracy will do! You only have a short sentence and you're still young. You will live to see the kind of autocracy that Russia has not known since the time of Peter! What am I saying?! There were no trains, airplanes, telephones or telegraph in Peter's day. The autocracy then was moderated by distance and patriarchal relations. The present autocracy will be something of the kind that history has never seen! It will bring extraordinary advantages to our state. And the losses to the people will also be considerable... There's no way round it...

"Markov, Khvostov, and the others in the Union[3]—they always aroused only shame and revulsion in me. They were boors and scoundrels, of course. His Majesty shielded them out of weakness of character and solitude. Some would suck money and awards from him, some openly despised him, others hated him and could only think about how to kill him... But he was just a human being and wanted at least someone to love him, and carry his portraits...

"The Pale of Settlement, and the *numerus clausus* for Jews were hangovers from a barbaric era, they came from an inability to rule. Instead of releasing the bowstring they kept the bow bent all the time. Then it unbent of its own accord... I respect Jews as people no less worthy of respect than others. Quite the reverse, in fact: they are clever, capable and reliable and as an administrator I always preferred to deal with Jews. But when I returned to Russia this time I felt like an Indian who has returned to India after a long absence. And in that India the Jews were playing the role of the English. I can understand, it's only natural: they made the revolution and so they want to enjoy its fruits. But the Jew is not the material of which the Russian state can be made. You are not a nation-minded state, you simply do not understand the intrinsic value of the state! And you will have to return to your old place in the new Russian state. I feel sorry for you, old fellow, but nothing can be done about it!"

Roshchakovsky excitedly continued to draw pictures of the Russia he wanted to see, that was so dear to his monarchist heart.

"Yes, there will be state anti-semitism. Jews will again only be permitted a percentage of places in the universities and they will be excluded again from the ministry of foreign affairs, the police, and the secret police. They won't be admitted into the state elite. There won't necessarily be a Pale of Settlement. It would be hard to restore and anyway it's not needed. And if the need does arise, why then it won't be as before when the Jews were given fifteen of the best, most fertile southern provinces to live in! Now if the state so desires, the Jews will be driven to the devil and beyond, into the tundra and taiga. And no one will so much as squeak! A Vlas Doroshevich[4] will not spit in someone's face over this in some feuilleton. Not that this will help the state—you should be able to understand that! Excluding several million talented and educated people from administration, production and scholarly pursuits will bring enormous losses to the state and the nation. But when a nation-state is being created and the ordinary people must follow a lead, then a slogan is needed that everyone can understand—like your famous "Property is Theft!" The semi-educated, half-civilized Hitler came to power in civilized Germany by saying, "Germany for the Germans!" And, there we are: the feathers flew and nothing was left of civilized, educated, philosophical Germany. So they'll come up with the same slogan here, "Russia for the Russians!" It's inevitable, unavoidable. And everyone who sees the Jew as a competitor will follow. The government officials, the professors, the journalists and the writers. The shop assistants and managers, dentists and doctors... Needless to say, it will not be a pretty sight and we shall have to suppress our stirrings of conscience. But we're already used to doing that! When there's an advantage to be had, noble words will be found to justify it. Nothing so inflames the national or revolutionary conscience as personal advantage! You're probably looking at me with horror, and thinking 'The old cynic!' What kind of cynic am I? I'm simply an old, rational man. Yes, indeed...

"Once in Livadia I got into a conversation with Stolypin. We were kept waiting for a long time on the wharf for His Majesty's ship to arrive. Stolypin was a most intelligent man. And he knew what he wanted to do—for a statesman that is almost the most important thing! But he had been spoiled (as though the moths had got at him!) by his provincial past. Too narrow he was, my good fellow. He looked at Russia through the eyes of a provincial governor. But ruling a country is quite a different matter. And he also was too closely tied to his environment. The land question he approached timidly, in a chicken-hearted way, as though Imperial Russia had centuries ahead of it. But there were only a very few years left then... If he had resolved on the obligatory alienation of the gentry lands, at a large purchase price, and then given them to the peasants, Russia would not have known or feared revolution for the next 100 or 200 years! Lloyd George had the brains and determination. And why? Because he was not a landowner himself, his family did not own land, but he looked ahead and thought of the state's needs and not his own class interests. Our gentry and even our capitalists lost Russia through their greed and stupidity. It's a good thing the Bolsheviks turned up, otherwise the Russian state would have vanished altogether."

"What's your view of the 'Smenvekhovtsy'?[5] Have you read the collection *A Change of Landmarks*?"

"I know, I know: I see what you're getting at! Yes sir, I did read those works and subscribed to their newspaper *Nakanune*, and talked to some of them when I went on the firm's business to Berlin. Of course, it was a sensible idea of theirs, that the Bolsheviks would come round to a nation-state as soon as the most clearheaded among them realized that world revolution was a fairytale for immature minds. And that they would see that they could not get by without autocracy. But the Russian intelligentsia still cannot abandon its own dreams: it wants a Russian state but on the Western model, with parties and parliament... An autocracy must rule Russia, but a civilized one, they insist, that would always watch the response of newspapers in Paris and London... But one behind cannot sit both on the throne and a parliamentary bench—it's a physical impossibility! They simply could not grasp that! But they were not a stupid lot, not at all, and many of them made adjustments, like that writer fellow Alexei Tolstoy. Or Professor Tarle. Yet none of them became statesmen of any kind, nor could they. They ended up by becoming lackeys. And sold themselves cheaply, moreover...

"How did I find living in Russia again, you ask? Interesting, of course, but dreary. I had grown unused to Russian ways. Filthy toilets, unswept corridors, poorly washed cold plates, tasteless food... I know this is trivial but ever since I came back I have not had one decent meal! There's nowhere!"

"What do you mean, nowhere? Is it really not possible to eat well in Moscow restaurants? In the Metropole or the Nationale?"

"How can I begin to explain to you, my good fellow, when you have never eaten well in your life. You don't know how they used to cook at Donon's, Cubat's or even in the Moscow restaurant or at Testov's tavern. Only in a very few Paris restaurants was the food that delicious! Even His Majesty did not eat as well. Your restaurants with their old names are simply canteens, and there's no one who can cook properly there. The old ways are forgotten quickly, oh so quickly! I went to the Art Theater one time to see *Anna Karenina*... I couldn't stand it. Since I had once been acquainted with Nemirovich-

Danchenko in Petersburg, I went backstage to see him and said: "Vladimir Nikolayevich, they may not know and haven't seen, but you used to attend imperial receptions and saw how it's done... How could you permit such a thing?! Karenin is wearing the dress coat for a grand reception and the tricorn hat for a minor reception!"

"You know that's one of our traits as Russians, we forget quickly! It makes you angry but, in fact, it is a great and positive quality. You'll experience it yourself. In fifteen years time no one will believe you when you begin to tell them what things were like before 1937. Executions? Executions are forgotten as rapidly as everything else. The Russian is the strongest, most adaptable character there is. He is capable of everything. One time Novikov-Priboi came to see me and brought me a whole novel, *Tsushima*. I couldn't help admiring him. A simple gunner but what a fat book, an entire novel, he had written."

"No, *Tsushima* wasn't really written by a gunner, but by a novelist."

"What?! Have you read it? I read from beginning to end, and with interest. It was written by a gunner, not a novelist! Novikov was no more than a gunner, and a gunner he remains. The only interest of the book is that it helps one understand how a gunner looks at great events and human destiny... Like a f-o-o-l, I say!

"I had a long talk with him and we drank vodka. He'd knocked around, seen the world, become one of your writers, grown rich and famous... But in his eyes there was fear and such servility. You must forgive an old man, dear fellow, but all of you have fear and servility in your eyes. You won't find that in the humblest British sailor..."

"I don't understand you, Mikhail Sergeevich. You regret the fear and servility in the eyes of Russian people. Yet you dream of a state founded on fear, injustice and inequality, the slave-like existence of some and the elevation of others... Don't you think that in place of greatness there will just be the most ordinary swinishness?"

"I see everything, my dear fellow, everything! I can see all the drawbacks. You Jews will have a hard time, and the Russians will also. People will hate Russia and fear her, but no one will ever despise her as the Germans did when His Majesty was on the throne! Years and years will pass, the generations will come and go, and Russia will stand up straight and gather other, small countries under her, and then the servility in the eyes of Russian people will disappear. You've never seen the faces of the English when they arrive in somewhere like Singapore, India or Arabia... that's what the faces of the Russians will be like!!"

Roshchakovsky had even half-stood on the board bed. His habitual calm had deserted him, his black skullcap slipped sideways, and he now resembled not so much a famous French writer as an unsuccessful prophet, a heretical defrocked priest... I needed to bring our conversation to an end. I was on the verge of shouting and breaking our unspoken gentlemen's agreement. Roshchakovsky also understood this. He gave me a charming smile, straightened his skullcap, waved his tiny dry hand dismissively, and denounced his over-excitement with a string of naval obscenities that on his lips sounded almost like polite chit-chat... It was time for the evening meal. Large cans full of lentil slop were carried into the cell and we returned to our simple everyday concerns. Unexpectedly, and for the first time, I felt sorry for the old man. He was alone, quite alone—in the cell, in the prison, in the city and the entire country. I was with my own kind. But he...?

* * *

Why was Roshchakovsky so alone, as if cut off from everyone else by an invisible but impenetrable wall? Why was this Russian nationalist, overjoyed to see his dream coming true at last, so out of place in that vast cell, when he was surrounded by a great many other Russians with whom, according to his convictions, he ought to have shared that great sense of belonging to the same nation? Why was the only person he would talk to and confide in a Jew and a Communist, who at most could have been his youngest son? Could the masters of the old Russia lose their sense of superiority and become members of another community without regarding it with revulsion and regretting what they had lost?

The cell was getting ready to sleep. The evening meal was finished; the quiet evening stories of books once read and people once met were also over. An unspoken but strictly observed rule existed: only during the day would we discuss what was happening now and what the future held in store. Only in daytime did the inhabitants of our cell describe their "investigators" and interrogations in every frightening or amusing detail. The evenings were always devoted to what Gribkov, our elder, used to call our "literary and artistic program." Evening roll call was over and we had laid out the clothes that served as a mattress on our narrow strip of the board beds. The first snores could be heard from different ends of the cell, and I was lying on my back, gazing up at the tediously familiar and grubby patterns on the underside of the upper tier's bed boards.

Had I ever known such people before I met Roshchakovsky? A lame young artist had worked with us at Molodaya Gvardiya publishers. Golitsyn was a simple lad, his drawings were very primitive and he happily dashed off any kind of work. He particularly liked illustrating adventure stories and when he was caught using the same pictures again and again, for the most varied works by quite different authors, he would laughingly justify his behavior. There was nothing majestic or pitiful about him and so it seemed strange to me when I learned one day that he was a prince, no less, one of "those" Golitsyns! Was there anyone else? Suddenly I remembered someone who had not been a young and carefree artist but a man from the Tsar's immediate entourage—an interesting and not entirely conventional figure who was well known to historians.

I glanced at my neighbor. Roshchakovsky had not yet gone to sleep. As always he had somehow made a neat and attractive bed of his thick autumn overcoat, placed his rucksack under his head and lain down comfortably, pensively combing his French beard with his fingers, waiting for sleep to come.

"Did you ever know Dzhunkovsky?"

"Vladimir Fyodorovich? Why, of course! The most handsome general in the Tsar's retinue. And, moreover, something like a brother-in-law to His Majesty. He lived openly with the Grand Duchess Elisaveta Fyodorovna, the Tsaritsa's sister. He became her lover when her husband Grand Duke Sergei Alexandrovich was still alive and then, when Kalyayev went to work with that bomb,[6] why, Dzhunkovsky entirely stopped concealing their liaison. And do you know, no one, even at court, condemned them... The Grand Duke was a quite exceptional monster. A boor and a pederast, he had his boyfriends among the grenadier guards and thought nothing of slapping policemen across the face... Tsar Alexander was very fond of his other brothers but he despised and felt ashamed of Sergei. He wanted to send him far away, to Tashkent, but another embezzling relation was already living in disgrace there and, in any case, it was somehow awkward, the Tsar's own brother! Still, they did throw him out of Petersburg and sent him off as governor general of Moscow. For decency's sake they married him off. The elder daughter of the Grand Duke of Darmstadt was brought to Russia. I knew her father and brother well, I had served as ambassador there. They were of the petty and impoverished minor aristocracy and Wilhelm treated them like a Russian merchant bossing about his shop assistants. What good fortune it seemed! One daughter married to the heir to the Russian throne, the other became the wife of his uncle, the Tsar's brother... Of course, they knew what kind of creature that brother was, into whose hands they were passing the girl, but do people ever bother about things like that when concluding a dynastic marriage?

"So the young little princess, a romantic creation who had been reared on Schiller and Kleist, fell into the lap of that monster! To begin with she sought consolation in religion. She had only just been christened but she became such a zealous Orthodox believer that even pious Muscovites were astonished. In church every morning, evening and at all-night vigils... Visiting all the monasteries, often spending the entire service on her knees... Yet she still had to perform her duties at court as well: receptions, dinners—she was a Grand Duchess, the Tsaritsa's sister and the Tsar's aunt, when all was said and done! Youth is youth, and beside her stood the most handsome man in Moscow, her husband's aide de camp, Colonel

Dzhunkovsky. What a handsome fellow he was; and there was a no-
bility about his good looks. He was also a chivalrous man. That was
why he did not make a career although no one else had all his advantages! He was a general in His Majesty's suite of guards, governor of
Moscow, assistant to the Minister of Internal Affairs, and chief of the
secret police... It was with difficulty that he gained permission to
fight during the war. Nor did he rise any higher than divisional commander. Elisaveta Fyodorovna looked most demure but she kept
pushing her handsome fellow forward. Vladimir Fyodorovich behaved
very strangely, though. He was a fine decent chap—but not a statesman of any kind! Just imagine, my dear fellow: he was made chief of
the political police, something like your GPU, and suddenly he found
out that a deputy in the State Duma was one of their secret agents.
What do you think he did? He rang up Rodzyanko, the speaker of the
Duma, and says to him something of this sort: Mikhail Vladimirovich,
one of my Okhrana agents has managed to become a deputy in your
parliament... I do not feel at all happy about it, this is going too far...
Call in that creature, please, and tell him to quietly and nobly submit
his resignation. Seriously. Yet that agent had almost become the
most important Bolshevik! I don't have to tell you how the Okhrana
howled!"

If anything, I knew more about the story of Malinovsky than
Roshchakovsky did. It was a rare stroke of good fortune for the
Okhrana. Their agent became a member of the Bolshevik Central
Committee, one of the party's main leaders, a close assistant of
Lenin, and a deputy in the Duma. His parliamentary immunity proved
most convenient: all the Bolsheviks around him could be picked off
but the provocateur was left untouched. Then the whole set-up came
crashing down, all because of the strange and old-fashioned views of
the chief of the political police.

"Next Dzhunkovsky decided to get rid of Rasputin, who was only
just beginning to influence the Tsaritsa through Vyrubova. Either
Vladimir Fyodorovich was counting on his illegitimate membership in
the imperial family, or he had grown accustomed in Moscow to act
without any great subtlety: in any case, he simply ordered his agents
to pick up Rasputin and send him back to Siberia, to his former place
of abode... Ha! What an uproar in Petersburg! Her Majesty now took
no notice of her sister at all. His Majesty immediately dismissed
Dzhunkovsky and ordered him to leave Petersburg; he was to go to
his estate in the Crimea and not leave there without His Majesty's
permission. Only when the war began did he barely manage to be allowed back into service..."

"And since you came back you've never heard what happened to
him?"

"No, I never had the pleasure of meeting him again, and I heard
nothing more of him, either abroad or in Russia. If he survived this

war between Russians, then, probably, he has emigrated. Perhaps he's dead; he must be getting on now. Why were you so interested in Vladimir Fyodorovich, my good fellow?"

"I knew him... To be more precise, I met him a few times..."

Our long, quiet conversation had come to an end. Roshchakovsky fell asleep, in an instant as always, curled up with his cheek resting on his right hand. He even slept elegantly—quietly, calmly, not disturbing those around with snores, wheezing or drawn-out, suffering sighs. But I could not sleep for a long while. I remembered meeting Dzhunkovsky and tried to set him beside Roshchakovsky and understand why they were so unlike one another.

* * *

It was only ten years earlier in 1928. I was twenty and had just finished my first time as leader in a Young Pioneer camp. I was young, healthy, happy and successful and each day was better, more interesting, than the last. My elder brother Solly was on vacation in the Crimea with Varya Grigorieva—either she was his fiancée or his wife but, much more important to me then, she was the secretary of our Komsomol cell. We had agreed that after camp finished I would join them in the Crimea. For the first time in my life I travelled to the South and, after Inkerman, as we approached Sevastopol, I glimpsed water between the rusty warehouses—the sea! My brother met me and together we wandered about Sevastopol; then we took the tram to Balaclava and persuaded a fisherman to take us over to Batiliman where Solly and Varya were living.

We rowed out of the quiet bay of Balaclava, past high cliffs on which there rose the ruins of a Genoese fortress, into the gray-blue, unsettled waters of the open sea. The fisherman raised the sail, the boat dipped and then rapidly flew past the cliffs of Fiolent, the tangled green of the woods and the sandy spits of the inlets...

Batiliman was an extraordinary place quite unlike the rest of the Crimea. Some time in the immemorial past half of the mountain of Kushkai had collapsed, leaving a sheer face, as abrupt as if a knife had sliced across it. The piles of rock were overgrown with groves of juniper trees and impenetrable thickets of dewberries. The sea washed the enormous sandy beaches, separated by the tilting, unstable cliffs. The builders of commercial dachas had still not reached this deserted place and several writers and artists had built their own summer houses there. Korolenko, Chirikov, Bilibin... They were very simple, for the most part small, wooden buildings. The only exception was Pavel Milyukov's two-storey brick house with its grand staircase, large sitting room and library. Now the sitting room was used as a small dining room for the two or three dozen holiday makers visiting Batiliman. They lunched and dined on what the local area could provide... And this was very modest. A narrow bridle path led through the mountains and the so-called Turkish pass from Batiliman to the nearest Tatar village of Khaity. From there one could ride on a cart to the shops in Baidary and buy something else to eat. We were not discouraged, though. Each morning we brewed up cocoa on a fire beneath the cliff, and during the day we gathered the crabs, which lived in countless numbers under the rocks, and boiled them up in an enormous bucket. Sometimes the surf washed up quite large fish and then we gorged ourselves. Our determined hunt for food was greatly aided, however, by an old peasant who used to visit us. Almost every day he appeared in our small settlement carrying a large basket full of tomatoes, eggplant, bottles of young wine, cheese, and tasty small bread rolls. The old man was tall, handsome and very picturesque, with a large curling white beard and lively black eyes beneath thick white brows. His trousers were canvas, he wore a long hempen shirt and on his bare feet, simple home-made leather shoes. His vegetables and other produce were always fresh and cheap. He was calm and courteous and we liked him.

Like most twenty-year-olds I was thoroughly absorbed all the time either in enjoying my vacation or in thoughts of someone I had left behind in Moscow. I paid little attention to those I met in the Crimea. I did not even register surprise when, one day, I came across our peasant acquaintance in the empty dining room. He stood next to some shelves, reading a book he had found there. Only later was I astonished how inattentive I had been. The Russian books in Milyukov's library had been stolen long ago. All that remained were those in foreign languages, chiefly English, and no one ever touched them. There they quietly lay, gathering dust on the mahogany book shelves beneath wooden busts of the wise men of Antiquity.

Once seven or eight of us went for a walk in the mountains around the Laspi inlet. The low, small hills were thickly covered with juniper and we quickly left the faint path and lost our way. Round and round we went, circling about the same hills, tired and exhausted, with no idea where even the sea lay. When the women in our group began to panic I found a footpath and we decided to follow it. It must lead somewhere, we resolved. And indeed, quite soon we had reached a clearing, quite free of all undergrowth. Beside a melon patch, vegetable garden and small vineyard stood a white cottage. A tall elderly man who was tying up bunches of grapes turned and with joy we recognized our old benefactor. He was also delighted when we gathered around him and, able to laugh again, told him how we had lost our way in the juniper forest.

He did not even inquire if we were hungry. He suggested we wash our hands and sit down at the large table under the windows of his house, and then his sister would feed us. A tall and—despite her age, gray hairs and simple garments—still very beautiful woman came out of the house. She quickly laid a rough but white cloth, and brought out clay bowls filled with a puree of eggplant, with yogurt and home-cured sausage. Our host took a large bottle of cold homemade wine and poured us each a glass. Then he sat at the edge of the table and observed with pleasure as we ate our fill and interrupted one another while merrily discussing our adventures. Every once in a while he got up to pour the wine, and bring more bread and sausage. Evidently he rarely entertained guests and he enjoyed our company. We all liked him and I was, probably, not the only one who wondered why we had never asked his name before.

"What is your name and patronymic?" I asked.

"Vladimir Fyodorovich."

"And your surname?" added the pedantic Varya.

"Dzhunkovsky."

"You weren't by any chance once governor-general of Moscow?" I asked in a flash, confirming my holiday reputation as a witty and well-read fellow.

The old man looked at me calmly and attentively, almost with a smile on his face.

"Well, young man, if you are that well-informed then you must also be aware that it was indeed only by chance that I became gover-nor-general of Moscow..."

Apart from my brother and me, the surname meant nothing to the rest of our young group. But for us to meet a living tsarist gover-nor-general was almost like encountering Neanderthal man in that thousand-year-old juniper grove. We leapt up and gathered round our host. Seated on the bench, he sipped his glass of red wine and calmly told us his story.

When the February Revolution broke out he was at the front. A commissar of the Provisional Government arrived and, evidently knowing more about him than we did, suggested that he resign be-cause of his links with the former Tsar's family. Dzhunkovsky left for the Crimea where he owned a small estate. He remained there and philosophically observed all the great events that shook Russia. He withdrew, once and for all, from politics. When the White Guards held the Crimea he refused outright to take any part in the "White Movement" and never left his estate to visit Simferopol, Yalta or Sevastopol. When the Soviet authorities took over he left his house without protest and moved into the groundsman's lodge. He calmly looked on as his former employees and wounded sailors, sent there to recuperate, took over his estate. Nobody touched Dzhunkovsky, even Bela Kun's fearful partner Rosa Zemlyachka left him in peace when she headed the Bolshevik party in the Crimea. He was of no use to anyone and, as a consequence, no one took any interest in him.

When the Soviet regime became firmly established Dzhunkovsky thought it improper to remain on his former estate where, as he put it, they continued to feed him and his sister out of habit. He took a job as a lighthouseman. We knew the small lighthouse at Sarych very well, standing at the edge of the Laspi inlet, close to Tesseli. A tiny house, made of dry stones, stood there for the man who each night had to light the clumsy kerosene lamp. Dzhunkovsky moved in with his sister, one of the last Tsaritsa's ladies-in-waiting, and they lived contentedly until 1924.

As a former tsarist office-holder he was now deprived of this job. It was obvious that he would not be able to find work anywhere else. It was then that he decided to become a peasant. He rented some abandoned land in the middle of the Crimea nature reserve, cleared it and planted melons and vegetables, and restored the wild vineyard. He took his time, and did all the work himself. There was no cause for him to hurry. During the long southern summer he lay by a winter store of simple farm produce. Any surplus he sold in Batiliman and Tesseli and used the money to buy simple clothing or a few books. In winter he seldom left the house, which lay surrounded by darkness: the wind howled in the forest, and the sea gave a muffled roaring below. Then spring would come, work began again, and rare encounters with other people...

"You may, of course, believe me or not," Dzhunkovsky said, finishing his tale, "But I consider I have been very fortunate in my old age. Like most of my contemporaries, my real active life finished long ago. There is nothing more foolish than trying to prolong life. There is only one way to end your days with dignity: try to stay healthy, so as to be as little of a burden to others as possible, and then you can think calmly about all the good and evil, the wise and silly things you have done in your life. Many of my former colleagues have added a great deal to the unkind and stupid deeds they committed before the revolution. They have no time to ponder this, to finish their lives naturally, but feel they must go on, although it's clear they're floundering. I'm better off. My sister and I are dependent on no one, only ourselves and our own labors. We are independent in our thinking, our habits and our preferences. Could there be a better life for an elderly couple? Believe me, my friends, my responsibilities introduced me to many old men who had formerly been famous and powerful... I would pay calls on them, visit them when they were sick, and accompany them on the last journey of all. They were profoundly unhappy people. Tormented by impotence and sickness, depressed by the loss of the power to which they had become accustomed, and also suffering from the insufficient attention they received from the authorities and the Tsar. And how happy we are!"

"And you don't...," one of us began to ask.

"I have no regrets!" interrupted Dzhunkovsky with uncharacteristic firmness. "I do not regret any losses. Old men must not lament the past, they have already taken from life all they can, the good and the bad. Let the young organize their own lives. We should not interfere or impose our views, tastes and preferences—what's the need?! They are the ones with a life ahead of them, let them decide! I believe that once a person is past forty he should bow to the ideas of the young, and once he is over fifty he should not have any right whatsoever to engage in politics..."

During that stay, I met Dzhunkovsky several more times in Batiliman, already as an old acquaintance. Hurrying to buy our supplies from him, we hardly talked and I thought I had endless time in hand to still ask the former head of the tsarist political police about a number of things that interested me... Soon, however, I returned to Moscow where new and, for me, more important impressions pushed my acquaintance with Dzhunkovsky to the back of my mind. It was only now that I remembered him, lying on the board bed in the transit block of Butyrki beside someone who had known Vladimir Fyodorovich in quite another life. How very differently these two men who had known power and been close to ruling circles were ending their lives. If I survived to old age, who would I resemble more: Dzhunkovsky or Roshchakovsky?

* * *

It was now over a month since we had been moved to a cell in the transit block. Here there was none of the horror, or fearful and mysterious expectation, that always formed part of our life when we were still under investigation. Yet neither did we any longer feel the hope that always accompanied that horror. We were so impatient to leave prison and reach the unknown world of the camps. Rationally speaking, of course, we fully understood how right a certain wise man in the prison had been when he scratched the following advice with some sharp object on the walls of the toilet: "Entering, do not lose heart: leaving, do not rejoice. Be patient, let nothing surprise you, and expect the worst." But we had such a longing for change—even if things did turn out for the worst. When we were taken out for exercise, and I walked in the inner slower-moving circle, I gazed up at the early autumn stars already shining in the evening sky and murmured some lines of Bagritsky:

> Though hungry I stand by the stove,
> inhale scents of another's feast;
> Though my clothes may tatter and tear
> And my boots wear out on the stones;
> Though I forget how to write songs—
> What care I? I long for some change.[7]

Suddenly the unexpected and irreversible was again happening, as in cell 29 a few weeks before. We had just finished the morning meal and returned to our places, we had wiped our spoon with a rag and hidden the rest of our bread somewhere safe, when "Transfer! Transfer!" rang round the cell.

In the silence that followed we could clearly hear the irregular and nervous step of tens and hundreds of feet marching past our cell. Doors were slammed shut and the whole church building was filled with the sounds of movement, restrained voices and ringing commands. Now the hatch opened, a screw looked fearsomely in, and did not speak but shouted a command, "With your things, all of you! Leave nothing behind!"

The cell was instantly transformed into an ant's nest. The same apparently disorganized, swarming, rushing activity. In fact, people moved rapidly and sensibly. All belongings were snatched up and laid out separately—underclothes, outer garments, food. We could not tie anything up in bundles and pack it away because they would throw it all about again when they frisked us. But we already knew how to prepare for a search and come out with the minimum losses as quickly as possible.

In the turmoil I forgot about Roshchakovsky for a while. Then I remembered and rushed to help, "Let me give you a hand!"

"My thanks, dear Lev Emmanuilovich. But I am a sailor and we were well-trained at the college."

When, indeed, had he found the time to pack all his things in the tough foreign-made hiker's rucksack and in his small but capacious travelling bag of excellent soft leather? He had changed out of his pyjamas into a sturdy, elegant costume that had come unscathed through the heat disinfection, searches and transfers from one cell to another.

The cell door opened and we could see part of the corridor, filled with guards. They were not our prison (almost family) jailers, unarmed and in soft boots. No, these wore shoulder straps, hung with holsters and bags, and they had a hasty, dry, unbending look about them: our future escort guards in transit. The Vologda transport. (All the experienced prisoners had warned us the most terrible and wicked transport was that from Vologda.)

"In ALPH-abetical order!"

"We shall be together here as well, my dear Lev Emmanuilovich!" Roshchakovsky stood beside me, calm and imperturbable.

A lengthy, almost interminable procedure now began. Each prisoner went up to the door and quickly replied to a rapid series of questions, "Initials in full! year of birth, offense, sentence!"

Then he vanished through the door, and joined the guarded transport. My name came before Roshchakovsky's and I went out into the corridor to one side, where I was frisked, passed on, checked off and allocated. While they were pulling me somewhere by the sleeve I watched the door out of the corner of my eye: Roshchakovsky would now appear...

But instead I saw how a gloomy Professor Rytov left the cell, clutching the long johns he used instead of a bag, and was followed by Sakharov, then Stenin... Already Grisha Filippovsky was beside me, the door of our cell slammed shut and all of us were here. Apart from Roshchakovsky. He was not summoned and remained alone in that enormous empty cell filled with the pathetic, crumpled traces of other lives and fates which the little, thin prophet had calmly cast into the jaws of his Moloch-state. In the fuss of the transport and its anticipation and tension, I quickly forgot Roshchakovsky. A great many years would pass and then my thoughts returned more and more often to him and our arguments. I now retained no anger, no desire to convince him or make him change his mind. Other wiser, kinder and more humane people than this former friend of the Tsar also fell for the same temptation.

I never heard of Roshchakovsky again. He may have been lucky. If he reached the camp in one piece, he might have immediately been allocated to the weak team and been made barracks orderly. He could have lived out his last years in comparative calm in the stench and semi-darkness of the barracks, resting during the day from the row, the shouts, the snoring, the obscenities of the work-distributors and work-team leaders, the crunch of lice being crushed, the groans of the dying.

Did he ever lose his sense of happiness, I wonder? Was his store of philosophical stoicism great enough to withstand the reverse side of his ideal?

Razgon in Chepets camp, Usollag, on his second day of freedom. July 2, 1955.

BORIS AND GLEB

Someone who has lived through my experiences can remember meeting people with astonishing biographies, striking personalities who have left their mark on history. Only a few years ago, when I wrote about some of them, it seemed they had been forgotten forever. Without any great optimism, I still believed that "manuscripts do not burn" and that what I had written might, some day, be published. But events proved far more unpredictable than I could have supposed, and today one can find references in dictionaries and newspaper articles to many of my one-time camp acquaintances. Their photographs also appear, although it is difficult to recognize in these strong young faces the worn-out, tormented individuals I met in transit between camps, in the camp offices, or on work teams in the forests.

I am constantly troubled, in particular, by the fate of two brothers, youths or practically still young boys, whom I met at a rather difficult period during my own time in the camps. They passed me by like a pair of shadows and I did not even learn their surname. I have no doubt that they perished then, and I am sure that none of the relatives or acquaintances who might retain the slightest memory survive. Millions were destroyed in the camps and disappeared without leaving a grave behind them or any other material evidence that they ever existed. But they had friends and relatives in the outside world, and their lives formed part of the biography of others.

Yet no matter how many of the latter I have known—peasants and priests, accountants and schoolteachers—they hardly ever come to mind. Memory is not a fathomless well. It is simply very deep, and it takes some effort to bring those faces, voices and stories back to the surface. Boris and Gleb, however, refuse to sink into such oblivion. To this day I cannot understand why: I met dozens of boys like them, and saw how they died uncomplaining, of cold and hunger, or from unidentified illnesses in the camp's medical barracks. The others, though, had relatives who grieved for them, and somewhere the photographs of their childhood and youth are preserved.

Nothing remains of Boris and Gleb. What happened to them was a mere drop in that vast ocean of injustice in which we then lived and continue to live today. Yet their bitter fate constantly troubles me and so, however briefly, I am writing down the story of the two boys. To say it is improbable would be wrong: everything that we then experienced defied belief.

It all happened at Camp No. 1 of Ustvymlag[1] during the terrible winter of 1942. The fanfares to celebrate the halting of the Germans before Moscow the year before had long died away. The victory at

Stalingrad still lay ahead. Meanwhile all the Ukraine and Belorussia and a vast part of Russia itself had been occupied: the Germans had advanced as far as the Caucasus and the Volga... Even when the news was severely distorted and read in the robust and reassuring voice of announcer Yury Levitan, the daily bulletins of the Informburo inspired an unrelieved gloom. There was very little to eat and a large box full of frozen corpses was taken to be emptied outside the compound more than once a day. The camp bosses were merciless in their attempts to fulfill what were now called "defense" plans. The security officers were on the lookout for "defeatists" and even "conspirators" among the camp's inmates. In the new transports that arrived were prisoners charged with wartime offenses. When a certain part of occupied Soviet territory was liberated (cities like Kharkov changed hands several times) the first priority was to round up "fascist collaborators." The real traitors, those who had served the occupiers as policemen and members of their punitive squads, had left with the retreating Germans. So our security men could only pick up the cobblers who had mended German boots, the cooks who had made their soup and, of course, the "German bedding," the term for women who, whether willingly or not, had become the occupiers' mistresses.

Strange, previously unfamiliar types of people began to appear at our camp. Among them the brothers Boris and Gleb somehow immediately stood out. The difference in age between the two was probably not great. Boris could not have been more than eighteen, Gleb no younger than sixteen. They looked very similar and yet there was no mistaking which was the older, and which the younger brother. They never left one another for a minute. Not only did they refuse to join any of the groups and cliques which prisoners always form, they rejected any kind of contact. They aroused universal compassion and even the most hardened zeks, in whom hunger and deprivation had erased all human features, were moved by the extraordinary and tender concern with which Boris looked after Gleb. When the work team returned in the evening, Boris would take Gleb's heavy tools back to the tool store; in the canteen he always poured part of his watery soup into his brother's bowl. When they had a free moment the elder would tell a story and the younger would look at him with the eyes of a child who is gazing at his only hope and defense, his mother.

Of course, there were those who tried to help the boys. This was no easy matter. Their forms contained a selection of the most terrible offenses: espionage, sabotage, terrorism and even "collaboration with the world bourgeoisie" (there was then such a crime). The chief accountant wanted to employ Boris temporarily in drawing up inventories. But Boris refused to stay inside the compound when his brother was being taken out to work in the forest each day. The doctor had great difficulty in getting Gleb allocated, for two weeks, to the weak team. Gleb obeyed his brother's order to stay behind but suffered terribly without him and would squat near the gates almost all day, waiting for Boris to come back from work. He pined for his brother and in the end the doctor angrily decided that it was impossible to separate them: they grew sick instead of getting better...

Who were they? Where did they come from? How had they ended up in our camp? Why had those who were barely more than children been convicted of such terrible offenses? The result was that they were never allowed anywhere without a guard or to take up work less murderous than felling trees. I was by then a major "trusty," already the senior norm-setter, and this removed almost any opportunity for contact with them. The brothers demonstratively rejected all expressions of sympathy and they never came anywhere near the office. Soon, however, events took place that enabled me to learn almost all that had happened to them in their short lives.

As far as I was concerned, those events were far from pleasant. The "godfather," our chief security officer, lodged an accusation of defeatist agitation against me, for reasons of his own that I describe later. Here I need only say that I was instantly deposed from my elevated position, arrested and put in the punishment cell, and subjected to a rapid "investigation." While waiting to receive the charge sheet and summons to appear in court, I was put back onto gang labor and went out to work in the forest. I found myself in the same work team as Boris and Gleb.

The daily roll call before being led out to work is one of the most important and memorable events in the daily life of a Soviet prisoner. It is always a grim experience. Even in summer, on a warm sunny morning, it is tedious to stand in a column of prisoners and listen to the yells of the team leaders and the work distributors, to be quickly and carelessly searched and then "handed over" by the camp screws and "received" by the escorting guard. This wearisome procedure could not be alleviated even by such innovations of the administration as "departure to music": an accordion-player from the Cultural and Education Section would sit by the gates, playing cheerful Soviet songs or melancholy old waltzes.

Roll calls in winter, however, were far more terrible. You stood around in the cold for an hour or more before the compound gates were opened. It was 6 a.m. but still absolutely dark. The compound was feebly lit by electricity and the work distributors ran up and down with kerosene "bat" lamps, dividing the prisoners into columns. A flickering light would reveal figures who had struggled into every scrap of clothing they possessed: padded trousers, quilted work jacket, short cotton coat, a towel in place of a scarf, and a sweat-stained hat with the earflaps down. When there was a very severe frost, below -30 C degrees (work only halted when it was minus 50 C), everyone had to don the "face masks" that formed a part of the winter uniform. Made from random scraps of cloth—bright cottons, towels or other rags—these masks had holes cut for the eyes, nose and mouth. The crowds of zeks then looked like some grotesque and frightening carnival scene by Hieronymus Bosch.

Even in that awful crowd, where it was impossible to recognize anyone, two prisoners caught my gaze. They were always side by side and, often, holding hands, just as in kindergarten. That was how Boris and Gleb sometimes walked the long road to the work site. Without a word, we went to the tool stores, picked up axes and saws and moved on out into the taiga. In the dark we stumbled over tree roots, stumps and fallen trunks. Soon even the light one-handed saw became heavy. Even so, the march was more pleasant than the loathsome procedures of roll call. We tried to walk more quickly. Not because of the constant yells of the guards, "Stop lagging behind!" but because we longed to reach the work site where we would have an hour or more to ourselves.

The early roll call and march to work in winter were quite senseless. We reached the clearing in total darkness when it was impossible to begin felling trees. We had to wait until it grew light. It was that wait which explains this story. Without any order from the team leader several of us would cut down a dead pine, saw it up into logs, split them and light two bonfires, a small one for the guards, and a large one for the team. We sat down on the felled trunks. Now we were free to think our own thoughts, and even do what we wanted. The warmth from the fire was so reminiscent of home, so invigorating; the flames recalled things that we had left far behind, the hearth or the fire on a fishing expedition... Most sat in silence. Some dozed, others stared fixedly into the flames. Yet others practically set about making rope shoes or even sewing on a button. A few talked quietly. Only there could one appreciate all the life-giving force of fire. Only in the forest at night can one really understand the feat of Prometheus!

We tended the flames carefully, pushing a whole tree into the bonfire so that it kept alight all the time we were at work. We would come back and sit by the fire again after dark had fallen; work had to be abandoned but there was still time left before we were due to return. That was another blissful gift, not of the camp administration but of nature, which was beyond their control.

The brothers sat side by side, sometimes snuggling up to one another. Occasionally Boris would quietly say something to Gleb. More often they would be silent, their eyes fixed on the flames. The sky grew gray and the trunks of the trees grew visible. Unwillingly the team leader would order: "That's enough lazing about, let's get started!" Usually we split up into pairs but the brothers did not work together. Boris helped someone to fell trees, while the leader put Gleb in charge of burning the waste. Of course, this was easier than cutting down and stripping a large pine or fir, but it was not an easy job either. For reasons of safety the branches, "felling debris" as they were officially termed, could only be burnt in the winter. The brush from the trees felled during the summer months, the thick pine and fir boughs and the "tops" (sometimes half of a large tree) which by now were buried under mounds of snow had to be burnt. First the snow was cleared off, then the already tightly packed pile was brushed down, and a small hollow made beneath it. A small fire of dead wood was lit. When the flames had taken hold, wet branches, "tops" and even entire trunks were gradually laid over it.

The dense smoke made the eyes smart and tiny ash particles clung to the face. Sparks might burn through one's clothes and since they were made of padded cotton, it did not take much to set them alight. You could easily be burnt alive or, what was almost as fatal, be left with only a shirt or even less in sub-zero temperatures.

Boris was worried about his younger brother but was in no position even to keep an occasional eye on him. He was the assistant to the tree-feller, the more important of the working pair. I have done the same job and know that it left no time for just a minute's rest. With two or three strokes of his axe the feller would make a deep cut in the trunk. He decided which way the tree should fall and then, bending very low, took up the saw. His assistant would run up and together they shouted, "Timber!" and pushed the trunk with the long pry lever. It fell in a blizzard of snow dust. After that the tree-feller could stand for a while, wiping his brow and smoking a cigarette.

The assistant could not halt for one minute. He had to strip off the branches quickly—not at all an easy job!—and then, levering up the felled tree with a pole, saw it up into six-meter plank lengths and four-meter "waste" sections. He was quick about it because the tree-feller, meanwhile, was already tackling the next tree. My tree-feller this time was a young and experienced peasant lad, sentenced for a criminal offense. It seemed to me that he was deliberately working fast in order to wear out his assistant. Probably that was not the case. I had gained the reputation of a decent person who never left a worker without his full ration. But I did not want to give in and be a burden to my partner. I tried for all I was worth. I did not ease up, so as to avoid those unpleasant minutes when the feller stopped work and began to help me cut up the trunks. He made no comment and did not give me reproachful looks. Nevertheless, if you are working as a pair then either both "take it easy" or both work hard so as not to let the other down. That is a universal law, even when the work may be hateful and performed in the service of an enemy...

Probably Boris was in the same position. Each time he heard the cry, "Timber!" he shuddered, turned round, and anxiously tried to spot his brother. Thank God, not one of us had yet been crushed by a falling tree. In other teams, however, it happened quite often and we feared and hated the forest. Several years after my release I still could not look without hatred at the beauty and wonder that is a forest!

Again the sky was turning gray. Winter twilight descended quickly. We could stop work, brush the snow, twigs and bonfire ash from our coats and hats, and sit around the flames that were once more blazing brightly. People rolled a cigarette, looked about them and had some more time to themselves. They could sit in silence or chat to the zek beside them. Many felt the need to hear human speech: all day long we had not said a word, even to our partners.

During one of those evenings "round the fire" I found myself next to the brothers. They, of course, were sitting together. Boris was examining Gleb's coat from every side, making sure the cotton padding was not beginning to smoulder anywhere. He took the remains of his bread ration out of his pocket and broke it into two very uneven portions. Without a murmur, Gleb took the larger. Slowly they ate and then snuggled together, motionless.

For some unknown reason, I suddenly remembered Nekrasov's verse about winter: "No storm but the forest is drumming, No mountain becks race to the plains, The Frosty Commander is coming, Patrolling his mighty domains..."[2] I stopped. "Can you remember much of that poem?" I asked Gleb.

"Which poem?"

"Nekrasov, of course, 'Winter, Red Nose'."

"We didn't study it at school."

"What town was your school in?"

"In Ostrava."

I tried to remember where it could be, in what province. My mind was a blank. Suddenly I guessed, "Is that in Czechoslovakia?"

"Yes." Gleb cast a frightened glance at his brother, as though he had betrayed some secret. But Boris said nothing, and continued to listen to our conversation.

"But it was a Russian school, wasn't it?"

"Of course, it was. And we learnt a lot of Russian poems there. Nekrasov as well, only different ones. Mostly Pushkin. I know all of *Poltava* by heart. And many other poems. 'O my bluebells, flower of the steppes...' Alexei Tolstoi wrote that. Are there bluebells here in the summer?"

I struggled to remember, "Yes, they grow here. Not quite the same as in Russia, but similar."

"But do the flowers here have a scent? And do the birds sing?"

He was like a child who finds himself in a quite unfamiliar country where everything is interesting and incomprehensible. A quite unfamiliar country, of course. The flowers here had no scent and in all the years that I spent in the Far North, I never heard a single songbird.

"Do you really know a lot of poems?"

"Yes, a great many."

Seeming overjoyed that he could speak to someone apart from his brother, Gleb began to recite poetry. They were old poems, about Russian history and landscape, that I had first read in pre-revolutionary collections: "I know a land where all breathes of abundance, Where the rivers run a silver lode...."

Sometimes Gleb forgot a word or a line and then Boris would suddenly prompt him.

From that evening I developed some form of contact with the brothers. We never actually became very close, it must be said. Boris did not smoke, nor of course did Gleb, so I could not share a cigarette with them. Once I offered them a rare treat, a sweet made of soya, but they turned it down firmly and at once. Still, now we would greet one another at roll call and Boris would listen to my advice when I explained how best to strip the tangled, dense branches from the fir trees. We had, in a word, become acquaintances. During the dark morning hours at the work site we would sit together by the bonfire. Once Boris confessed to me that they did not know Russia, but had only seen two or three villages. Then they were in Moscow and several other towns but had only visited the prisons there, nothing more.

"If only we could just have a look at Ivan the Great's bell tower in the Kremlin, at least once," Boris said with a sigh.

"You'll still get there."

"God willing... " and rapidly, so it almost went unnoticed, he crossed himself.

Such faith was rare among us and the brothers did not often reveal it in this way. But when the team were led to the canteen they would immediately pull off their old, dirty fabric hats, as though in church. At work, no matter how cold it was, they would always bare their heads when eating their bread (Boris's cropped hair was chestnut, Gleb's the color of wheat) and then whisper to themselves. At first it did not occur to me that they were praying...

Once Boris, observing an unusually-shaped fir, said, "How like a white acacia it is..."

"Do white acacias grow in Czechoslovakia?"

"No, they don't. I've never seen one."

"How do you know what they look like then?"

"From the story."

"Which story? What author do you mean?"

"No author. The cover story we had to learn at spy school."

Noting how my expression changed, Boris suddenly began to tell the story of how he and Gleb had ended up in a camp, in the distant and quite unfamiliar northern Komi republic. It took him two or three of our free hours by the fire to tell me everything. He never attempted to continue our talks back in the compound where he again became distant and would do no more than politely say "good morning" or "good evening" when we happened to meet there. But there was nothing remotely good about those mornings and evenings as I listened to their heart-rending story. How I wished I could help them in some way and alter the course of their terrible and unjust fate. Thinking about them, I sometimes forgot the uncertain lot that awaited me in the near future. It was the first time I had encountered quite such extraordinary lives.

* * *

They were emigres, of course. Or, to be more exact, from an emigre family. The boys themselves had never emigrated from Russia or seen it before; they had not even been born there. Their father was a professional soldier. He served as a company commander in Denikin's army during the Civil War but before that had been a colonel on the General Staff. When he reached Constantinople he was already middle-aged and had lost his own family. There he met a young girl, the daughter of a Moscow lawyer. Bitter fate was kind to them and they did not become separated by the checkered fortunes of emigre life. After they married they were able to settle down in the most attractive part of Europe for all Russians abroad, the newly-founded state of Czechoslovakia.

Perhaps it was common Slavic sentiment, perhaps it was because Masaryk, the first president, had long admired Russia. Whatever the reason, Czechoslovakia seemed a part of the old Russia to the Russian emigres. They set up schools and lycees there, even the semblance of a university. There was a cult of everything Russian. Boris and Gleb were born in the Moravian provincial town of Ostrava. Their mother died soon after the younger brother was born and their elderly father not only became their sole support, but also brought them up himself and was their model and their ideal.

The old colonel worked as the modest employee of some trading firm. His convictions placed him on the left-wing of the emigration. He was against the idea of military intervention in Russia and did not join any of the numerous emigre military associations and unions. His life was devoted to his sons and he nurtured in them a passionate love for all things Russian—the people, their customs and their way of life. The boys went to a Russian school, then on to the lycee, and Boris was about to enter the university...

All the plans of this little family were swept aside by the terrible catastrophe that befell Czechoslovakia in 1938. The country became a mere bargaining chip in the attempts of France and Britain to sate Hitler's excessive appetite. The Munich pact handed him a part of the country and he took over the rest when the war began. After the Germans invaded the Soviet Union on 22 June 1941, the Russian emigres were divided over what to do. It was the position then adopted by their father that led to his death. He joined the "defensists," those who believed that Russians should help defend Russia and that they had no right to collaborate with the enemies of their motherland. What actually happened is hard to say, and I could not question Boris closely, but one night their father was "accidentally" shot by a patrol.

The children were left on their own. All on their own. Neither in Czechoslovakia nor in any other part of the world did they have relatives or anyone they could turn to. They were left behind in a large apartment and survived by selling off their possessions. Boris occasionally found some work. For the younger brother he now replaced their parents, teachers and friends... What did they have to live for now? What occupied their thoughts? Where did they place their hopes?

All they had left was Russia. The Germans were pushing towards Moscow and the radio, newspapers and everyone around them crowed over the successes of the German soldiers. Boris did not believe them. Neither, as a consequence, did Gleb. Their one childish dream now was to make their way to Russia and join the Red Army. Only a miracle could have made such an unrealistic dream come true.

A Russian who had probably gone over to the Nazis much earlier proposed a way. After carefully observing them, he suggested that they enter the service of the Germans and enroll at a special school; knowing their love for Russia he persuaded them that they could "ride into Moscow with the Germans." Soon they understood what kind of school he meant. The Germans were training Russian emigres as spies to be dropped behind the Soviet front lines. Two Russian teenagers who still looked hardly more than children and had an unmistakably Russian appearance seemed suitable candidates for the job.

It was then that sensible, quiet Boris, who felt so burdened with responsibility for his younger brother, had an idea that might have come straight from one of the adventure stories by Louis Boussenard that they loved reading. They would enroll at the school, learn all the Germans' secrets, and be dropped behind the Russian front lines; then they would immediately report to the Soviet military authorities, tell them everything and ask to be enrolled as volunteers in the Russian army. Even if they were not accepted as soldiers, they would at least reach Russia and stay there. The Germans would not defeat the Russians, their father had said. And he was not just a Russian patriot but a colonel of the General Staff who knew more and understood better than anyone else.

So the brothers went to the German spy school. Judging by what Boris told me, the training was not intended for the most advanced agents, who could handle radio transmitters, write in code, and engage in sabotage. A more modest role was being prepared for the brothers. They were to pretend to be refugees who had lost their parents and were making their way to Moscow or another city, to find help and somewhere to stay. According to the cover story they were given, they were supposed to come from Rostov-on-Don and have lost their mother long ago. Their father had gone off to fight at the very beginning of the war and a month later the aunt they were living with received notification that he had been killed. She had enough to worry about, without two almost grown young lads to look after, so she decided to pack them off north to a better-off relation in Vyshny Volochok. They had hardly arrived before the Germans began to advance on the town. Their relation did not want to evacuate but it was far too risky for her if there were two children of a Soviet officer living in her house as well. The boys fled back, towards Moscow.

Boris and Gleb studied the map of Rostov-on-Don, learnt all the names of the streets by heart, and memorized its various attractions. They could describe the river where they swam, the gullies where they played "Cossacks and Robbers," and name the school they had attended, recalling the surnames, appearance and nicknames of their teachers. They memorized code names for those they must report to in towns along the way, and the necessary passwords... The brothers had excellent memories and the German intelligence officers intended to make good use of them. Nothing could be written down. All they should do was to look, memorize the numbers on the tanks and cars, count how many vehicles there were on the road, and note which direction they were moving in. They were taught to recognize all the types of artillery and tank, and distinguish the different branches of the armed forces and the various officers' ranks by their collar tabs and stripes. Then they were to report all this to certain individuals whom they would find in the cities and large villages. Soon, very soon, they were promised, they would be in Moscow. There a wonderful and comfortable life awaited them, as it did all those who wholeheartedly served the German Reich.

The brothers were good students and quickly learnt all they were taught. They also memorized the surnames, code names and appearance of their present teachers and fellow students, and all the conversations they overheard at the spy school: everything, in fact, that in their view might later be of value to the Russian military authorities.

All went according to plan. They were dropped behind the Soviet front line at night. They parachuted into Russia. The night was dark but already had a summery translucence. There was no wind at all. Boris and Gleb landed without mishap and acted on their instructions: they buried their parachutes, and marked the spot with a stone so as to be able to show it to the Red Army officers later.

Then they set out. They asked the first Soviet soldier they saw how to make contact with SMERSH. They knew all about Soviet military counter-intelligence (and its acronym "Death to Spies!"), from the German school. It took some time for the soldier to understand what this pair of boys, covered in dust, in thin, worn clothing wanted from him. He was about to tell them to stop being a nuisance when they spotted a military unit moving towards them down the road. The boys found its commander. He was not a little taken aback, when Boris told him, in answer to his question, that they were German spies.

Finally, they reached Soviet counter-intelligence. The brothers were rapidly and doubtfully cross-questioned, given something to eat, and sent on. Everything was going as they had imagined. They were cross-examined by Soviet officers, and each time of a higher rank. Of course, it was upsetting being kept under lock and key all the time, and that their first encounter with Russia took this form. But they were well fed, given better clothes and promised that they could enroll at the Soviet officers' training college.

In this way they indeed reached Moscow. They did not see anything of the city, though, not even the bell tower of Ivan the Great. They were taken off the train, put into a closed truck and driven straight to prison. It was a real prison and there the most terrible thing that could happen, occurred: for the first time in their lives, they were separated and held in solitary confinement. This time there were no kind promises, but an interrogation with threats and fists waved in their faces. Soon, however, the brothers met again. They were put in a cell together with the most varied and repulsive people they could imagine—deserters, traitors and real spies.

They were called out and told their sentence: ten years in the camps for offenses committed under articles of a Soviet Criminal Code which meant nothing to them. Next they began their journey into the heart of Russia, to which they had so longed to return. It took the usual form: the Krasnaya Presnya transit prison in Moscow, a prison train of converted goods cars, and a very long journey north to Kotlas (every military train took precedence over theirs), where they continued along the recently constructed railway as far as Veslyana station. I know this journey well. But when I made it, the part from Vogvozdino to Knyazhpogost was still covered on foot. I doubt that the war had softened the hearts of the camp administrators in any respect. The brothers were not separated, however, although long-established rules said that relatives should not be sent to the same camp, let alone be put in the same compound. Probably, for all the inhumanity of those who then resolved our fate, even they could see that these youths would not survive if parted. And the value of "labor resources" had risen greatly during the war. A vast amount of timber was required, since powder for the ammunition was made from cellulose... American corned beef and powdered egg even began to appear in the camps. There was no longer anywhere for Soviet trawlers to catch the stinking cod they gave us before.

The concern of the highest authorities for their "work force" went so far, indeed, that only prisoners, of all Soviet people, were allowed to receive food parcels. Despite the universal semi-starvation in which people then existed, food parcels from relatives trickled into the camps from various towns and cities. A "black market" appeared in our camp where you could exchange a packet of crude tobacco for a piece of lard, and abandon a warm scarf still smelling of home for a day's bread ration or a packet of buckwheat-porridge concentrate. Boris and Gleb, however, had nothing to swap and there was no one who might send them the briefest of letters, let alone a food parcel. My friends working in the camp office and I tried in some way to help the boys, to tempt them into accepting our gifts. With a dignity we had long forgotten, Boris and Gleb calmly rejected such offers. There was something in their old-fashioned, pre-revolutionary courtesy and breeding, and in all that they said (they not only would not use the usual camp obscenities, but even the common camp terminology) which evoked respect. We felt it, the "educated" prisoners, and so did the other categories of camp inmate. Everyone was well-disposed towards them, from the team leaders and foremen to the lowest caste of degraded prisoners, the lackeys who had to serve their more powerful and well-fed fellows.

What made Boris and Gleb behave this way? I wondered then, during the two to three weeks we worked in the same team, and later when I had become a free worker and had my own separate, even lockable room, in a barrack outside the compound. Decades later, and after a long and eventful life, I continued to ponder their behavior. To this day I return, time and again, in my thoughts to these two youths and try to enter into their minds, and understand what made them so resistant and alien to our camp existence...

Boris was then already quite grown-up and his character, fully formed. Instinctively, by force of his upbringing and personality, he chose the only correct way, as it seems to me, for he and his brother to survive. Only by remaining equally alien to all in the camp, and not becoming a part of the prisoner's small world, could they preserve their individuality, remain as their father, a colonel on the General Staff, had raised them. It was, moreover, an absolutely correct tactic. Once I had somehow got the brothers talking, and become close enough to them to learn their story, I imagined I would be able to understand them fully. For even at the most difficult moments I kept my saving interest in others. But in this case I did not have enough time.

One evening, after we had returned the work distributor came into the barracks.

"Don't go out to work tomorrow," he said. "Get ready for transfer."

Transfer? Where to? To the court in Vozhael? But I had still not received the charge sheet, although I had signed note No. 206 certifying the completion of the preliminary investigation. Yet the charge sheet was handed to prisoners a week before they were taken to court: I was already very familiar with the procedures of our strict and impartial judicial system and knew they were observed with the most senseless tenacity.

Next morning I nevertheless went to roll call. I wanted to say goodbye to the two brothers. Our work team was already lined up, and I had a chat with the leader. "Chin up! Damned if we'll die!" he said, and slapped me encouragingly across the shoulders.

I agreed with him, and shook hands with the brothers. Boris said nothing but gave me an adult, understanding look, filled with compassion and warmth, that I had never seen in him before. As I said farewell to Gleb I automatically pulled him towards me, and he nudged his head into my coat. Suddenly I realized that I was seeing him for the last time.

At Records and Distribution they told me I was being sent to Camp No. 2, until ready to be tried. Our "godfather" Chugunov had evidently decided that a prisoner should not be left in a camp where everyone knew and sympathized with him and tried to make his life easier in all kinds of ways. According to their methods, an individual should appear broken, and physically and psychologically defeated, when he was brought to court to be given a new sentence. This made the prisoner seem capable of penitence and a sincere confession of his crimes. Why they found this necessary, I'm damned if I know. To this day I cannot see the reason!

It was not far to Camp No. 2, only 18 kilometers. I had an escorting guard all to myself, the deputy commander of the platoon, who had his own business there. Friends helped me fill a skimpy knapsack—since we were going on foot I could only take the essentials. The day dragged by unbelievably slowly and I sat in my old office in the planning section, smoking and chatting about neutral subjects with my friends, as one always does after some misfortune.

The work distributor rushed in and yelled at me, "Razgon, to the guardhouse!"

I embraced and kissed my friends. Some of us had actually arrived here together and there were people in the camp whom I had become very close to. Each transfer in effect was a new arrest. When would we meet again, if ever?

My escort was waiting in the guardhouse. I had known him for a long time. The deputy platoon commander was a middle-aged fellow who had spent all his life as a soldier, working as an escort guard in the camps. Not a vicious man, he was not alarmed by "enemies of the people" and calmly carried out his duties, without excessive zeal. In my conflict with the "godfather" he was, if anything, on my side. At the guardhouse he said, "Let's have a smoke before we go, shall we? And we shan't make a race of it. I've no reason to hurry, and as for you... !" he tossed up a hand expressively.

We smoked a small cigarette in the guardhouse, and then the gates of Camp No. 1 of Ustvymlag closed behind me. The greater part of my sentence since October 1938 had been spent here.

It was the middle of a winter's day and we could still reach Camp No. 2 in daylight. Quickly and silently, walking side by side, not as prisoner and escorting guard, we covered the familiar road which led past the tool store into the forest. We had not yet managed to join the main road when we saw, ahead of us, a horse harnessed to a timber-hauling drag and some people. On the sled lay a body covered by a coat. There was no hat on his head and I noticed blond close-cropped hair. Behind, his eyes wide and glassy, walked Boris. He glanced at me as if I was a stranger or simply an object, and nothing altered in his deathly pale face.

A guard lazily shuffled behind, bringing up the rear.

"What's up? Who's that under there?" my companion asked.

"Huh! a young zek, got crushed by a tree."

"Dead?"

"He's dead. Standing right under the trunk. How he got there, the devil knows!"

The terrible procession moved past, and I gazed after it, half-believing, half refusing to believe, what had happened...

"Pity about the lad, he was hardly more than a boy... Well, we'd better get moving. Don't want to be walking after dark."

* * *

One and a half months later, in March, I was escorted with two "refusers"[3] from Camp No. 2 to Vozhael to be tried. The snow was already loose underfoot, and the going was hard. We set out in the morning but by evening we had only reached my old camp. We were to spend the night there and carry on the next day to Zimka, the Machinery Depot and then the capital of Ustvymlag, Vozhael. After a perfunctory search at the guardhouse we were taken off to sleep in a little building in the corner of the compound that I knew only too well, the punishment block. This time it was heated and the prisoner on duty was someone I knew.

"You remember those two brothers?" I asked him. "One of them was crushed by a tree. Perhaps he survived?"

"No chance. He was already cold when they brought him in. I remember it."

"And the older boy? He's here, is he?"

"No, he's not. They sent him away, probably, with some transfer or other. There've been two transports, one to Vorkuta and the other no one knows where."

* *

Early next morning, even before roll call, the escort came for us. I did not have a chance to see any of those I knew. So I could not find out what had happened to Boris. Where was he? Still alive somewhere else? I rather doubt it. I cannot imagine how he could have lived with the idea that he had failed to look after his brother and protect him. As though he could have done anything in the terrible and incomprehensible world where they found themselves instead of the country they considered their motherland!

Why did their father give them those names, though? Why did he name his late and beloved sons after another pair of brothers, famous early Russian martyrs? Did he not feel any qualms of unease in doing so? The first young Boris and Gleb were killed by their older brother Prince Svyatopolk, in 11th-century Kiev. In different times, and under different circumstances, this story is repeated from century to century...

My Boris and Gleb, after all, were also trying to reach their brothers...

Razgon with Kostya Shulga, Ust-Surmog, 1953.

Razgon listening to Moscow on the radio in the camp office, February 28, 1954.

STRANGERS

I want to write about the "strangers" in the camps, the "others." They were seized, sentenced and sent to join us by the same organization that arrested me and all my other fellow inmates. Nevertheless, they were in some definite sense different. It all happened many years ago and now I am much wiser and more experienced, yet I continue as before to think of myself and those like me as basically the same, as "our people." Consequently, I include in this term those who arrested, tortured and killed us. Even though it is quite obvious that to our tormentors we were as infinitely alien as those who, lacking our passport and citizenship, had previously lived somewhere like Teheran or Warsaw.

Still, we were all the same, we were all Soviet. Hundreds of peasants from Smolensk, Archangel and the Kuban were convoyed on foot to our camps: they were ours, they were Soviet. So were the Chechen and Kabardians plucked from their mountainous North Caucasian homes; so were the Kazakhs and Kalmyk driven from the steppes. We thought of those who worked for the Comintern and lived for years in Moscow as "ours." Likewise we accepted as our own those foreign women who, by some miracle in times long past, had married our diplomats or engineers. Then there were prostitutes with foreign-travel passports[1] licensed to serve their non-Soviet clients—they were also "ours." And of course there were the Odessans with Greek passports and Turkish passport holders born in Baku. They were all "ours," because they had either been born and grown up in the country or else come to live there of their own free will. Even when they spoke Russian very badly or did not speak it at all, they were ours. And in the melting pot of the camps they quickly ceased to stand out or appear in any way different. Those of them who survived the first year or two of camp life could thereafter only be distinguished among "us" by their poor Russian. The Chechen and Kabardian mountain people often did not know how to speak Russian at all. It did not matter: they were still ours.

The strangers, on the other hand, appeared from elsewhere, swept from their own country to the far North of Russia by an alien and hostile historical force which they could not comprehend. No one offered the Moldavians or those from Bukovina the choice of being Rumanian or Soviet. No one asked the Poles whether they wanted to move to the forests of the Komi-Zyryansk area. A flood of events simply descended on them and they fled before this calamity without any idea where they might end up. And once they reached us they could neither understand nor assimilate; they did not try to adapt and survive. They merely huddled together instinctively, forming a small island constantly eroded by deaths and transfers else-where.

Large batches of such strangers began joining us in the camps in 1939, expelled from Galicia, Moldavia and Bukovina under our amica-ble arrangement with Hitler. Before they reached Camp No. 1 we were alerted to their arrival in Ustvymlag by the appearance of exotic items of clothing among our criminal inmates: the shaggy tall hats and colored sashes of Moldavia and, from Bukovina, embroidered fur waistcoats and fashionable close-fitting jackets with high, padded shoulders. The camp prostitutes began to parade about in incongru-ously elegant summer coats with white silk linings, Angora shawls and even silk jumpsuits provided with numerous zippered pockets. All this told us that new transports had arrived at Camp No. 11 and the transit camp next to the Kotlas-Vorkuta railway. There, in an expres-sion that almost all of us used, they had been given the usual "frater-nal welcome." Every experienced criminal inmate did his best to get moved to those two privileged camps so as to cream off the new-comers' best possessions during the few days they had to wait for medical examination, allocation of work category and distribution to other camps.

Only after the desirable items turned up were the strangers them-selves marched into our camp. By this time they had already passed through numerous distribution centers, prisons and transit camps, and they were thoroughly distraught. They understood nothing and their only thought was how to get through the day alive. They would give away their clothes and in return receive someone's bread ration or a matchbox full of rough tobacco or nothing at all. Terrified by the frightful and unheard-of obscenities and the threatening fists, they were issued a set of rough prison clothing and often this struck them as a very fair deal. Padded trousers and a good quilted work jacket were, in fact, of more importance to a prisoner in the camps than a fashionable suit from Warsaw. Yet this was not a "market" or even "the bartering of commodities." What happened was unmitigated robbery. It was encouraged by the camp administration, moreover, because they themselves had ample access, through their trusted se-curity officers and work distributors, to all the best wares taken off the strangers.

Who were they, these strange birds, these "foreigners"? As far as those from Moldavia, Bukovina and the Baltic states were concerned, things were fairly straightforward. Those territories had been incor-porated into the USSR and so all the well-tested and current methods for the "liquidation of classes" were extended to them. Lists were hastily drawn up and during a few days, or even a single night, mem-bers of the bourgeoisie, government officials, and the most noted party leaders, journalists and lawyers were rounded up and loaded onto trucks. All with their families as well. Of course, petty traders, dentists and even couriers from some insignificantly tiny government department also found themselves on this list. For, when all is said and done, the local "well-wishers" who helped to provide these names were only human. The temptation to settle scores was too strong to resist...

Those arrested were allowed to take with them no more than they themselves could carry; they were herded onto trucks or railway cars and dispatched to the distribution centers. There the majority of women, and the children and old men, were taken away and sent off into exile—to Siberia, Kazakhstan and the other vast expanses with which God saw fit to provide our country. The men, meanwhile, were transported to the camps. They were sentenced by arbitrary and rapid decrees of the local troika to five, eight or ten years for the same abbreviated offenses of which we had supposedly been guilty: SOE, KRA, KRD and PSh (Socially Dangerous Element, Counter-Revolutionary Agitation, Counter-Revolutionary Activities and Suspicion of Espionage), and so on. These verdicts were added to their forms at the distribution compound before departure or, if they were not ready in time, were sent on later to the camps. Sometimes the clerks of this infernal bureaucracy made mistakes and the decrees were sent to the wrong place, or were not sent at all. The strangers remained in the camps all the same. For as old and experienced camp hands rightly said: show me the man and I'll show you the article to send him down.

Still, it was astonishing how rapidly the Soviet mentality took hold. The prisoners from the "reunited" territories, whether they came from the Baltic states or from Bukovina and Bessarabia, all accepted everything that happened to them as natural and inevitable. It was the response to a chronic, incurable disease with the most dismal prognosis. After a certain length of time they would become zeks like the rest. They may have still spoken Russian badly and retained certain customs and distinctive ways but they were now zeks. We saw numerous such cases, from Persians and Indians to Tasmanians (one of them even landed in our camp). Only once did I have the chance to follow, with mixed emotions, the behavior of not one but, to use the biologist's term, an entire population of "stranger" zeks. This happened when large numbers of Poles flooded into Ustvymlag.

* * *

This was in 1939, of course. To be more precise, in autumn 1939. By then Stalin and Hitler's bloody conspiracy had led to the Fourth Partition of Poland. Molotov announced that Poland as a state had ceased to exist and rightly so, since the Poles had no right to have a state of their own. All that remained now was to deal with the Polish nation, for centuries torn between the bandit states with whom it had the misfortune to share frontiers.

Over the years people in Russia have acquired a basic sense of how the Germans behaved towards the Poles at that time. I am writing about a less familiar story. The erstwhile citizens of former Poland who ended up in our camp belonged to the most varied categories. For the most part, they were Jews. The new frontier drawn across the territory of the former Poland (and confirmed by Stalin's dashing and Ribbentrop's more modest signatures) presented a choice to the many who had fled before the Nazi push to the east. Either they could return to the German "Polish General Government" or they could continue moving eastwards, into the limitless hinterland of Soviet Russia. For some the draw of their abandoned homes, factories and old and settled ways proved stronger than their fear of the Germans. To such people the invaders still seemed to be the Prussians in *pickelhaube* helmets whom they remembered from the First World War. Conquerors, of course, but still human beings like anyone else. They did not yet know of Hitler's intention to implement the "Final Solution." So they returned to "their" Poland, to their home towns and houses, only to depart two or three years later for Auschwitz and the other vast factories of death.

Those who remained escaped this appalling fate. Despite their uncertainty and foreboding (the Soviet Union had, after all, just become the ally of Nazi Germany) they decided to remain in this alien and terrible country. Not all of them survived, but the majority did. When I recall the horrors they experienced, at the same time I cannot forget that they stayed alive only because they ended up here.

Who were these human beings, now reduced like the rest of us, to just another "contingent" of expendable labor? Far from all found themselves in the camps. A great many were sent vast distances eastwards within the Soviet Union and became accountants, factory hands, engineers and even collective-farm workers. They were given Soviet citizenship. They received food ration cards. And, somehow, they survived the war and the chaos of the post-war years to see the restoration of the Polish state. Not a very independent state then, it may be said, but one to which they could return.

And the others... well, the others were sent to the camps. We can only surmise what our anonymous decision makers were thinking about as they fought "their" war against unarmed and defenseless people. One category, though, was obvious. The surviving members of the Polish aristocracy were sent to the camps for no better reason than their proud surnames, which we were familiar with from reading Sienkiewicz's historical novels.

A few years ago, during some writers' tour, I went to speak at the town of Nesvezh, not far from Minsk. It was a very interesting little town, people told me, since the Radziwills had their family estate there. Yes, those Radziwills... And indeed, the architecture was un-usual and there remained something un-Russian about the people and the life they led. A military sanatorium now occupied the princely palace and its enormous park. However, the Catholic church in the very center of the town was still functioning, unlike the closed Russian Orthodox churches. Nesvezh's large and wealthy Catholic congregation kept up the standards of the past: the church building retained its extravagance and grandeur and continued to be deco-rated with statues, coats of arms, military standards and the banners of various artisan guilds. As distinguished guests we and the accom-panying town officials were shown around by the elderly priest, a clever and ironic man of eighty-two who knew just how to cope with the Bolsheviks. It was some feast day or other. The church was crowded with people praying and we looked on as the elaborate ser-vice, complete with organ, choir and processions took place. When it was all over and everyone had left, the priest unfastened the great lock hanging on one of the doors and led us down into an enormous crypt that extended the entire length of the church. This was the burial vault of the Radziwills. The bright electric light revealed dozens if not hundreds of lead coffins, some large, some small, and some tiny children's coffins. They all bore one and the same surname, with unfamiliar first names and different dates. Here lay the heroes of his-torical novels about the Rzeczpospolita, immensely wealthy feudal lords who had been courtiers of the tsars, kings and emperors of Russia, Prussia and Austro-Hungary respectively. On one of the coffins lay the dusty tricorn hat of a man-in-waiting with its ostrich plume: this was the most "recent" Russian Radziwill, who had been laid to rest in the crypt in 1913.

Any graveyard prompts reflections about the transience of our earthly existence. Yet I have rarely felt it so intensely as in that old, formerly Polish town. Suddenly, I remembered that there had been Radziwills in Ustvymlag as well... Not in our particular camp but at the machinery depot nearby. A Prince Radziwill had found himself a comfortable job as a bathhouse attendant; two princesses were cleaners in the workshops and, according to the cynical assertions of the drivers there, did not rate their favors more highly than the usual camp sluts. So this was how a family history extending over centuries could end: hundreds of dusty lead coffins, and common prostitution in Ustvymlag...

It would be unjust, though, to give the impression that such was the fate of all the aristocratic Polish families who found themselves stranded on one of the islands of the Gulag. In Camp No. 1 we had our own real Polish count. None other, in fact, than Count Tyszkiewicz. Apart from being an extremely wealthy businessman and owner of the Palanga resort on the Baltic, Tyszkiewicz headed a major conservative party and was a noted political figure in Poland.

He behaved just as we are told a count should. He categorically refused to go out to work each day. So he became a "refuser" and was
confined to the punishment cell on a punitive ration. His was such an
unusual case, however, that he became prized as a subject for re-education.

Every morning before the prisoners were marched out of the
camp to work and the columns of zeks were lined up in the yard, two
warders would fetch Tyszkiewicz from the punishment cell. Gray
stubble covered his face and shaven head, and he was dressed in
remnants of an old overcoat and puttees. The camp security officer
would begin his daily educational exercise, "Well you f-r, Count, you
stupid f-g f-r, are you going to work or not?"

"No, Pan. I cannot work," the count would reply in an iron-firm
voice.

"Oh, so you can't! You f-... " The security officer would publicly explain to the count what he thought of him, and of his close and distant relations, and what he would do to him in the very near future.
This daily spectacle was a source of general satisfaction to the camp's
other inmates. The count would listen calmly and majestically until
the security officer yelled, "Oh, take this son of a bitch off to the shit-
house!" and added a pair of Polish curses for good measure. The
warders then escorted the count back to the punishment block
where, it was said, he was admired and respected by the other "refusers."

I don't know which was uppermost in the count's mind, his sense
of honor or cold calculation. Old convicts would often refuse to work
because they knew they were more likely to survive on the 300
grams of bread they received in the warm punishment cell than on
the full kilogram ration they would get in the terrible timber-felling
area. Whatever the reason, the count refused to work at the cost of
participating in this daily demonstration of re-education techniques.
This went on until suddenly the boss of all Ustvymlag sent his jeep to
our camp. The count was brought out of the punishment cell, put in
the vehicle and instantly swept off to Vozhael. A few days later the
work distributors, who knew everything, said that overnight an elegant suit had been made for the count (some even insisted that it
was a morning coat!), and then he was put on a plane and flown to
Moscow.

After a while those newspapers that filtered through to us reported the formation in London of the Polish government in exile. It
was led by Sikorski and more or less friendly towards the Soviet
Union. The minister of foreign affairs was none other than our old
"refuser" and inmate of the punishment cells, Count Tyszkiewicz...
Miraculous are thy ways, o Lord! Some time passed and in one of the
main Moscow newspapers I came across an article that was indignant about Tyszkiewicz's behavior: forgetting who had saved him

from the Nazis, along with thousands of other Poles, it said, the minister of foreign affairs in the new emigre Polish government was pursuing an anti-Soviet policy.

And it was nothing but the truth. I was always amazed in the past, and indeed today remain astonished, by the ability of the "organs of information," to use official jargon, to tell the most appalling lies while not actually saying anything formally untrue. I can remember how the idiotic movement of "women furnace-workers" first appeared in Soviet metal-working plants. "Nowhere else in the world, only in our country," rapturously proclaimed the newspapers, "has a woman first stood by the tap hole of a blast furnace." This was nothing but the truth, of course. A woman who had worked for a month by the furnace, our Dr. Stefanov told me with horror, would not be able to have any children. Female labor in such workshops was strictly forbidden throughout the world. What the papers wrote was nothing but the truth, "only in our country"!

On 1 January 1939 a population census was held throughout the Soviet Union. This was hardly the best year to choose and there were good reasons why the results were subsequently discounted and even made classified information. At the time, however, it was carried out everywhere and, naturally, in the camps as well. Otherwise the figures for the total USSR population would have looked very peculiar... I recall only two of a long list of questions: level of education and occupation. We answered quite honestly: education higher, occupation lumber-worker. About half a year later, we accidentally got hold of an issue of the Syktyvkar newspaper, *For a New North!*, the mouthpiece of the Party regional committee. The leading article discussed the results of the census which, it declared, had shown what strides the Komi Autonomous Republic had been making. At the last pre-revolutionary census there had been only one person in the Ust-Sysol district with higher education. Today, the 1939 census demonstrated, there were more people with higher education in the Komi Republic than in France and Belgium put together. Moreover, this was not a piece of propaganda but an incontrovertible fact. As one of Babel's heroes says, "What I'm telling you is not one of those facts, comrade: it really did take place..."[2]

What next happened to the ungrateful count I do not know. Soon we quarrelled with the London-based Polish government, Sikorski was killed in an air crash, and Count Tyszkiewicz disappeared from the news altogether. I think of my former fellow camp inmate only when I'm in Palanga (now a part of Lithuania) and being shown round what used to be his mansion. Today there is a museum of amber there. So much for the aristocrats. There were several other social groups in our camp left over after the abolition of Polish society.

They differed a great deal. There were ethnic Poles, most of whom were young men who had not been accepted by the army for some reason. The commonest type, however, were middle-aged or even elderly Jews. These were not our impoverished Russian Jews, artisans and craftsmen from the shtetls. Evidently the Polish Jews sent to the camps had been selected for their class origins. In the past they had been major industrialists, managers and owners of factories and timber yards. Perhaps it was no coincidence that the majority of former Polish-Jewish capitalists in our camp had been involved in the timber industry. You might suppose that this should have helped them adapt to work in a timber-felling camp. But nothing of the kind. They could not make head or tail of this horrific new world which shared nothing in common with their previous lives.

We were greatly amused when one former timber merchant who had been taken out to fell trees for several days requested to see the camp commandant and firmly told him, "I have examined the trees you are felling very thoroughly, citizen commandant believe me, I know what I'm talking about and I have to tell you that it is quite unprofitable to cut down such timber."

"So what should we be doing with it?" asked the commandant with interest.

"Sell the trees as they stand. That will be much more profitable."

"But we don't sell timber for others to cut down in our country!" said the commandant, amazed by such a proposal.

"That's because there's a lack of experience," proudly responded the former timber magnate. "Entrust the job to me and I shall sell it as it stands and make a large profit for you..."

These negotiations between representatives of two different worlds had an unhappy ending. Lacking a sufficient sense of humor and humanity to appreciate the old man's good intentions, the commandant did not fix him up with an easy job inside the compound. The old man carried on felling the unsuitable trees until he caught pneumonia and died straightaway. All he left behind was the story, which soon became legend, of how they tried to sell our forests as they stood. Need I add that the rest of us all bitterly regretted the administration's failure to take up this suggestion.

After the Polish transports the work of the norm-setters grew and grew. I took on a young Pole called Andrzej as my assistant. He had been studying at Cracow University and was rejected by the army because he had limped from birth. A very capable and pleasant lad, he spoke Russian rather well and told me a great deal about a Poland that we did not then know. I don't think we know it to this day in Russia.

It was upsetting to see how defenseless the descendants of the Wolodyjowskis and Zaglobas[3] suddenly found themselves, not only against their jailer bosses but also the most petty camp hooligans. It was no surprise to us, though. Even our own Civil War heroes sometimes proved as vulnerable. In this case, however, there was an added feeling of pity because it was impossible to explain or help—the majority did not speak Russian. Several days I watched from the office window as an emaciated and still young Pole walked across the compound, nursing the bread ration he had just received. Almost every time a group of four or five of the lowest type of criminal inmate attacked him and took his bread away. The Pole would remain alone in that terrible yard in front of the barracks and weep helplessly... How could we help him?

"Lev Emmanuilovich," said Andrzej (With difficulty I had taught him not to address me as Pan Chief Norm-Setter), "Do you know, that lad was the middle-weight boxing champion of Poland. He used to win international competitions as well."

"What, him? Call him in here."

With Andrzej's help I tried to find out why a professional boxer, even though emaciated, did not resist a gang of equally emaciated prisoners.

"But there's a lot of them and only one of me. They know everyone else but I'm alone and a stranger."

"Have you forgotten how to box?"

"Of course not, how could I!? I was among the top ten middleweights in Europe."

"And even in your present shape, could you deal with that gang?"

"Of course, Pan. But I wouldn't dare!"

"Listen carefully. I'm now going to give you my bread ration and you carry it, as always, across the yard. When they attack you, show no mercy and knock them out cold! If you do that, you'll survive—they only respect force. But if you give up this ration as well, not one of us will help you again and you'll die here."

Through the office window, Andrzej and I watched this strange experiment, devised not to satisfy my curiosity but a natural desire to save a man otherwise doomed to die. The champion left the office, timidly clasping my 400 gram bread ration. A few minutes later criminals from the "weak team" (to which he also belonged) attacked. The former champion helplessly glanced at our window and I raised my fist threateningly. I saw then what professionalism meant. The wasted Pole tucked the bread under his armpit and, in an instant, laid three of his attackers flat in the dust. The others fled.

"Andrzej," I said, "let the whole camp know that this guy is a boxing champion and can easily break the nose of the biggest fellow here."

Andrzej set to work and soon all the camp's criminal small-fry began to avoid the former champion, who now had no fear for his bread ration. The real hardened criminals did not snatch bread from other prisoners and were even impressed that there was a former boxing champion in the camp. In this way I saved a good soldier for the future Anders army. For the end result of our complicated policy towards Poland was that all the surviving Poles capable of fighting were sent to join the army formed by General Anders somewhere in the sands of Persia. Even my lame Andrzej talked a visiting Polish emissary into signing him up since, as he explained, his lame leg had not prevented him being a champion marksman at Cracow University. The ones who remained were the old Jews who could patch work coats, make rope shoes and serve as duty orderlies, sweeping the barracks.

I was sad to part with Andrzej. I had grown accustomed to him and though he had not worked a great deal—there was no way I could teach him to use the slide-rule—he had told me many interesting stories. Still, I needed to find a new assistant. The search introduced me to one of the most interesting people I have ever met.

* * *

Cautiously an aged man entered our office.

"May I see the Pan Norm-Setter?"

His nationality, previous social status and even his character were immediately obvious. The coat was worn, of course, but it was spotless, with all its buttons neatly sewn on, and his elderly intelligent face was shaved and clean.

"I heard that the Pan Norm-Setter is in need of an assistant and I wanted to offer my services."

He spoke a pure Russian and even lacked that indestructible accent that almost all non-Russians have.

"Yes, I do need an assistant. But it would be desirable for that person to have at least some idea of forestry work."

"I owned almost all the large timber yards in Poland," modestly replied the old man. "I had three Bollinder timber-working factories. I was a well-known and respected exporter and I can determine the volume of any trunk with my bare eyes to within a percent or two."

"But do you know how to use an abacus? Or a slide-rule? Or a simple mechanical calculator?"

"No, Pan. I can't do that."

"Then how will you do the work? I know you're used to doing all the sums on paper. But that's impossible here. The norm-setter must constantly divide and multiply two and three-figure numbers. And he must do it quickly because all the work teams must have their norms fixed by morning."

"I can do all that without paper and quicker than a calculator. I do the sums in my head."

And there and then he demonstrated a phenomenal ability. I gave my visitor two and three-figure numbers and he divided and multiplied in his head instantaneously. I checked his answers, using the slide rule, but the mysterious cells in his brain worked much faster... I was astonished.

"You will start working here tomorrow. I shall tell the senior work distributor."

The old man bowed politely and left. After half an hour he returned with a neatly rolled packet in his hands.

"What's that? Who's that for?"

"For you, Pan. With gratitude. It's a very good almost entirely new suit. I bought it in London just before the war started."

My high-minded Komsomol training was still firmly engrained.

"Take back the suit and don't come here tomorrow. Unfortunately, I cannot employ you here. A norm-setter must be free of such behavior. Neither I nor my assistants ever give or accept bribes!"

I admit it was painful to watch how cautiously and hopelessly he closed the door behind him, unable to feel himself in any way guilty. I did not have the intelligence or kindness to call out and summon him back. It was even more painful to see him trudging past in the filthy column of prisoners that was driven out to work in the morning. Soon I could stand it no more, and I appealed to my friend, Konstantin Ravinsky, the camp's chief accountant. An intelligent and cultured man, Ravinsky had avoided being a member of the Komsomol himself and had worked as a lawyer in Leningrad before his arrest. One of his constant worries was the frequent need to replace the bread cutter. I hardly need emphasize the importance and responsibility of the man who lived alone in a building crammed with loafs of bread, those thick and delicious blocks that he then cut up into normal, bonus and punitive rations... To prove how precisely he weighed out this vital ration, a tiny sliver of bread was pinned to each half or quarter loaf. Preparing slivers was an extremely desirable occupation for some weakened fellow inmate whom the bread cutter had taken under his wing.

Yet despite the accuracy with which the rations were weighed out, as emphasized by the slivers, and in spite of the total impossibility of verification, every inspection revealed that the bread cutter had either been thieving right, left and center or was quite incapable of managing this simple business. Even bread-cutters imprisoned under Article 58, people of indisputable honesty, were also found wanting. The chief accountant despaired of ever employing someone whose work he could rely on.

I honestly admitted to Ravinsky that my conscience was troubled. My Komsomol puritanism had condemned an elderly man to heavy manual work and someone, moreover, with a phenomenal capacity for instantaneous calculation. Once again there was the usual crisis in the bread-cutting section: an experienced and apparently reliable bread cutter had been stealing large quantities of bread. So Ravinsky agreed to replace him with one of Poland's greatest timber dealers.

The name seemed more Polish than Jewish, Jacob Pavlovich Svienticki. Although I have not just referred to him as an old man but felt him to be one, he was probably not much over sixty. He was nothing like the petty traders or craftsmen I knew from the shtetls of Belorussia. Tall, calm and deliberate in his movements, he still retained remnants of the dignity of a very rich and, consequently, independent man.

Svienticki proved an ideal bread cutter. My friend the chief accountant could not praise him enough. Any inspection revealed that the bread had been weighed out with impeccable honesty. But that was not all: numerous people in the camp who needed the food, were given extra rations. The work commandant had no inhibitions about walking into the bread-cutting section and saying: "Give ten extra bread rations to work-team leader so-and-so—they've worked well today!" He did not wonder where Svienticki would find the extra, and he was right not to worry: the new bread-cutter could always provide extra rations. Not only of bread, either, but of sugar and even certain products from the commissary for free workers. Evidently, Svienticki knew about more than just timber, and the fundamentals of a capitalist existence were more firmly engrained in him than my anti-capitalist past was in me.

By then my life had changed considerably. I had finished my first sentence and, after my second conviction was lifted, I became a "free" employee of the camp. Such "freedom" chiefly meant that I no longer lived inside the barbed wire but outside, with my own small room in the barrack for the camp's free workers, and when I walked through the guardhouse on my way to work and back they did not frisk me or make me undress. Still, I remained one of theirs... And everything else was unchanged. I would arrive at the office each day and, before sitting down to work, chat about the latest news from the front with my deputy Nikolai Lisovsky. (A military man, he had at one time been a corps commander and deputy head of the General Staff, and he always added his own commentaries and prognoses.)

On rare occasions, and only when work required it, Svienticki would visit the office. Not once did he remind me of my behavior when we first met, nor of my subsequent patronage. I liked this calm and melancholy man who accepted everything that happened to him with an ineradicable fatalism. One day he said to me, "Lev Emmanuilovich! I have some very good real tea and I would be most happy if you came to drink it with me this evening. We do not work together any longer and I am not dependent on you. So your convictions, which I respect deeply, will not be offended in any way."

I began to visit Jacob Pavlovich, at first once in a while and then more and more frequently. And it was not to drink his tea, which really was delicious, so much as to talk to him. There was an enticing smell of fresh bread and strong tea in the bread-cutting room, and it was always warm and comfortable there. The trestle bed was clean and neatly made-up, and on a nail in the corner hung an old but very respectable-looking fur coat.

Svienticki had travelled all over the world. He had been in almost every country in Europe and had visited the East, including Palestine. This last was not from any religious feeling (something, in my opinion, that he lacked entirely) but rather the result of curiosity. He told his stories intelligently and laconically, and would always select the most graphic turn of phrase, not the common banalities but usually a striking paradox. I never asked him about his family or what had happened to them, or how and in what way he had ended up, quite alone, in the Soviet Union. Solitude, it seemed, was one of the main qualities of his character. Unlike all the other "trusties" he did not make efforts to get on friendly terms with the elite who ran the medical unit. Neither would his fellow Polish Jews drop by, to chat about this and that. He lived alone with his thoughts and I cannot explain why he picked me to discuss his ideas about the fate of the Jewish nation, though I listened more than I argued.

"The Jewish nation has fulfilled its historic mission, if we are to believe that it ever had one. It will now cease to exist, just like many other tribes and nations, even great nations that created great civilizations. In one or two hundred years time only history students will know about the Jews. All the European Jews have perished. They have been killed, cremated, or worked to death in the camps."

"That's only true of Germany and Poland."

"And in other places? What are we doing here together?"

"But quite a lot of Jews have survived in European countries."

"You've never planted a new forest, have you? In order for it to survive and for the individual trees to form a forest, the majority of saplings must stay alive or there won't be enough trees and there will be no forest. It's the same with the Jews: some trees remain standing but those individuals will never now make a forest. The surviving European Jews have been mortally terrified and, more than anything else, fear to appear to be Jews."

"But there are millions of American Jews."

"They're not Jews, they're Americans. They're no different from the Anglo-Saxons, Italians and Irish there. Some of them eat spaghetti, others eat stuffed pike, but they're all Americans and share a single country, America."

"You've been in Palestine, Jacob Pavlovich. What do you think of Zionism?"

"A childish conception, the idea of quarrelsome children. The British and other Europeans will never let go of Palestine. And

surrounding those isolated groves that dream of becoming a real forest, there is an entire tropical jungle of Arabs who rightly consider
the land to be theirs. What do they care about history! The Crusaders
also once ruled Palestine—so the Europeans should also lay a claim to
the Holy Land, should they? If the Jews do manage to grab a piece of
Palestine, they'll be fighting continually. But a fighting Jew ceases to
be a Jew—he becomes just as stupid and revolting as all who engage
in killing. It's not the business of the Jews."

"Well, what then is the business of the Jews, Jacob Pavlovich?"

"To be an outcast and therefore lay no claim to power. To build
factories for others, make discoveries, dream up new ideas and write
books (also for other people) and publish newspapers (for others, as
well). And to gradually lose their Jewishness. That was how the Jew
Disraeli became the English Lord Beaconsfield. That is what would actually happen if the Jews did not arouse a hatred that I find incomprehensible, and a desire in others to exterminate them. It's better
when they finish the job straightaway, the way my family were murdered: when the thing goes on year after year then you grow infinitely weary of such senseless cruelty. Yet we must also learn to survive these wearisome years and find some way of living through
them. Do you have any relations left out there? And children?"

"Yes, some family and a daughter."

"There you are. You're still young and have already finished your
sentence here. You still have a life ahead of you, as many years as
God sends. Your descendants may also survive for several more generations if those Hitlers do not take control of the entire world. Don't
make such a tragedy of my remarks. I sound like Job because for me
and my family everything is already finished. I can see that you are
embarrassed to ask, Why am I still struggling to stay alive? I wanted
to be a norm-setter and now I live, quietly and well-fed, in the bread-
cutting room... That's just a matter of habit, dear Lev Emmanuilovich.
The indestructible habit of living that only very strong-willed people
or madmen can overcome. I am neither one nor the other."

Svienticki's attachment to me was quite sincere. Once he even
suddenly decided to make a present of his furcoat, which was, it
seems, the only memento of his former wealth. And, as it later
turned out, rather more than just a simple memento.

"You've probably noticed that I am a very solitary individual.
That's because I'm rather intolerant, I suppose. I'm very thankful to
you for listening patiently to views that you cannot accept or believe,
and helping relieve many a lonely evening. You are the closest person
here for me. So I would like to leave you a present."

"Whatever present do you mean, Jacob Pavlovich?"

"My furcoat."

With difficulty I held back an indecent smile as I imagined myself
wearing that heavy garment, which probably dated from the last

century, about the camp.

"Of course, you cannot walk about the streets of Moscow in such a coat. The cut is out of fashion. But all the rest is still valuable. The cloth is excellent and has not worn out, and it is padded with camel hair of the kind used by only the best London tailors. If you unstitch it any halfways decent tailor in Russia will make you a superb coat that will last for ever. But there is one condition: you must take out the lining yourself, and separate the material from the lining and the filling... If I believed in an afterlife I would then be very satisfied that I had made the life of someone I like easier."

"I'm touched and thankful, Jacob Pavlovich. But you talk as though you were making your will."

"You're right."

"The time hasn't come yet. I'm convinced that the war will end soon and you, as the citizen of another country, will be among the first to be released. Then your old-fashioned furcoat will again grace your shoulders."

"All right then. I already know what your views are. Let's reach a compromise. This furcoat is my one and only possession and it would be very easy to steal it. You're a free man and live outside the camp compound. Take it home with you. Then if, as you so naively suppose, they free me I shall be grateful to you for keeping it safe. If I die here, as is my fate, then consider that I have bequeathed it to you. In that case I want you to treat everything I have said to you as my last request."

"Very well, Jacob Pavlovich. I shall take your coat home with me. But no one here is going to steal it: it's of no value to any prisoner."

I did not take the coat that evening, however, nor the following night either. I put off doing so, time and again. I felt uncomfortable about going through the gates carrying that heavy fur coat: "So our norm-setter finally got itchy fingers," the amused and knowing gaze of the guards would say. "And they all boasted that he wasn't one to take things..."

I probably would have carried out the old man's strange request in the end. But before I did, they killed him.

"Have you heard? They bumped off our bread cutter—someone's chopped him!"

I ran to the bread-cutting room. It was already full of guards and the "godfather," the chief security officer, was in charge. On the bed, covered by a blood-stained cloth, lay the man I'd visited the day before and, thank God, I could not see his disfigured face... It was a quite commonplace story. One of the hardened criminals had come to the bread-cutting room and demanded an extra loaf. When Svienticki refused, the criminal pulled a hand-axe out from under his jacket, and struck the old man across the head with it. Then he calmly took one loaf (one, only one!) and went back to his barracks.

Now he was eating that loaf, just as calmly, in the punishment cell. Instead of going out to work in the forest, the murderer would receive food parcels from his admiring companions and go to chat with the "godfather" in his office. Then he would be sent to Vozhael, and see many of his acquaintances in the transit camp, before being tried and given a quite minimal sentence. He'd get ten years "with reduction of time already served" and since he had served six months of his last conviction, he'd be getting half a year off for murdering the old man.

So Jacob Pavlovich's tragic premonitions had been quite correct. He was indeed fated to be buried in an unmarked grave in the camp cemetery and disappear forever, just like his family before him...

For two whole months the furcoat he had bequeathed to me became the subject of conversation and legend not only in our camp but throughout Ustvymlag. It was found to contain an enormous number of large cut diamonds.

"All as big as walnuts, they were, those diamonds! Two kilos of them," said the slop-bucket carriers, who passed on all the rumors in the camp.

Evidently before the war, or at its very outset, Svienticki had transformed his enormous fortune into portable form, and then sewn the diamonds into an old furcoat that would be of interest to no one. I had been the intended heir of this fairy-tale Golconda! Sad as I was at the loss of a tormented old man whom I had liked, I could not restrain a laugh when others started to list all the vanished opportunities of my diamond-financed future. It seemed incredibly funny then (and today I still cannot help smiling) when I imagine being released "for good" and returning to Moscow, my pockets stuffed with walnut-sized diamonds... Whatever would I have done with them? Even now that I have abandoned so many prejudices and convictions I would not have any idea what to do with a small sackful of diamonds. Those who pocketed one or two of them before handing the rest over to the state had a much better idea how to dispose of them.

Those evenings together in the bread-cutting room remained much more vividly in my memory than the vanished diamonds. I remember that former capitalist's painful reflections and in my mind I continue our debate to this day. He might have erred in some of his historical predictions but the moral presuppositions on which he based them were sound. Fifty years have passed since he died and his prediction that the Jewish nation would perish has not come true. However, he himself perished, as did my relatives and his, and millions of others. People may continue to be born but that does not make it any more acceptable that any individual should suffer such a fate and vanish. In the famous American documentary *Holocaust* a bulldozer pushes hundreds and thousands of naked male and female bodies into a trench. It is impossible to think of such things without despairing. Just as it is impossible not to despair when remembering how we were killed and buried in unmarked graves in our tens and hundreds of thousands. In the Nazi camps they were killed because they were Jews. And in ours? Because such murders were a way of solving any problem, racial, class or political. They are the simplest and most reliable means for disposing of each and every problem— and that's why I feel hatred and contempt for all "great" military leaders. After one of his victorious but very bloody battles, Napoleon was told that the losses of the French army were enormous. "A trifle!" the great leader calmly responded. "One night's work in France will make good the entire deficit."

Curse them, these "great" men. I can do nothing to them and they can do anything they please with me. Apart from one thing, that is. None of these Alexanders and Napoleons, these Stalins and Hitlers, can make me feel the slightest respect for them, let alone love them. No one can alter my contempt for them. Let those who admire such men do their ass-licking in articles, studies and novels. For me they will always be shit.

* * *

The Poles disappeared from the camp almost as abruptly as they had appeared. They were all pawns in a political game and those in charge treated them with the indifference of men driving cattle to the slaughterhouse. Some of the Poles were needed for Bierut's Communist army, some for Anders's army, and others for still different purposes. They spent only two to three years in the camps and, unlike us, who had been rounded up in 1937-38, most of them survived. The rare exceptions were our timber merchant, who had wanted to sell stands of trees, and Jacob Pavlovich, who was killed in passing by a professional thug. The only reason the others survived was that the camps had undergone major and fundamental change. This was due to the introduction of the "trusty" system. And here I must take issue with such an authority as Alexander Solzhenitsyn.

For it was he who created a contemptuous attitude to "trusties" in *Ivan Denisovich* and *The Gulag Archipelago*. Ivan Denisovich and ordinary people who found themselves in the camps were indeed "stubborn": they died working out in the forests and down in the mines while members of the intelligentsia had comfortable "trusty" jobs in the camp offices and after a day's paperwork could indulge in discussions about art and literature. Yet this is a profoundly unhistorical and, to put it baldly, immoral way of describing things.

In the *Gulag Handbook*[4] the only work of its kind, the Frenchman Jacques Rossi, who spent twenty years in Soviet camps, gives the following definition: "a trusty is an individual with a cushy job; a prisoner who has arranged an office job or work that is not physically demanding." Yet, as he adds, the law of 1930 specified that "Individuals convicted of counter-revolutionary crimes may not be employed in the administration or work within the compound." To the very last possible moment, this law was unswervingly observed in the camps. All the "contras" were sent out to fell trees, work in the mines, and so on, and they died very quickly there. As a rule, in 1937-38 the camps were extermination camps.

However, it was the intention of those butchers who organized the camp system that this form of execution should also make a profit. The prisoners were supposed to work and, consequently, like those in the world outside, meet plan targets. This was the universal economic and political "law" in the Soviet Union. Ustvymlag was a timber-working enterprise, and very large. It contained 24 separate camps and numerous further outposts spread over several hundred kilometers of thick coniferous forest. It was supposed to supply the country with millions of cubic meters of timber and was larger than even the largest state logging enterprise. A great number of trained people were therefore required to work there: from doctors, economists and accountants to medical assistants, car mechanics, railroad engineers and many others.

As I tell elsewhere, the plan exerted an implacable pressure of its own which tolerated no excuses. Under its influence even the most zealous camp bosses who expressed the greatest hated for the "contras" were obliged to break the 1930 law and put political prisoners to work where their skills were needed. For there were no doctors, engineers or economists to be found among the "socially acceptable" inmates, i.e., the thieves, murderers, rapists and delinquents. Many prisoners were thus able to avoid heavy and killing labor and serve their time in warm workshops, design bureaus, offices or medical units. There was nothing amoral or reprehensible about this. Every prisoner who was driven out into the forest to work envied the "trusties" and dreamed of getting their kind of job. Solzhenitsyn himself became a "trusty" when he worked in the research institute he describes in the First Circle. Anyone with a training remotely of use to the camp was termed a "trusty." Ivan Denisovich, for instance, knew how to lay bricks and so was not sent out into the forest. In our camp there was a young postgraduate from Moscow University and even at that time his professors were not afraid to appeal in letters to the camp boss to take especial care of him: he was a brilliant mathematician and would be the glory of Soviet and world science. Our director put him onto clearing the stumps from the unmetalled forest roadways, and deliberately chose an area of pine forest. (How difficult it was to get those pine stumps up by hand!) Once when riding around the worksites on horseback, the director trotted up to this brilliant mathematician and asked: "Well, which roots are easier to find?" The bosses always like a joke, don't they? Within two months this potentially brilliant mathematician was dead. Who needs a Lobachevsky or a Gauss in a timber-felling camp?

Timber-felling work as it was then, was simply murderous: there were no chain-saws, no timber-haulage tractors and no mechanical loaders. With good reason people in the camps referred to such work as "slow" or "green execution." It was not the consumptive intellectuals who died fastest in the camps, because they had certain skills and knowledge to offer. No, it was the sturdy peasants who were accustomed to hard physical labor. They all fell victim to the "big ration." They actually did receive large portions of food. While ordinary prisoners would get 400 grams of bread and a bowl of hot water with some rye flour mixed in it, each morning the forest worker would receive a further 600 grams of bread, a bowl of the same slops, and another 200 grams in place of a second course each evening. That was for fulfilling his norm; for over-fulfilling it, there would be another "premium" of 200 grams. In all, the "big ration" therefore amounted to almost one and a half kilos of bread. It may have been raw and badly baked, but it was real bread. For peasants who had lived in semi-starvation for years this appeared an enormous quantity, even without any cooked food. A man could easily live on such a ration!

In fact it was impossible to survive if you were felling timber. Our wise old doctor, Alexander Stefanov, told me that the discrepancy between the energy expended in work and that provided by the "big ration" was so great that the healthiest forest worker was doomed to death by starvation within several months. Quite literally he would starve to death while eating one and a half kilos of bread a day. The only peasants to survive—and they made up the majority in the camp —were those who knew how to sharpen and set instruments, and those given familiar agricultural work to do, who could make up their diet with a filched potato, radish or any other kind of vegetable. It hardly needs adding that the theft of any piece of camp property, be it a bread ration or a vehicle spare part, was not considered shameful —it was regarded as quite natural, and aroused only admiration and envy. I thought so then, and I do so now. A master like the Gulag, the Main Administration for Camps, has no right to demand that its slaves respect its interests at the expense of their own. The "strangers" among us could not instantly cross this psychological threshold. If they survived at all it was to a great extent thanks to the existence of the "trusty" system.

Whether they wished to or not, the camp bosses were forced to hand over a part of their unlimited powers to the "trusties." For them the Plan, officially termed a "state law," was no less severe or terrifying than the articles of the Criminal Code for us. Not only the career but the very life of the camp administrators depended on the work of experienced timber assessors, planners, accountants and foremen, because the war had started and unsuccessful camp bosses were sent to the front. The "trusties" acquired very real powers. They could choose their assistants and appoint people to "soft" jobs and, quite naturally, they began with the educated and cultured people who had some skill or knowledge. It was not that they were indifferent to the Ivan Denisovich's who went out to fell timber or that they felt estranged from them. Simply, they could not help those who did not know how to do anything other than physical work. And even among the latter they sought and found people with the most unexpected skills: those who knew how to make shaft-bows and barrels were sent to the outpost where skis were produced; those who could weave baskets began to fashion basketwork armchairs, chairs and sofas for the bosses.

It is impossible to overestimate the activities of the camp medical staff. Camp folklore and tales told outside the camp are full of anecdotes about the medical assistants and "trusties" attached to the medical units. In reality the prisoner-doctors performed their professional and human duty despite the inhuman conditions under which they were constantly humiliated, threatened and dependent on the jailers and restricted by quotas for the numbers they could take off work. They did not have enough medicine or instruments and yet they treated the prisoners and operated on them, taking them off work and saving them by transferring them to a lighter work category. Anyone who was in the Gulag and survived has no moral right to think of camp doctors without a feeling of deep gratitude.

* * *

The "strangers" survived to a large extent because the trusties found them the kind of work where they could stay alive. I hope that those today who still remember the past (and we cannot forget it!) will remember this also.

KOSTYA SHULGA

Over the telephone an unfamiliar woman's voice hastily told me between stifled gasps that she was Kostya Shulga's sister and she had found my number in her brother's address book. Knowing how much he had respected me, she was ringing to say that Kostya had died in May, quite suddenly, of a heart attack. He had been in a terrible state. His wife had written a letter denouncing him to the Department for the "Struggle Against the Misappropriation of Socialist Property" in the internal affairs ministry. Kostya started smoking, he paced up and down all the time, and would not talk to anyone. On 18 May when she came to visit him, he was lying dead on the floor. The woman stopped speaking, began to cry and hung up.

So Kostya was dead! How very strange that even he could not survive. There was always something reassuring about his unbelievable steadiness, his optimistic outlook and the irrepressible conviction that it was always possible to adapt, get out of a tight spot, escape unpleasantnesses, do a deal, hold out, or start all over again... He was, it seems, only forty-six when he died and almost all his life he had survived like one of those old-fashioned children's toys that, no matter how much you try to knock it down, bounces upright again: however hard they hit him he always bounced back, there and then... Even physically there was something reminiscent of such a pleasant, old-fashioned toy—a round, kind face, large intelligent eyes, and a mouth that was almost always smiling.

When our transport of prisoners arrived at Ust-Surmog, the first camp in which I was held during my second term inside, Kostya gave me a little time to lay out my things and stretch out on the board beds before he approached. Then with a smile on his face, he introduced himself and explained that he was the ledger clerk at Supplies. While I had not yet settled in, he simply wanted to offer me some sugar, rough tobacco, bread and a tin of corned beef. I looked at him very carefully. There was not the slightest trace of charity or compassion on his crafty, good-natured face.

"You offer food and tobacco to every new prisoner, do you, Shulga?"

"Dear, oh dear—now why talk like that? We can be open here, we're not in a prison cell! No, I'm just helping out a future colleague. I was there when you were all checked in and I know that you're a norm-setter... "

"For the time being I'm on gang labor, like the rest."

"But you'll be a norm-setter again, mark my words!"

Kostya was an old hand, and knew what was what... Some time later I did indeed work as a norm-setter again. But I didn't accept his invitation to join the privileged company in which, along with the construction foreman and the senior works inspector, he ate his better rations. A norm-setter could not belong to such cliques without losing his independence. But I did work alongside Shulga and found it interesting to follow his progress. Usually people who held his extremely important job in the camps were insolent and had an ineradicable predatory taint about them. These traits were totally absent in his case. Kostya, like all those in charge of food distribution, did deals, fiddled and made sure he and his circle were very well fed. In this, he was no different from the rest. Yet he would never bully others, never take anything away from anyone else, and tried to help everyone. I cannot say he did this from a natural and selfless kindness, although he was undoubtedly a kind person. It was part of his philosophy in life to be good-natured, and was something he had acquired over many years as a waif on the streets, during the war and in the camps and prisons. A kindness was never forgotten, Kostya was convinced. Whenever he did someone a good turn, he knew that this created a potential helper against the time when he himself might fall in need. Shulga was a crafty, keen-witted and very resourceful fellow, who could turn his hands to anything practical.

Of course, as might be expected, Kostya came unstuck numerous times and spent periods in such terrible punitive outposts of our camp as "Bloody" Sim. Nowhere, however, was he ever out of his depth, and he would trim and fiddle and become once again a merry, smiling and privileged prisoner. It would be inaccurate to describe our relations as friendship. During my second term in the camps I was already a rather tired and alienated character, little suited to friendship with a cheerful fellow many years my junior. But Kostya, for his part, displayed something like a respectful tenderness towards me. There was nothing the slightest bit servile or otherwise ingratiating about his attitude: he trusted me and I trusted him. So I came to know most of the story of his life. Kostya was a victim, one of the millions of victims, of the most peculiar judicial system that has ever existed.

* * *

I shall never understand why such laws and courts were necessary! Our judicial system might well have been, like the 1936 Constitution itself, the best and the "most progressive" in the world. That would have been quite in the spirit of its founder. Stalin hardly ever wrote or said anything that contradicted the principles of justice, humanity and respect for the law... It was simply that he said one thing, and did quite another. If he declared at the plenary session of the Central Committee, "We shall not give you the blood of our beloved Bukharin, the darling of the Party and one of its leaders," then it was clear that Bukharin's fate was sealed. If Stalin declared, "the most valuable capital we possess are people," this meant that entire factories had already begun producing barbed wire for the camps. Once, his voice almost shaking with emotion, Stalin said that "children did not answer for their fathers" and straightaway issued instructions that not only the children but all the relatives of executed Party and state officials should be arrested without delay and despatched to the camps or sent into exile...

During Stalin's time the courts and the Criminal Code represented an insignificant part of the means of repression. "Extra-judicial procedures" were a legal and quite public institution. Everyone who was working at a secret plant or institute, everyone who signed a declaration committing them to silence, anyone who went abroad or committed what was, for the average Soviet person, a similarly such unnatural act would have to fill out a form acknowledging that he or she was aware they would "be dealt with under extra-judicial procedures" if he or she, wittingly or not, committed any infringement.

These "procedures" gave one or more individuals the right to sentence people in their absence and without a trial to any length of imprisonment (up to and including a 25-year term), to forced labor, exile for life, or to be shot... The term "sentence" sounds barely appropriate. It is hard for me to find a better word, yet what kind of sentencing actually took place?! Lists were simply drawn up and people were shot. Or people were shot, and then the lists were compiled. Or people were shot and no record was made or kept. High-ranking enthusiasts, like Stalin's secret police chief in Azerbaijan, Bagirov, would dispose of people in his own office. Incidentally, he was not the only one: other lesser figures also developed the same habit—they were pleased by its dramatic impact.

During this era executioners lost the evil reputation their profession has had throughout history. When educated people could publish and read the memoirs of Saint-Saume, the Paris executioner throughout the French Revolution, Pushkin considered this a sign of declining public morality. More than one hundred years after Pushkin's death, Sverdlov's son Andrei showed me the literary work he had created from the memoirs of Malkov, the head of security at the Kremlin. Several pages of these crude and not very truthful reminiscences were devoted to an extremely detailed account of the execution of Fanny Kaplan, Lenin's would-be assassin. Malkov described how he shot her himself, dragged her body into the Kremlin garden, doused it with kerosene and burnt it. I told the co-author of these memoirs that this boastful description of the execution of a woman was revolting and would undoubtedly be cut by the publishers.

Nothing of the kind. They left everything in, the book was reprinted three times and, I do not doubt, will continue to be reprinted. Mikhail Koltsov wrote, in one of his early sketches, that we had advanced immeasurably since the Civil War days when a semi-literate sailor, chairman of the local Cheka, could scribble on a piece of wrapping paper: "Shoot Merchant Kutepatkin, as a hydra of the international bourgeoisie, and with him the other twenty-nine inmates of his cell..." Now we shall never know whether Koltsov recalled this sketch during the weeks and months he spent in the hands of the NKVD before he himself was killed. To us, however, it is quite clear that the fate of merchant Kutepatkin and his cellmates was preferable to that of Koltsov, and those like him, who became the objects of the Stalinist "legal order."

These extra-legal forms of repression and revenge, of preemptive "isolation", "liquidation" and so on, and so forth, gave their exponents unlimited powers. Yet the tiny proportion of cases that came before the courts might, even so, have still been heard with all the trimmings: public and open hearings, prim judges in wigs, captious, fault-finding and begowned lawyers, a jury...

In fact, the published laws and the courts that applied them were as frankly and openly thuggish as the "extra-judicial procedures." To begin with, the laws themselves were not only unrestrainedly cruel but as infinitely adjustable and flexible as the "one-size" elastic socks they sell nowadays. They could be applied to any individual for any act, and the judge could give whatever sentence he wanted or however much he was told to impose by secret instructions and orders, or by a telephone call from one of the numerous bodies that could give orders to a judge.

There is a universal and popular Christmas story about the hungry boy who stole a loaf of bread or a bun. Let us imagine the same moving and dramatic plot unfolding on the charmingly snowy streets of Moscow, or any other Soviet town, in the winter of 1937-38. Soviet children, for the first time in years, have again been allowed to have a Christmas tree and the celebrations that go with it (though only at New Year). Our hungry boy, who has just turned fourteen, steals a three-kopeck bun (a French bun, they used to call them). If he has gained some skill in jurisprudence and acquired a clear idea of legal norms, he will hang around the shop until some fellow citizen buys a bun and then, and only then, will he steal it for himself. Caught red-handed at the scene of the crime, he will get a year in prison under the Edict on Petty Theft. If our young criminal, on the other hand, has not acquired any experience of the law and, driven by such an untypical motive in our society as simple hunger, he snatches the bun directly from the counter, this is already a different offense and it demands a different punishment. This act is qualified, under the 1932 law, as the "misappropriation of socialist state or cooperative property." No matter how the judge may pity the unwise lad, he cannot give him any less than three years imprisonment. Moreover, that is only when there are "extenuating" circumstances: usually he would receive a seven-year sentence for his bun. God forbid, moreover, that there be more than one boy involved! In that case, the offense is already "collective misappropriation" and the upper limit for such a theft can be more than ten years.

There was one young fellow at our camp who, after being demobilized, went to work at the Dagestan Lights glass factory near Makhachkala. There was no electricity in the dormitory, only kerosene lamps. He and a friend from the same room found two unbroken funnels for their lamps in a vast pile of shattered glass. They were caught when leaving the factory. Both received fifteen years. But they were grown-up, you say, and in our story it was a mere boy who stole the bun? Well, when I imagined my Soviet version of this Christmas tale I quite deliberately specified that he had turned fourteen. For from that age on, a child was subjected to the same sentences and punishments as an adult.

I am afraid I cannot maintain this dispassionate tone any longer when talking of the children who were swept into the camps and prisons. Of all forms of cruelty, the sheer inhumanity of cruelty to children is the most terrible and unnatural.

I was seventeen, and taking my first uncertain but determined steps as a journalist. *Komsomolskaya Pravda* commissioned me to write a piece about the Moscow children's prison and I spent several days behind the massive brick walls of the former Danilov monastery.[1] Then I wrote a sketch that borrowed the title of the prison wall-newspaper: "A Factory for Turning Out Well-trained Citizens." Everything in that sketch was true and, at the same time, it was a lie from beginning to end. The children were certainly not cold and hungry and they did have a wall-newspaper, clubs, film shows and almost clean sheets on their metal cots. Yet I wrote not a word of how they shuddered when the guards shouted, how the older children mistreated the younger, and of the prison hierarchy in which the smaller and weaker you were, the worse it was for you... I didn't mention that the little children became the hostages of their semi-criminal elders since the prison authorities could only keep control with the help of the latter. For the rest of my life I avoided writing about many things, but to this day I feel a particular responsibility for this piece of dishonesty. It is the most unforgivable of the many falsehoods I have written and uttered.

I don't know how much our children's prisons have changed since then. They have a different title today. I doubt that they have altered much. Still, these were prisons specially organized for children. From 1938 onwards I witnessed something else—children in ordinary prisons and camps. Of all the terrible sights, that was the worst.

The "juveniles," as they were called, varied greatly. Alongside the under-age urban prostitutes there were peasant girls arrested for gleaning a few ears of grain on a badly harvested collective-farm field; as well as the professional thieves, there were teenagers who had absconded from the special homes where the children of arrested government and Party officials were sent. The reasons why they found themselves in the camps and prisons were different, and they came from quite different backgrounds. Soon, however, they became alike. All displayed a frightening and incorrigibly vengeful cruelty, without restraint or responsibility. Even in an ordinary camp, where they were treated like the rest, the juveniles enjoyed certain unwritten privileges. The guards and the escort did not kill them. The juveniles were aware of this, but they would not have been afraid even if they had faced death.

They feared nothing and no one. The guards and camp bosses were scared to enter the separate barracks where the juveniles lived. It was there that the vilest, most cynical and cruel acts that took place in the camps occurred. If one of the prisoners' criminal leaders was gambling, lost everything and had staked his life as well, the boys would kill him for a day's bread ration or simply "for the fun of it." The girls boasted that they could satisfy an entire work team of tree-fellers... There was nothing human left in these children and it was impossible to imagine that they might return to the normal world and become ordinary human beings again.

In 1942 entire consignments of children began to enter the camps. Their story was brief, terrible and clear-cut. All had been sentenced to five years for infringing the war-time law "On Unauthorized Departure from Work at Military Enterprises." They were the same fourteen- to fifteen-year-old "Dear Boys" (as Lev Kassil called them in his book by that name) and teenage girls who took the places of their brothers and fathers after they had left for the front.

Many touching and emotional words have been written about these children who worked for ten hours on end, standing on boxes because they could not otherwise reach the lathe. All of this was quite true.

The only thing not mentioned was what happened when, through force of wartime circumstances, the enterprise had to be evacuated somewhere else. Of course, its "labor force" went with it. This was fine when mother and sister, or some other relative, also worked there: but if the mother was at the textile factory and her little girl was turning out shells? The new locations were usually cold, frightening and uncomfortable, and without much to eat. Many children and teenagers could not stand it and gave in to the natural instinct to run back to mother. They were arrested, put in prison, sentenced to five years and packed off to the camps.

After the shattering succession of arrest, search, prison, investigation, court and transfer to the camps, these boys and girls had little resistance left in them. Hunger and the horror of what had happened had deprived them of all defenses. They found themselves in hell and sought the protection of those who seemed strongest there. These, of course, were the male and female criminals in the camp.

The entire criminal class pounced on the "fresh" arrivals. The women would sell the girls to the drivers, work-distributors and the camp bosses, for a tin of meat, a day's bread ration or, most valued of all, a glass of vodka. Before the sale, the girl was prodded and probed like a chicken: virgins went for a higher price. The boys became the lackeys of the criminal bosses, the strongest and best-off. They were servants, mute slaves, jesters, hostages and everything else. A criminal, once he had acquired such a boy for a day's bread ration, could beat him, starve him to death, take away everything he wanted and vent all the misfortunes of his own unsuccessful life on him.

We "politicals" could do nothing about it. In the eyes of these children and teenagers we were trusties who had no power or authority and possessed none of the others' attractive contempt for the camp bosses and their laws. When the daily march to work was about to begin none of us could tell the camp director, in front of a thousand others, "Fuck you, your system and your work" and calmly walk off towards the punishment block...

* * *

One summer when I was already a "free" employee, living outside the compound, I visited Alexander Zotov, the doctor at one of the outposts of our camp. He had been released, sentenced again and returned once more to an outlying part of our camp.

Zotov was performing surgery, so the well-trained assistant brought me a patient's generous lunch in the medical unit shack. I was not hungry but it would have been stupid to send the meal back to the kitchen. Outside a very young fair-haired girl was sweeping the empty camp courtyard. There was a rural simplicity about the way she performed her undemanding task.

I called her over and asked what she was doing there. She had been stripping bark, she replied, and her finger became infected and swelled up. The doctor had lanced it and she had been off work for several days...

"Sit down and have something to eat," I told her.

She ate quietly and neatly and one could tell that she had been brought up in a family. It was this quiet domesticity and the cleanliness of her faded, much-washed dress of camp fustian that made her attractive. For some reason, I imagined that my Natasha must look much the same, although this girl was a pure blonde while my daughter already had a head of chestnut hair ten days after she was born.

The girl finished eating, and neatly piled the plates on the wooden tray. Then she lifted her dress, pulled off her pants and, holding them in her hand, turned her unsmiling face in my direction.

"Lying down or what?" she asked.

At first not understanding, and then scared by my response, she said in self-justification, again without a smile, "People don't feed me without it..."

She ran out. Of course, I must have been a frightening and unattractive sight if, thirty years and more later, I still begin to cry each time I remember that small girl with the frowning face and the tired submissive eyes.

* * *

Each new law was drawn up in such a way as to permit its much harsher enforcement.

There was a woman with us in Camp No. 1, who had been convicted of breaking the law against abortions. I remember her because her husband, an air-force officer adorned with numerous awards, was permitted by his superiors to come and visit her in the camp while the war was still going on. Her story was as follows. Her airman-husband had been rewarded for his feats of military valor with a week's leave at home. He returned to his unit and his wife found she was pregnant, which was evidently also in line with state policy. She did not comply, however, with the lofty intentions of the state. It was 1942, with no end in sight to the war, and she already had two children. So she persuaded her close friend, a nurse, to perform an abortion on her. The attempt was unsuccessful, and official medical authorities quickly established that the law had been broken. The tireless guardians of justice immediately went to work. A woman who had aborted her own child was not subject to criminal prosecution. Only two types of "criminal" were punished: those who performed abortions, and those who concealed the former... In short, the unfortunate woman was supposed to name her friend who, at risk to her own liberty, had agreed to such an illegal act. Probably, the stubborn unwillingness of my heroine to name the criminal infuriated the judge. He sent her to prison for five years for "concealment of an abortion." The commanding officers of her husband's unit deluged every legal authority with petitions. They sent her pilot husband to Moscow and to the camp, but all was in vain. The woman was only released under the 1945 amnesty.

The courts—any one of them!—had quite unlimited opportunities for their arbitrary behavior. Some of the subtleties of our legal system were so extraordinary that, had I not read the documents with my own eyes, I would never have believed such things were possible.

The famous 1954 post-Stalin amnesty did not extend to those sentenced for "particularly large-scale misappropriation of socialist property." Here large-scale meant anything from 50,000 rubles upwards. A middle-aged, unfamiliar zek came to me almost in tears and asked me to write an appeal for him: "So at least there's a chance they can understand." For some reason, I was considered to be adept at drafting these declarations and I wrote many such appeals.

He handed me the lengthy text of his sentence (unlike mine, it took up several pages!) and I immersed myself in the study of a case that astounded even me, although I thought I had seen everything by then...

He had returned from the war and become chairman of a collective farm. Evidently he was good at his job. In spring 1947 when the country was on the verge of starvation, he carried out the spring sowing, quickly and efficiently. He stored the seeds so carefully that not a single kilo went to waste. Even so, while storing the seeds provisions were made for a certain amount of waste. As a result, when the sowing was finished, the collective farm had eight centners of wheat left over. Since field work was still going on and the tractor drivers were fainting from hunger, the chairman persuaded the collective-farm's board of management to issue a decree permitting these eight centners to be distributed to the tractor drivers in accordance with the number of labor days they had worked. Among the various government decrees that were then considered the only way of running the economy, however, there was a very recent edict "On Raising Responsibility for Wasteful Use of Seed." Naturally, well-wishers did their bit, and the chairman was arrested. The fact that he had not taken this wheat for himself but distributed it according to the amount of work each had done was, of course, of no relevance. He had "misappropriated" and that was it. But how much had he stolen? The state paid the collective farm eight rubles per centner. Elementary multiplication gave a total of 64 rubles. This did not suit the court's purpose. It was possible to calculate the value of the wheat at the price at which flour was sold in the shops (if any was being sold, that is). This did not suit the high priests of our judicial system either. They came up with something more original. To begin with they calculated how much grain there might have been if these eight centners had been sown and given the maximum yield for the area. They then sold this hypothetical harvest on the black market at a hypothetically inflated price. The sum misappropriated now reached 53,000 rubles. It was this sum that was written down, as though it was not hypothetical but quite real, in the sentence which condemned my chairman to fifteen years imprisonment. Most resourceful! In this case, though, I really did prove to have a lucky touch and in response to my text Moscow extended the amnesty to the unfortunate chairman as well. They did not revoke his sentence, of course, but pardoned him after he had already served a third of his fifteen years.

* * *

"Extra-judicial procedures" and "judicial procedures" were inextricably bound up together; as our literary critics like to say, they "mutually enriched one another." It was up to the investigator on a case to decide which to use. For the prisoner it made little difference. Even when it was the court that handed down his sentence, in practice it was his investigator, his interrogator who decided. I learned this from my own experience.

When "extra-judicial procedures" were being applied the definition "socially harmful element" was often used, just as in Shkvarkin's comedy...[2] The "harmfulness" of an individual was determined by an anonymous figure in a well-known institution. Naturally, no one could ask how he had reached the conclusion that his charge was "socially harmful"... But it was only a seven-year sentence and one should be thankful that the offense was criminal, not political.

There were always analogues of the unpublished "extra-judicial procedures" in the public laws. Take, for instance, the famous Article 7:35 in the Soviet Criminal Code. This punished those "without fixed place of residence or specific employment" with a sentence of up to seven years. The sixteenth-century English law against vagrancy is considered to be of unparalleled cruelty in history but it was child's play compared to our own Article 7:35. For under it not only prostitutes, beggars, and homeless cripples but anyone could be sent to the camps. An individual might have a place of residence but the court resolved that it was not entirely "fixed," or he might be employed but his work also lacked certain necessary qualities... There is little need for me to explain about this particular law, however, because it survived Stalin's death. To this day it remains on the statute book[3] and all remember how, under the liberal Khrushchev, the poet Joseph Brodsky was arrested and exiled under the law against "parasites."

In either of these two systems, one law could replace another depending on the requirements of the moment. Occasionally this worked to the benefit of the prisoner. The story of Friedrich Platten springs to mind. It is not to be found in any book or encyclopedia written by our historians. It was Fritz Platten, as leader of the Left Social Democrats in Switzerland, who organized the return of Lenin and other Bolsheviks across Germany to Russia in 1917 in the famous "sealed train car." He is also famous for an incident in January 1918 when the car in which he, Lenin's sister Maria and Lenin himself were travelling was attacked by bandits. Platten threw himself in front of the Soviet leader to protect him and was wounded. Afterwards Lenin was extremely indignant that neither the chauffeur nor any of the passengers carried a weapon. In gratitude, Krupskaya gave Platten a small Browning with "To the savior of our Ilych" engraved on the handle. This gun, as per Chekhov, did indeed fire in the last act...

The last act, naturally, came in 1937. Because Platten worked for the Comintern and his native tongue was German, his young, inexperienced interrogator tried to make him confess that he had been working for the German intelligence service the whole time. Platten was then almost sixty and could not resist the enthusiasm with which this young healthy lad, with iron fists and no conscience, went about his job. With tears in his eyes, however, he pleaded with his tormentor to accuse him of spying for any foreign country—for the English, French, Brazilian or Papal intelligence services—but not the Germans. If he were to sign such a "confession" that would confirm the accusation of Alexinsky and others that Lenin's return to Russia was organized by the German General Staff. Even the brutal and ignorant young thug in charge of Platten's "case" was disturbed by the stubborn pleas of the old man. He stopped beating him and sent him back to the cell so as to inform his superiors about his strange prisoner. For a long time Platten waited without further interrogation while his fate was decided. Of course, Vyshinsky was probably tempted to obtain documentary confirmation of allegations he himself had made in 1917 and as late as the beginning of 1918, when he was editing a right-wing Menshevik newspaper. He was forced to desist, though.

It was at this moment that the gun fired. While searching Platten's apartment they found Krupskaya's treasured present. He was sentenced to eight years for "unlawful possession of a firearm," and sent to the camps where he died of dystrophy during the first years of the war.

* * *

The first article in the many volumes of the Tsarist Legal Code, if I remember rightly, reads: "No one may plead ignorance of the law." This is quite natural. Once gripped in the suffocating, stifling coils of our judicial system, anyone could perfectly understand this. The vast majority of Soviet citizens, though, had no idea of the legal risks that they ran every minute. And even when they did know, they found it impossible to believe.

Like the hundreds of thousands who were sent into exile "for life," my wife Rika signed a document stating that if she left the village to which she had been assigned without permission, this would be considered an attempt to escape and be punished under "extra-judicial procedures" by twenty-five years hard labor. This was not an ordinary camp sentence. The prisoners were identified by the numbers sewn on their clothes not their surnames, and performed murderously heavy labor twelve hours a day. The exiles calmly signed the agreement. Not only had they no intention of trying to escape: they simply could not conceive of such an improbably horrific fate as a further twenty-five-year sentence.

In the winter of 1951, however, I met a teenager, still hardly more than a boy, at the Georgievsk transit prison who wore a number on his hat, his back, the sleeves of his coat, and on the knees of his padded trousers. His story was as follows. In 1941 his father had gone into hiding rather than fight, and spent the entire war in Siberia or even the Far East. One of the unpublished laws of the time condemned the family of a deserter to arrest and exile. His wife and under-age son were picked up and sent from Cherkessk to somewhere in Kazakhstan where they could barely make ends meet. In 1945 an amnesty was announced for all deserters. The father returned to his native town, reported to the authorities, received an official pardon and his identity documents. Naturally, he was penniless but relieved and, probably, already used to the irresponsible life of a man on the run. Whatever the explanation, he was in no hurry to bring his family back. This went on for several years until his wife died, still in exile. Moved, he wrote to his son, inviting him to return to Cherkessk. The boy could not wait and—what happened next is Grand Guignol. Neither father nor son had much experience with the law. No one, it turned out, had yet revoked the boy's sentence of exile "for life." The security officer in Kazakhstan, to whom the boy and other exiles had to report regularly, issued an alert that he had escaped. He was arrested in Cherkessk and under "extra-judicial procedures" given 25 years hard labor. The stunned boy was on his way to begin his sentence when we met, in the territory's transit prison.

Yet why expect that boy to know such things when educated and informed people had no more idea of what went on in our Soviet judicial system than he did. In Autumn 1971 in Yalta I got into a fierce and bad-tempered argument with Vadim Sobko. We were discussing the Crimean Tatars, and Sobko, who was considered a liberal among Ukrainian writers, asserted that all the other nationalities had been illegally deported during the war, but not the Tatars. They really had been allies and accomplices of the Germans and deserved their punishment. When I retorted that women and children were not accomplices of the enemy, Sobko offered an unshakeable argument: all the other unfortunate nations, the Kalmyks, Chechens and so on, had returned to their native lands but the Tatars had been neither amnestied nor rehabilitated.

Shortly afterwards I was browsing through the latest volume of the *Literary Encyclopedia* when I came across an article about the literature of the Crimean Tatars. There I read the following paragraph: "In May 1944 the Tatars living in the Crimea were, as the result of infringements of socialist legality, deported to Central Asia, the Volga region and the Urals. On 5 September 1967 the baseless accusations against the entire Tatar nation were revoked by a decree of the Presidium of the USSR Supreme Soviet." It was understandable that I had not read the work they gave in reference (pages 531-32 of the *Bulletin of the USSR Supreme Soviet*, No. 36, 1967). Yet how could Sobko, who was a public figure at home and often travelled abroad, not be aware that the Crimean Tatars had been pardoned and amnestied for the last four years? They had not been allowed to return home but that was a question not of laws but of practical problems and local politics.

Once I asked my brother, an authoritative professor of history who taught about the Soviet period, whether he knew that during Stalin's time work in the villages had officially been forced labor. He stalled, of course "there were elements"... but "officially"?! Did the professor know, I asked, about the edict issued by the Presidium of the Supreme Soviet sometime (I do not recall the exact date) in June 1947? No, he had never heard anything about it.

Well, I had. Moreover, when I was working in the Stavropol territory as an assistant in the educational department I attended meetings at the collective farms where the edict was read out to the peasants. It had not been published in the newspapers but the collective-farm workers were conscientiously informed of its contents. It was certainly of direct interest to them. It made work on the collective farm obligatory for all those who lived in rural areas and were not engaged in other non-agricultural work or employed as white-collar workers in Soviet institutions. Every man, woman, youth and girl was obliged to work on the collective farm. The necessary quantity of work days was also established. For the Stavropol Territory, it seems, the minimum was 176 work days. Each individual who refused to work on the collective farm and failed to achieve the minimum annual requirement of work days was to be deported for five years, with all those members of the family too young or old to work, to "distant regions of the USSR" where he or she would be obliged to work as exiles. The decision was to be taken, moreover, not by the court or by some troika, but simply by the local village Soviet! I met a great many such exiles in the transit camps and in the taiga around Verkhnyaya Kama. Those living in the countryside have very little protection from the law, but I'm not writing about that here. It is the degree of universal ignorance about our ingenious judicial system that I wish to reveal. What could one expect from those living in the cities if a professor, teaching about the history of Soviet society, had no idea there had been such an edict!

* * *

There were two paragraphs in the Criminal Code, however, that were in some sense the greatest achievement of our legal theory and an undoubted embellishment of Soviet judicial procedures.

Paragraph No. 17 of the Criminal Code was the product of Vyshinsky's legal genius and showed how far we had advanced since that naive time when twenty-nine men were shot solely because they shared a cell with the "hydra of the world bourgeoisie," the merchant Kutepatkin. In essence, exactly the same thing continued to happen but now it was veiled in the extravagant terminology adorning the highly sophisticated theory of "complicity." That was the name of a thick volume produced by Vyshinsky. He received an honorary doctorate and other awards, and was made a member of the Academy of Sciences for his "doctrine of complicity." I have never read the book but cannot help being amazed that it was possible to write an entire volume when, in his time, the chairman of the district Cheka had set it down so much more concisely on that scrap of wrapping paper.

In the most general terms, paragraph 17 said that each member of a criminal group (and membership in that group was expressed by knowledge of its existence and failure to report it) was responsible not only for his own individual criminal deeds but also for the deeds of the criminal group as a whole and for each of its individual members, taken separately. It did not matter that the individual in question might not know the other members of the group, might be unaware what they were up to, and might not have any idea at all what the group he belonged to was doing. The purpose of the "doctrine of complicity" was to alleviate the exhausting labors of the interrogators. Undoubtedly, however, it also lightened the burden of those under investigation. The techniques of cross-examination became far simpler. Several dozen people were linked together in a group and then one of them, the weakest, was beaten almost to death in order to obtain confessions of espionage, sabotage, subversion and, of course, attempts on the life of "one of the leaders of the Party and the government." The others could be more gently treated, only requiring beating until they admitted they knew the individual who had given a "complete and full confession." Then the same crimes, in accordance with paragraph 17, were automatically attributed to them as well. What this sounded like during a court hearing I can describe from the words of a man I came to know in the camps.

Yefim Shatalov was a very high-ranking manager and for years he headed the State Cement Administration. Why they needed to send him to prison, God only knows! He had no political interests or involvements and did not wish to have any, since he was always prepared to serve his immediate superior faithfully and truthfully, and was unquestionably loyal to his ultimate chief, Comrade Stalin. Furthermore, he was incredibly circumspect and every step he took was protected by an entire system of safety measures. When he was baldly accused of sabotage he conducted himself so aggressively in court that the judge, in panic, deferred the hearing of his case. Some time after, Shatalov was presented with a new charge sheet and within an hour he was summoned to appear before a new sitting of the Military Tribunal. The chairman now was Ulrich himself. For the defendant Vasya Ulrich was an old, dear and kind acquaintance. For many years they had always sat at the same table at the Party elite's sanatorium, The Pines; they went for walks together, shared a drink or two, and exchanged men's jokes. Evidently the chairman was observing the old principles that justice must be rapid, fair and clement in his conduct of this hearing. What follows includes almost everything that was said, as recalled by Yefim Shatalov.

Ulrich (in a business-like, quiet and jaded voice): Defendant! you have read the charge sheet? Do you recognize your guilt?

Shatalov (with all the force of his love and loyalty to the judge): No! I am not guilty in any respect!

Ulrich: Did you know that there was a counter-revolutionary Right-Trotskyist organization in the People's Commissariat of Heavy Industry?

Shatalov (throwing up his arms): I had no idea whatsoever. I had no suspicion there was such a hostile gang of saboteurs and terrorists there.

Ulrich (gazing with affectionate attention at his former drinking companion): You were not in prison during the last trial of the Right-Trotskyist center, were you?

Shatalov: No, I was not.

Ulrich: You were reading the newspapers then?

Shatalov (slowly, trying to grasp the purpose of such a strange question): I did...

Ulrich: So you read Pyatakov's testimony that there was a counter-revolutionary organization in the People's Commissariat of Heavy Industry?

Shatalov (uncertainly): Of course, of course.

Ulrich (triumphantly): Well, there we are! So you knew there was a counter-revolutionary organization in the People's Commissariat of Heavy Industry. (Turning to the secretary of the court.) Write down: the defendant acknowledges that he knew about the existence of Pyatakov's organization...

Shatalov (shouts passionately, stuttering from horror): But it was from the newspapers, the newspapers, that I learnt there was an organization there!

Ulrich (calm and satisfied): But to the court it is not important where you found out. You knew! (Hurriedly, like a priest at a poorly-paid funeral.) Any questions? No. You want to say a last word? No need for repetition, we've heard it already! (Nodding right and left at his assessors.) I pronounce sentence. Mmmh... 15 years...

I shall not insist that this trial strictly met the requirement for fairness. Yet compared to others it was clement, leaving Shatalov among the living. And it was indisputably rapid. Evidently the speed was typical. In the late 1950s I attended a memorial evening at the Museum of the Revolution for Kosarev, the 1930s Komsomol leader executed by Stalin. The head of the Central Committee administrative department told me that Khrushchev had entrusted him to re-examine Kosarev's case: "The hearing began at 11.00 a.m.," read the record of the trial, "and ended at 11.10 a.m."

* * *

Everything I have described above refers to paragraph 17. It was the second paragraph, no. 16, that led Kostya Shulga to become sucked into our judicial system. This paragraph enabled a judge to pass sentence "on analogy." If it seemed to him that the crime he was examining did not fall under any article in the Criminal Code he was allowed to try it under another article, quoting paragraph 16 in justification.

The story of Kostya's life and crime now becomes comprehensible. He lived in Krasnodar in south Russia and when the war began his family was rapidly scattered. Kostya was left alone there, but he did not mind—he was a strong and resourceful boy. As far as I recall, he led a rather free and reprehensible way of life. In particular, he was not above wringing the necks of other people's chickens and boiling them in an old bucket. One of these birds led to his downfall. Perhaps it was a very important chicken or perhaps the judge was feeling irritated. Whatever the cause, the judge did not wish to apply the Edict on Petty Theft to Kostya, which would have earned him only the maximum of a year in prison. Using paragraph 16, the judge invoked the article covering horse-theft, that is, he equated the chicken with a horse, Kostya received five years and was sent to the local camp. There an elderly and experienced criminal persuaded Kostya to escape with him. They succeeded, but in doing so Kostya's companion killed a guard. When the fugitives were quickly caught, the older man was shot and Kostya, as an under-age accomplice, was sentenced to ten years under Article 59:3 (armed robbery).

The camp where Kostya began to serve his new sentence was not far from Stalingrad. It was summer 1942. The front was advancing so rapidly towards the camp that the bosses could not consider evacuating the prisoners. They quietly slipped away themselves and the more energetic prisoners also left. Kostya was among them, although he did not flee so much as calmly walk away. He got as far as Stalingrad, which by then was already very near the front. He reported to the military commissariat, gave his real name, adding eighteen months to his age, and asked to be sent to the front. He had lost his passport and other documents, he said. They had no time to check up on Kostya and they saw no reason: before them stood a tall, fit lad who might be much older than eighteen.

Kostya left for the front. He served in the infantry and the artillery, was slightly wounded and sent to the hospital, then fought for the rest of the war on an armored train. He reached company sergeant and I can well imagine how popular he must have been with everyone. He received his awards and medals, one by one, and became so well loved that in 1944 in East Prussia his superiors suggested that Kostya join the Party. There was nowhere he could turn. Apart, that is, from SMERSH, army counter-intelligence. He offered his repentance and the story of his life before he arrived at the front. They confiscated his weapons and belt and arrested him. He remained under arrest while his superiors checked his words and decided his fate. After some time he was summoned to appear. His belt, his weapons and his awards were returned, and he was told that it was premature for him to become a member of the Party but he could fight, since he had shed his blood and proven himself, etc., etc.

Kostya Shulga was arrested on 9 May 1945, two hours after the war had finished. They did not even leave him time to celebrate. Nor did they send him to court. He was simply sent back to the camps to complete the sentence he had received in 1942. But first, of course, they relieved him of all his awards and medals. For years Kostya waged a long dispute with the judicial system over the way he had been treated and I, as an adept writer of appeals, actively helped him. Since the years he fought at the front were not spent in captivity, the legal authorities ruled that they could not be counted as part of his sentence. Kostya could not accept such injustice and sent appeal after appeal to all the middle-ranking and highest legal institutions, insisting that his war years be knocked off his sentence. I hardly need add that all was decided in accordance with Emperor Ferdinand I's maxim: "... let justice be done!" It was, and Kostya was only freed in 1954...

A year before his release Kostya began to spend days on end in the dentist's office at the medical unit.

"I survived in the camps, and I'm going to survive out there," he told me, calmly and confidently. "I'll learn to be a dental technician and get married. I'll build myself a house and live like a normal human being! Do they think I'm going to work for a measly 700 rubles a month? I can think for myself and know how to use my hands. I'll always be able to earn my keep. The most important thing in this life is to be adaptable. I'm good at that, I'll adjust..."

* * *

What Kostya called the most important thing was the main problem facing any prisoner. And, for that matter, anyone who was not yet in prison. How could they adapt, with the least harm to their health, dignity and risk to life itself? Sometimes the decision had to be made in a moment; sometimes long, sleepless nights were needed: in either case, a decision had to be made.

With disgust Rika told me about a woman who was in her cell at the NKVD prison in Stavropol. The woman categorically objected to the "poor committees" and other forms of prison self-help by which the better-off aided those without food parcels and so on. She thought that in a Soviet prison everyone should sincerely fulfill every rule without exception. Prisoners should do everything that their interrogators demanded of them: they should sign any testimony against any individual since all was being done in the interests of the Soviet state and, consequently, served higher goals than the fate of a single individual. Was it fear that drove her to behave in such a way? Ordinary fear, justified by torture and the threat of death? I also knew this woman a little, however, and had heard still more about her from others. Sokolovskaya was a fearless, well-educated, properly brought-up woman, famous for having headed the Foreign Collegium in Odessa during the Civil War intervention by foreign forces. In his famous play[4] Slavin called her Orlovskaya and made his heroine the most beautiful and charming creature. Her husband Yakovlev, who was a favorite of Stalin's, first served as a secretary of the Central Committee and then headed the Committee's Agricultural Department. She was a far more gifted and intelligent person than he.

Whatever induced someone like her to participate in such a false and immoral show? The same offer was made to every prisoner, after all, openly and without any shame: participate in this charade, but we shall not guarantee any reward.

* * *

If only there had been such a guarantee! If only it had been possible to reach an agreement with these people. It would have been an agreement between hostages and their kidnappers, but what of it? Then, at least, a certain predictability would have entered our lives. Perhaps not legal norms but at least some some agreed rules of play!

But the fact that no rules existed was the whole point. There were no guarantees that any sacrifice, any compromise with truth, conscience and those other (in our jailers' eyes) quite ephemeral considerations, would be recompensed. The jailers, for their part, had no need of theoretical justification. Still, there was an authoritative formula, "Only that which helps the cause is moral..." Which cause, and whom to help was up to them to define.

Who actually decided was also quite important. There were, of course, authorities who were termed "directive," i.e., the Central Committee, and could give orders to the NKVD men. History long ago revealed, however, that torturers are always very unwilling to part with their victims—even when told to do so on the highest authority. Therefore, orders from the latter or the next rank in descent also provided no guarantees. The story of my camp acquaintance, Pavel Zdrodovsky, is an example.

He was a renowned member of the Academy of Sciences, and had received every prize and award, including Hero of Socialist Labor. We finally met in the camps although we had known about each other before our arrests. Shura Vishnevsky, who today also possesses every award and order of merit, was a common acquaintance.

It was autumn 1941. The next transport had arrived at Camp No. 1 and our doctor Alexander Stefanov went to examine them. Panting, he came up to me and said, "Professor Zdrodovsky, the famous epidemiologist, has arrived in the transport. I've got him in the medical barracks. Come quickly..."

I ran. Could it really be the man Shura had told me about? Yes, it was. His form was appalling to read. Struck through by a large cross, which meant "inclined to escape," it also forbade him to be allowed anywhere without an escorting guard. There was an almost fatal note there, moreover: "Must only be used on escorted gang labor."

The year was 1941, however, not 1938. Such an ominous comment now might be of only artistic interest. In any case, at our camp there was no power that could make the doctor force a medical professor to go out to work in the forest with the rest. Zdrodovsky was immediately listed as sick and placed in the medical barrack. He would be able to remain there for an indefinitely prolonged period. He had enough free time each evening when I left the office to unhurriedly tell me his vivid and instructive story.

By 1937 Zdrodovsky had become the leading epidemiologist in the Soviet Union and was renowned throughout the world as a major expert on the treatment of infections, especially brucellosis. Dozens of veterinary stations throughout the country treated animals according to his methods. It was therefore not surprising that he was put in charge of the special commission in 1937 when a mass epidemic broke out among horses in the Ukraine. After several months work he gave a report on the necessary measures to be taken to a session of the Central Committee or of the Council of People's Commissars, I don't remember which now. In any case, Khrushchev, who had only just been promoted to the first rank, was chairing the discussion.

Zdrodovsky reported, with scholarly dispassion, that the epidemic was caused by a virus. From time to time it spread in a wave across Europe and Asia. The present outbreak had come from the East. In order to combat it, the following measures... Khrushchev impatiently interrupted the professor's report, "What are you going on about epidemics for, Professor?! The horses ague is the result of sabotage. They were poisoned with powders! The powders are there, lying in front of me... Those responsible have confessed their crimes and suffered their just punishment. And here you are going on about some epidemic or other!"

Zdrodovsky reached out, picked up the fatal powder, poured some onto his tongue and swallowed it. Then he explained to Khrushchev, just as calmly, that he was not in the least concerned about sabotage or the confessions of the saboteurs and so on; that was a matter for the law. As far as horses and powders went, it was impossible to poison anyone with this powder since it was mainly composed of baking soda. His task was to report on how the epidemic could most rapidly be halted. That was what he was doing now.

He was arrested quite soon after. They did not spend much time on him (they were too busy!) and the Special Board simply gave him ten years. But then they sent him to an extremely dangerous camp from which almost no one would return alive. It was part of the Ukhtpechlag system and was responsible for building the road between Chibiu and Krutaya. The work was no more than a drawn-out form of murder. The prisoners had to tip barrow after barrow of sand into bottomless bogs. The ones who pushed the barrows changed constantly, and no one lasted more than two months. Zdrodovsky had already survived many others but he had no illusions: he knew he could not hold out much longer.

Then occurred the unexpected and fateful event that may descend on a prisoner at any moment, saving or dooming him. Zdrodovsky was taken away from his barrow, fed, washed, given a haircut and an unheard-of brand-new prison uniform, and driven off to the central Ukhtpechlag administration. There he was most respectfully and carefully escorted by his special guards to the airport and put on a plane sent for the occasion. The prisoner Zdrodovsky set off in an unknown direction, as in a fairytale, making numerous transfers at other airports to other planes. Only later, after a great deal of time had passed, did Zdrodovsky learn exactly what had happened and why he had been saved in this unusual way.

A brucellosis epidemic of unprecedented severity had broken out in Kazakhstan, and was affecting the cattle and, most important, the sheep and goats there. Millions of animals were dying and the disaster had become so serious that it was discussed in the Politburo. During the discussion there occurred a scene that might have come from one of numerous films. Stalin was walking up and down beside the table and then he took the pipe from his mouth and said, "What are the Zdrodovsky stations doing in such exceptional cases?" (His memory was quite extraordinary, and could store an unbelievable quantity of the most varied information.) "And what, incidentally, is Zdrodovsky himself doing to stop this epidemic? Where is he, in Moscow?"

One glance at the face of the man whose job it was to know where someone was immediately told Stalin the answer, "If he's still alive, find him and send him there!"

They managed to locate Zdrodovsky in the Russian Far North and sent him south to Kazakhstan. There this notable prisoner, personally sent by Stalin, was met as a plenipotentiary. He was allocated a mansion filled with servants who doubled as his bodyguards and jailers. Direct telephone lines linked Zdrodovsky to the Central Committee and Council of People's Commissars in Kazakhstan, and with the various ministries and regions. He had airplanes, cars and hundreds of subordinates at his disposal. Each order of the invisible dictator had the force of law, and his praise created an aura around Zdrodovsky that made visiting high-placed officials talk to him reverently and smile obsequiously.

Zdrodovsky managed to achieve an almost exceptional feat. In a few months, and with a speed unheard of in medical history, he was able to halt and eliminate the brucellosis epidemic in Kazakhstan. The danger that it might spread to the European part of the country was removed. The leaders of Kazakhstan almost shed tears of relief and thankfulness. They would send Zdrodovsky to Moscow to receive his well-deserved award. The entire government accompanied him to the station and saw him into his *de luxe* compartment in the international carriage. He travelled back to his native Moscow, alone, a free man, just as in former times. At the station the Kazakhstan People's Commissar for Internal Affairs had taken him aside and said, "Pavel Felixovich! Take this sealed envelope. I advise you to go straight to the Commissariat, deliver it and get the necessary certificate there. You are still formally under arrest and the janitor won't allow you into your apartment. He'll go straight to the police and report you... First you'll get the certificate and then, later on, all the necessary documents. Let me congratulate you now on the awards you are about to receive, please do not forget us here..."

With what relish Zdrodovsky described the long train journey from

Alma-Ata to Moscow! The comfort of the international-class carriage; the starched linen napkins in the restaurant where you could sit at an elaborately set table, sip an expensive brandy, and watch the landscape slip past the gleaming windows... Alerted by a telegram, he was met at the station in Moscow by his friends, relatives and students. There were flowers, hugs and tears. On the way home in the car Zdrodovsky suddenly remembered, "Let's stop for a minute at Lubyanka Square. I'll pop into the Commissariat, hand in this envelope and collect a certificate. It will only take a few minutes. You can wait for me in the car..."

With the new and confident gait of a free man, Zdrodovsky strode into the entrance and handed over the letter to the polite duty officer. He waited and then a captain came out and asked if he would accompany him. They walked along endless corridors and passages on different storeys until in the confused geography of that labyrinth he began to recognize where they were... His companion stopped by a painfully familiar door and with a polite gesture asked Zdrodovsky to go first. The sign read "Reception for detainees." There followed the all-too-familiar procedure: "...undress, take off your underwear, arms up, legs apart, bend down, open your back passage..." Metal buckles and buttons were cut off, and laces removed. An hour later the newly-processed detainee was already in solitary confinement in the Inner Prison, impatiently waiting to be summoned. He waited for a day, a week, a month, half a year... No one summoned him, no one disturbed him, and only the mysterious muffled night sounds made him uneasy. After eight months he was called out "with your things," shoved into a Black Maria and taken to Lefortovo. That same day he appeared before the Military Tribunal and within ten minutes the ten years had been slapped on him. Only this time (honor of honors!) it was for an ordinary criminal offense. The article of the Criminal Code and the additional phrase "wartime" enabled Zdrodovsky to guess that while he had been in his cell, war had broken out.

Some time later he turned up in a transport at Ustvymlag, at Camp No. 1. Alexander Stefanov kept him in the small hospital there for a long time. The camp administration agreed, very unwillingly, that the professor could be sent to work as a medical assistant in the most remote camp outpost. Zdrodovsky did not have long there. In autumn 1942 it started all over again, and once more they came from the Administration, shaved and dressed him, and put him on a plane. As he was leaving, Zdrodovsky sighed and said it would be more difficult to cope with military typhus than brucellosis.

For a very long time I knew nothing more of him. In Moscow at the end of 1945 they told me that Zdrodovsky was a free man and the head of an institute. And in the 1960s I saw him speaking on television: he had just been awarded the Lenin Prize. He was old but still very hale and evidently most pleased with himself. He could not say enough to express his joy and thankfulness. He was so successful and well-off that I had no desire to meet him. In his present majestic triumph, he would experience, or so it seemed to me, a certain discomfort at being forced to recall the past. For my part, I couldn't stand the company of those who didn't want to remember and wanted to forget it had ever happened. Perhaps, I was wrong and Zdrodovsky was not one of those who tried to forget. I was told that at the very height of his success as chief designer of the rocket program Korolyov liked to gather his former prison comrades from the Tupolev *sharashka* (or prison institute) at his vast dacha and, seated at the most lavishly provisioned table, recall the past, "I would walk past the guards and they sprang to attention and looked respectful... But even so I used to think each night that they might burst into my bedroom and yell: 'Come with us, trash!'"

Perhaps Academician Zdrodovsky could also never again feel certain that there were any guarantees? I did not try to find out.

One way or another, he, too, had to participate in this game without any guarantees or rules.

* * *

A great many, if not the majority, of prisoners consented, in one way or another, to take part in this game. I'm not referring here, of course, to those whose consent was forced out of them by tortures exceeding the threshold of human resistance. These others agreed to participate. But their motives for doing so were very different.

One of the closest assistants of the aircraft designer Tupolev was in cell 29 with us. Timofei Saprykin was a middle-aged, embittered and gloomy man. Unsociable, he hardly said a word to any of his cellmates. Once during the night they brought him back from interrogation when everyone was already asleep and only I, weary with insomnia and yearning, was up, sitting on the bed boards and smoking. Saprykin wore the face of a thoroughly shocked man. Yet he was unharmed and did not display any other traces of investigative zeal. Evidently the need to share what had happened with someone else was so overpoweringly strong that Saprykin's inherent taciturnity deserted him. He was even glad to find such an unfamiliar companion as me.

I gave him an interrogative look. He drew on his cigarette, let out a cloud of smoke and sighed, "I've just been at a face-to-face..."

"?..."

"With Tupolev..."

"And?"

"It's enough to drive a man crazy! They bring me in and there is

Andrei Nikolayevich Tupolev sitting at the investigator's table. He's calm, looks well and unharmed. The interrogator, of course, is a vicious bastard. Are you acquainted, do you have personal vendettas, and other nonsense. The usual performance. Then he asks: 'Do you acknowledge the testimony of prisoner Tupolev that he recruited you for his counter-revolutionary sabotage and espionage organization?' 'Lies! This can't be true! Andrei Nikolayevich, how could you?!' Tupolev, calmly, as though we were at a planning session in the Aviation Institute, says to me: 'Do you trust me?' 'I've always trusted you in every way, Andrei Nikolayevich,' I reply. 'Well, then. You will now sign testimony that on a certain date I called you into my office and proposed that you join the sabotage and espionage organization that I was leading...' 'Whatever are you saying, Andrei Nikolayevich?!' 'You always used to obey me, am I right?' 'I most certainly did!' 'Obey me now. Do what I say! Acknowledge all the testimony which I have given and which I am now confirming in your presence. Sign all the testimony that the investigator will now dictate to you. Consider that I am still your superior and do everything that I command!'"

Saprykin smoked one cigarette after another. He grunted to himself, and waved his hands. Observing prison etiquette, I didn't ask whether he had carried out the orders of his former boss. Of course, he had. Some time later they took him out of our cell and during the war I came across his name in a list of those given awards for their work on designing and building airplanes. Saprykin received the highest reward of all, the Order of Lenin.

Rika was also being held at the very same time in the Lubyanka, and became friendly with one of her cellmates, Yulia Tupoleva. Once Tupolev's wife came back from interrogation, uncharacteristically quiet and distressed. She was very disturbed, she explained to Rika, by the unusual politeness of the interrogator and his praise for her husband. "I have the feeling that Andrei has agreed to something unworthy...," she admitted to Rika.

But can one be so categorical, and call this behavior "unworthy"? By agreeing to play his role in the proposed performance, Tupolev not only saved his life and that of his wife but also the lives of Nekrasov, Petlyakov and Korolyov. And can we accuse Tupolev today of behaving immorally when he agreed to participate in such a "show" to save his life? Vast numbers of irreproachably well-brought-up, educated people, on the whole quite decent individuals, have been taking part in such performances their whole life; and in their case, a refusal would risk only their career and high pay, their trips abroad and other valuable things. That cannot remotely be compared to the life and death choice others faced before them.

* * *

But this is the story of Kostya Shulga, not Andrei Tupolev. If things had been as simple for Kostya as they proved for Tupolev, then he would have lived just as well at liberty as in the camps and not burdened his conscience with excessive worries. But no one offered Kostya a part in such a well-paid performance. That was just the trouble. Only those who were needed were rewarded. Sokolovskaya participated with total self-sacrificing sincerity and her performance ended with a bullet in the back of the head. She was not needed— she didn't know how to build aircraft. For Kostya there would never be any clear signposts or hard and fixed rules to follow in that strange existence he had led since being a teenager, in the camps and during the war, back in the camps and once again as a free man...

At first, this suited Kostya. It seemed to him that he could outplay the bank in this game without rules, and that he was fitter and craftier than his opponents. With what passion Kostya began his new life as a free man! Strangely, he never lost contact with me in all his ups and downs. Once released, he went back to Krasnodar and I received letters from him in the camp and even a food parcel. He was not permitted to stay in Krasnodar, however, with his record as a hardened criminal who had served time for a vicious murder. So he left for Solikamsk in the Urals and soon was known as one of the best dental technicians there. He found a job at a polyclinic and equipped a small workshop in his apartment which brought him a very good income. He had chosen well. No one released from the camps of Usollag or Naryblag could avoid spending some time in Solikamsk. Almost all of them had lost most of their teeth and they desperately wanted to return home with at least a set of steel false teeth.

Those who visited Solikamsk reported that Kostya was leading a very comfortable existence. A recently-released and pretty female convict shared his life, he was smartly dressed and generous and hospitable towards others. Later Kostya would assure me that he had broken no laws, and had not used gold in his work: he only lacked a license to practice and was operating on someone else's since he had no diploma himself. Kostya was officially the other man's assistant. Nevertheless, the end result was that Kostya was arrested, convicted of some offense and given two years imprisonment. He served half the sentence in a camp near the town, was released early for good conduct, and took off for the inhospitable North.

The subsequent stages in Kostya's life were always marked by his unexpected visits to me in Moscow. First he lived for several years in Krasnodar. No longer confident that he could outwit his fate, he decided from now on to play by the rules. He settled down, quite offi-

cially, just outside the city and started studying to be a dental technician. In rapid succession he qualified, found a legal job, married his
girlfriend and had a small son. He energetically patched and repaired
jaws in outlying farmsteads, and earned large sums doing so. He built
himself a house in Krasnodar. It all ended with a visit to Moscow, during which he came to see me, temporarily deprived of his characteristic buoyant self-confidence.

"Why won't they let me alone? I just can't understand it," he said.
"I'm not breaking any laws now. I only go out to the farms on my
days off work, and I'm not taking a job away from anyone else.
There are no dentists there and everyone is overjoyed to see me. I'm
not robbing people but charging almost the official rates. It's honest
work, with no cheating. Why do they hunt me like a mad dog? The
police called me in and wanted to distrain the house. Of course, I
made it over in Mama's name. I had to give up my job quickly and
get the hell out—they were threatening prison again!"

"Where now?"

"To Siberia, the Altai region. I'm through with dentistry! A man
works honestly and does no harm to anyone, and he'll end up behind
barbed wire again! No, I'm going to lead a different life from now
on. My father-in-law lives in a remote village in the Altai region. He's
a famous, very experienced beekeeper. I'm going to live with him
and keep bees. You don't need any diploma or license or tools to do
that. The hives will be mine, and the flowers are God's, for anyone to
take... I'll earn as much as the honey I produce, and according to the
rules I have every right to sell it at the collective-farm market..."

For the first few years of this new semi-monastic existence, Kostya
made rare appearances in Moscow on his way to Krasnodar and
back again. He would buy instruments and literature in Moscow.
Each time he brought a jar of exceptionally delicious and aromatic
honey. He went about his new profession with characteristic effi-
ciency and skill. He got hold of vehicles to transport his bees to the
most fertile stretches of wood and meadow; he invented a hive with
a particularly convenient construction; women eager to trade at the
market would sell Kostya's honey for good commissions where the
demand was greatest.

Kostya was cheerful and contented. He began to build himself a
new large house in Krasnodar, intending to settle in his beloved
south again some day. He described with enjoyment what a wonderful house this would be, and in the orchard and garden around it
there would always be a few hives just for himself and his chosen
guests. Rika and myself, for instance, who would come and stay with
him each summer.

On one of his visits Kostya sat in front of me, shrunken and gray,
breathing with difficulty. The new life he had so energetically put together had fallen apart. While he had been breaking his back in that

accursed Altai, saving up the money for a decent future, his wife had been living a high old life in Krasnodar, behaving no better than the lowest type of camp prostitute. Someone sent word, he arrived immediately, caught her in the act, and she threw him out. The house, garden, everything was in her name! He went back to the Altai and that saintly old man disowned him. Formally, Kostya owned nothing, it was officially the old man's property. Kostya had put all his money into the hives and the new house. He had nothing left. He began to demand his rights and the old man threatened to call the police. Who do you think you are? A sponger and good-for-nothing ex-convict! He went to stay with his mother in Krasnodar and the police came round that night: Where's your residence permit, where do you work, why are you threatening your former wife?

It was no longer the confident young ledger clerk from Supplies with the brilliant white teeth whom I first met in Ust-Surmog. Something had snapped irreparably, he would never get back his confidence.

Kostya vanished for a long while and I heard nothing about him. Then unexpectedly the phone rang. The voice was calm and satisfied, "I've become a Muscovite like you. Yes, I'm living in Moscow. Working for a military organization, and married... May I come and visit you? I'd like you to meet my wife and see both you and Rika Yefremovna."

Kostya paid us a family visit. He was dressed up in a suit and wearing a tie. He looked handsome but the corners of his mouth turned down, and his eyes lacked their former brilliant energy and sparkle. His wife was vulgar and pretentious with a sharp little nose and a bossy manner. She watched jealously to ensure that the visit met all the rules of Soviet etiquette and that Kostya, whom she called Konstantin Porfiryevich for some reason, behaved himself. When referring to herself, she spoke in the third person.

While the ladies discussed the problems of running a household in Moscow, Kostya sat in my study and hurriedly, in whispers, told me about his new life.

"I met her in the train one time... I'd never met such an independent woman before! A member of the Party, and head of the personnel department at a little factory. She set me up at a military polyclinic and I'm working as a dental technician there: they even have my photo on the honor board as an exemplary worker! I'm registered as living near Moscow, but I stay in her apartment. It's a separate, one-room apartment with all conveniences. She's got everything, she's very much respected and the local administration come to visit her, just like that... She has the police wound round her little finger... Well, you can understand, she's in charge, personnel and all!"

"So you're living on your own salary?"

"Lev Emmanuilovich! I couldn't live off her?! No, I'm living like everyone else. The dentist sends me a client, I take a mould at work, make it up at home, try it out at work and then fit it. The dentist takes half, and... Well, as I said, like everyone else. Only I keep to the dentist she recommends. I couldn't do anything without her! I'm like her lackey. She likes me to jump to as soon as she glances at me."

"And that suits you, does it?"

"It doesn't matter what I want, I've got to settle down! I can't go on shifting around, afraid all the time. Damn it! I'm going to play by the rules. She's promised to get me a residence permit for Moscow and then we'll get married and I can start living like everyone else, as best I can. It didn't work out in Solikamsk, in Krasnodar or the Altai, perhaps I'll be able to live like a normal human being in Moscow. How much can one man take?"

I'm ashamed to say that we did not return the visit. Not only because we didn't like the lady from personnel but because it was painful and unusual to see Kostya as a lackey, jumping to... Nor did he himself try very hard to persuade us to come and see his new home. After that he rang, every now and again, and was evasive when I asked questions or invited him to drop by. I had the impression that he did not want to come with her, and she would not allow him to go by himself. Then for almost half a year we were away from Moscow. That autumn the telephone rang, and there was his sister crying at the other end of the line...

* * *

As I have written elsewhere, a prison is one of the most conservative and settled institutions. At least, this is true of Russia. The same cannot be said of the camps. They are inseparable from the wider society, and any changes that take place there, whether political, social or economic, immediately affect what goes on behind the barbed wire. So the camp in which I found myself at the beginning of my new sentence in 1951 was very different from the camp I had left in 1946.

Among the many changes one of the most striking was the character of the criminal world there. The post-war criminals differed from the older generation in their extremism. What had happened to the good old criminal occupations of swindlers, pickpockets, frauds and con men? The post-war criminals were cold-blooded killers, vicious rapists and organized robbers. That was not the only distinguishing mark of the new generation, however. Now they were split up into castes and communities, each with its own iron discipline, with many rules and customs, and if any of these were infringed the punishment was harsh: at best the individual was expelled from that group and at worst, he was killed. The most widespread criminal community of this kind in the camp were the "honorable thieves."[5] To be "honorable" meant: going out each day with the rest but only performing the semblance of work; not working for the administration, even as cook or hospital orderly; never having any but the most murderously hostile relations with the "ratters" (i.e., those who in criminal terminology had ceased to be "honorable" and begun to work for the camp administration); and to submit wholly and unconditionally to the criminal "leaders" and unswervingly carry out their orders.

The life of the "honorable thieves" in the camp were surrounded by rules of behavior that were observed with an almost religious fervor. If a criminal was "honorable" and then broke the rules he had no alternative but to "run for the dead zone." This was a ploughed and raked strip of land between the high fence and a low barrier of barbed wire. Each prisoner who found himself in the "dead zone" had to lie face down on the ground immediately. Otherwise he would be shot dead, without any warning, by the armed guards on the watchtowers. The "ratters" would run for the "dead zone" when they were being persecuted by their former comrades. The guards then led them from the safety of this stretch of earth and locked them up in the punishment block. From there, after some time, they would be put in a transport to another camp in the same system. They could no longer remain where they were, since they had been declared outside the law...

It would be wrong to conclude, from what I have said, that the "honorable" thieves led a severe, almost ascetic existence. They did not work but they were allocated a full ration; they levied a money tribute from all the "peasants," those who did work; they took half of the food parcels and purchases from the camp commissary; and they brazenly cleaned out the new transports, taking all the best clothes from the newcomers. They were, in a word, racketeers, gangsters and members of a small mafia. All the ordinary criminal inmates of the camp—and they made up the majority—hated them intensely. After Stalin died and a breeze of liberalization blew through the Gulag, the "peasants" engaged in bloody uprisings against the "honorable thieves."

In the Chepetsk camp, where I was from 1954 onwards, the main "boss" among the local "honorable thieves" was Vanya the Frenchman. There was nothing remotely Gallic about this bald, very quiet and calm man. He was past fifty and had spent most of life in prison or in the camps. He became a thief while still a juvenile and had never done anything else. Vanya was not at all stupid and he was well-balanced. He enjoyed an unlimited power over his subjects but he exercised it without extremes and even observed a certain degree of tact. As far as I, or any other useful person, was concerned, Vanya was always impeccably polite and reasonable. Once we got into a conversation at the office.

"Ivan," I said, "I've been wanting to ask you for a long time: you're a clever man who's no longer young—why do you, keep on leading this kind of life? How much time have you ever spent on the outside? Does it really suit you, this way of life? Don't you want to start living like a normal human being: start a family, have children, stop being afraid of the informers, the rats and the knock in the middle of the night? You've got a good head on you, and know how to use your hands. You'd be valued anywhere you chose to work. Well, you might not get so much money but that's only of interest to a young man, not people my age and yours!"

"Well, 'Manuil'ich," he answered, after thinking for a moment, "thank you for spotting my gray hairs. Do you think I really chose such an old age for myself? Do I really want to go on knocking around the camps? I can see you want to ask me: why don't you cut free? I did. And more than once. I was released early from the Volga-Moscow canal, given an award and a certificate... They gladly employed me as a free worker and I tried, like a 'peasant,' and honestly put my back into it. They picked me up again, and gave me a sentence for fuck all. I served five, came out, looked around and everywhere they treated me like a mad dog. No one would employ me, I couldn't live in any city, and then I was sentenced again. I served three, settled down with a woman on parole, went to live with her, and I thought this is it... The pigs came and woke me up in the middle of the night: what right do you have sleeping with this woman when you've no residence permit? I ground my teeth, and went back to my old ways. As soon as our Mustachioed Benefactor kicked the bucket, I was let out under the amnesty. I got as far as the nearest town and there they roped us in like quails. They said nothing, slapped on a new sentence, and that's that. Someone was cuddling up with his woman, another was robbing a shop—they just picked everyone up without bothering to find out who did what!

"That was when I understood, 'Manuil'ich, that I could not play their game. There must be some rules in any game! If I play by the rules, then let them keep them too! But there I am with a pontoon in my hand and suddenly the bank says: 'Today those with twenty-two win!' Then I get twenty-two and he says: 'Today those with nineteen win!' He doesn't keep to the rules and I can't play his game. The bank is always in their hands. So I've got to remain an 'honorable' thief until the end of my life. There's nothing else left for me to do..."

"You know, Ivan, it's strange to see a boss like you following all these rules... They're like some game or other. Well, the young are always thinking up something new... But the criminals didn't do that kind of thing before..."

"No, they didn't. Because people were still living according to some rules or other. Now there are no rules at all out there! But it's impossible to live like that. Our laws may be ridiculous but at least we observe them! No messing! To the finish! Whatever they may be!"

* * *

I witnessed the end of Vanya the Frenchman. In spring 1955 an uprising of the "peasants" against the "honorable thieves" began in the camp at Chepetsk. Almost all knew that such an uprising was being prepared. At least, among the prisoners. Despite the thorough searches at the guardhouse, both the "peasants" and the "honorable thieves" brought weapons into the compound: iron bars, home-made knives, hatchets... The administration, of course, also knew what was brewing. Machine-guns were set up on the watchtowers and the guards ran back and forth across the compound. Evidently, they were keeping their eyes on Vanya. For all his experience, he overlooked this. When the two sides hurled themselves, with a savage brutality, at one another and rounds of automatic gunfire rang out from the watchtowers, for the time being shots fired into the air, two guards seized Vanya when he was standing near the "dead zone." They grabbed him and in a second had hurled him over the wire. Vanya fell on the accursed earth of the "zone" and he wanted to get up, but bullets whistled over his head and he understood that this was the end...

This happened right next to the office and standing by the window we could see the dramatic end of the leader of the "honorable thieves." The guards leaped over the wire, and lifted Vanya off the ground. He looked around him, as though with blinded eyes, and began like one of the musketeers due to be executed on Red Square, to bow in all four directions. They took him out of the compound to the punishment cell and the uprising continued. It was already quite obvious, however, that the "honorable thieves" had lost. Two hours later they surrendered and the camp was cleaned up, and all the prisoners were segregated. the dead and wounded were carried off to the medical barrack, the "honorable thieves" were led out of the compound to be transported to another camp where they would find their own kind. Vanya, however, was now faced by a quite new and unfamiliar life. He would be sent to a camp inhabited by "ratters" and there he would have to live the unfamiliar and shameful life of a "ratter"...

* * *

That evening when Kostya's sister told me he had died I remembered the unhappy story of this old thief. They were quite different kinds of people, Vanya the Frenchman and Kostya Shulga. Yet they both died because they were caught up in a game without rules. Evidently not only they but each one of us faces the same choice: either we must accept that we are always going to lose, or try in one way or another to outwit the merciless opponent who deals the cards and fixes the rules. Even Kostya did not succeed in this, though. For some reason, in the enormous list that I keep in my head of victims in this game without rules, I feel especially sorry for Kostya. And so I have written about him here.

JAILERS

"Is no prison, no prison: only jailer!"

Antonio—I now only remember his first name (and perhaps I never knew more)—spoke in his usual categorical way. Everyone in cell 29 took his words quite seriously. And Antonio deserved such attention. There once was a man who collected echoes (it's a famous story). Well, Antonio evidently collected prisons and enjoyed considerable success in this pursuit—he had seen the inside of almost all the world's prisons. He was an Italian and an anarchist. In 1924 he fled his native land and ever since had wandered the world, engaged in his mysterious anarchist activities. Naturally, he was imprisoned wherever he went.

Antonio reached us in a roundabout way. When the civil war started in Spain he immediately went to the classic homeland of anarchism where his comrades were the masters of Catalonia. Since anarchism was an extra occupation for Antonio, who was a navigator by trade, he signed on with a Spanish ship transporting arms from the USSR. On one of these voyages when the ship docked in Murmansk Antonio was invited for a chat by an unfamiliar organization. Within half an hour he realized his collection was about to be considerably "enriched"... Imprisoned with us in Butyrki he was talkative and full of life. Once a month we were given a small piece of paper on which each prisoner could pour out his heart and write a complaint to someone or other. Antonio neatly divided the paper in two and wrote one letter to "His Excellency the USSR Procurator General, Signor Vyshinsky" and another to the "Ambassador of the Spanish Republic in Moscow, Comrade Marcel Pasqua." After this he felt better and would resume his endless tales.

Since he was a natural polyglot and had already spent more than a year hanging around in Soviet prisons, we could understand his odd-sounding Russian. He had tried the prisons of the Old World and the New. The worst of all, he asserted, were in China. There he had been held in a pit covered by a grating. From time to time something edible was thrown to the prisoners and a bucket of water was lowered down. The best prisons in the world were in Brazil. They were former monasteries and the pleasant monastic cells where the prisoners now lived were left open day and night. Each was free to do as he pleased: draw, read, argue, grow flowers in the extensive monastery courtyard, or even make love to the kind senoritas who charitably brought the poor prisoners a rich meal each day. The jailers could not have cared less. Their job was to make sure that none of the prisoners went beyond the monastery walls. For loss of liberty here meant that the prisoners remained entirely free within the monastery courtyard.

Antonio, the great prison specialist, used to tell us that for the prisoner the jailer is much more important than the jail. Better be held in a very bad prison with a good jailer, than a very good prison with a bad jailer. Our experience was minimal and although we listened to Antonio with interest we were a rather absent-minded audience. Later, however, during my years in prison and in the camps, my thoughts often returned to the words of this Italian anarchist. I think Antonio was right. Both in general and in particular. Hippolyte Taine wrote in his *Origines de la France contemporaine* that Napoleon transformed the country into an enormous barracks, which fully reflected the personality of its creator. But no state institutions so reveal the character of their creator as its prisons. They are the most perfect embodiment of the thoughts and emotions of the man who heads an authoritarian state. For he himself is the chief jailer.

* * *

When I say "jailer" I do not just mean the individual who walks through the prison corridor with a bunch of keys, opening the cells, counting the inmates once or twice a day, and leading them out for exercise and on toilet duty. Because it is not he who decides to imprison people or to lock them up in solitary. He does not say when they are to be released—temporarily for interrogation or forever as free men, for transfer elsewhere or to be shot. In addition to those faces that became familiar to us, the jailers to whom we gave nicknames, not knowing their real names, there were innumerable other jailers who never visited the prisons. They sat in ordinary offices with shiny oilcloth divans, carpet runners on the floor and portraits on the walls. All they did was to read and write reports, talk over the phone, and go to their superiors for the latter to countersign their documents. They would ring up their wives, mistresses, parents and children several times during the working day to find out how they were, and to ask about their health and other domestic matters. Then, if there were no meetings, they went home and gave themselves over to the pleasures (or torments) of family life. Like everyone else.

These were the people who drew up the rules of our prison existence. They decided when and how exercise was to be taken, the quantity and quality of food. They discussed what kind of beds there should be in each cell (with a mattress or without?), how many letters the prisoner might receive, whether food parcels could be handed in and what they might contain... In a word, they were the ones who devised that world of rules we call a prison. Each cell, before it became a dark and stinking box or a dazzling bright hell, existed in plans and descriptions. The plans were signed by their authors and in the corner, or down the side, were added the signatures of their superiors under a typed or rubber-stamped "Agreed" or "Confirmed." If someone had to be hanged, then they drew up plans of the gallows, as required, from various angles: if shooting was preferred then they explained how to perform the execution and how and with what to wash away the blood afterwards. They compiled the detailed technical description of the prison and camp cemeteries; they indicated how to extract the gold from the deceased's teeth so that valuable material did not go to waste; they decided how old the underclothes in which the dead person was buried should be; they determined on which of the deceased's feet the board with their prison number should be attached; they specified with what to smash the dead person's skull before burial so as to make sure that no one was trying to use death and interment as a cover for escape...

All these decisions were taken by people we never saw. For that very reason they were terrifying in their mysterious anonymity. I always wanted to know: who are they, what do they look like? They were of every kind, after all. Apart from the unsuccessful architects, tempted by the rations and high salary to design prisons, there were judges, public procurators and still others. What, for instance, did he look like, the public procurator who replied to Auntie Pasha's letter?

Auntie Pasha, a kindly middle-aged woman, washed the floors in the camp office. She pitied the office workers because they were so helpless and impractical: and she darned and sewed patches on the trousers and quilt jackets of the "trusties" who were not yet privileged to wear first-hand clothing. The story of her life was simple. Auntie Pasha came from Zlatoust in the Urals. Her husband, a furnace man, died during an accident at work and she was left with two teenage sons. Their life was predictably hard. Someone taught Auntie Pasha to go to Chelyabinsk to buy stockings and then sell them (naturally, at a suitably higher price) in Zlatoust where they were not to be found. The rest was recorded in the charge sheet and the sentence passed by the court. "For the purposes of speculation" she had "obtained 72 pairs of knitted stockings in Chelyabinsk which she then tried to resell at the market in Zlatoust." Auntie Pasha was reported, arrested, tried and sentenced to seven years imprisonment with confiscation of all her property. The children were taken in by acquaintances and, besides, they were almost old enough to take up any profession at the trade school. Five years passed, the war began, and Auntie Pasha's boys had reached the age when they could defend the Motherland. So off they went to fight. First Auntie Pasha was informed that her younger son had been killed. Staying behind in the office at night to wash the floors, she moaned and beat her head against the table.

Then one evening she came up to me with a glassy-eyed expression and handed over a thick package which she had been given in Records and Distribution. This contained several medical reports and the decisions of various commissions. To these was added a letter to Auntie Pasha from the hospital administrator. It concerned her elder son. He had been severely wounded and was in the hospital. The doctors had done all within their power and he was, as they put it in his medical history, "fit, to all intents and purposes"—apart, that is, from having lost both arms and one leg. He could be discharged from the hospital if there was some close relation to look after him. Evidently the son had explained where she was because the administrator advised the mother of this wounded soldier to send an appeal to the USSR Procurator General's Office, including the enclosed documents, after which they would release her and she could come and fetch him.

"'Manuilich, dear heart,'" Auntie Pasha said, starting to cry, "You write for me."

So I wrote, and very persuasively. I attached all the documents and handed in the letter. Two or three months passed, and each day I reassured Auntie Pasha: they received a great many such appeals, I told her, and it would take time to process her release. I described in detail the lengthy procedures as her application passed from one level to another. Auntie Pasha wept, but believed me and each day I gave her paper on which to write her son a letter.

One day I went into Records and Distribution myself. A great pile of mail lay on the table, already sorted out to be handed over, or its contents communicated, to the prisoners. Auntie Pasha's surname caught my eye. I picked up the flimsy sheet of headed paper from the USSR Procurator General's Office and read it through. A public procurator of a certain rank or class informed Auntie Pasha that her application had been examined and her request for early release turned down because there were "no grounds." I carefully placed the single sheet on the table and went out onto the verandah, terrified that I might suddenly meet Auntie Pasha... Everywhere, in the barracks and in the office, there were people I did not want to see. I ran to the latrines and there, clinging to the stinking walls, started to shake uncontrollably. Only two times in my prison life did this happen. Why was I crying? Then I understood: I felt ashamed, terribly ashamed, before Auntie Pasha.

She had already served five years for 72 pairs of stockings. She had given the state her two sons. Now, there it was, there were "no grounds"... In France during the First World War prisoners serving any sentence, even life, were set free if their son died at the front.

I promised myself that if ever I was released I would go to Moscow, track down that procurator and look him straight in the face. There are many things I have not done in my life, and this was one of them. I even forgot his name: Dmitroshchuk, Dmitriev, or perhaps Dmitrievsky...

* * *

Yet however much these distant officials affected our lives as prisoners, we had most of all to do with our immediate guards and jailers. This was true of Butyrki and of the vast Kotlas transit camp in the northern Komi republic. We could already distinguish the more from the less vile, and the time-servers from the enthusiasts. The comforts of our unattractive existence depended on them. Yet it did not occur to a single one of us that our very lives were in their hands. I only understood this during my first transfer on foot.

We were taken from Kotlas by barge to Vogvozdino, the transit point on the Vychegda, a tributary of the River Dvina. I remember the place well. It was there that I made friends with Alexander Lizarevich. And it was in Vogvozdino that Oksana, my first wife, died, five months after I had passed through.

From Vogvozdino we were marched along the recently-cleared Ustvym-Chibya dirt road. Cut through the forests, it ran across bogs and was already broken up by the heavy truck wheels. Sand and road chippings shifted and swayed beneath our feet and we walked through pools of water that never dried out. We made twenty-five kilometers a day and by evening would arrive at the transit station, a fenced-in area surrounded by watch towers where prisoners spent the night. That August was warm, even hot, and it was hard to walk on the crumbling sand. In addition, our escort proved particularly vicious. Each morning we stood in line and the man in charge of the escorting guard, a short pock-marked lad, looked us over severely and slowly recited the following litany, spelling out each word, "When we are moving, observe the established procedures: no talking, and carry out all the guard's orders. A step to the right or the left, and any infringement of the rules, is considered an attempt to escape. Rifles will be used without warning. Is that clear?!"

The prisoners were supposed to chant in unison: "Clear!" If it seemed to the head of the convoy that our reply was not sufficiently loud and disciplined he would ask again threateningly, "Is that clear?!" This went on until he heard the answer he wanted.

All the guards resembled their leader: stumpy, pock-marked and overeager to perform their duties. On the second or third day of our march I started talking to Lizarevich who was walking beside me. I was telling him the story of the dictionary I had once edited and became so engrossed that I forgot all precaution. Suddenly we heard a shouted command: "Column, halt!"

We stopped, not understanding what the matter was. Beside me at the edge of the road stood one of the guards. Holding his rifle at the ready he yelled: "Lie down, lie down, you Trotskyist!... fuck you, lie down!"

I did not realize immediately whom he was yelling at. I looked about me and saw I was standing in a deep and dirty pool. And this pock-marked young idiot, this armed brute, was proposing that I lie down there! I won't lie down, I thought to myself. Go on, shoot, you bastard...

"Lie down! You're resisting the guard..."

He slid back the bolt on his rifle, his eyes blazing with a triumphant joy and fury.

"Lie down, go on! lie down..." the whisper of my fellow prisoners reached me. It was then that I realized he was indeed about to shoot. Everything would end. I should never learn what had happened to my family nor finish telling Lizarevich my story...

Slowly bending at the knees I lowered myself into the pool, laid my cheek against some stone there, and closed my eyes. Lord! If I could just lie there and never get up again.

"Get up!"

I stood up very slowly and looked at the guard. His eyes were now dull and the thrill of imminent murder had left them. Probably he liked being able to kill. All he had to do was pull the trigger and one small universe of thoughts, emotions, friends and acquaintances that existed quite independent of his will, would disappear.

I then understood that the jailers had one strength: they could kill us. But no more than that. Lizarevich would quote Seneca: "It cannot be avoided but it can all be held in contempt." He taught me not to feel humiliated and to regard all these ordeals with disdain. Yes, the jailers could kill me. And also increase or diminish the measure of my physical sufferings.

* * *

Since jailers are at least originally human they each retain certain unique traits of character. The jailers whom I shall now describe were not all alike. They varied greatly in rank and ability. Among them were both the clever and the stupid, good and evil men, the bureaucrats and the fanatics. I and millions of others were at their mercy. I shall tell about my jailers. Let others tell about theirs. I think it is useful for all those who do not share our experience and knowledge to be told these things.

Ivan Zaliva

Our transport walked for a whole week. Behind us lay the un-metalled dirt road to Knyazhpogost, the unfinished railway from Knyazhpogost to Veslyana, and the large wooden gates on the un-ballasted road over which there rose something like a triumphal arch bearing the handsome inscription: "Ustvymlag NKVD USSR." Behind us lay the transit camp and Camp No. 11, the "Zimka" outpost, and the Machinery Depot. Now we were walking along a broad sandy roadway, which climbed up one hill after another. A pine forest of exceptional beauty stood on either side. The smooth bronze trunks reached up to the sky and between them the ground was covered with an even, silvery-velvet carpet that I had never seen before. It was reindeer moss. We were tired after a week on our feet, and so were our escorting guards. They no longer gave us the usual ten minutes rest after two hours of marching, they cursed more often when prodding those who lagged behind, and they were in a hurry to hand us on to other masters.

Finally, after a sharp turn in the road, a river glistened ahead of us. It flowed rapidly over the shoals and calmly in the backwaters. Veslyana. A beautiful name, perhaps of early Slavonic origin. On the far side of the river stood an architectural structure to which our eyes were already quite accustomed: the tall logs, set upright in the ground, the posts of the compound fence; beyond them the low barracks; some way off, the unattractive houses of the camp administrators and free workers; the long stable building and the smoky chimney of the bakery... Our column crawled slowly across the pontoon bridge and approached the entrance to the camp. Various people stood outside the gates. Sharp young men in brand-new quilt work jackets held clean plywood slates and pencils in their hands: the work distributors. Other individuals in white coats who looked like prisoners—evidently doctors. The jailers and camp escort guard, who were not dressed up or there for show. And, in front of them all, a tall man in a well-made overcoat, with a blue NKVD cap and boots polished to an unbelievable shine. Wound about with the straps of his shoulder belt, his hand firmly placed on the wooden butt of his Mauser, he surveyed us with a condescending but severe gaze. This was our first camp boss, the head of Camp No. 1 in Ustvymlag, Senior Lieutenant Ivan Zaliva.

I am writing about him not only because he was my first jailer in the camps, but because he was also a curious phenomenon. It was the first time I had come across someone of his kind and for several years I was able to follow his career. The personality of Zaliva affected the many and, for us, very important changes then taking place in the camps. I do not know about Zaliva's biography before he came to the Gulag—where he had studied or worked earlier, and how he had reached the by no means insignificant rank of senior lieutenant in State Security.[1] He was a man of astounding ignorance and rare stupidity. In these respects he stood out among the camp bosses, and they were not a profession known for exceptional wit and education. He did not steal, like most of his colleagues. Neither was he a despot: on the contrary, he kept strictly to his instructions. Zaliva was no sadist and when, during 40 degrees of frost, bound and completely naked "refusers" were taken on sledges to the punitive outpost he would follow their departure with sad regret in his eyes. He even had a certain Ukrainian kindheartedness and cheerfulness about him, tempered by the strictness necessary for his post.

Zaliva always tried to do what his superiors demanded. When they required that he accept as many zeks as possible he agreed to take one transport after another. Unlike some camp directors he did not try to refuse new prisoners on the grounds that there were insufficient barracks, tents, clothes, tools or food. The interests of the state governed all his activities. He crossed rice, semolina and sorghum off the list of cereals supplied by the food depot and replaced them with cheap barley chaff; salt beef and horsemeat was replaced with dried cod; he would check the prices of medicines and demand cheaper substitutes. Instead of new expensive coats and felt boots he eagerly accepted second- and even third-hand clothing from the depot. He took great care, though, of the camp's most valuable possession, its horses. Early each morning he himself would walk round the stable and make sure that they were being fed with the scarce oats. He checked how the feed was weighed out and given to the animals. While Zaliva continued to visit the stable the prisoners could not get their hands on this ration: the strict and incorruptible head of the camp would look on as the horses munched their oats. In the monthly reports from all the camps in Ustvymlag the lowest wastage levels for horses were consistently recorded at Camp No. 1. Zaliva was always praised for this.

To begin with, no one checked what he did with his "contingent" of zeks. During our first year in Camp No. 1, from 1938 to 1939, the transports arrived one after another, and Zaliva was held up as an exemplary boss who always found room for new "contingents." The explanation was simple: in his camp places were rapidly freed. There were 517 in our Moscow transport, which reached his camp in late August 1938. By spring the next year only 27 of those Muscovites remained. About 20-30 people were, probably, transferred to other camps in Ustvymlag where their professional skills were put to use. All the rest died that first winter. The same fate awaited those then transported from Smolensk, Stavropol and Mogilyov.

In November 1938, 270 Chinese were driven to our camp from the Far East. They were inhabitants of Manchuria clad in enormous wolfskin fur hats, long fur coats and peculiar quilted boots of their own design. Each summer they had been accustomed, for years un-counted, to cross the invisible border with Russia and work as market gardeners until the winter. In 1937 and 1938 they were all arrested, given eight years for "illegal crossing of the frontier" and sent to the camps. Zaliva could not find sufficient words to express his delight. He set them hauling timber by hand. Usually horses pulled the felled trunks to the roadways where they were carted away. There were few horses, however, and they were valuable; moreover, special paths had to be cleared for them at the work site. It was much easier to use manpower. Depending on the weight, a team of six, eight or ten men lifted the trunk onto their shoulders and carried it. I have done the work and know what it's like. Your eyes strain from their orbits and, as you walk, all thoughts except one fly from your head: how to drop this terrible, crushing and murderous burden as quickly as possible. None of us could take more than a week of such work. The Chinese, steadily, quietly and calmly, worked day after day. Each of them took a pole in his free hand, carefully using it to test out the path ahead. Ten men carried a log that weighed almost two tons, and carried it very well, with great care.

They were good-hearted, honest and hardworking men, the Chinese. Even in the camp they managed to keep as clean as was possible. For a month or more Lizarevich and I lived in the Chinese barrack, and it was a joy to be there: there was no robbing or steal-ing, and it was always swept clean. The Chinese came back from work when it was pitch dark, ate the thin soup, and then repaired their torn fur clothing. (Zaliva had economized here too, since they did not then require camp issue.) They would sit on their heels on the bed boards and, holding the lighted splinter (then the only source of illumination) in their mouths, deftly and quickly sew up their fur coats. By February 1939, 269 of these Chinese had died. Only one re-mained alive, working in the kitchen.

Every day Zaliva called in the work distributor and the planner and asked for a detailed and strict account of the morning roll call. How many Group A (workers), he asked, how many in Group B (services in the compound), and how many in Group C (excused on grounds of illness). He would check carefully that all these figures fell within the limits laid down by the Ustvymlag authorities. Only after that did he enquire about the night's "C figures." This meant those who had died. Higher authority did not set any limits for this category and, therefore, did not expect reports on them. During our first winter the daily "C figures" amounted to about 25-30 people. There were no particular diseases involved. It was simply that Zaliva strictly enforced all the instructions. A transport arrived and for the first three days, until the new prisoners began working, they were given the standard food allowance. Then they were transferred to an output-related diet. Even experienced and trained lumbermen, with good tools, found it difficult to fulfil the norm. For those unused to hard physical labor, weakened by prison and transfers, and lacking the right clothes or footwear, they were quite unattainable. After the three days all those who had just arrived found themselves on the punitive ration—300 grams of half-baked black bread, and two bowls of thin gruel a day. Nothing else. A week, ten days or two weeks later, people began to swell up strangely and then, over two to three days, an uncontrollable diarrhea would finish them off.

Before my eyes good-natured, bluff Zaliva killed off 1500 people in the course of a single winter. Perhaps, even more. Yet, amazingly enough, the prisoners treated him with a kind of humorous disdain, and without hatred. To a great extent, we judged our jailers by how easily they could be hoodwinked. The stupidity, ignorance and cowardice of Zaliva offered considerable opportunities. He prevented the prisoners from stealing the horses' oats only for as long as he continued to visit the stable.

"I can't help admiring your bravery, citizen director!" the vet said one day, with respect and a certain mournful pity in his voice.

"Indeed," Zaliva agreed condescendingly. "But why did you say that?" he suddenly inquired, pale with fear.

"Well, just think what our horses are sick with! In-fec-tious anemia..."

"You damn Trotskyist!" howled Zaliva. "Why didn't you tell me right away there was something contagious?!"

He never set foot in the stable again.

In accordance with an old instruction, never revoked, 58-ers could not be permitted to work within the compound. Zaliva not only forbade us to be work distributors and managers but also quartermasters, ledger clerks in Supplies, bakers, and medical or barrack orderlies. All these posts were filled by the "socially acceptable," as thieves, robbers, rapists and other criminals were termed in that instruction. Naturally, in such circumstances, the workers did not even receive half of a ration that had already been cut in the interests of the state. The most unbridled thievery and lawlessness reigned among the prisoners.

Yet it was under Zaliva's rule that the "politicals," the 58-ers, began their irreversible takeover of the camps. Only during the first winter did Zaliva flourish. At that time no one demanded that he meet the plan for timber supplies. A year later, when the peak of excess zeks had passed, Moscow firmly told the camps that they must not only guard their zeks but also give "performance": this was the term applied in official documents to the labors of millions of prisoners.

It was then that the formerly clear and precise distinction between what was permissible and what was not began to blur for Zaliva. In order to retain the goodwill of his superiors he needed clever planners and accountants, experienced engineers, capable organizers and honest warehousemen. He could only find them among the "politicals." Zaliva's sense of self-preservation was so developed and strong, it turned out, that he began to send the "socially acceptable" on gang labor out into the forest and appoint to all the decisive posts those recommended by the head of planning, the chief accountant and the doctor. The foreman and the planner blatantly exploited Zaliva's stupidity. They concealed almost half of the already very modest output and after the daily report, Zaliva, pale with fright, would not summon the planner but himself run into the planning office and, stuttering, beg him almost obsequiously to "throw in" a few more dozens or hundreds of cubic meters... By nighttime the formerly fearsome and self-confident boss became a pitiful wretch, sweating from terrible fear. For now, every night, the administration called up each camp in turn for a report.

At about midnight the most important figures in the camp would gather in Zaliva's office. The director sat behind the lavish desk made for him by his own personal cabinetmaker, surrounded by jailers of various rank—the head of the guard, the "godfather" or security officer, and the heads of the medical and culture units. A little way off sat the prisoner heads of sections—the planner, accountant, normsetter, works inspector and the foremen. It was at the latter that Zaliva now gazed, with fear, suffering and hope in his eyes. How he was probably cursing that damned radio and the prisoner, a radio operator, who had so skillfully and quickly set up the equipment and, if need arose, was sitting here to correct any defects in transmission.

All sat, talking in a whisper, as if they might be overheard by their yet more powerful bosses, at this very moment assembled in Vozhael at Ustvymlag headquarters, and sitting in the awesome director's office. Zaliva could not take his mournful, dog-like eyes off the little box sitting on his desk. Finally, it begin to crackle, gasp and clear its throat. The voice of the head of production could suddenly be heard, calling all the camps participating in this roll-call report. Then the calmly insolent voice of the director himself rang out of the box. Since poor Zaliva was in charge of Camp No. 1 they began with him and he was the butt of most of his superior's anger and zeal.

"Zaliva! Report on output!"

Zaliva's shaking voice was interrupted by a roar, "How much? How much? What are you up to there, you lazy good-for-nothings? What about the state plan? I sent you a contingent, and chucked in a few extra horses, now where's the output? I'll have you pile the logs on your prick, you idiot, and carry them here yourself!"

When Zaliva tried to interject a timid word of self-justification or a promise to do better in this stream of abuse he was shut up in such a way that even our experienced jailers began to look firmly at the floor. At last, this torment drew temporarily to a close, "If you don't raise output by 150 cubic meters tomorrow I'll send you bare-assed into the forest to fetch the wood yourself! What else is left if you can't force your zeks to work!?"

Then the director turned to the other camps, more fortunate and, often, less fortunate. From time to time, he would remember Zaliva, "Are you there, Zaliva? You hear how they're working at No. 14? And they've less men, and fewer horses! They know how to make people work there. They know what the state plan means. They've probably organized a health resort at No. 1, since they can see what a fool their boss is!"

Yet Zaliva believed that he also knew how to make people work. He had often forced the doctors and all the camp "trusties" to go out and fell timber. But those cubic meters, where was he to make up those damned cubic meters?! Only by appealing to the "Trotskyists" could he get them. Zaliva pleaded an extra hundred cubic meters from the planner "for his own personal needs"; he agreed to let the foreman's mistress live in his cubicle with him; he was agreeable to anything, in fact, that could help him keep his difficult but still desirably superior position. Apart from the nightly radio reports there was also the daytime. Then he sat in his office, punishing and, where necessary, pardoning; he rode around the "work sites" on superb light sledges pulled by a pure-blooded ("anemic") trotter; and, having survived another twenty-four hours, he would sit down and calculate the day's profits and losses. For, apart from everything else, Zaliva was also unbelievably stingy. He was afraid to steal because he was almost as great a coward as he was a miser. He tried to spend as little as possible on himself and his wife. His dinner came from the prisoners' kitchen, to be "tried first" by him. Since the meal he received was always filling and delicious he took away the unconsumed part for his wife to eat. Even his bread was brought from the bakery "for testing." When his wife, nevertheless, had to pay for his food ration—it couldn't be allowed to go to waste!—she wrote down the quantity and price of each item. Zaliva would then come to the accountant's office with this slip of paper and check for himself that she hadn't cheated him. Sometimes he would weigh out the food again. Everything in his house was under lock and key and Zaliva took the keys with him. In the morning he handed his wife the food she needed to survive the day.

As the value of those working in the camps rose, comparatively, and the demands for output continually increased, Zaliva was steadily demoted. He was made deputy director, then sent to a small camp producing skis, and then somewhere else. Towards the end of the war I came across him in charge of a small outpost of another camp. After the war ended he discharged himself and sold off all his belongings. The prisoners were able to buy a few worn-out greatcoats and his large ginger cat. Zaliva bargained long and passionately with the zeks, listing all his pet's exceptional qualities...

He returned to the Ukraine, taking with him his tormented wife, vast trunks packed with goodness knows what, and a fat pile of banknotes earned over years of zealous and loyal service to the state. He did not leave any friends behind him at Camp No. 1 but he bore no one any malice. Several months later, the chief of the escort guards received a contented and self-satisfied letter. They had appreciated him, after all, wrote Zaliva: he had been put in charge of a district MGB section in his own Poltava Region, and not sent back to the ferocious and tedious North.

Korabelnikov

I never once saw him in the transit camp at Kotlas. Nor did he catch my eye when we were led to the wharf. It was only towards the end of our first day on the barge that I noticed him. The tug slowly pulled us down the North Dvina river and then it and the two barges full of prisoners set out along the Vychegda. About four or five hundred of us were crammed into the hold. There was no room to sit and we took it in turns to lie down and sleep. There were no bed boards; we simply sat and lay on the filthy, damp floor. Rain beat against the deck and the sides of the barge and sometimes the waves on the river rose so high they flooded the deck above over our heads. For some reason we were given herring to eat. Admittedly, it was the real Far Eastern herring, small, rich and incredibly delicious. We devoured it all—skin, scales, innards, the head, the tail and the bones. The only drawback was that it made us thirsty, and we were given no more than a mug of water, fished straight out of the river, twice a day. A long line formed, round the clock, to get out onto the deck. Shifting from one foot to another, and cursing the guards with every insulting name they could think of, people battered impatiently at the hatch. Many could not restrain themselves and urinated and defecated in a corner of the hold itself. Meanwhile, on the wet deck, the guards, blind drunk, bawled out songs and danced. From time to time they opened the hatch and, with kicks, chased out a dozen prisoners who rushed to reach the little boarded toilet at the stern. The guards stripped the most insolent naked and made them squat on the wooden bollard. Sitting out in the rain, the punished zeks could observe all the guards' drunken antics.

It was there in the barge that I first saw Korabelnikov. Solidly-built and showing no signs of the usual prison pallor, his self-confidence and calmness set him apart. He was well-dressed and, every minute or so, he shook his straight blond hair with a sharp toss of his head. There was something strange about his eyes, so pale they were almost the same color as his hair, and this gave his round face an unusual appearance, like that of a blind man with cataracts over his eyes. Most of those on the barge split up into gangs and stuck together. We were first put with criminal offenders at Kotlas, but the 58-ers had separate barracks there as well. In the hold of the barge we were now all together, but like oil and water we did not mix. People kept with their cellmates, and small cliques were formed based on common, if not entirely clear, interests.

Korabelnikov did not belong to any group or mix with the other prisoners. He somehow gave the impression of being neither a criminal nor a political. He received his herring separately and ate it all himself, not joining one of the small prisoner communities based on the great principle of "share and eat alike." This alienation did not disturb him in the least. Confidently, he would step over those lying on the floor. He inhaled the air in the hold—tainted with urine, herring, farts, and tobacco—as easily and freely as if he were walking in the forest or across a flower-strewn meadow.

Our acquaintance began unexpectedly. I had left our small group and made my way to the side of the barge. Fresh cold air forced its way through gaps in the planking and one could press one's face to these cracks and breathe deeply. Near me sat the man with yellow eyes, whom I had noted sometime before. Not far away, stretched out on their pitiful knapsacks, some criminal offenders were singing an old song from Solovki:

> The hold is deep
> We're crammed like sheep
> We're sailing on "Gleb Boky."

"Yes," said Yellow-eyes, with a toss of his head, "Gleb Boky! Now there was a man!"

I turned to him:

"You didn't know Boky, did you?"

"Most certainly! And not only him. I knew them all! Artuzov, Molchanov, Berman... Pauker, of course. But how do you know Boky? Or did you also work...?"

"He's my father-in-law."

"Oh! that's clear then, isn't it... "

Yellow-eyes came to life and the strange expression disappeared from his face. Until now I had not understood its meaning: it came from his sense of superiority over all those in the barge. He wore this expression almost all the time. Only on those rare occasions when I saw Korabelnikov (that was his name) talking to his superiors, any superiors, did it disappear. His yellow eyes would light up with a canine intelligence—attentive, respectful and understanding. Then the light faded and, once again, he gazed on the rest of us indifferently and calmly. There was even no malice there. And this was surprising, because of all the many villains whom I met in that strange world it was Korabelnikov who made the most terrifying impression on me. After I was released from the camps the first time, and then, after a second term in prison and in the camps, Korabelnikov with his straight pale blond hair and yellow indifferent eyes would continue to haunt my dreams, and I would groan in my sleep and wake up in a cold sweat.

Even such a monster as Korabelnikov evidently suffered from loneliness and the impossibility of discussing the only thing that he considered valuable and interesting in life. He immediately accepted me as "one of ours." After all, I knew all the gods in his pantheon and since I was the son-in-law of one of them he believed I must know all the secrets that nourished and sustained him. It was not difficult to maintain this illusion. I did indeed know a great many such secret matters and talked of those I did not know as if they were something long familiar. From the very first sight of him and the first sound of his voice, I found Korabelnikov terrifying and, in some inexplicable way, repulsive. But an unquenchable curiosity burned within me and carefully, so as not to alarm him, I began to probe the sticky, frightful and revolting matter with which he was stuffed.

Korabelnikov had occupied a quite insignificant post in the NKVD hierarchy. He was a low-ranking officer, working for Pauker's active operations department. It was they who kept people under surveillance, and they were responsible for the security of the chiefs, and for arrests and executions. Yet, to judge from Korabelnikov's tales, if his rank was lowly (a junior lieutenant or plain lieutenant) he was a trusted employee. I now regret that I could not suppress my horror and fastidious distate and, after two days in his company, began to hide from Korabelnikov and his stories in that hellish hold. I remembered Korabelnikov for all time, though. Today I can quite clearly conjure up his round, flat face, straight, back-brushed hair and his cataract-like eyes. I can hear his calm even voice, "Of course, it's possible to work anywhere. But for our job you should have some knack and, you know, a grasp of things. I did a little surveillance but it was dull work so I transferred to active operations. There you must understand all the subtleties. When I'm out on a job I immediately form a picture of the people there. I don't look at the person I've come for— he'll get what's coming without me. But I have a look at the whole gang in his apartment. Straightaway I can see who he loves most— mother, wife, son, daughter—and who he's most afraid for. Then I go for that person... And I go to work so well that the dear fellow arrives at the Lubyanka ready and willing, just sign him in... I carry out the search and can tell, watching their eyes, where everything is, what they value most of all. There's no need for any nonsense, like a doll belonging to their dead daughter... but I can tell what to grab so as to turn them inside out! You know, they used to fall at my feet and would agree to anything. And the women, so pretty and proud, were ready to lick my boots. Any one of them, there and then, I could have... Not allowed, of course, impossible. Pauker was very strict about that, and I didn't want to get myself in trouble. Some of our boys would give their telephone numbers, quietly, so the others didn't notice, and then make use of it. The old man had already been taken to Lefortovo and finished off but his woman or his daughter, say, went where they were told, gave themselves enthusiastically, thinking it would help and he would be released... A risky business, and I never tried it. My superiors were always sure of me: I would never step out of line, but do everything as required! I didn't need to screw them anyway, it was enough to know that if I wanted, I could do anything I liked with them.

"Pauker's deputy Volovich himself noticed me and he sometimes called me up and gave me the kind of tasks that he couldn't entrust to any old bumpkin. All kinds of jobs, enjoyable work, yes... "

"Matters of state?"

"And matters of state, important jobs. And other kinds. Well, you yourself know, all these bosses are only human and they all feel tempted by forbidden fruit. They'd pull someone like me to pieces if I nicked anything during a search or took a girl into the next room, for a personal investigation... But they themselves got up to all kinds of things, you wouldn't believe! You always needed a trusted man, whether for matters of state or personal business. And I could always be trusted!

"In 1934, on 1 December, we were called in from all over Moscow. Pauker and Volovich personally selected who to take. I was the first. That night we travelled in a special train up to Leningrad. We arrived, and the platforms were sealed off. Medved and all the local NKVD chiefs met us: into cars, and straight to headquarters on Liteiny Avenue. There they summoned me and gave me a job that not everyone would get. Me and another guy. For almost a month we were in the remand prison..."

"Whatever for?"

"I wasn't under arrest! I was in the same cell as Nikolayev. The one who bumped off Kirov. I wasn't a stooly either, he knew who I was. Me and my partner did six-hour shifts. They didn't leave him alone for one minute. Only once, when Stalin himself came to the cell to see Nikolayev, did we leave him with someone else. They talked there in the cell for a whole hour while we stood outside the door. And who do you think was with us? All the chiefs were there!"

"And then?"

"And then Stalin left and I went back in."

"What was he like, Nikolayev?"

"Funny fellow. As though he was bit off his head. He'd throw himself down on the bed and lie with his head covered up. I ordered him to not to do it. It wasn't allowed, head and arms had to be visible at all times so the fool couldn't do anything to himself... That, or he'd run around the cell, muttering to himself. Or he'd start to ask me things."

"Like what?"

"About life outside, the weather. They didn't take him out for exercise. Suddenly he'd ask me what was on in the theater. Once he asked how they shot people. The joker! What a laugh! 'Why are you asking,' I says to him, 'you'll find out all right.' So I spent all the time with him and, you can imagine, I got tired. Just think. I'm in jail and don't see daylight. When I leave the cell I sleep there in the prison because I was always supposed to be wide awake when I was on duty. When they took him out to be shot, I sighed with relief. I saw him off, then me and my partner went back to our dormitory, put on civilian clothing, took off to the Astoria and had a hell of a party! He got hold of some girls and we had a good, entertaining time. We had a decent rest like normal people after such work."

"So you didn't go with him?"

"Who? With Nikolayev, you mean? You think I hadn't seen all that before! I know how they plug them. What's the point in that? Now if they had asked me to do the job, another matter entirely! And even that's not really my line. Mag was the main one for that sort of thing. The top bosses were always ready to do anything he said—immediately, you're most welcome. Always drunk, he was, always having women, and they kept a special secret apartment for him to take them to. It was guarded as well. After he'd knocked off Zinoviev, Kamenev, Bukharin and several others, he asked for the Military Red Banner award and for the decree to be published in all the newspapers. And there it was! The award and the announcement. And for what, I ask you? I had no wish to be his assistant! Once, after they bumped off Kamenev, I saw what his little helpers did. There was blood everywhere, like cutting a pig... Drag him out to the van, drive him away, wash down the floor—what was I, some cleaner or something?! No, to be an assistant was not interesting at all. I wanted to be in charge myself. I like independence. Until I stupidly got in trouble I had a very nice job. When I think of what my stupidity cost me, the job I lost, it makes me sick."

"Why, what were you doing?"

"It happened last year. Me and my partner, also an educated, knowledgable guy, used to go the Metropole hotel in the evenings. We were dressed in the latest fashion, the most expensive gaberdines and coats, from the atelier where the bosses themselves have their clothes made, and our pockets were full of money. A man would remain in the car by the entrance and we would sit, like some foreigners, in the best seats. A table was reserved for us, not far from the fountain, and we could see everything from there. Well, the waiters and maitre d' knew who we were. Of course, we paid for everything—why not when it was the state's money? But the bill was one thing, our tastes were another. We'd have two bottles of the most expensive Spanish brandy and there'd only be a half-litre of Russian vodka in the bill. We'd eat the best salmon and cutlets de volaille and in the bill, only goulash and cheap Pacific salmon. They would serve us respectfully. But a glance at their eyes and you could tell they knew who we were: who were they compared to us?

"We sat there the whole evening, eating and snacking, in no hurry, like foreigners, all very proper. There were real foreigners there, from the embassies, and we already knew who they were, where they were from. We watched to see if any Soviet guests approached them. Were they winking at anyone there? Because people who came up to them just like that knew what to expect. But they could still wink, so you'd hardly notice. They couldn't hide anything from us, though!

"It's good to be independent, to know that you're the boss! Sometimes you were sitting there, finishing off the second bottle and watching. All that riff-raff were dancing round the fountain imagining themselves to be the devil knows what! Just think, he'd been to the university, had a good salary, the girl was a very smart piece, maybe his fiancée... He dotes on her, their eyes are shining happily—with passion. They don't know about us and if they did, they wouldn't pay any attention. But we are the masters. They'd irritate my partner and me until we lost patience and I'd say: 'let's pick him up. Come on!'

"Then we get up, quietly, and my partner goes to the cloakroom where we had our own special room. I come up to the man, politely, apologize to his woman, I do beg your pardon and so on, and ask him for a word. She nods and I take him, softly-softly, to the cloakroom and when he asks what the matter is, I pull out my identity. Then, into the room. We immediately empty his pockets, take all there is, my partner takes his cloakroom check, brings his overcoat: get dressed, boy, the party's ended. Into the car, round to the Lubyanka and hand him over. Sometimes we went back again. His woman sat there, stunned, she probably had no money to pay the bill. What a joke! Her boy's vanished, gone, kaput! She knew that was it. If I wanted I could come right up to her and take her to my place—she would have agreed to anything, the silly bitch! But I knew there were more of our lads sitting there. Pauker's lot and others from special section, just keeping an eye on us—so why should I drop my guard??"

"Wait a minute! So you brought in that man and handed him over... But what for? What had he done? What would you say?"

"You're slow, aren't you? It wasn't our concern what they did with him. The lads there were no fools and could fix him up all right. Arrested under suspicion, say, exchanging winks with foreigners...

Our job is to pick up the suspect and yours is to investigate, and then charge him if there's something... An experienced and skilled fellow will get him to admit to everything. And if the investigator is feeling lazy, then it's eight years, Suspected of Espionage, and that's that! And not a squeak..."

"What if you suddenly met one of your 'god-children' here, on the barge or in the camp?"

"Of course, there might be an unpleasant moment. But, then, the guards know. Don't imagine our work has ended. If we fetch up in the same place you'll find out what kind of a man Korabelnikov is! Stick to me and you'll stay alive."

"What did they pick you up for, then?"

"I was stupid. I always did everything right at work, and earned the best reports. But once when I was drinking I blabbed to my best mate—we were that close!—about one of the bosses' women. How I could have been so stupid, I don't know! Of course, he reported me. They hauled me in. I had made a mistake and admitted it—guilty, do what you will, I'll make it up. A crazy business. I was still in the remand prison and they arrested the boss I'd blabbed about and he was in very serious trouble! But it made no difference. I had lost their confidence, and must be punished. Five years as a Socially Dangerous Element and into a transport with the rest. But I'm not like the rest. I'll make it up, I won't go under!"

With that conversation my acquaintance with Korabelnikov effectively came to an end. Had I found the strength within me, I could probably have learned many more things of interest to a historian and student of his times (as I considered myself to be). But I could not force myself to overcome the revulsion that his face, his eyes and his tales aroused. I concealed myself among my fellow prisoners. When he made his way up and down the hold, evidently searching for me, I hid...

In Vogvozdino we were taken off the barge and he vanished somewhere. I did not see him there at all. Neither did he march in our transport. Yet Korabelnikov turned up again and, by some irony of fate, at camp No. 1. We had already worked for a month, clearing a path through the forest for the unballasted road. The weather had turned bad—day after day of cold autumn rain. We would come back soaked to the skin, dressed in the remnants of our civilian clothing which retained none of our body heat. The vast tent in which we lived was hopelessly dirty and damp. On the rough bed boards, made from small logs, we slept packed like sardines, pressed one against the other. The dirt and soot from the bonfires became so ingrained on our faces that we did not try to wash it off. Within a month Senior Lieutenant Zaliva had transformed us into walking skeletons, and our faces were now disfigured with a growth of filthy stubble.

So when I noticed Korabelnikov on the verandah of the camp office I had no fear that he would recognize me—it was impossible. He wore a new camp uniform. One could tell he already held an important post by looking at his jacket: well-made quilting had been carefully added, and two side pockets into which Korabelnikov shoved his large pale hands.

"Who's that?" I asked an experienced prisoner who had arrived at the camp with me.

"The head of the new camp outpost. Sent here by special order."

The outpost Korabelnikov had been sent to organize was, I discovered, to be used for punishing disobedient prisoners. There was always a special punitive camp in each division of the Gulag; in Ustvymlag it was No. 9. Apart from this camp, however, to which prisoners were sent on the orders of the central Ustvymlag administration, the larger camps were allowed to set up their own "local" punitive outposts as well. Zaliva petitioned for permission to have one and (he was then still in favor with the administration) his wish was granted. Korabelnikov was sent to him as an expert. He had apparently been right—his faithful service was rewarded.

The outpost was set up ten kilometers away from the main camp. The prisoners who built it whispered dreadful tales about it. Two low barracks of small-caliber timber were erected inside the compound. The walls were not insulated; there were rough continuous bed boards inside, and bars on the window. During the night, as in prison, the doors were always bolted and a slop-bucket stood inside. The food was brought to the barracks and people ate it there: 400 grams of bread and two bowls of thin soup a day, the punitive ration. But it was the punishment block that most astounded the builders. It was quite unlike the usual cells. Logs driven upright into the ground formed something resembling a well. A man was placed inside, tied up, with his head pressed to his knees. There was no entrance; simply a round lid was lifted to place the individual inside and then closed, resting on wooden pegs. There was room only for one person at a time. But since there was no heating, the cell became free very rapidly: in an hour or two the punished individual had become a frozen, unbending corpse. And that was how he was buried. Special round graves were dug to take the bodies. During that first winter the worst threat our bosses made was, "I'll have you in the round pit!"

The second small barrack at the outpost was for women. Only from them did the camp later begin to learn of all Korabelnikov's activities. Only they (and, of course, not all of them) came back from the outpost. The men perished. With almost no exceptions. To be sent to Korabelnikov's outpost meant certain death. Each time someone was taken there, the departure was transformed into an incredible and barbarous spectacle. Some of the criminals, trying in any way to delay this transfer, used to resort to an old tactic and strip themselves naked: they would not be transported like that in winter, they thought. This had no effect on Korabelnikov, however. Like the angel of death, he himself came to collect the raw material for his punishment cell. The naked man was bound, carried from the barrack across the entire compound, taken out through the guard house and thrown on a sledge. Then he was slowly driven off. The howl of the man as he gradually froze would fade away into the distance. Sadly and reproachfully shaking his head, Zaliva would gaze after another bad and foolish zek.

Korabelnikov did not see me once. The fear that he might do so was one of the greatest of all the terrors I felt in the camp. I avoided him and hid from his gaze, and it was thankfully easy to do. At the end of December 1938 I was sent to outpost No. 3. I was brought back the next spring when almost everyone there had died. It was quiet and there were few people at our camp. There had been no new transports during the winter and most of its former inhabitants were already in the cemetery. The punitive outpost had been closed down and Korabelnikov himself sent by special order back to the central administration to carry out new tasks.

In summer 1940 I was given a pass and allowed to go without an escort to the timber float. When I was on my way back I used the opportunity to visit the former punitive outpost. The compound fence had begun to lean over and, in several places, had collapsed. The barbed wire of the dead zone was trampled into the ground. A terrible deadly dampness possessed the crooked barracks. How many people had been sent here? A well-built house stood outside the compound, in which the guards and a single prisoner, Korabelnikov, had lived. The camp prostitutes who had visited the outpost said that the head of the camp had got on with the guards; he lived well and enjoyably there. Women had been brought from the camps to wash the floors and entertain them. Korabelnikov knew what his superiors needed. Not far from the compound I saw a strange construction, like a well-shaft. An absurdly large and clumsy round lid lay on the ground, almost invisible among the thick willow-herb. Around this curious structure the ground was uneven, and in several places formed humps. I did not guess immediately that this was the cemetery with its round graves...

I never met Korabelnikov again. I know nothing more about him, although when I became a "free" worker I asked the fellows at the central administration and in other camps if they knew anything. I think he was shot when all those who had been involved in Kirov's assassination and the subsequent investigation were tracked down. Tireless and faithful servants of the state, similar to Korabelniov himself, probably dealt with him. No good service record would help him now. Orders were orders: he simply had to understand.

Knowing that Korabelnikov was shot gives me no pleasure or satisfaction. When I think of him—something I try to do as rarely as possible—he seems just as alive as ever and I begin to shake with insatiable hatred. In my eyes, this tiny, insignificant man has achieved a very high rank and stands close to his chief idol, Stalin.

Colonel Tarasyuk

"Only the first ten years are terrible. After that, you get used to it." Apart from gallows humor there is a good deal of truth in this common camp saying. Under more or less routine conditions a zek who survived two to three years had a chance of serving out his whole sentence. By the summer of 1941 we were already calm and settled camp regulars. Those who couldn't stand it became part of the night's "C figures." The survivors adapted and grew accustomed to the work; they established contact with their relatives outside and regularly received letters and parcels. By then we had made firm contact with other prisoners: we were friendly with some, and others were already almost family. We received many books from Moscow and some of us were allowed to move about without an escorting guard. Zaliva was demoted and the new bosses proved more reasonable. In their attempts to get more out of the prisoners they realized that it made sense to feed them better. It didn't require particular intelligence or humanitarian enlightenment to grasp this truth: most of the bosses were former peasants and they knew how to look after livestock.

This went on until 22 June 1941, the day Hitler attacked the Soviet Union. The shock affected all without exception and among the bosses led to an idiotically pointless burst of warning and preventative measures. During the very first day of war all radio amplifiers were taken down, correspondence and newspapers were forbidden, and no more parcels were allowed. The working day was extended to ten and, by some enthusiasts, to twelve hours. All days off work were also cancelled. And of course they immediately introduced very severe cuts in the food given to the zeks.

By autumn people were beginning to be struck down by pellagra. It was the first time we had heard this awful word. With horror we began to observe in ourselves the primary and then progressive symptoms of the "disease of despair," as even the medical textbooks call it. The skin on our elbows became dry and rough and it peeled; dark spots appeared on our knuckles and rapidly turned black; around our throats a dark ring of patches blending with one another became ever clearer. Then followed a rapid loss of weight and uncontrollable diarrhea. That was almost the end. The diarrhea removed the mucous lining of the intestine and it could not be restored. Nothing could bring someone back to life after that.

Within two to three months the camp was full of living skeletons.

Only in the photographs presented by the prosecution at the Nuremburg trials have I seen such a degree of emaciation. Indifferent and without any will to live, corpse-like figures covered by a taut gray skin sat on the board beds and calmly waited for death. Carts and then sledges carried the almost weightless bodies to the cemetery each morning. By spring of 1942 the camp had ceased to work altogether. It was difficult to find people still able to cut firewood and bury the dead.

And here the military enthusiasm of the camp administration was exposed as being quite inappropriate. The war could not be fought, they discovered, without timber. It was needed for building airplanes, for making skis and pit-props. Most important of all, it was essential for explosives. Cellulose is the basis of all modern gunpowders and it is obtained, as everyone knows, from wood pulp. No matter how great their need for more soldiers at the front, timber-industry workers were almost all exempted from service. Our bosses were also exempted—but they couldn't supply the timber required of them, there was no one to cut it... Only then did their NKVD superiors start to do the minimum that reason required. Timber-felling zeks began to be fed as much as free workers. Correspondence was restored, the amplifiers were put back and newspapers started to arrive. Prisoners were the only people in the country who were allowed to receive food parcels. The old bosses were quickly removed and others sent in to replace them.

It was then that we first heard the name of the new boss of Ustvymlag, Colonel Tarasyuk.

At this time the remaining prisoners from the evacuated Berezlag joined our camp. When they described the man who had been their boss and was now to head all of Ustvymlag, they would give a very significant shake of the head and explain that Tarasyuk was the worst bastard of all. (The word they actually used, following the peculiar jargon of the camps, was "pederast" but it meant misanthrope rather than sexual deviant.) The former Berezlag prisoners also recounted at length the Colonel's staggering administrative abilities. Yet they could not keep silent about this other, still more vividly pronounced, side to his character.

In fact, Tarasyuk represented the most extreme and fully-developed type of slave owner. Before working in the camps, it was said, he had been in charge of "Internal Affairs" in Dagestan, in the North Caucasus, and was later removed from that prestigious post for "excesses." If he was really in Dagestan in 1937 then it becomes understandable why a column of centenarian Caucasians could appear at Kotlas while we were in transit there. I do not exaggerate. An entire trainload of old men aged eighty and more suddenly arrived in the Russian North from Dagestan. They did not know any Russian and expressed no desire to mix with anyone else or say how they came to be there. They sat silently on their heels with their eyes closed, in their homespun clothes and distinctive tall shaggy fur hats. Only when it was time to pray to Mecca did they rouse themselves from this immobility. They had been "withdrawn" from Dagestan, explained the zeks who hung around Distribution, as part of the elimination of feudal survivals. Many Dagestanis did not recognize the Soviet courts and preferred to go to the elders who would judge them according to *adat*, their own customs and traditions. In order to reorient the republic's inhabitants towards more progressive forms of justice all the old men were rounded up and given ten years a piece. Then they were sent to the North to die. This certainly bore the hallmark of Colonel Tarasyuk.

Now Tarasyuk was in charge of our camp and we soon felt his purposeful and iron will. He travelled around all of Ustvymlag and drove the criminals out of any work linked with food, replacing them only with "politicals." The ledger clerks in Supplies, the quartermasters and the cooks grew pale with fear when Tarasyuk appeared. Those who could work in the forest were even better-fed than their escorting guards and the free workers. Medicines appeared and non-prisoner doctors arrived. Special anti-pellagra rations were introduced. Tarasyuk restored the capacity of the camp to work with all the energy of a gifted and determined administrator. But the methods he used!

I first saw him at close range when he visited us in spring 1942. Accompanied by a vast entourage of bosses of all ranks he examined everything in the camp, including the latrines. If he came across someone working in the office or doing another job inside and it seemed to him that person was fit enough to cut timber and not idle about in the compound, he beckoned the unfortunate with a flexing of his finger (rather like the mythical giant Viy in Gogol's tale).[2] The name of the unlucky zek was immediately written down on the work distributor's plywood slate. In the evening Tarasyuk summoned the section heads. I was then standing in for the senior norm-setter and so, with all the prisoner-administrators (head of planning, chief accountant, works inspector, foremen, vets and doctors) I found myself next to Tarasyuk.

He had the face of a Roman patrician, and a coldly calm and indifferent look. The way he sat down in the camp director's armchair, lifted the telephone receiver and ordered the switchboard operator to connect him with headquarters—and the way he then spoke with them—all conveyed that he had been accustomed to giving orders for many years. He was used to having the power of life and death over those around him. The last phrase should be understood in the most literal sense. Moreover, it applied to the free workers just as much as the prisoners. The free workers were all exempted from fighting. Tarasyuk merely had to say "remove their exemption" and any of the bosses could be sent straight into battle. Telegrams "regretting to inform..." came for them with astonishing rapidity, as Tarasyuk was well aware.

He ordered the camp director to report on the condition of his "contingent," as the prisoners were termed in all official documents. Breathless with nerves, our boss listed how many of our zeks were fit "for any work," for "medium" or for "light" work; how many were in the weak team and in the sickbay. How many of them worked in the forest, in the office and doing other jobs around the compound.

Tarasyuk listened calmly and negligently to this report. Suddenly he interrupted, "How many bonus meals are handed out in the compound?"

A "bonus meal" meant a little runny porridge which was poured onto a wooden platter and cooled to form something like a jelly. The administrative and technical staff got it as well as the tree fellers and all those service personnel who did piecework, such as the laundry-workers and water-carriers. After hearing the reply, Tarasyuk calmly said, "Cut it. Use it to increase the amount for those working in the forest."

The head of General Supplies wanted to say something but Tarasyuk almost imperceptibly flashed his eyes at the man, who swallowed his words and kept quiet.

"And who are those? What did you call them?" inquired Tarasyuk.

He was referring to the "convalescent team." There were 246 of them in our camp. Our boss looked at Dr. Kogan who was the acting head of Health and Sanitation. Still young, Kogan had been sent to work in the camps after being wounded at the front. He stood up and, not without some pride, said that these people had been "plucked from the grips of pellagra." We could now be sure none of them would die... The following dialogue ensued:

> *Tarasyuk:* What are they getting?
>
> *Kogan:* They are all receiving the anti-pellagra ration established by the Gulag Health and Sanitation department (and he specified the quantity of proteins in calories).
>
> *Tarasyuk:* How many of them will go out to work in the forest, and when?
>
> *Kogan:* Well, none of them will ever go to work in the forest again, of course. But now they'll survive and it will be possible to use them for light work within the compound.
>
> *Tarasyuk:* Stop giving them any anti-pellagra rations. Write this down: these rations are to be given to those working in the forest. The other prisoners are to get the disability rations.
>
> *Kogan:* Comrade Colonel! Obviously I didn't explain clearly. These people will only survive if they're given a special ration. A disabled prisoner receives 400 grams of bread. On that ration

they'll be dead in ten days. We can't do that!

Tarasyuk looked at the upset doctor, and there was even a sign of interest on his face. "What's the matter? Do your medical ethics prevent you from doing this?"

"Of course, they do..."

"Well, I don't give a damn for your ethics!" said Tarasyuk calmly, and with no indication whatsoever of anger. "Have you written that down? Let's move on..."

All 246 died within a month.

We had both clever and stupid, kind and cruel camp bosses. Tarasyuk was something quite different. He resembled in some ways the slaveowners of classical times. The idea that his slaves were human beings never worried or concerned him. I said that his face recalled that of a Roman patrician. And he lived like a Roman who has been appointed governor of some barbarous newly-conquered province. Vegetables and fruit, and flowers quite alien to the North were grown for him in special hothouses and orangeries. The best cabinet-makers were found to make his furniture. The most famous couturiers of the recent past dressed his capricious and willful wife. When he felt unwell he was not examined by some freely-hired little doctor who had sold himself to the Gulag as a medical student. No, Tarasyuk was treated by professors who had headed the biggest Moscow clinics and were now serving their long sentences in the medical barracks of remote forest camps.

The Roman matrons, as we know, stripped naked in front of male slaves not because they were shameless but because they did not consider those slaves to be human beings. Tarasyuk, like these figures from antiquity, lacked any similar inhibitions. Moreover, he showed it not only in front of the zeks but also of the free workers who, in origin and situation, hardly differed from the prisoners. Once he gathered all the norm-setters and economists together at headquarters in Vozhael for the latest "bawling out." It was the middle of the war when the ration of even the free workers could sustain a semi-starved existence only with difficulty. The meeting had gone on for a long time and people were sitting exhausted and worn out from hunger. Suddenly well-dressed young waitresses in lace pinafores and with silk grips in their hair entered the room.

Tarasyuk was seated, as was the custom, in front of us behind a separate table. With professional speed and in silence the waitresses covered it with a spotlessly white cloth, stiff with starch. Then they laid out various-sized dishes in front of the colonel. Without interrupting the meeting Tarasyuk tucked a dazzling white napkin into the stiff collar of his uniform and uncovered the dishes. The delicious smell of some wildfowl prepared by his personal cook (formerly chef in a famous St. Petersburg restaurant) wafted over the room. We felt faint. Indifferently Tarasyuk bolted the fowl, only interrupting this activity to roar imperiously at someone or cut another short with an intimidating glance of his clear, cold eyes. So little idea had he that those before him were in any respect his equals that he could have performed any physical function in front of us, if it proved more convenient for him. It would be difficult, moreover, to call him particularly vicious.

He encouraged zeks who worked well. Those who broke production records were allowed to take women to their barracks without fearing the warders. After doctors and tailors had visited him in his mansion the cook would take them out a slice of white bread spread with butter... An unbending order was maintained throughout Ustvymlag under which those who could cut timber lived well, and those who could not, irrespective of the reason, suffered. There was order. There was even a kind of justice, if one can use that word in this context. For the camp bosses were careful not to be tyrannous under Tarasyuk, and did not steal from the prisoners—they gave them what they were due. And this meant, we found out, that we should have mattresses and even sheets. They appeared from somewhere and the prisoners slept in sheets. Truly, he was a just boss!

We hated none of the bosses like we hated Tarasyuk. Fortunately he was only with us for a short while. Once Ustvymlag was working properly again he was transferred to put another camp back on its feet.

* * *

When Rika and I found ourselves free at last we lived in Stavropol. There we went hungry all the time and counted each kopeck. One day Rika gave me her last three rubles and I went to Stalin Avenue to buy garlic sausage and bread. In the shop next door they sold newspapers which had come by the evening train. Usually I just read the copy of *Pravda* hung up in the showcase by the concert hall. My eyes lighted on *Izvestiya*, however, and a familiar surname in a black frame at the bottom of the last page made my heart almost stop. I bought the paper. "With deep sorrow the Chief Administration of the Timber Industry Camps announces that after a severe and protracted illness, the great organizer and award-bearer Colonel Tarasyuk..."

I went into the food shop and instead of sausage bought a 250 gram bottle of vodka and some bread with the remaining 30 kopecks. When I reached home I held out the newspaper to Rika as she looked at my purchases with incomprehension. I watched as her tired and worn-out face lit up with an irrepressible triumph! We sat at the table, cut up the bread and poured out the vodka. Rika did not drink as a rule but now she didn't even pretend to pour more into my glass. Sighing with relief that Tarasyuk had died, and probably in terrible pain (he must have suffered!), we drank all the vodka... He was dead and we... we were free. So there was Justice after all! Or a God? I don't know what to call it. Anyway, that's not important. The thing is, it exists.

Captain Namyatov

Namyatov was not in Tarasyuk's class at all. It was not just that one was a colonel and the other only a captain—Tarasyuk in charge of a vast camp complex and Namyatov, of a single camp. The times had changed. Tarasyuk enjoyed virtually unlimited power over many tens of thousands of people. Namyatov was head of the Chepetsk camp in Usollag when I came across him in the summer of 1954. The excitement of the post-Stalin squall had already passed and died away—the amnesty, then the new Criminal Code, and the new, unaccustomed liberal procedures. Now a refuser or someone who had broken camp rules had a long time to wait while the charge against him was drawn up. Then the charge was signed and the "quack," a doctor or medical assistant, provided a written assurance that incarceration in the punishment cell would not be harmful to the all-important health of the prisoner. After this the charge sheet was taken to Namyatov, who studied it carefully before summoning in the offender in order to make his own assessment—what was he like, how guilty was he and how capable of penitence? Then, and only then, would the actual punishment, the number of days, be determined. According to the new instructions this was how each such case was to be treated, and Captain Namyatov carried them out unswervingly.

Finally, the jailers took the offending zek to the punishment block. Formerly it had openly been called the shit house, the cooler or a number of other explicit names. Now it was "the free-standing premises." I remember my childish delight, in reading about Russia after serfdom was abolished, when I came across exactly the same term! The serfs became free men and women but still needed to be locked up or whipped from time to time. The "cooler" where these punishments had taken place before was now referred to as "the free-standing premises."

How stable our prison vocabulary and terminology has remained! Exactly the same words can be found in Dostoevsky, Doroshevich and Solzhenitsyn. Naturally, cells, peepholes and slop buckets continue to perform the same functions. But even the verbs used remain distinctive: you are not "escorted" to an interrogation or on a new transport but "taken," not "imprisoned" in the punishment block but "chucked" there. And so on. Almost nothing in this language has changed, testimony to the hellish stability of the system that gave it birth.

And perhaps it's just as well. Because one of the phrases or terms I most hate belongs exclusively to our own Soviet era: I'm referring to "special," that ubiquitous prefix. Not the most attractive-sounding word but, it might seem, a quite normal, rather bureaucratic sort of usage. Yet this prefix almost always added sinister meaning to a word. A "special operation" meant shooting people, a "special corridor" meant the strict regime solitary-confinement cells, and the "special tribunal" was the court that examined political cases. The "special section" attached to almost every Soviet organization hardly requires explanation. Even the "special canteen" is repellent because it is restricted to the privileged while a "special construction site" arouses unpleasant suspicions: either a prison is being built or a mansion for some high-ranking member of the new aristocracy...

So the zek was now taken to "the free-standing premises" or punishment block and the warder walked behind him, carrying a thin mattress. For if he had committed a simple breach of camp rules, and was not a "malicious" offender (someone to whom Namyatov applied a special new post-Stalin instruction), he was allowed "bedding" in the cell. In practice this meant a rotting straw mattress.

I have already used the word "instruction" a dozen times in recalling Namyatov and it was his attitude to such orders that most distinguished him from Tarasyuk. Tarasyuk was a satrap who made policy himself and he did not follow instructions. He did not give a damn about such papers since he issued and annulled them himself. Namyatov kept strictly to the word and spirit of each of these documents.

He was not a particularly cruel man. He never inflicted pain on another unless it was laid down in the instruction. The limited kindnesses that the instructions permitted were also dished out, without holding back a single gram. Yet when one mother travelled for weeks by train, car and boat and, finally, on foot through the forest and the bogs, Namyatov would not let her see her prisoner son. She had not known she must first get permission in Solikamsk, and no one could make Namyatov change his mind.

It is hard to convey just how much the prisoners hated him. And not just the prisoners. Once I witnessed an entertaining scene, not far from the compound, when Namyatov encountered a peasant woman who distilled spirits. Forty-two kilometers of bog-ridden forest separated the nearest village from the camp. However, many women there earned some extra money by selling vodka or spirits to the camp's inmates. The prisoners had money to spend since they were now paid almost the normal rate for the job—after all the taxes had been deducted, that is, and the costs of maintaining the guards, warders and Namyatov himself. Even so the prisoners still retained quite large sums. Most of it was then taken away by the work-team leaders, the criminal "bosses," the "honorable thieves" and the many other parasitic types there. They were the ones who bought the vodka, with the help of the escort guards or prisoners who were allowed to move about without a guard. It was the only opportunity the soldiers in the escort, with their monthly pay of 3 rubles, had to drink.

Namyatov caught a suspicious female near the compound fence and found two three-liter bottles of spirits in her bag. All who could, ran out to see what was going on. The captain followed instructions to the letter. He explained to the woman that she had committed an offense under two articles of the Criminal Code and that he would now take her to the camp office and draw up the charge sheet. Then, seizing one of the full three-liter bottles (with its red-wax seal) by its neck, he smashed it against a tree. Behind me something struck the ground. I turned. One of the young soldiers had fainted.

Namyatov was a man of great faith. He did not believe in God, of course, but in all that he had been taught in the course for future camp bosses, and in the political study classes where he worked devoutly. He implicitly believed everything in the periodicals and books that he was advised to read. This also set him apart from Tarasyuk who, of course, did not believe in anything at all. Namyatov had passionate convictions and did not allow himself the shadow of a doubt. In particular, he was certain that the institution to which he sincerely devoted all his energies was a thoroughly socialist organization. Namyatov frequently and enthusiastically declared this to be the case during the educational work with the free workers and the "contingent" that was required by his superiors' instructions.

Once when I brought in the daily work results for his signature he began to complain. He was dissatisfied that in his socialist enterprise the output per tree-feller was extremely low. I became fed up and said, "Why should you be disappointed, Citizen Captain, that the output in an ordinary timber-felling combine is higher? Ours isn't a socialist enterprise."

Namyatov sat back in his armchair and gave me a strange, frightened look.

"What do you mean, not socialist? What are we then?"

"A survival of capitalism."

"What?!? So I'm working in a survival?"

"Of course. As Lenin wrote in 'State and Revolution' certain survivals of the capitalist state, such as prisons and so on, will be preserved in our state. Marx says exactly the same. You've read everywhere that our factories and plants and our state farms are thoroughly socialist enterprises?"

"Yes."

"Have you ever, anywhere, seen the words 'socialist prison,' 'thoroughly socialist corrective labor camp'? Never!"

Our theoretical discussion concluded in a rather banal way. Namyatov summoned the warder, ordered him to handcuff me and take me to the "free-standing premises." No note from the doctor was required, neither was I given a straw mattress.

The next day the warder took me from the punishment block back to the boss. Namyatov was scowling, pale and somehow deflated.

"Go back to work," he told me severely. "And remember this: Marx and Lenin weren't writing for prisoners. The teachings of Marxism-Leninism do not apply to them..."

Evidently he had spent the entire day getting through to the political section at the central Administration so as to establish how criminal my assertion had been—and also to reinforce his own faith in socialist infallibility.

I could not help admiring the iron logic of the low-ranking official (or, perhaps, more important figure) whom Namyatov consulted. Our world, of course, led a separate existence to that inhabited by the rest of Soviet society, and to which we ourselves had earlier belonged. At the same time, we remained inseparable and indivisible from that world. The artificial division formed part of the system of illusions on which all was built. But I shall discuss that elsewhere, when I try to describe the peculiar socio-economic system of our corrective labor camps.

* * *

I want to slip in another story here, into the tale of Namyatov, that confirms Antonio's words. That it is not the rules that are important in prison, but the jailers.

Rika and I were imprisoned as "second-timers" at different moments. She was arrested almost a year earlier, in March 1949. For six months she was held in the Stavropol remand prison, then for a short while in the city jail, before being sent to the territory's transit prison. There she waited to join a transport to the Krasnoyarsk Territory, to "exile for life." I found all this out in Stavropol where I went through a routine familiar since 1937. I joined the line to see the procurator, went to the local MGB information desk each week, and found the money to pay for parcels. Then I would wait impatiently to be allowed to hand in my parcel, and then spent the whole of that exceptionally important day waiting in line outside the remand prison. I had time on my hands. After Rika was arrested I was immediately sacked. At night I worked as a drudge, writing lectures on Marxist-Leninist philosophy, the history of the Party, and the state of Soviet literature for the lecturers of the Party Territorial committee. I found a generous patron who ordered lectures for himself and several of his colleagues. The fees fed me and paid for Rika's parcels.

I had already learned that there were no new charges against her. She had been arrested again for the same "offense" and was simply waiting for the Special Board to sentence her to life exile. I was told all this by the procurator for "special cases" after I had spent several months visiting the MGB reception. When the calm gray-haired colonel explained this to me, I could not restrain myself.

"How can that be?" I demanded. "She's already served her time. Does the law really permit you to punish a person twice for the same offense?"

The procurator looked at me in amazement.

"Of course not. But what's the law got to do with it?"

On another occasion when I wanted to know if Rika's transport would be sent in a goods truck or a "Stolypin" car he answered with dignity, "We don't have any Stolypin cars, only Soviet cars. Your wife will travel in one of those..."

Half a year later they would not accept my food parcel and I learnt that Rika had been sent to Georgievsk, to the Territory's transit prison. As is always the case, people display the most uncharacteristic energy, initiative and inventiveness in such circumstances. Somehow I managed to get an acquaintance to write a letter to the head of the Georgievsk prison, borrowed money for the journey, and was so quick about it that I almost arrived there before Rika did.

I had the home address of the prison director and a letter asking him to provide help. I found the house in a quiet street on the outskirts of Georgievsk, opened the gate and entered the yard. There stood a sawhorse, and a tall elderly man in military uniform was cutting up a trunk with a two-handed saw. I could not help feeling sorry for him, I knew only too well how difficult it is to use a cross-cut saw by yourself. Did the prison director live here, I asked.

"I'm the director of the transit prison," replied the old man. "What did you want? Take a seat. Over there, that bench is clean..."

This was quite unexpected. I had some idea what prison bosses were like. Especially those in charge of transit prisons, where there was no demand to account for the "use of labor resources." And here he was, cutting up firewood on his own with a two-handed saw!

He read the letter carefully. Then he gave it back to me.

"Ivan Ivanovich asks me to help your wife. But, perhaps, you are aware that what will happen to her now is beyond my control. She comes to us with her ultimate destination already decided. Neither does the time it takes to fill up the transport and despatch it depend on me. The only reassurance I can offer is that nothing will harm her health here. You don't need anything from me in order to give her a letter or a parcel, or to send her money or visit her. Come to the prison at the fixed hours and they'll do everything for you."

I left this unusual prison boss cast down by my failure. But that day, having spent only two or three hours in the very fast-moving line, I was able to do everything I had dreamed of. My parcel and letter were accepted and they explained that I could send Rika letters and money each day from the city post office. She would receive the letters the following day and the money would be transferred to her prison account and be released as she requested. A visit could be quickly and simply organized and, moreover, it seemed that it would be arranged with the kind of punctiliousness I had not encountered even in such neutral organizations as the savings bank.

Much later, when Rika told me of her various experiences in prison she would stutter with amazement as she recalled the transit prison in Georgievsk. She had plenty to compare it with. In early 1938 she had passed through a vast number of transit prisons on her way from Moscow to the Mariinsk camps in Siberia, and then back from Mariinsk to Ustvymlag. In the autumn and winter of 1949 she travelled into exile in the car proudly termed "Soviet" by the procurator. This meant that she passed from one transit prison to another on the long route from the North Caucasus to central Siberia. Oh, we knew very well what transit prison meant! A clinging sticky filth left behind by previous transports; bedbugs and lice; hours waiting for the bathhouse where you were given a bowl with so little water that it served only to smear the dirt over your body; the heat disinfection chambers where buttons melted and fur burnt but, by some miracle, the parasites survived. Then there was the insatiable hunger (because it was almost legal not to feed the prisoners in transit), the thieving and robbery of the staff, and the bestial ferocity of the guards. Everyone was a "stranger" there. Here today, gone tomorrow, never to return. This prompted a total lack of responsibility towards the prisoners. Anything could be done to them. And it was.

Yet here was the transit prison in Georgievsk. The cells were not only swept but washed, both the floors and the bed boards. The food was so filling that the constant hunger of prisoners in transit disappeared. You could really get clean in the bathhouse. There was even a special and fully-equipped room (and this amazed Rika more than anything else!) where the women could primp and perk... In this prison letters were quickly handed out and telegrams delivered at any hour of day. Each morning fresh newspapers were brought to the cell, and not once were prisoners denied their exercise period. Every day it was possible to buy a wide selection of items for the forthcoming journey: rusks, processed cheese, sugar, tobacco, matches...

Yet the most important, unaccustomed and incomprehensible thing was a certain atmosphere of compassion. Perhaps, it seemed to us, it was by following the instructions that they showed their compassion? No, that was not it. Before her transport set out the head of Culture called in Rika and said that she should only have 99 rubles with her on the journey. Rika was sufficiently experienced to take the hint: anything above that sum would be taken by the guards and lost forever and should therefore be hidden so as not to be found during the search. This was not a very difficult task. During the most thorough search in transit an experienced prisoner could take virtually anything, up to a dismantled medium-sized tank, with him!

Incidentally, while I unfailingly believed my wife's stories I was given the chance to find out for myself. A year later I also ended up in Georgievsk prison and the months I spent there did not cease to amaze me. It was not the cleanliness or the nourishing food that astounded me but the exhibition of the maximum humanity possible in prison.

A jailer is obliged to carry out innumerable instructions, each of which is intended to restrict the prisoner's life and make it as tormenting as possible. This affects everything. If he takes you out for interrogation or on toilet duty, he makes you walk with your hands behind your back and the moment he strikes his key against his belt buckle, you must face the wall and freeze. If he brings you a food parcel he cuts everything up, crumbles it and tastes it, doing everything to make it lose its most important quality—that it's straight from home. When he leads you to the toilet he doesn't care how your insides are working but drives you straight back again, without allowing you to rinse your hands and face... Most important of all, a jailer must never develop any remotely human relations with a prisoner. He does not have the right to chat, ask questions, listen to the answers or himself answer questions. He must not sympathize, smile, laugh or cry—in a word, he cannot demonstrate his human qualities.

Yet you can come across jailers who, while eagerly observing every instruction (and they cannot do otherwise!), still break the most important unwritten rule of their profession—do not show any humanity. Rika and I, and many of my comrades, sometimes met such jailers. Rika told me about a warder at the Stavropol remand prison. They all knew that her name was Klava. She did everything according to the rules but, for some reason, she took a liking to Rika. She did not hurry her in the toilet, never raised her voice and always chose Rika to carry out the garbage after the cells had been swept. This was practically a second exercise period. The garbage had to be carried to the distant third prison courtyard. The yards were vast and on the way she and Rika conversed. Actually, only Rika spoke and Klava did not reply, since Rika knew from experience not to ask her any questions. It was simply pleasant for Rika to be able to comment: what fine weather it was, how nice not to have to wear an overcoat, look how the flowers in the corner of the yard have come into bloom. Klava would listen, and smile.

The smile of a warder is, of course, the first deviation from instructions. Then Klava was put in charge of food parcels. That was where I made her acquaintance.

Such parcels were immensely important in our lives. It was the only chance of letting the person in prison know you were still there and of finding out something about them. Parcels were accepted once a week, and then once every ten days. I would prepare long in advance. I got hold of some money, thought what to buy and decided what to pack it in. This last was so important! To see the butter dish from home for a few minutes, or a familiar plate or cup you had noticed at a friend's place, was like a conversation, an entire language of its own. Our friends are sending you some home-made curds—do you recognize the cup? I'm fine, staying with Zhenya: you remember this plate, don't you, with the chipped edge?

Then there was the list of contents. Of course, you could only write down the items included. But how important to see familiar handwriting! Klava never hurried Rika when she had to sign her name at the bottom of the list. Patiently she waited while Rika carefully (and using as many words as she could!) wrote out: the day, month, that she had received everything, absolutely everything, and then her name and surname. It was a letter in itself. It was also possible to pass on a request through Klava, please bring this or that. Once Klava gave me back the cigarettes and, with a smile—yes, she was smiling!—said, "Your wife is returning the cigarettes because, from today, she is giving up smoking. She asked me to tell you that from now on..."

It was our day, my present, and Klava understood that and rejoiced at my happiness. Once, however, on Rika's birthday, I succumbed to a foolish recklessness and poured some wine into the jar of fruit-juice I was handing in for her. Klava rapidly brought the jar back, "Your wife doesn't want any fruit juice," she said and, lowering her voice, added: "Don't ever do that again, they might stop her getting any parcels."

Klava developed, quite against the rules, some kind of fellow feeling for Rika and myself. One day she returned the parcel and with a certain anxiety in her voice, added, "She's left the prison." Then, rapidly, "Go straight to the city prison. It's parcel day there today, and you'll still be in time."

I do not know if she remembered my surname—there were so many of us!—but she remembered me. When, seven months later I was in the remand prison myself, and the woman from whom I had rented my room prepared me a parcel, Klava and the warder entered the solitary confinement cell where I was being held and placed the parcel on the table. She turned to me and, though I was already gray, with a shaven head covered with a whitish stubble, she instantly recognized me. She grew pale, even in a prison cell it was noticeable, and her eyes became so scared and sad that it was very difficult for me to maintain my composure. I was glad this was the only parcel I received and that I never met Klava again in the prison.

* * *

But I must finish the story of Namyatov. He did not get on in the Chepetsk camp. First he was appointed head of a large construction site, building a single-track railway each kilometer of which cost a million rubles. They built the depot, the workshops, warehouses, the timber stores, a settlement for free workers and compounds for the prisoners. It was then that various "clever" NKVD men or very foolish economists decided that the same rules ought to be extended to the camps: the same norms, calculations and various complicated and ridiculous "indicators." Well, I don't know what was going on outside but in the camps it was only possible to get anything built by brazenly and openly infringing all instructions, rules, laws and "indicators." In other words, by disregarding everything in which Namyatov believed so passionately. All the free camp bosses from the foremen to the lieutenants worked hand in glove with the criminal work-team leaders—boosting their nominal output, paying vast extra sums, adding credits, letting the criminal "bosses" drink vodka and take the zeks' wages, and pocketing this confiscated money themselves with no inhibitions. Namyatov could see that he was surrounded by the most blatant and insolent thieving but there was nothing he could do.

What could he have done, in fact? A railway was under construction. As in any normal construction work, the bank transferred the money as each separate stage was completed. Some bright fellows from unknown organizations had dreamed up their own system of incentives for the work force. The major part of the finance was to be transferred after the last stage in construction, when the rails and sleepers had finally been laid. They thought this would speed things up, unconcerned that the most labor-intensive and time-consuming work was not laying the rails but clearing the stumps from the future line and building up the ballast. The crafty foremen quickly found a solution. They rapidly chucked down the sleepers and bolted on the rails along a tract that had only just been cleared, leaving the stumps in the ground. The work was approved and was considered to have been two-thirds completed. Only then did they begin to dig out the stumps from under the sleepers and pour down the ballast. It does not take much to imagine the extra cost and the unnecessary work involved in meeting these numerous "indicators."

Namyatov walked around in a daze. Most of all it worried him that he was handing out phoney credits that earned the prisoners remission. He could not avoid it because then they would not have worked at all, and his superiors would have got rid of him. His bosses knew the game well enough, and turned a blind eye. Namyatov, however, found another way of salving his pristine conscience. Following his instructions down to the very last letter, he did everything to deprive the prisoners of those credits. There were vast, almost unlimited, opportunities for doing this. A credit could be taken away for talking when lined up, for not urinating in the toilet, for not clearing up bedding properly, for answering back, for trying to get around the camp censorship when writing letters... It was very hard to accept. You thought you would be free in nineteen months and then they told you that you had lost your credits for the last six months: that meant you had almost another eighteen months to serve and, consequently, would only get out in something over three years time. It was hard enough for an ordinary prisoner to take but most of the zeks were "peasants" not criminals. The majority had been sentenced for misappropriation of state property and were working as hard as they could, counting each day, each kopeck.

Several times he deprived me of my credits, for "answering back," "lowered norms" and avoiding camp censorship. I was not especially worried: I was in for a full ten years and, anyway, I was sure I would be released any day now, even though more than two years had passed since the "Boss snuffed it", i.e., since Stalin's death. It still affected me, though, being deprived of my credits, and Namyatov knew this. So I was amazed that when the telegram confirming my release arrived, he called me in and suggested that I stay on as a free worker.

"What are you laughing about? If you all go crawling back to Moscow who's going to be a free worker here?"

"You will, Citizen Captain. We're the ones with a sentence to serve. You signed on forever."

"Get out!"

When I left the compound I was searched as I had never been searched on arrest or in transit. Namyatov's orders. Probably he was sure I was taking a lot of money with me.

I later learned that Namyatov, as if to prove me wrong, left his job a year afterwards. He took his well-earned pension and went to live a free and clean life in Kislovodsk where he had bought himself a house, and an orchard a little way off, and roses around the balcony. He was still physically very strong, a man only in middle age who might have enjoyed the happy life his honest labors had earned him for a long while yet. But a year, or at most a year and a half, later Namyatov did not return home from a walk. The next day they found him in a grove outside the city. He was hanging, with his hands tied, from the branch of an old pine tree. There was an outcry in the resort town and the police did everything possible to track down his assassins, organizing raids to pick up all the known criminals. I know perfectly well, however, that it was not they who killed Namyatov.

Dignified peasants who had never harmed another creature, unless it was a German during the war, had at last been released and could not resume a normal existence until their natural feeling of justice had been satisfied.

Major Vypolzov

Vypolzov replaced Tarasyuk as head of Ustvymlag, and his appointment was received by the zeks with much the same feeling as, eight to nine years later, they greeted Stalin's replacement by other leaders. Life did not "become better" (to adapt Stalin's notorious declaration), but it did "become merrier." More human, somehow... Tarasyuk placed himself above everyone else and, probably, did not consider others, including the free workers, to be human beings at all. Vypolzov was like the rest, he lived among real people and he understood every human weakness and desire. Prisoners get to know all about their bosses and they enjoyed the fact that he liked his drink, liked his women and frequently shifted his light-hearted affections. It's very good when the boss is not without his weaknesses!

Furthermore, Vypolzov loved all beautiful and elegant objects; he was an art lover. This meant a great deal to many of those in the camp. All the surviving artists, sculptors, wood carvers and cabinetmakers were gathered together at the "Zimka" outpost. Officially it was reserved for the disabled, who produced various consumer goods there. They did actually make wooden and clay toys, simple pottery and certain wooden household trifles. That, however, was the work of ordinary craftsmen. The artists produced quite different objects. There were superb ceramic pots and dishes that would have enhanced any museum or exhibition. Caskets, cigar and cigarette boxes of original design, which played tunes when they were opened, were fashioned from birch knots, with decorative inlays and secret locks. Carloads of oak, beech, walnut, maple and ash were transported by clever dealers from camps to the south. Then the cabinetmakers—but they too were artists, not simple artisans!—made furniture that would have graced any palace. At the small leather works suede was prepared from deerskins and Warsaw tailors made costumes that were striking in their non-Russian elegance. They also prepared the most valuable furs there and sewed blankets of ermine... And a great deal else. Vypolzov loved beautiful objects, paintings, furniture, pottery and other trifles.

This was very important. Had Stalin felt the need to decorate his dozens of dachas and mansions with items that had some connection, no matter how vague, with real art then, I am convinced, we would have lived much better. At the very least, a great many lives would have been saved. But the Leader preferred to pin up pictures and photographs reproduced in the "Ogonyok" weekly and to use tables and chairs of the kind to be found in station waiting-rooms.

The artistic output at "Zimka," of course, was not for sale, was not registered by any organizations or sold on the market. But, in addition to his love of beautiful objects and the pleasures of life, Vypolzov was neither tightfisted nor greedy. He appreciated it when others displayed good taste and so most of the items made by his artists and craftsmen were sent to various of his superiors in Syktyvkar and Moscow. Large, sturdy trunks were got ready and filled with numerous presents for the different bosses who came on official visits to Ustvymlag. Vypolzov was very familiar not only with the tastes of his various superiors, but also the ethical principles of each. A suede suit and ermine blanket were prepared for one boss, a complete bedroom suite for another, while others received some little souvenir carved from elkhorn to amuse the children. The disabled prisoners were allowed to roam the bogs and forests without escort guards, gathering the discarded elkhorns.

Since Vypolzov loved art he also acted as a patron of the arts.

It is only fair to add that all those in charge of the camps, with the exception, naturally, of Tarasyuk, loved art and encouraged the formation of amateur and professional artistic ensembles. These had existed since the building of the White Sea Canal in the early 1930s but then they were quite definitely amateur performers. Now it was possible to put together an excellent troupe made up of thoroughly professional and even famous actors and singers.

Vypolzov put art in Ustvymlag on a very high footing. Actors and musicians were brought from all the nearby and distant camps to the base camp outside Vozhael and organized into an ensemble. They did not go out to work but were registered as Group C or with the "weak team" (at the expense, of course, of those who really were ill and enfeebled because there was a very strict limit on numbers permitted in these categories) and they enchanted the bosses with their talents. They staged the most fashionable plays of the day: Gusev's "Glory," Korneichuk's "Plato Krechet" and other highly artistic, life-affirming theatrical works. Singers performed "The Blue Scarf," "Seagull," "You are waiting, Lizaveta" and similar popular songs from the cinema and elsewhere. The ballerinas and folk dancers dashed about the stage in ardent, similarly optimistic dances. With weakened fingers the violinists and cellists would play Saint-Saens "Rondo capriccioso" and Mendelsohn's "Song without Words." For although the bosses preferred the positive and life-affirming, they were, nevertheless, still human and sometimes found it pleasant, in the comfort and warmth of the club, to become a little maudlin to the melancholy strains of such soft melodies.

The club in Vozhael was, actually, an enormous centrally-heated building with a fine stage, a handsome auditorium, and a foyer decorated by superb artists. It provided work and food for a large team of artists, stage designers and prop makers. Sometimes all of them were loaded into a truck and taken out to reward the camp with the best "output." This was always a major event for everyone involved.

In all the camps of the Komi republic—and there were a great many of them!—there were directors who patronized the arts and paraded their serf ensembles in front of each other. The most fortunate, it seems, was the head of Ukhtizhimlag. He maintained a real opera troupe in Ukhta, which was directed by none other than Konstantin Egert, the handsome and famous actor of the Maly Theater who starred in the film "Bear's Wedding." The superb leading soprano of the Harbin operetta sang with them, Radunskaya of the Bolshoi danced for them, and the orchestra was made up of first-class musicians, including the viola-player Krein who had led the famous trio.

Sometimes the head of Ukhtizhimlag would pay his neighboring colleagues a visit. Although the official purpose was "to share experience," this flat description belies the elaborate preparations and protocol which more resembled a visit by a foreign head of state. The bosses were accompanied by a large entourage of their section heads, special hotel accommodation was prepared for them, routes were carefully planned and presents were brought in from "Zimka." The Ukhtizhimlag boss also brought his best performers with him so that his hosts could see that the arts were just as flourishing there, if not more so.

I once had a chance to see the Ukhta operetta. I was already a free worker and had been summoned to Vozhael for the planning meeting that formed part of the Ukhta bosses program. So I was also able to enjoy a long-forgotten spectacle, admittedly from the very last row.

It was the most enchanting sight. The war had ended and trainloads of clothing gathered from abandoned homes reached the camp from East Prussia. They were sold at knock-down prices to the free workers and other camp staff, who then had them successfully altered by the camp's tailors. When it came to costumes for their performers the bosses were most generous with the booty. They were staging Silva³ at the club in Vozhael and, by God, it was as good a show as the Stanislavsky operetta theater ever put on in Moscow!

I found it impossible to take my eyes off those beauties in their wonderful, extravagant costumes. Their eyes shone as brightly as the paste diamonds they wore on their fingers, in their ears and round their necks. The handsome men were dazzling in their elegant frock coats, worn with style and panache. The foolish desire to believe that somewhere, in some distant kingdom or state, people really lived like that was so intense and overpowering. Could people somewhere really take such dramas, such happiness and misfortunes, seriously?! "Do you recall," sang Silva in joyful suffering, "how fortune smiled on us?" and I took a physical delight in this suffering, the languor in her voice, and all the dazzling theatrical extravagance of this joyous and beautiful spectacle.

The show ended. In the foyer a jazz band of zeks from the base camp played the latest Polish tango. The NKVD officers began to circle the dance floor with their plump, rosy-cheeked partners and, despite all alterations, their dresses still retained something of the elegance and style of that foreign existence. It was almost depressing to gaze at the dancing couples after the beauty and artistry of the performance, so I went outside. It was the end of November and a recent snowstorm had whipped up enormous drifts around the building. The sky was clearing, with the beginnings of a severe frost, and the stars glittered, as always in winter, with a gloomy power and a remote indifference to all that is alive.

By the "stage" entrance I heard a commotion and the familiar cries of the escort guard: "Stop slithering around like a louse on a wet prick!" "Move it!" "Up, up, quickly!" "No talking!" I turned the corner and encountered a totally familiar and accustomed sight: prisoners, men and women, dressed almost alike in padded trousers, crumpled work jackets and ugly short coats, were forming up, tired and unwilling, into an escorted column. The guards hurried them along, cursing obscenely. They wanted to get the prisoners back to the base camp and return in time to watch the dancing, even if they were not allowed to dance themselves. For some reason the prisoners' faces seemed familiar. It took a moment to realize where I had just seen them—handsome, young, happy and elegant despite all the misfortunes and upsets of their operetta love affair. Of this, though, not the slightest trace now remained in those captive faces. They were just like the rest of us, showing their age, the effects of numerous transfers, of exhaustion and of the desire, which I knew only too well, to reach the warm barrack as soon as possible, where they could undress, drink a mug of hot water and chew a piece of bread.

Still, they were probably thankful, all the same, to their patrons that they would not have to get up for roll call and go out in the darkness to perform an unbearably hard and murderous job in the forest!

Vypolzov was a patron of the arts and therefore a kinder boss than many. He did not enjoy a very spectacular career—such people do not usually attain the highest posts. After Ustvymlag he was in charge of other camps and stayed long enough to earn the large pension of an MGB colonel. Without in the slightest having lost his zest for life and his love of elegance, he is probably now living in a fine house built long ago somewhere in the south, surrounded by beautiful and expensive objects. Well, let him!

Major-General Timofeyev

The many hundreds of thousands of prisoners who passed through (or would never return from) the timber-cutting camps of the Urals, Komi, Karelia, the Archangel region and Siberia all knew the name of Major-General Timofeyev.

Each morning at roll call the latest orders were read out. Fugitives and refusers had been shot for "counter-revolutionary sabotage." Certain prisoners had been given new sentences for negligent treatment of the horses, vehicles, their clothing or other state property. (The zeks themselves came under the last category, and "self-mutilation" was also an offense.) All of these orders concluded with the words: "signed by the Head of the NKVD Main Administration for Timber-industry Camps, Major-General Timofeyev." He was, in other words, almost the chief jailer as far as we were concerned. Not everyone has had the opportunity to see such a high-ranking jailer. I saw Timofeyev no less than twice. But to explain how that happened I must provide the lengthy prehistory to our meeting. I hope my potential future readers will forgive me.

For reasons beyond our control, any term of imprisonment eventually comes to an end. Those sentenced with me to only five years should have been freed while the war was still on; and in a few years time, the eight-year convicts, who then formed the majority in the camps, were also due to be released. So something had to be done. There were a great many ways of coping. New sentences could be handed out for new "offenses" committed in the camps. Releases could be held up either "until the end of the war" or, simply, "until special instructions" were issued. Those released were then considered free but restricted in the same way as exiles: they received no identity documents and did not have the right to leave their particular camp, let alone the area covered by the central camp administration. They were obliged, even when living outside the compound, to continue performing the same work as inside, cutting up timber, mending vehicles, sewing coats, working in accounts... This was termed "remaining assigned to the camp until special instructions." I fell under two of these categories, as a "second-timer" and then as an "assigned" person.

My sentence was five years and it was due to expire on 17 April 1943. I did not draw attention to myself as a prisoner and so they probably would not have bothered to give me a new sentence had it not been for one circumstance. At the beginning of the war the bosses at each camp, carrying out some instruction "on raising vigilance," began hauling in all those prisoners whom they did not want to release or, for reasons of their own, simply wanted to kill. It was quite simple. The informers wrote down in their reports what the security officers dictated to them. Criminals were bribed with a packet of tobacco to provide the necessary eyewitness testimony. The accusation was always one and the same, defeatist agitation. It earned a sentence of ten years and where necessary the offense became collective, "group agitation": this was the equivalent of "setting up an organization" and under Articles 58:10 and 58:11 carried the death sentence. People were arrested again, held in the local prison and interrogated before being sent on to Vozhael from all over Ustvymlag. There they were tried by the special collegium and either shot or given new sentences and sent to the punitive camp, where there was no certain guarantee of survival.

Among those picked up in Camp No. 1 was the former director of an electric power station, Oleg Staskevich. A young man of an ironic turn of mind, he already had a checkered past despite his youth. He also had a loose tongue. We lived together in a small barrack for only fifteen persons. In the vigourous campaign to raise the country's defensive capacity, camp security decided to make an example of Oleg. He was arrested and all his associates were taken in turns to see the "godfather," the camp security officer, in his little house with its special separate entrance and exit.

Our godfather, Chugunov, very much wanted to make me testify as a witness. For this he needed to "turn the screws on me." He went about it in the usual way. I was seized during the night and thrown in the punishment block. The next morning I was accused of having delivered a long and passionate speech, in the presence of A and B, in which I implored Hitler to speed up his conquest of the Bolsheviks, liberate Russia and, naturally, me as well. The investigation got under way and, like any primitive, well-oiled and functioning machine, it went to work: an indignant statement by one eyewitness, the testimony of several others, face-to-face encounters... It was quite amusing to read the bombastic patriotic declarations, often stolen from the newspapers, in depositions provided by semi-literate petty thieves and "jackals" who had sunk to the last stages of degradation and humiliation in the camps. Yet I understood what the result would be—and there was little to laugh about. A few days later Chugunov finished the investigation, gave me form No. 206 to sign and, finally, came to the point of the whole exercise. If I would sign a testimony he had already drawn up against Staskevich then, "on his word of honor as a Communist" (yes, he actually used those words!), he would immediately, in front of my very eyes, throw my new case file into the stove.

The two sides, as they say in communiques, could not reach agreement and the enraged godfather took the obvious next step. As someone due to "appear in court" I was transferred to another camp and after working there, felling trees, for two months it was my turn to come before the judge. (The line was quite long and no one was in any hurry to get ahead.) We set off on foot for Vozhael. It was February 1942 and a snowstorm had just obliterated all the roads, sweeping away the ballast, so that the guard led me and three refusers along the snowdrifts, following the barely visible markers that indicated the routes of the former roads. It took us four or five days to cover sixty kilometers, spending the nights in the punishment blocks of the camps along our way. For me it proved a very important journey. I had nothing to hope for and could think back, in complete freedom, over everything—my own life, that of my friends, all my actions and beliefs—without concern for the consequences or self-deception.

We finally reached Vozhael, were put in prison and within two days were tried. The court if not just, was at least rapid. I was summoned from a corridor crowded with others taking the same "exam" and in half an hour was awarded a new sentence for "defeatist agitation in war time." It was already dark when they led me from the court through the free workers' settlement to the base camp. Now, I knew, they would send me off to Camp No. 9 and I would probably never again see the normal human world that I was now passing behind its gauze-draped, lighted windows. Orange lampshades, made from gauze dyed with crushed red streptocide pills, hung above white tablecloths. The silhouettes of women and children moved freely and easily in the rooms, laying out a meal on the table. They were waiting for husbands to come back from work before they could eat... There was something touchingly domestic, almost Dickensian, in these flickering family scenes. I did not somehow grasp that it was the jailers who lived there. To me it was just one more part of that old, kind, familiar world, with its great and little joys, that I was now leaving forever. I said my farewells because I was convinced I would not be strong enough to survive.

People usually consider themselves weak and have no conception of their physical malleability or their extraordinary ability to adapt to almost any circumstances. I then thought that I would reach a limit of exhaustion beyond which all desire and capacity to resist disappeared. I had watched many very young men die because, it seemed to me, they had grown tired of living.

That was in spring 1939. They brought me back from the outpost where I had spent the winter to the main camp. I was half-alive and covered, like a panther, with large black spots, the result of scurvy; they would not completely fade for many years. My life was saved by a handsome and exceptionally amusing scallywag who had been working in Camp No. 1 as a doctor and had treated me when I first arrived. In the meantime he had finished his three-year sentence and on release he told his successor that he should track me down and, if

I was still alive, help me to survive. The new doctor Alexander Zotov informed Zaliva that he must have a medical student in his last year of studies to assist him, and gave him my name. They found me at outpost No. 3, put me on a sledge and took me to the hospital at the camp.

What they called a hospital was a quite ordinary barrack where the starved and emaciated patients lay dying. Zotov quickly brought me back to life, fattening me up like the cannibal's wife feeding Hop o' My Thumb. When I was myself again, he sketched for me the magnificent prospects of becoming a medical worker. While I was listed in the weak team he appointed me as orderly. This meant that I stayed alone on duty in the barrack at night. The three weeks I did the job were probably the most terrible in my life. My duties were quite simple. I was given a syringe and three ampoules (never more) of camphor. It was left up to me which of the dying I should inject. I walked around the board beds and when I saw someone who had died, I closed their eyes and bound their arms and legs. The first was a traditional and largely aesthetic operation. The second was purely practical: it made it easier to toss such a corpse, already beginning to stiffen, into the box used to take them to the cemetery.

I had a naive faith that the ampoules really helped and tried to use them on the young. I felt most sorry of all for them. I saw teenagers there, however, who died fully conscious and without the slightest sign of fear in the face of advancing death. (They were mainly "fragments," as the Lubyanka poetically referred to the children of the exterminated Party and state elite.) It was as though they were very old men, weary after a lengthy life and looking on death as a welcome release. These seventeen- and eighteen-year-olds were so worn out by the arrests, searches, interrogations, transfers, hunger, cold and unbearable labor that they had no fear of it all ending. They made no efforts to stay alive and when I injected them with camphor they quite calmly asked, "What's the point? I'll be dead by morning."

In the morning the head of the medical unit, a tall pimply young medical assistant in a junior lieutenant's uniform would come round. He would summon me and, briskly pulling a notebook from his pocket, demand, "How many fatalities during the night?"

Neatly he noted down fifteen, or twenty, or still more, and left. He did not come back to the barrack all day.

I imagined, therefore, that I would also experience the same loss of resistance as those dying boys. So I calmly said my farewells to this world, without especial fear, simply with regret and a certain mild sorrow. Later I understood I had been quite wrong. Those poor children in the medical barrack died like old men because they were fatally ill with scurvy, pellagra, dystrophy or totally undiagnosed pneumonia. No one was treating them, no one took their temperature and if they had, it would have been below normal. All the life functions of someone with dystrophy pursue a different course to those of a healthy person.

Today I know from experience that of all the advanced forms of life, or at least among mammals, human beings are the most malleable and adaptable. No other animal, be it a cow, a pig or a dog, could withstand what the prisoners endured in our camps.

In February 1942, however, I still did not know that. And it would certainly have never occurred to me then that a whole decade would pass, during which I would be freed, visit Moscow and again undergo arrest, trial, transport, prison and the camps. Nor that I would eventually be released and enjoy many happy years as a free man. I could not have imagined myself sitting here, writing these memoirs in Yalta, on a warm and sunny November day. I shall just finish this page... and then I'll go down to the sea with Rika. We'll walk along the always lively seafront, stand by the parapet and then go to the park where the melancholy, southern autumn breathes of fading leaves and the last blooming roses. In a few weeks time we shall return to Moscow and, once back in my cramped study, surrounded by books, I shall take out a manuscript and continue my biography of a wonderful and sorrowful scientist who died in 1912...[4] Of course, as a form of youthful bravado one can use mechanical logic to refute my naive faith in the individual's capacity to resist his circumstances. Yet how many times, when my back has been up against the wall, have I recalled the way I said farewell to past and future on a February night in 1942...

* * *

Like Pushkin's Yevgeny Onegin, "I did not die, nor yet go mad" (the causes were quite different, of course)... I did not even end up in Camp No. 9. A friend of mine, who had already completed his sentence and been appointed head of labor and wages for Ustvymlag, managed to persuade them to send me back as norm-setter at Camp No. 2. There were very few who could perform this much-needed work and once I had acquired the skill, it stood me in very good stead all my years in the Gulag.

The result was that I found myself back in the office at Camp No. 2 but now under escort, serving a new sentence. The following months I survived without any great enthusiasm. It was difficult to take: six weeks before my release I had been given a new sentence. Even if the prospect of freedom had been relative and fairly illusory, it was very hard when 17 April 1943, the day of my supposed release, came and went. As at the beginning of any sentence, the future appeared difficult and almost without end.

This was my mood through that spring and the early summer. At the end of June, as I was passing the head of the guards in the compound, he called out, "Some papers came about your release, it seems."

I remained quite unmoved. There had already been such cases. A prisoner was convicted of a "new" offense. A while later someone in Distribution came across a list of those due for release where they had forgotten to add the poor devil's new sentence. A paper summoning him to the transit camp was issued before the mistake was discovered. I went to the director. I shall find time elsewhere to write about Anatoly Yepanichnikov. He was young and a rare figure among jailers—kind, polite, filled with goodwill towards the prisoners. There was a paper about my release, he confirmed, and added that it had evidently been an oversight. He would not send me off since it was too exhausting to be transferred there and back again, and to spend frustrating days at the transit camp for no purpose. He would simply inform the Distribution department of the misunderstanding. I thanked Yepanichnikov and went back to my office.

Suddenly, I felt I could not work. What if it was not a misunderstanding but true? For the first time in all those months my thoughts were no longer under my control. I could not think about anything else. I went to Distribution. There were several free workers there, among them a wonderful girl named Zhenya (her father, one of the bosses, had fallen out of favor with Tarasyuk and been sent off to fight). I began begging Zhenya to ring up Vozhael and find out from Distribution why a paper for my release had been sent, when in fact... Zhenya gave a sigh. It was very difficult to get through to Ustvymlag headquarters and she thought there was no hope in my case. But she was a kind creature and felt sorry for me. She began cranking the telephone handle, and she went on for an hour, and then two. She could not stop because I stood over her and did not take my eyes off her. At last she got through, was connected to the relevant inspector and began patiently to explain the misunderstanding that had arisen. Suddenly her expression changed. She turned pale, added, Yes, yes, I understand, and slowly replaced the receiver. Tears burst from her eyes and then, unexpectedly and without any provocation, she threw her arms round my neck.

"Lev Emmanuilovich!" she began to tell me, through her tears, "It's true, it's all true! You've been released! they've revoked the sentence, completely revoked it!"

You do not forget such moments. I went through almost the same thing once more in 1955 when (it was again summer) I was released five years before the end of my sentence. That night Yepanichnikov achieved an unheard-of feat. He took one of the trucks that carted the timber, put me and an escort guard inside and sent it off to the transit camp, ordering the driver to let us out several kilometers away. Had his superiors caught him it would have gone very badly for him! A week later I returned alone, like a free man, to

Camp No. 2. This time I had a paper not from Distribution but from the personnel department, appointing me to the same post I had held as a prisoner. I was now "assigned to the camp" and left the compound to live in a separate room in the free-workers' barrack.

Why did they release me? I became quite celebrated in Ustvymlag as the only person sentenced for "defeatism" to have his conviction quashed. The story is as follows. Everything, even in the camps, follows a strictly observed law and so when I received a new sentence I was given twenty-four hours to write to the Appeals tribunal. They gave me a piece of paper and I sat down in the empty barrack at the base camp and began to think over the literary task I now faced. Although the chances of success were minimal they still existed. Chugunov had turned in very sloppy work when he drew up the charge sheet. He used the same accusation against everyone and so far it had worked. In my case, however, he had forgotten something. I was Jewish. Almost all my close friends and relatives were Communists and were fighting against the Germans. For me to become a defeatist meant that I must have gone off my head, at the very least! There was a chance here. But how could I make that unknown official take any notice of my appeal? There were thousands of similar sentences and appeals and they probably did not read any of them. So I had to write in such a way as to draw their attention. First, the text should be written very clearly, using that library script I had been taught on my special courses, and it must occupy no more than half a page. Second, it had to open with a phrase that would intrigue this custodian of the law and end in a way that could not leave him unmoved...

I consider this appeal to be the best thing I have ever written. "My case must be the only one of its kind in the world," it began. "I am a Jew and some fifteen of my relatives have been murdered by the Germans in Belorussia; the other half of my family is fighting at the front. Yet, being of sound mind, and five months before I was due to be released, I am accused of publicly inviting Hitler to conquer the Soviet Union." This was followed by a laconic and extremely sarcastic description of the "case" against me. I stopped, and began to think how to end the appeal. "My conviction is not a private matter but is of fundamental significance. I am sure that the Jewish Anti-Fascist Committee will appreciate this. If necessary I shall turn to them for help."

I began to picture what would happen when the procurator (or whoever it was) pulled my text out of the pile of papers and lazily began to run his eyes over it. He had never seen such a short appeal before! He read it to the end and then began, so I imagined, to look through the charge sheet and sentence which were stitched to the appeal. "The idiots! the lazy, sloppy idiots," I heard him muttering aloud or to himself, cursing Chugunov and the court: "Couldn't they have thought up something different for this zek? They've got so lazy they've stopped using their brains at all!" Then, glancing at the personal details in the charge sheet, And he's a journalist as well! This bastard'll certainly write to his Jewish Committee (or perhaps he said that bunch of Yids?) and then we'll never hear the end of it! Roundly cursing his Gulag colleagues again, he added his decision, "Sentence revoked!"

I shall never find out what really happened. Yet I believe that my suppositions are quite close to the truth. In any case, the appeal board did not send my case for re-investigation or to be heard again but simply revoked the sentence. I don't even know what justification they provided. I was released but, of course, as someone "assigned to the camp until further instructions."

My new status permitted me, as a free man, to live outside the camp compound, marry and become a member of a trade union. I received a wage and I could attend meetings and take part in political education classes. I could move freely about Camp No. 1 but I had still to work there and, since a forestry camp was considered to be a defense enterprise, unauthorized absenteeism would result in a five-year sentence... Incidentally, the "assigned" individual was also kindly relieved of the (by now) tediously familiar procedures of arrest, investigation, trial and transfer: if the bosses found something they didn't like in the free man's behavior the camp procurator drew up a decree that released him from his "assignment," and drove him back inside the compound where he was interned as a prisoner "until special instructions."

Several months after the war ended, unknown to us, an order was issued that permitted bosses to grant the status of almost free citizens to former prisoners with particularly good conduct and work records. They received a passport, could move about outside the camp and even go away during vacation periods, which had now been restored again. The passport, it is true, was restricted by Article 39 of the law governing passports and so the holder could not visit the main city in almost all the Regions, or the capitals of the fifteen Union republics and many other cities and towns. Neither could he leave the camps. There were also a great many other things he could not do but since those on the outside were also deprived of these rights it was not important. Now no one could drive you back into the compound without a trial. Most important of all, you could take leave and go and see all that remained of your life—home, family, native town and friends. It was true freedom and the desire to attain this much became the most important thing in our lives.

I gained this status as well but I shall not go into all the details here. It was not easy, and the deputy camp procurator responsible for such decisions would not release me at first. He was a small, dark Ukrainian Jew, an ignorant scoundrel, a drunkard and a boor, who feared most of all that he would be suspected of protecting "his own." He possessed only one redeeming feature, he feared his father. The father, a tiny, stringy old man worked as a despatcher for the automobile depot. I had not met him before but I when I came to the bus station after visiting the procurator's office he demanded to know who I was and what was the problem. When he found out, and learned that my mother was alive and waiting for me, he instructed me severely, "Stay here, don't take the bus! That ne'er-do-well will sleep out in the open tonight if he doesn't let a Jewish boy see his mother! You'll get that paper tomorrow, you can trust me!"

The next morning I indeed was given the paper and I left for Knyazhpogost. There in a quite ordinary district police station I was handed a passport. It wasn't quite the real thing but I already knew enough not to treat it with condescension. Millions of people in the country areas and elsewhere who had never been convicted of anything dreamed of having such a passport but had no hope of getting it. With it I could now go on leave and travel to Moscow. For the document stated that I worked for NKVD Ustvymlag, or more simply the NKVD, or simpler still, for THEM. With such a text I could risk coming to Moscow, even with a defective passport.

October 1945 found me already in Moscow. I shall resist the temptation to relive my arrival, to recall how I saw my mother, brothers and cousins, and the little girl, now in pigtails, whom I remembered as a plump year-old baby. I also met some of my friends and discovered that the past had not vanished completely but continued to survive, even if in a strange and deformed condition.

I was back and I lived without a residence permit in my childhood house. I ate the treats that my mother concocted for me, took my daughter to the zoo and the circus, and sat in unfamiliar apartments, passing on a greeting or a letter, listening to the tears of a mother or wife who still had long to wait to see their loved ones return. In the evenings I celebrated with friends who looked at me as though I had returned from the next world. They felt obliged to ply me with every kind of drink I had forgotten.

One day I sat in my good friend Tusya's apartment in an old building off Petrovka Street, drinking weak tea and strong vodka, and we recalled all our friends, living and dead, as if I had never been away. Apart from being a very faithful and reliable friend, Tusya was also quite fearless. One source of this courage and of her conviction that the impossible could be achieved lay, as I understand, in the charm that she was so accustomed to exercising on others. Another was an unwillingness to acknowledge the extent of the difficulties that had to be overcome. In any case, she was so convinced that I must stay in Moscow and begin working as an editor for a literary magazine (nothing less!) that she almost convinced me it was possible.

The most important step was to discharge myself from the camps.

Here Tusya remembered that when she was evacuated she had worked for the newspaper of a large defense industry plant where she became acquainted with the Central Committee representative. This man was working in Moscow now and, it seemed, was the person in the Central Committee who supervised the activities of the security services. From time to time he would ring her up, though she had no idea what they could find to talk about! This time she immediately found a subject for conversation. After finding his telephone number, she rang him up straightaway and for a few minutes exchanged a few idle and sociable words in her rapid, cawing voice before adding, as if on the off-chance, that she had a friend who needed help in taking up a literary career and abandoning another, in the far North where there were no prospects...

It was like a fairytale. The next day saw me sitting in the office of Tusya's friend at the Central Committee. He was straightforward, attentive and calm as people in that organization are supposed to be. He questioned me in a business-like fashion: where did I wish to be discharged from, how many years had I served, what was the conviction for, and evidently he was quite satisfied with my answers. Then, while I was still sitting there, he lifted the receiver of his special government telephone, and rang up "Comrade Timofeyev" (he did not even call him general). He conducted the conversation in the calm and indifferent voice that Tarasyuk used in addressing some petty free camp employee. There was a certain Razgon, he said, who formerly worked in publishing, who now wanted to return to his old profession and so Comrade Timofeyev should issue an order releasing him from his present work. As he replaced the receiver the man from the Central Committee said that Comrade Timofeyev had asked me to visit him the next day.

Comrade Timofeyev had *asked* me...! Well, in that case I had no choice. The next morning mama wept as she saw me off and answered all my reassurances with the words, The only thing I want is for you to come home. I was more confident of that than my mother. I boldly arrived at Kuznetsky Street and found my pass ready waiting. First I was received by the head of the personnel department, a lanky colonel, who gazed at me oddly with something like pity in his eyes. I filled in a form and then wrote out a formal request to be discharged from the NKVD's Ustvymlag. After this the colonel led me upstairs to the general and I found myself in a lavish reception room, decorated with panels of expensive wood in the taste of Stalin himself. All the bosses had their offices decorated in this style.

Soon the leather-covered door opened and the colonel indicated that I should enter. I walked across a tiny lobby and opened a second similarly soundproof door. Beyond lay a vast study. Major-General Timofeyev sat opposite the door, far away, at the end of a wide red carpet runner. It was the first time I had seen a real, live general close up. It was a real general's uniform, with a tight-fitting collar, broad golden shoulder boards, and colored strips of medals. Timofeyev's face was just what one expected of a general, the kind of caricature Kuzmin produced for the tales of Leskov or Saltykov-Shchedrin...

Despite my anxiety, I found it difficult to suppress a smile as I noted the extraordinary, almost implausible coincidence between the classic literary conception of a general and Timofeyev's appearance. However, I restrained myself and, stopping at a respectful distance from the table, boldly announced, "Good morning, Comrade Major-General!"

The general made no reply. Tucking in his lower lip he examined me attentively with deeply sunk eyes the color of bottle-glass. Then he slowly said, "It seems you imagine you are still your former self. You visit the Central Committee, make plans for your future..."

"I have not committed any act of insubordination, Comrade Major-General," I replied, trying to repress the tick that was beginning to affect my left cheek. "Any individual can appeal directly to the Central Committee..."

"They can, they can..." Timofeyev answered in a conciliatory calm tone. "Do you think we need you? Let THEM appoint you chief editor of *Pravda*, if they want. No objections. We have no need for you whatsoever."

"Of course, you don't need me," I said, regaining my courage. The tick had already gone. "I'm of no use to you, and you are of no use to me..."

"Exactly. Give me your appeal!"

Taking the paper from my hands he wrote in the corner in large letters using a thick blue pencil, "I have no objections, Timofeyev". He then handed me back the appeal and, leaning back, said, "You may leave! An order will be sent."

I staggered out, quite literally. I went straight home and began to wave the paper bearing Timofeyev's resolution in front of my weeping mother. Then we discussed how I would live in Moscow and where I should work, in a magazine or somewhere else—an unwise and infantile conversation. But my friends also thought it would work and Tusya was overjoyed that she had proved you could even influence THEM...

They were wonderful days, before I departed for Vozhael, taking nothing with me (I was going to return very soon!), and then after I arrived there and delivered the precious document with its thick blue pencil marks to the personnel department of Ustvymlag. And they continued when I reached Camp No. 2 and began to gather my things and write down the addresses of the numerous zeks originally from Moscow—on my return I was to visit their relatives.

Winter began and they still had not called me to be formally discharged. I rang up Personnel and they answered coldly, there is still no instruction. They stopped summoning me to meetings in Vozhael, and Yepanichnikov warned me that if I left on a Sunday I should be back to start work at 9 a.m. on Monday. They had rung him up from headquarters and told him so, and there were other people in the camp who kept an eye on such things. I wrote to Vypolzov, the head of Ustvymlag, asking to be allowed to see him. Only one and a half months later was I permitted to go to Vozhael.

Vypolzov gritted his teeth like a snarling wolf. He heard me out and then said coldly, "Yes, that's correct, General Timofeyev has no objection to your discharge. I do. I cannot let you go until I can find a replacement of equal worth. Those you have named will not do. Dismissed. Go back to your camp."

Not until a year later, when the instruction allowing former zeks to go wherever passport regulations permitted reached our camp, did I learn the reason for Vypolzov's unusually bold attitude to his superior's decision. As the inspector in Personnel, a tiny young Komi, handed me my papers, he said, "I thought being educated, you're a clever man. I found out you're very, very silly. Why did you start interfering by making an appeal? Two papers arrived here immediately a year ago. One was from the central personnel of the Timber-Industry camps in Moscow and it had everything on it, release so and so, discharge him... With it there was a simple slip of paper and on it the general himself, in his own handwriting, had written, Do not discharge, keep him out in the forest, the farther away the better. Understand? If your Yepanichnikov had not been so stubborn you would have ended up as norm-setter at the punitive camp, at No. 9! Then you wouldn't have had a chance in hell of getting back to your woman! Think yourselves clever! The bosses are tougher than any of you clever boys!"

* * *

It was seven years before I saw Timofeyev again. I was in the Ust-Surmog camp of Usollag when, in summer 1952, I learned that Major-General Timofeyev himself had arrived in Solikamsk with all his entourage. It was clear that he would come to Ust-Surmog because it was a large camp and only 40 kilometers from the town. The camp feverishly began to prepare for its high-ranking guest. The bosses relied most of all on the impression the outer appearance of the camp would make on the general. The chief doctor, an old man who had even worked for the zemstvo before the revolution, was a great lover of flowers. He still had a long term to serve and he planted a vast and staggeringly beautiful bed of flowers around the sickbay and the office. He had every opportunity to do so, using two experienced gardeners, whom he kept in the weak team, to tend the flowers. I supplied the seeds. Like any normal person I adored flowers and at my request mama sent me entire parcels full of seeds.

In the beds, carefully bordered by a sharp upright brick edging, bloomed Turkish carnations and nasturtiums, primulas and begonias, lavish dahlias and curly asters. There were also many scented flowers: mignonette, tobacco-plant and mattiola. By evening the flowers gave off a scent so full of reminiscences that sometimes you simply held your breath. The flower bed was the pride of the camp and the lowest "jackal" would not have dared to pick a single one. Everyone would have minded. And nobody in the camps, naturally, ever wanted to annoy a doctor.

Timofeyev actually did arrive. I thought out very carefully where to hide so he would not spot me. What if he caught sight of me and found out where I was now? Why give him the pleasure! He enjoyed himself quite enough without seeing me. From my hiding place in the store of Culture and Education, where the old banners (calling on prisoners to "burn away your sentence with honest labor") were piled up, I watched through the tiny, unglazed window as the procession of bosses poured out of the guardhouse. Ahead of them all, slowly and majestically, strode Timofeyev on his tiny legs. The sunshine joyfully played on his wide golden shoulder boards. Behind, in strict order of precedence, according to rank and position, came the colonels, lieutenant-colonels, majors and captains, the senior lieutenants, the plain lieutenants, and, even, the junior lieutenants... All of them, to the last man, officers in State Security! A major-general, a captain—even senior warder Yeremchuk, who brought up the rear, was a sergeant in the MGB hierarchy. However many of these generals, officers, plain soldiers and civilian employees were there defending the security of our state?!

I saw how the first thing our bosses did was to lead the general to the sickbay and the flower beds. What happened next was quite outrageous and incomprehensible, the kind of thing you only see in nightmares. It was all taking place so far away that I could only watch, as during a silent film, when something starts to happen but the subtitles do not yet explain what or why. Timofeyev stopped beside the largest and most beautiful flower bed, stretched out his arm and beckoned with his finger. The boss of our camp ran up to him. Having heard the instructions, he in turn called Yeremchuk and the latter ran off somewhere. Timofeyev and his suite continued towards the office. A few minutes later the senior warder trotted back, accompanied by a dozen people, barrack orderlies, office staff and some other trusties. They all carried spades and immediately set about destroying the flower bed. Chopping down the vast clumps of dahlias, pulling up the primulas and mignonette by their roots, trampling down the mattiolae, and scattering the carefully selected and placed brick borders over the besmirched and now desecrated earth.

I could not make any sense of it. It was frightful to observe this destructive, pointless activity. Within ten to fifteen minutes all that remained of the flower bed was a disfigured and filthy waste. Yeremchuk who himself helped the zeks in their work, stood up straight, wiped the sweat from his brow and surveyed his handiwork with satisfaction. Then he dismissed his chosen team, directed a last kick at the broken but still standing Georgina plant, and ran off to report the job done.

Timofeyev did not return to the flower bed. He knew that his orders would be carried out. I never saw him again. The general and his entourage left the compound, without entering the barracks and other buildings and the cortege set out for the timber floats. The bosses always liked visiting the timber floats. The enormous stacks of tidily sorted timber, stood with their pale stumps sticking out. Marx's idea about the impersonal nature of the end product of labor has no more apt expression than these handsome stacks of timber. Here it lay and nothing cried out, spoke or even whispered, how human beings had been brought here, had felled and cut up the timber, walked out into the snow-covered forest, rolled over the trunks with poles, cut them into segments of different quality, and then loaded, unloaded them and pushed them into the river. If the bosses ever felt a need for justification (which seems unlikely) then they could derive it from the endless banked routes of the railroads, the meandering green line of the canals, the towns of Angarsk, Vorkuta and Norilsk or the monstrous bulk of Moscow University—all of which were earlier termed "installations", "sub-divisions" or "enterprises" and located at mysterious disguised "post box" addresses...

The words Timofeyev had uttered by the flower bed were no more than an unattributed quotation. Stalin had said that "prison should not resemble a sanatorium." Quite right too, it is hard to disagree with such a sentiment. In the nick of time Timofeyev brought them to the attention of our petty bosses. The next day the warders went round all the barracks, pulling down the paper cutouts with which the enthusiasts of domestic comfort had decorated the board beds; they threw out the flowers that someone had picked in the forest and were blooming their last in a tin can; and they ripped off the pillowcases embroidered with flowers and sent from home, which the prisoners put over their stalk-padded pillows.

When I heard what Timofeyev had said I experienced a strange sensation. Like all of us I knew that we were living under Stalin, and if our lives had a discernible end in sight, his life was endless. Almost like the universe, Stalin seemed to have no end and no beginning. Yet it was very rare that Stalin made himself felt in the material, direct way Timofeyev had left his mark. Now I started thinking about him again. A melancholy abruptly descended on me as I thought that his advanced years meant very little and that Stalin would outlive me. All of them, from General Timofeyev down to Sergeant Yeremchuk, would survive me. I did not then know what lay only eight months ahead.

* * *

That March of 1953! By then we had been moved from the old compound into a new compound which they had been building for almost two years. Our camp had an assured future and the new compound had been built to house many thousands of zeks for many years to come. The fence was made of thousands of thick, commercially saleable pine trunks, sunk deep into the ground, and closely packed, one against another. Four months later we would pull this fence down with haulage tractors and burn it on enormous bonfires: the camp was being hastily reequipped to house a settlement for freely-hired timber workers.

We did not know this then, and it was depressing to live in the spacious new compound with its damp and as yet barely habitable barracks. In our small barrack lived the ledger clerk from Distribution, Kostya Shulga, a man with an extraordinary biography and limitless capacity. They had not yet strung the radio transmission lines as far as the new compound and so I was deprived of one of the pleasures of my work: I used to sit through the night in the empty office, drawing up the work assignments for the next day, to the muttering and musical burbling of a home-made amplifier. However, Kostya greatly respected me and doled out the dry ration to the radio technicians and gave them tinned pork which they preferred to the slimy and rotting cod. On 1 March they stretched a single line to the office and the small barrack where we lived, and to the medical barrack (the technicians were also prisoners and knew perfectly well whom to suck up to).

Do you remember that pause in the broadcasts on 3 March 1953? That unbelievable, implausibly long drawn out pause, followed by no word but only music... that miraculous, amazing and exceptional music? Without a single comment, one after another—Bach, Tchaikovsky, Mozart and Beethoven, pouring out all the funereal sorrow of which they were capable. To me it sounded like the "Ode to Joy"! It's one of them, all right. But who? No, it can't be... O God, could it really be...?

The longer this extraordinary musical interlude, this lengthy prelude to the unknown, continued the more certain I became: it's Him, it's certainly Him! Finally the familiar, grieving and sombre voice of Levitan (at last he could make full use of that famous timbre, that low, velvety tone!): "Moscow Calling! All the radio stations of the Soviet Union are on the air..." The first government announcement was made, and the first health bulletin issued.

I do not remember whether it was then, or during the second bulletin, that "Chain-Stokes respiration" was mentioned, but as soon as we heard that we rushed to the sickbay. Kostya Shulga, the norm-setter Potapov, myself and two others from the office demanded that Boris Petrovich, the head doctor, summon his subordinates for an urgent consultation. What, we asked him, could we hope for on the basis of the information given in the bulletins?

The others who participated were the former military surgeon Pavlovsky and the medical assistant Vorozhbin. They spent an intolerably long time, discussing things in the head doctor's study. We sat outside, silent, in the hospital corridor. I was shaking uncontrollably and could not stop my teeth from chattering. At last the door on which our eyes had remained fixed all this time swung open and Boris Petrovich appeared. He looked radiant and before he spoke we had understood: "Not a hope, lads!"

Potapov, a career officer and intelligence man, a former captain, who still remembered his countless awards, threw himself on my shoulder and burst into tears.

All the next day, or for several days, I don't remember, we sat by the amplifiers and listened to music, that miraculous, divine music, the sweetest melody on earth. On the evening of 5 March one of the guards brought Kostya Shulga a bottle of vodka in exchange for ten tins of corned beef and a hundred rubles. Kostya and I went behind the unfinished washhouse, and poured the vodka into the tin cans prepared for the purpose.

"Drink, Kostya!" I said: "This means freedom!"

I was not released until two years and several months later. Kostya had to wait even longer. Nevertheless, all that time I lived with a sense of incipient liberty. Stalin was no more. Major-General Timofeyev was also finished. It made no difference that the stumpy general from the picture-book illustrations was still physically alive. He was on his way out. The time for those who came after, however, had not yet arrived...

Razgon in Stavropol prison, July 1992, sitting in the same cell where he had been imprisoned in 1950.

FEAR

A judge arrived at Georgievsk transit prison. Well, in this case, "arrived" is not quite the right word. He was on his way to serve a ten-year sentence handed down by another of his colleagues.

The Georgievsk prison was of standard design. It was intended to hold 25,000 inmates and serve the needs of the vast Stavropol Territory. If, in some respects, it was more liberal than many other identical institutions, the rules were strictly observed and no contact was allowed between the cells. Nevertheless, any event in any of its cells rapidly became common knowledge throughout the prison. So the news that there was now a real judge among the prisoners spread like wildfire. His first cellmates, naturally, gave him one beating after another. Had the administration been a little wiser, they would have left him where he was: after the first few beatings he and his fellows would all have got used to one another. But the prison authorities, responding to the judge's complaints, moved him to a different cell, and then another... Everywhere, of course, his new cellmates also began to thrash him. Who among the prisoners, after all, could resist the temptation to hit a judge, even if he was no longer sitting on the bench!

This went on until the day his transport left the prison. The Chief Jailers, in their Moscow offices, looked after every detail. The cars in our prison train were to be allocated, they instructed, according to sentence. Since I had only a "short," ten-year sentence I was chucked in a car with those who had been given between ten and fifteen years.

For the first few hours we had been kept kneeling in front of the train. We answered roll call and were assigned to our cars. The doors into the converted goods car were locked and sealed. Now we were settling into our new "home," where we were fated to spend at least a month, if not more... The arrangements were quite standard. Along both sides there were bed boards, each accommodating twenty men. In the middle of the carriage, a hole reinforced with tin edging replaced the slop bucket. There was a tiny metal stove. Each day during roll call the doors were unsealed and opened and they began to drive the forty prisoners from one end of the car to another, for some reason belting each prisoner with a wooden hammer as he passed. The hammer was part of the guards' equipment: they tapped the walls and bottom of the carriage with it, in search of cracks, hollow rings or other signs of a forthcoming attempt to escape. After the roll call was completed, they handed out dry rations and a bucket of water. Everyone was given 600 grams of bread, several herrings and a tiny lump of sugar. Then the prison car was locked again and for the next twenty-four hours it would become a quite independent organization with its own codes, customs and hierarchy. From the very first kilometer of our long, long journey we began to look around us and find out who was who.

The judge was in our car! Naturally—he also was a man with a short sentence. The excitement at this discovery was incredible: all took an interest and looked forward to the entertainment it would provide. Of the forty prisoners in the train car, thirty-eight were criminal offenders. Some had been convicted of embezzlement but most were simply thieves, rapists and robbers who had already been in the camps more than once and did not regard the prospect of returning there as any great tragedy. I and a very young soldier just demobilized from the army were the only "politicals." A year before, the young soldier had received a letter from his very own collective farm that ingenuously described all the realities of the system there. He did not just shake his head but naively read the letter aloud to some of his platoon comrades. In order not to spoil the statistics (there should not be any anti-Soviet agitators in the army!), they had not picked the boy up until now. He was demobilized without trouble, but arrested immediately as soon as he left his army unit compound. Now he was a civilian and had nothing more to do with the army.

Our position in the car was special. The others regarded the soldier with amusement and even compassion. As for me, I was an old lag. The rest were slightly shaken to think that when they were still only teenage delinquents I was already in prison. And not just anywhere, but in Butyrki! I also knew more about the camps than anyone else. So they regarded me with the appropriate respect. I occupied the best place on the bed boards, under the little window, and even acted as arbitrator during the quarrels which naturally arose between individuals who were not the most honest and decent kind, shut up together in a cramped car.

The judge is here with us! The engine had steamed its way past the first hundred kilometers, we had been through roll call, night had fallen and in our car, lit only by the flickering kerosene bat-lamp, the impatiently awaited kangaroo court began! What should be done with the judge? Kill him off, the most authoritative "honorable thieves" said, without hesitation. No one was surprised when murders occurred during transfers. People would settle scores and allowance was probably made for such "losses." The court followed all the established rules. Each could give his opinion. The verdict was almost unanimous: "This snake piled on our sentences while he took bribes, freeing those who had some cash to give! I say we crush the viper!"

The judge, on his knees, cried and insisted that he had not taken bribes. He had his own sentence with him and he pulled it out and shoved it at his accusers. Read that! Indeed, it was clear from the sentence that he had not taken bribes. Instead he and the court bailiff had simply pocketed all the money paid over for maintenance payments and so on. The former judge considered this to mitigate his guilt, but it did nothing to ease his position. For the inhabitants of our car this trial, the passing of sentence and its execution offered an educational form of entertainment which they could not deny themselves!

"You viper! You sentenced us for nothing while you took the last kopeck from some little child! Kill off the bastard, and have an end to it! We'll tell the guards that he did away with himself..."

I knew these kind of people very well. They easily became worked up and were capable of the most unpredictable behavior. It would be wrong to say I felt sorry for this character—he revolted me. Yet I could not stand by while they murdered him, a defenseless man faced by a mob of executioners.

I bent down to the weeping, kneeling figure, "Have you ever read any books?"

"Yes! I used to have a large library and I read a great deal," sobbed the judge, from fear and hope that a miracle might still save him.

"Men!" The car fell silent and all turned to me. "The judge can 'tell novels'! We're going to the Urals, they say. We'll be a month, or even more, travelling there. We can finish off the judge at any time. So meanwhile let him 'tell us novels.' Two times a day. Once in the morning and once, after roll call, in the evening."

To "tell novels" meant to recount the story of a book you had once read. Such a talent was very highly valued in the prisons and camps, proving that even the most desperate criminals were still human beings.

The mood in the car changed at once. The trial and execution would not, in the final analysis, occupy very much time but two novels a day—that was much better value. So began that unusual repetition of the *Thousand and One Nights*. The judge proved to be not only a scoundrel but a man of talents. He began with the *Island of Doctor Moreau* and then went on with all the other novels of Wells, Jules Vernes, Dumas and Conan Doyle. Our Scheherazade not only had an excellent memory, but also undoubted literary ability. His performances were emotional and vivid, and he chose the most striking episodes. But he did not stop there. I knew the books he was retelling and found, to my amazement, that he was thinking up and cleverly inserting exciting new events.

Within a week or two the "novel-telling" had become the favorite activity of all those in our car. In the evening the prisoners impatiently awaited roll call so that they could seat our Scheherazade between the rows of bed boards and listen to the continuation of the exciting novel. Following his fairytale predecessor's practice, the judge would break off at the most tense and mysterious moment. Of course, during that period the zeks' hearts had softened and no one now reminded them of the sentence they had given the novel teller. On the contrary, they began to feel protective towards the judge and even award him something edible for the most successful stories. For his part, the judge lost his fear. Not only did he pluck up courage, he also began to appreciate his new importance and demand a better place on the bed boards—or else he might catch a cold and be forced to stop his story-telling.

Once I asked him, "Don't you ever feel ashamed?"

"What for?"

"For having deprived children and old people of the money to live on?"

"Everyone was doing it. They were all stealing from each other. Why should I be the only one to feel ashamed?"

"And you always passed just sentences on people, did you?"

"I was a judge! What has justice go to do with it? I handed down the sentences indicated in the laws and instructions, in accordance with orders from my superiors and the behavior of the accused. If he was quiet and gave me an imploring look then I gave him a shorter sentence. If the man was impudent, why then I gave him the maximum..."

"Didn't you ever think you might find yourself in their place, in prison among those you had sentenced? The others wanted to kill you. And they would have done it."

"My thanks to you. I shall never forget. And if I once again begin to work as a judge and you come before me, then I shall return the favor."

"You still think you might go back to your old work?"

"Why not? Of course, people in my position do face unpleasantnesses. But our superiors never forget us. We can say I've already survived this transport and I won't be put among the honorable thieves or the criminal scum in the camp. The administration know who they're dealing with and where to send them."

He was quite right, too. When our train came to a halt in the siding at Solikamsk station and they began to take us out of our cars the judge vanished right after the first roll call. "Those bastards look after their own," experienced old lags explained. "Either he's been made duty orderly in the security officer's house or somewhere else like that. They won't drive him out into the forest. And he wouldn't have stood a chance there (not like in our car): they'd drop a tree-trunk on him and that's that!"

* * *

That was in autumn 1951. Much earlier, in 1940, a new transport arrived at Camp No. 1 in Ustvymlag and when the prisoners had been sorted, Stepan Gorshkov pointed out a tall, still not old man, in riding breeches and a faded military shirt. Although a prisoner, Gorshkov had reached the highest post a zek could hold in the camps. The work supervisor had handed in his notice shortly before and until a replacement was sent Stepan was performing his job.

"You can tell there are almost no Muscovites left here, if no one recognizes him," said Gorshkov.

"Who is he, then? I'm from Moscow but I don't know him."

"Your case was dealt with at the Lubyanka and so had nothing to do with him. His surname is Kupchinsky and he was deputy head of the Moscow and Moscow Region NKVD. A bloodthirsty beast! I've heard a lot about him. Just look, damn it, how many of them have been shot but he's alive and in the camps. And he'll survive, what's more, because of sentimental idiots like you and me."

"What can we do about it?"

"Wait a minute. In your last food parcel you got some Kremenchug tobacco. Give me two packs. I'll give them to one fellow who's a sly character but very handy with an axe. The second time they're out in the forest, he'll drop a tree on Kupchinsky. He won't miss, he's a past master."

This was 1940, as I said, not 1951, and then I did not feel the slightest pity towards such people. I had never killed anyone in my life but, if need be, was sure that I could. Still, to die under the first falling tree and never know what it was like to rise at six, march out to work at minus 30 degrees with a biting wind blowing, cover the long and tormenting road to the work site, then working up to your waist in snow, bending down and sawing through the trunks by hand, tugging the trunks out from under the snow, returning wet and exhausted to the compound where you lay down, hungry after the thin soup, on the hard bed boards waiting for reveille again... to miss all that would be most unjust!

"Stepan, let's try something else. They're about to go for medical examination. I'll have a word with the doctor and he'll pass him for heavy work. Let that bastard taste it all before he pegs out!"

"That kind never die! OK, go ahead."

The plan was simple. By then a shortage of labor was already becoming noticeable. Not just of prisoners, but of those who could fell trees and fulfil the plan. It was therefore strictly forbidden to use a "heavy labor" zek for anything other than forest work, unless he possessed quite irreplaceable specialist knowledge. Each time a zek in this category was found anywhere but felling trees a fine was deducted from the camp chief's salary, a most effective deterrent!

Kupchinsky looked highly emaciated and obviously was not capable of "heavy labor." But I explained my cruel plan to our kindly doctor and he felt no misgivings. Why should he? He, his wife and their
two sons had all been arrested at once, during the same night...
Neither was I asking him to disregard his medical ethics: no one was
demanding that he maliciously polish off this malefactor. On the contrary, as someone evidently in weak condition Kupchinsky was
quickly placed in the medical barrack. Within a month the former
deputy NKVD boss was quite ready—plump, rosy-cheeked and very
healthy. When anyone left the medical barrack he was examined by
the commission and assigned a new work category. Without any
qualms, the commission allotted Kupchinsky to "heavy labor,"
thereby preventing him from doing any easy "trusty" jobs. For this
torturer had no professional experience, apart from his ability to
force the necessary confessions from enemies of the people.

Some time after the work supervisor was summoned to the security officer's building. Prisoner Kupchinsky was standing next to our
"godfather" Chugunov, and the condescending expression on his
face said that he felt at ease there.

"Gorshkov! Appoint this prisoner as work-team leader."

"No, citizen senior lieutenant, I shan't. He's one of yours, not
one of mine. I need work-team leaders who will be respected by
their team and fulfill the plan. They won't listen to this prisoner,
they'll beat him. Each of them will remember how Kupchinsky beat
up people like them. No, Kupchinsky will go out and work. Like everyone else."

"Listen, Gorshkov! If you finish off this zek I'll have you for stealing from the prisoners. It won't bother me that you're work supervisor: I'll bring charges against you. Just you try to cheat him!"

Gorshkov summoned the security officer's orderly and ordered
him to call in the leader of the team that was uprooting trees along
the new road. The latter, alarmed, ran up. Without raising his voice,
the work supervisor instructed him, "Put this prisoner in your team.
Give him a separate section to work on and I shall myself check on
his work. I'll also send the works inspector to check. If you reduce
his work norm by half a percent I shall take you off the job and
send you back out felling trees. And if you give him an extra half
percent then as long as I'm in this camp you'll be in the worst team
doing the most exhausting work. Do I make myself clear?"

"Quite clear, comrade chief."

So out went Kupchinsky to uproot pine stumps. He only received
the punitive ration because without the usual norm-fiddling even a
hefty slob like the former deputy NKVD boss could not meet plan
targets. I had the pleasure of watching Kupchinsky marching back
from work with the other prisoners, line up for his ration and, unlike them, only receive a tiny 200 gram bread allowance. I soon no-

ticed, incidentally, that the "godfather's" orderly would slip him a good hunk of bread and even something else from time to time. In the evenings, after the order to sleep, this delinquent prisoner would quietly leave the barrack for the security officer's building. There, undoubtedly, he was well-fed—rewarded not just for past services either, probably.

I did not enjoy my vengeful feelings for long. Less than a month later Kupchinsky was suddenly transported somewhere else, on special orders. A while after, Stepan Gorshkov returned from Vozhael where he been attending a meeting.

"I saw Kupchinsky at the base camp," he told me. "In a white coat. 'Who's that?' I asked. 'The new doctor,' they said. He's been appointed medical assistant. So now he'll finish his sentence in style: well-fed, as much drink and smokes as he wants, and backhanders for getting people off work. You shouldn't have been so stingy about your two packs of baccy!"

* * *

I wasn't worried about the tobacco, of course! I would have given anything to quench the flame of hatred, revulsion and shame that was consuming my soul—even in such an underhand and vengeful way.

The hatred is easy to understand. There were any number of justified reasons for hating. Revulsion can also be explained. I was revolted by all of that way of life, all those rules which, if truth be told, were basically the same on both sides of the barbed wire. But shame? The shame I felt for the fear that had crippled me when I was still a free man and reduced me, as Raskolnikov puts it in *Crime and Punishment*, to a "shivering animal." Oh, how I had tried to repress that fear and overcome it! I tried irony, humor, vodka and the pleasure I experienced in watching my daughter grow up, observing how that tiny bundle of flesh was changing into a small human being. Sometimes I even succeeded. For a while, at least.

It was summer 1937. The hurricane of devastation had passed. My wife's parents had been arrested, so had my brother, my cousins and numerous friends. I had been evicted from that elite building and moved into a vast communal apartment. And I was already without a job: when I walked into Detgiz, the Children's Literature Publishers, I realized from the reactions of those around me, from their pitying, shamefaced, compassionate expressions, that I had been sacked. I went up to the notice board and read (I do not now remember the exact phrasing) that Tsypin, the director, Yekaterina Obolenskaya, head of pre-school literature, and I had been dismissed.

I became unemployed. To begin with I went from one publishing house to another, looking for work. Some of the directors knew me and liked me. They would be frank, "You know only too well that I think highly of you and could make very good use of your abilities. But they might arrest you, mightn't they?"

"They might."

"So, in that case, what would they do with me!"

"But they might arrest you anyway, even if I was not working for you."

"They might. But then I wouldn't care any more. If I take you on now, however, I shall be shaking with fear all the time. What kind of life will I have then?"

The things we did then to relieve ourselves of that crushing, all-engulfing fear! Sometimes Tsypin and I managed to suppress it for a while.

Grigory Tsypin was a most intriguing and pleasant person. He was a superb organizer, as good in his own way as Sytin had been in his time. It was Tsypin who transformed Detgiz from a tiny disorganized publishing house into a vast enterprise that began to issue large print-runs of the classics and the old favorite children's books. The illustrations were by the best artists and the bindings were excellent and lavishly gilded. Perhaps they did not display the most refined taste but they provided everything that children adore. Book connoisseurs referred ironically to "Tsypin's gold." Yet his old-fashioned tastes entirely suited the hunger for large beautiful books that the reading public began to feel after years of skimpy brochures and slim books about the great construction projects of the Five Year Plans. Now Tsypin, like me, was out of work.

The summer of 1937 was hot, without a cloud in the blue sky. We always kept almost exactly the same routine. We would meet at the beginning of Prechistenka Street, Tsypin carrying a basket and I, a lidded can. First we went up the street to the Museum of Modern Western Art.[1] We left our modest belongings in the cloakroom and entered the exhibition. Almost always we visited the same rooms and looked at the same favorite paintings. We sat on the benches opposite a Renoir or Gauguin and enjoyed the view in silence. Then we left the museum, went into the shop at the corner of the Boulevard Ring, bought beer and crayfish and went back to Tsypin's apartment. He lived nearby on Sivtsev Vrazhek Street, in a large new house built for the Old Bolsheviks. But by then it was already half empty and half occupied by the new "administrators."

Tsypin possessed an amazing library. At one time he had been director of the Soviet Writer publishing house which owned the largest old and second-hand book shops. Tsypin was a discerning collector and had works from the grand dukes' libraries and rare editions that had been found and treasured by Moscow's book lovers. I recall a complete collection of Dostoevsky's works in bindings of unique quality. On the frontispiece of each volume, across the entire page, was written "From the library of Fyodor Chaliapin" and the dashing signature of the great singer followed.

While my host was boiling the crayfish according to some subtle recipe, involving herbs and beer, I would look through his books. A feeling of peace and calm descended on me and I quite forgot the apartment to which I must return and the coming night with its inexorable anxieties. Soon Tsypin came back and we began our delicious repast. He would tell me the history of many of his books and the complex ways they had come into his hands; we remembered the libraries of Demyan Bedny and other noted book collectors; and during our conversation we forgot the time, and our fear disappeared for the present. Suddenly this antediluvian, thoroughly peaceful conversation was disrupted by a horrifying shriek: neither human nor animal, but some unknown creature. It was a parrot on the balcony of a apartment on the last floor. Bette Glan, the organizer and director of the Moscow Zoo lived there. They had arrested her and sealed off the apartment, forgetting that a large parrot was sitting in a cage on the balcony. Now he was dying of hunger and shrieking like sinners during the Last Judgment. The whole building or, to be more exact, those who were still living there, would shrink with pity, horror and fear. Not one of them plucked up the nerve to ring up "that" organization, though, and tell them what a dreadful misfortune had befallen a once beautiful and merry creature. No one wanted to draw attention to themselves...

This cry immediately put an end to our conversation. Instantly it lost its peaceful and abstracted quality and returned at once to the thought that occupied us constantly, almost for days on end.

"Lyova!" Tsypin began, "Just imagine: there were eleven people on a course at the Institute of Red Professors, nine were picked up and I was left alone. Kaganovich had six of us as his assistants: five were picked up and they didn't even call me in for questioning. There were five of us assistant editors to Bukharin at Izvestiya—four were picked up when they came for Bukharin but they didn't touch me. So they don't take everyone! That means there must be a reason why they pick up some but not others. If they didn't pick me up earlier, why should they come for me now after working for Detgiz. I've already been promised some publishing work. Of course, not such a good job but who cares about that now?! They're leaving me alone. So that means they may not arrest me at all. Well? What do you think?"

Turning the same thing over and over in my mind, I inadvertently and cruelly spoke my thoughts aloud, "I feel sorry about the books. They never return them. And no one knows what they do with them."

Nevertheless, by the end of the year we both found ourselves back at work. Tsypin started a job as a middle-ranking clerk in some ministerial publishing house and I became secretary of the Moscow Society of the Friends of Green Spaces. When I first arrived there it seemed to me as though I had entered paradise, so little did it have to do with the surrounding reality. An organization where there were a "Roses" section and "Chrysanthemum" section and a "Department for House Plants." Here was a place to rest one's weary soul, to forget and be forgotten. Very soon, however, Pushkin's words proved all too true: "Flawed passions everywhere abound, there's no salvation from our fate."[2] I was made secretary because my predecessor had been arrested. Shortly before I began work there, the chairman of the "Roses" section had been arrested. The chairman of the "Citrus fruits section," meanwhile, had been denounced. He wandered, pale, from room to room and everyone tried not to look at him...

Almost every evening Tsypin and I phoned each other up. We had nothing in particular to discuss, we were just checking. On 1 January 1938 I rang to wish him a Happy New Year. For the first time no one answered the telephone. I understood immediately—they had got round to him at last. Tsypin was arrested on New Year's Eve, 31 December 1937. To be more exact, it was by then already New Year. When Lebedev, the former director of the Leningrad section of Detgiz, returned after miraculously surviving ten years in the camps, he said that he had been accused of belonging to a counter-revolutionary organization of wreckers in children's literature. It was supposedly led by Samuil Marshak and among its members was Grigory Tsypin. Later I often met Marshak but I never mentioned this to him. Why remind an elderly man of the shameful and pitiful fear in which he, and everyone else, then lived? Tsypin disappeared. They did not shoot him, apparently, so he must have perished in transport or in one of the camps.

* * *

We used every means to disguise our fear, driving it deep within. We joked about it, told funny stories, and in our frank private conversations "They" appeared not only cruel but stupid, and deprived of those characteristics that distinguished our species as "homo sapiens." Despite all these ploys, fear sat deep within us, and even if we managed to overcome fear for ourselves, fear for our near ones was quite insuperable. No personal qualities could provide the necessary immunity to that constant anxiety.

Nineteen forty-eight was the happiest year of my life during the camp period. The whole year I was a free man, in the full sense of the word. Rika and I lived together in the attractive southern town of Stavropol. I was a legal resident, renting our one room and even working for the state (there were, in fact, no other employers there!) My job in the bizarre "methods" section of the territory's Cultural and Educational Section was to "study and generalize" the work of the cultural and educational institutions in rural areas. This involved frequent visits to the large territory's different districts. I enjoyed these trips. After many years spent in areas where there was nothing but forest, and more forest, I liked the wide expanses of the steppes without a single tree in sight, the vast fields, and the large villages where I found the people interesting, friendly and attractive, not worn-out by hunger like those in the cities.

In late August 1948 I was working my way across the Blagodatnenskoe district. The main town in the area was an old Cossack settlement. The sound brick buildings where well-to-do merchants and cattle breeders had once lived were now occupied by a great number of district offices, of one kind and another. The Cultural Center occupied the spacious old church. In other words, it was a typical small Soviet town. I took a great liking to the man whose work I was to "study and generalize" as head of the district's department of Education and Culture. He was a very young soldier, no more than seventeen when he went to the front, who had been demobilized only two years earlier. He returned to his home town not only fit and well, but decorated with numerous awards and among them, the highest of all, the star worn by a Hero of the Soviet Union. He had been in military intelligence. If he's lucky, an intelligence officer can stay in one piece and pick up a bucketful of medals at the same time. The man in charge of culture for the Blagodatnenskoe district was a strongly built and fearless character. While giving me dinner at his home, he told me ingenuously and without any posing, how he had captured enemy soldiers behind the front line. And when I asked, did he never feel afraid, I believed him when he replied, "If you're afraid when you set out, you better not go at all—you'll slip up. No, I wasn't afraid of the Germans!"

They had to find an appropriate job for this hero with his rare award. He had left school at fourteen but that did not prevent others from occupying positions of influence in the local nomenklatura. Evidently he lacked certain other requirements, for they appointed him to the least desirable job, putting him in charge of culture. There really wasn't much for him to do. The villages had tiny libraries, each with a couple of dozen brochures and a copy of *The Knight of the Golden Star*, a novel by the local author Semyon Babayevsky. Then there was the former church in Blagodatnenskoe where, once a year, competitions for amateur dance and song groups were held and all the various official gatherings in the district took place.

On 1 or 2 September I arrived in Blagodatnenskoe from the country area and found the little town bustling with preparations. The

Soviet people had lost one of their leaders, Andrei Zhdanov. Black ribbons were tied to the flags, the Cultural Center was being given an extra cleaning and its banner, changed: that evening all the important and humble local organizations were due to attend a memorial meeting there. My hero, together with the center's director, was running here and there, hammering, painting and decorating, and I only caught a word with him that evening at the ceremony itself. Everything had been done according to "the best standards"... On the stage, draped with black ribbons and surrounded by flowers, stood the portrait of the departed leader. All the local bosses sat behind a long table, from the district Party secretary to the head of the district MGB department. The head of Culture did not belong to that elite and was not seated with the presidium. Instead he sat next to me in the second row of the audience and as always, in his undemanding line of work, listened attentively and seriously to the speaker. The latter, head of Public Education, stood behind his plywood tribune. Sometimes stumbling over a word or two (evidently the speech was written by someone else) but with a tearful voice, he told his listeners what a great humanist and educator the deceased had been, and how he had worn himself out in his concern for the development of Soviet culture, literature and art... It was interesting for me to listen and I even felt a certain joyful twinge at the thought that Zhdanov, that plump boor, had proved powerless in the face of death. It was somehow encouraging...

As I studied the mournful presidium, however, I felt I might any moment emit an indecent giggle. For the portrait on the stage in its funereal border was not that of Zhdanov, but the very much still alive Shvernik. How it had happened, was anyone's guess. They all had the same mustaches, and similar faces. I tugged at my neighbor's sleeve.

"Just look whose portrait it is up there!"

"What do you mean?"

"That's not Zhdanov, it's Shvernik!"

I had never seen such a reaction before. The head of Culture and Education turned as pale as the white shirt he had donned for the occasion, and sweat started pouring down his face. Gasping, he began to get up.

"Where are you going?"

"I've got to change... I've got to..."

This hero, who had snatched Germans like so many sausages from the pan, was dying of fright, and did not know what to do. I pulled him back down beside me.

"Sit down! You'll only get the sack but they'll give the director ten years!"

"So what should we do?"

"Sit still. Then when the meeting is over, go up to the stage, take away the portrait and hide it. And, most important of all, don't say a word to anyone! Not to the director, your own wife or anyone else!"

The meeting cheerfully disbanded and I stood outside, waiting for my hero. The lights had been turned off and the doors of the old church locked when, from behind the building, the former intelligence officer appeared. Now he was comparatively calm. Only his heavy and irregular breathing showed what he had been through.

"So what did you do with the portrait?"

"I broke the frame and threw it away, then I tore up the portrait and scattered the pieces in different places."

"And you didn't tell—?"

"No! But didn't anyone else notice, besides you?"

"I don't think so. Otherwise there'd already be a hullabaloo..."

"You're right there. But what if...? What if, after you leave, they call me in. Someone reports on me..."

"No one will say a word, believe me. You're not afraid of me, are you? You don't think I would sneak on you?"

"You're OK, but..."

My hero had no idea where I had been before my present job. Yet he trusted me, an outsider, someone he did not know well. But his fellow townsfolk, the people whom he had played with as a boy and now had to work with—he did not trust them, and was terrified that he might be "called in."

Was the fear of such a summons really greater, I wanted to ask, than his feelings when he left at night, without documents or uniform, to capture a German informant? But I didn't have the heart. I felt sorry for him. Could this brave, good-hearted fellow have explained something I did not understand very clearly myself: where did it come from, this terrible, crushing fear we lived with? We were all living in a fragile world, in an unstable boat, shaken by fear. My situation was clear. But why was this Hero of the Soviet Union, apparently protected by his glory and a petty position that no one coveted, so scared? What must others, of greater rank, be feeling? Not all of them were as fortunate as the unmasked judge and the lucky executioner.

The judge survived. So did Kupchinsky who today, probably, has a decent pension. And a great many murderers and torturers of the most varied rank and profession have survived to the present, pretending to be just like everyone else. Yet what about the most powerful of all? Did they really believe they would survive to the end, that they could go on living without the same fear?

Our Moscow transport was unloaded in Kotlas at the Ukhtpechlag central transit camp in September 1938. While we were squatting on our heels next to the cars, waiting for the order to stand and line up, we took a look at the main entrance to this enormous prison, which millions had already seen. It almost resembled a triumphal arch. A vast poster, instead of an ironical "Welcome," bore a simpler and clearer message: "Death to the Enemies of the People!" Above the arch hung an enormous waist-length portrait of the Commissar General of State Security, Nikolai Yezhov. The colorful details of his uniform were lovingly emphasised—the straps and belts, the shoulder tabs and awards. His arms folded, that terrifying dwarf gazed down at the people being marched through the prison gates and nothing recalled the quiet fellow in a satin peasant blouse with whom I had drunk vodka several years earlier.

Yet, and this was extraordinary now, he no longer instilled any fear in us. We had lost all fear the moment the doorbell rang in the middle of the night and our eyes immediately picked out the words "… and arrest" on the paper they shoved under our nose. In Kotlas we said farewell to all kinds of fear. We could no longer be arrested or interrogated: we had already been sentenced. We were extraordinarily interested, on the other hand, to learn what became of "them." Above all, the man on the portrait.

Yezhov was then at the zenith of his bloody career, omnipotent and all-powerful. However, almost no one in that small but close group of acquaintances that immediately drew together in our transport had any doubt what awaited Yezhov. He had already fulfilled his purpose, his job was done and his patron would just as calmly remove him. I do not remember which of us began reciting from memory: "Cesare Borgia was a great ruler/ Whose kind had not been seen of old."[3] Soon Borgia, the poem related, felt the same need as all tyrants. "Only the weak seek the aid of the law" and he summoned Vittorio de Colonna. Vittorio only trusted in murder and robbery, but when he had outlived his usefulness Cesare had him arrested and declared he had killed innocent men on the orders of foreign malefactors. Colonna was executed in accordance with all the brutal customs of the time.

In this poetic tale we saw the past and future of the Commissar General of State Security. We even argued how soon retribution would come. Those who said it would take a year and a half, or two years, lost their bet. Yezhov had only a year left. Some of the few who survived Sukhanovka, the worst NKVD torture center, say that Yezhov himself was interrogated there. He would be brought in a filthy sweat-stained shirt for a confrontation with some unfortunate prisoner and, like Gogol's monster Viy,[4] would point at the man and say: "Yes, I recruited him." Of course, he knew and followed all the rules of the game—he had made them up himself. Did he know that he was also inevitably doomed? That is a question we can leave to the novelists.

In summer 1953 the company assembled at the new Kushmangort camp outpost were far less select or knowledgeable about history, and no one knew Machiavelli's poem by heart. Still, there were a few people it was safe to talk openly to, and I tried to persuade them that the same fate now awaited Beria. They were not very convinced but listened to me hopefully. For my part, I was sure that Beria would be removed since he was a mortal threat to the group of "chicken-necked" leaders who had now come to power. And removed in exactly the same way... I even gamely invited them to place a bet that he would be gone in a year's time. Luckily no one took up my offer because I would have lost.

The outpost was new and the only radio that worked all the time was in the guards barracks outside the compound. There was one telephone line linking the outpost to the main camp with two parallel telephones, one on the gate and the other in the guardhouse. Every morning after the march out to work I went to the gate, called up the planning office and reported on norm fulfillment for the previous day. This ridiculous accounting, for some reason, had to be provided each morning. Evidently this was so that General Timofeyev on Kuznetsky Street could be informed by mid-day how work had gone the previous day in the numerous forest camps under his command. The sentry would hand me the receiver and if I heard the guards talking with the main camp I would put it down and wait till they had finished their conversation.

This time I overheard the head of the main camp and the commander of our guard (I already knew their voices well). For once I did not immediately replace the receiver but for a moment continued to hold it, pressed to my ear.

"Did you listen to the radio this morning?" asked the head of our camp.

"I heard."

"Well, then: quickly take down all the portraits in the command post and the guards' barrack, and remove all the books and brochures in the Reading Corner in the barrack and in Culture and Education inside the compound... "

I heard no more of this unusual conversation. The guard on duty gave me a suspicious look and reached out for the receiver. I slowly put it down and left the room. My head was spinning but my thoughts were quite clear. Portraits and books meant it could only be a member of the Politburo. And whose portrait could be hanging in the command post and the guards barrack? I had no doubts at all that I had lost my bet. Six months earlier than I had estimated, Beria had gone the way of Yezhov.

You know what it feels like when you learn something that you can't possibly keep to yourself.

The last prisoners had been led out to work, the refusers and the petty hooligans who had tried to skip the roll call had been sent to the punishment block. In the middle of the compound, sitting on a log and sweating from his exertions, was the junior lieutenant who headed Culture and Education. The poor fellow was panting. Probably he had been dragging those shirkers who today had not wished to "burn away their sentence with ardent labor" out from under the bed boards. I sat down beside him. In search of sympathy, he remarked, "Oof! Razgon! There are some real sons of bitches, plain scoundrels, among your fellow zeks!"

"Indeed there are, Citizen Lieutenant. But then, what scoundrels one finds among those on the outside!"

"Who do you mean?" The junior lieutenant regarded me suspiciously.

"Take Beria, for example... "

The lieutenant's reaction was most peculiar. He leapt up, looked at me with dull eyes, uttered a shriek and ran to the gate. Half an hour later he followed me round the compound, like a calf, "Come on, Razgon," he whined, "you knew, didn't you? You did, didn't you?"

Of course, the whole incident was reminiscent of Russian roulette. It might not have been Beria, after all, but Malenkov, Molotov or Bulganin—if Beria had seized power there were many candidates for the first bullet. But now as I read the memoirs of Khrushchev and many others I realize that I was right in all my suppositions. It required no great intelligence but simply a familiarity with the rather simple functioning of mass terror. I had read Taine, Michelet and Jaures. It had already happened 150 years earlier, in one of the most civilized countries in the world.

The fate of Yezhov and Beria was quite clear. But what about the greatest Chief of all?

Things had turned out in a less satisfactory way as far as he was concerned. "To the shame of his people," wrote Naum Korzhavin of Stalin in one of his poems, "He died a natural death." Some satisfaction may be derived from his posthumous fate. Universally execrated, despised and hated, Stalin has become a money-spinner for petty journalists and insignificant writers, who turn his private life inside out, exposing all his foul habits. Yet the man who murdered and tormented millions of adults, old people, women and children "died a natural death." To this day it strikes me as an appalling injustice. I do not want to kill or take to court the Kupchinskys or those other torturers who are now quietly living out their lives (and even occasionally get invited to "Memorial" meetings as victims of Stalinism!) Let them be, the devil take them. I do not want be overpowered by a degrading desire for revenge. But Stalin, Stalin!... None of us managed to get him, unfortunately. I would have not regretted two packs of Kremenchug tobacco in his case!

24 KUZNETSKY STREET

The crane arm swings sharply and a massive iron ball smashes against the wall. Window bars crack apart and through the gaping holes one can see the traces portraits have left on the faded wallpaper. A very common sight in Moscow.

I'm standing on the opposite side of the street, looking on, and something within me also starts to give way with despair, like the walls of this building. For a moment it doesn't seem that dust is obscuring the demolished house but rather that tears are clouding my eyes. Probably I would feel the same if a similar crane were destroying my parents' home on Ordynka Street, a place linked to all the joys and sorrows of my youth and most of my young adult life. But they are not knocking down my home! This is an accursed, hateful and terrible building, and if people were once happy here it was in long-forgotten times, a hundred or two hundred years ago, when it was still owned by Prince Golitsyn or when it was inhabited by artists and sculptors and Pushkin came to visit Karl Bryullov who had just returned from Italy... But that was so long ago—who now remembers those times?

For year after year people only cried in this building. So many tears were shed here that if they had all been gathered and saved as they ran in streams towards Neglinnaya Street, the house would be standing on the shore of a salt-water lake. There were, of course, still more terrible buildings in the vicinity. I can remember myself how "that organization" (as we used to refer to it) spread like a cancer through the neighboring streets and alleys. It took over all of Greater Lubyanka Street, from the square up to the Boulevard Ring, and Lesser Lubyanka Street; it swallowed up a multi-storey department store and a nine-storey apartment block. Gradually identical silk curtains appeared in all the local buildings and for long hours in the evenings their windows remained alight with a cosy and infernal glow. There were certain places here it was frightening simply to walk past. That was where they tortured and killed. But there were no tears. People could and did scream from the pain, or from horror and fear...

But they did not cry there. At least I do not remember them doing so, and no one has told me since that they did. No, the most sensitive part of this vast cancerous growth was here. It was in this house that they wept, at 24 Kuznetsky Street. Here was located the reception office of the NKVD, NKGB, MGB, KGB... The names changed but not the organization. Until the very last day before its demolition the "KGB Inquiries" plaque hung there, and a tidy notice in gold on black announced for decades and for all time: "Admission 24 hours a day."

Yet there was a time when I used to visit this building without the faintest idea of what it would later mean to me. It was probably around 1925, when I was seventeen. The Berlitz Language School was then located at 24 Kuznetsky Street.

I enrolled there because at the time my cousin was in charge of Chiang Kai Shek's Soviet advisers. I terribly wanted to participate in a revolution in China and my cousin promised to take me on if I learned French. Why French, God only knows! Of course, I believed him and rushed off to 24 Kuznetsky Street.

It was an old three-storey building and there was then no reception office downstairs. That appeared later, probably in 1935 or 1936.

I would quickly dash up to the second floor, past the other people who were always moving up and down the staircase. Apart from myself and those who, like me, were cheerful, carefree, often elegant and almost always young, others also climbed these stairs. Whether young or middle-aged, well or badly dressed, they all bore the mark of suffering on their faces, and all of them were unsmiling and preoccupied.

We came in or mounted the stairs together and then parted: some to the right, to the Berlitz School, and others to the left. Because the door on the left was almost always open I did not immediately notice its small sign, "The Political Red Cross." A long corridor could be seen through the open door and it was always full of people. It's terrible to admit, but never once did I then wonder about this strange sign on the door or who those people were. I ran on to my idiotic classes where an attractive young woman pointed to the pretty pictures hanging on the walls and gave explanations in French: this is a beautiful country cottage; this girl is playing shuttlecock. And other such nonsense. We were forbidden to use a single word of Russian at the school. For several months I learned to recognize the French names for various quite useless objects. Once I overheard a conversation between two ladies sharing my box at a concert in the Hall of Columns: they were conversing in French and I was suddenly astonished to find that I understood what they were saying. It was an extraordinary feeling. Yet it did not prompt me to continue my studies after my cousin, together with the other Soviet advisers, fled China when Chiang Kai-Shek turned on the Communists in 1927. I lost any interest in the Berlitz School and stopped going to 24 Kuznetsky Street. And I quickly forgot about the door opposite, on the left.

I learned about this organization and the people working there much later from the stories of Rika, my second wife.[1] She had actually been there. For years she visited this strange organization, quite unlike any other in Moscow, which was not to be found in a single

Soviet guide or handbook. It was so alien to our entire political system, in fact, that after the war the experienced majors and colonels
in the labor camp administrations in Siberia, Stavropol or even
Moscow simply refused to credit Rika's stories. They could not believe
that this strange and quite inconceivable organization, the "Political
Red Cross," had existed openly and legally for almost twenty years.

Not only I but also these professional prison officers and policemen knew nothing about it. For them it was something mythical and
unreal. But not for Rika—nor for the many hundreds of others like
her. She went there regularly for twenty years, the first time as a
young girl. Each time she came to find out which new prison her father had been transferred to. They would inform her: what the latest
charge and sentence was, prison or exile; where he was at the moment; and when visits could be made and parcels handed over. There
she was given food to send, and money to go and visit him or take
him a parcel in Suzdal or some other prison town...

Some day historians will certainly begin to study this extraordinary
organization and the no less extraordinary woman who set it up and
devoted all her considerable determination and energy to running it.
Why had she been given this rather mysterious privilege? The name
of Gorky is insufficient by itself to explain how his first wife,
Yekaterina Peshkova, obtained the exceptional right to help political
prisoners and their relatives. She was entitled to find out where they
were, who was being transferred, and where to... Everything that
later became a major state secret could then easily be learned by visiting the strange organization across the landing from the Berlitz
School.

The corridor led into four small rooms. In the smallest there were
two tables. Peshkova sat at one; at the other, her irreplaceable assistant, Vinaver. Another room was something like the accounts department. The biggest room was almost always crowded with people
waiting, while the other large room was packed with boxes of food
and clothing. It was all quite incomprehensible. Who were these people sitting behind the tables for days on end, weighed down with the
woes of others (and perhaps their own as well)?

The relatives of jailed Socialist Revolutionaries, Mensheviks and
Anarchists came here. So did the relatives of people from the imagi-
nary "parties," "unions" and "groups" that were invented and fabri-
cated round the corner in Lubyanka Square.

Here women, old men and children found someone who would
listen, someone who comforted and reassured them. Here someone wrote down addresses and then, with extraordinary prompt-
ness, informed visitors where their father (husband, wife, brother,
son) was being held... They said when it was permitted to visit the
prison and when parcels would be accepted; and if the relatives
had no money they could come to 24 Kuznetsky Street and collect

food and clothing for those being sent on the long journey north or to the boundless East.

Where did the food and clothing come from? Who paid for it all? For the most part, goods and money came from abroad, from the American Relief Association, Social-Democratic parties and organizations, various charitable societies, and wealthy people. Or perhaps those donors were not wealthy, perhaps they were poor themselves. Who knows how this money was collected, or how it reached the Soviet Union? Only Yekaterina Peshkova herself probably knew the answer. Each day after her office at Kuznetsky Street closed she climbed into her motorcycle sidecar and was driven to the prisons, the customs office, and the warehouses. Still more often she walked around the corner—the Lubyanka was just next door—and negotiated with the people there: this person should be moved to the prison hospital, that one should be transferred somewhere nearer Moscow (it was difficult for his elderly mother to travel to the North or the Urals to visit him). She arranged for prison libraries to be expanded, and concerts and recitals to be given for the prisoners.

As though it was an unbelievable fairy tale, I listened to Rika describing how her father had been released "on parole," at Peshkova's request, when his wife fell seriously ill. He did not go back to prison, moreover, until she was well again. I heard of the New Year's Eve celebrations for political prisoners at Butyrki prison at which Chaliapin sang just before he emigrated.

This went on until 1937. Then one day Peshkova said helplessly to Rika: "That's it. I can't do anything more. Now there'll only be 'downstairs,' only those people on the ground floor." But for Rika and people like her there would be no "downstairs" either. She, and almost all the others, were sent off to the same prisons where they had visited their relatives. The Political Red Cross and all the problems with which it had dealt were abolished using an old and well-tried method. Just like Enver-Pasha resolving the "Armenian problem" or Hitler solving the "Jewish problem," all the exiles under the care of Yekaterina Peshkova were arrested, collected together in prison and shot. Vinaver and the unknown men and women who had worked in the Political Red Cross were also arrested and evidently shot. Only Peshkova was left alive, to suffer and die a free person. She took the key to the secrets of this mysterious organization to the grave with her. How and why had they allowed her to maintain the concept of "political prisoner"? Who was behind this decision? The very idea that there could be such prisoners in Soviet society thereafter in some way itself became illegal: it was denied and almost regarded as a criminal suggestion.

The time had now come when what Yekaterina Peshkova called "downstairs" began to spread upwards. "Downstairs" swallowed up the Berlitz School and the Political Red Cross and spread to the small neighboring buildings which until then had sheltered other obscure offices.

When people were taken away at night only a single address was ever given now: 24 Kuznetsky Street. If someone disappeared, in broad daylight or after dark, distraught relatives would ring all the frightening telephone numbers before trying the very last resort, the police "duty officer." "You've been to the police? And you've contacted the hospitals?" If the answer was positive then the "duty officer" would advise with satisfaction, "Then go to 24 Kuznetsky Street." The most terrible and hopeless answer. People came back from the hospital, and might even return from the police. But no one had yet come back from the last address. The majority never did return.

I then paid in full for my lack of interest in the organization opposite the Berlitz School.

At that time I had never had the occasion to go behind the cream-colored curtains of the reception office. Not everyone was allowed there. Only those who had been summoned, only those who came in search of their relatives—and, of course, the ones with information, who were received "24 hours a day." I went in through the courtyard behind the solid steel gates. How many times I went there, both by myself, and with my mother and Oksana, my first wife.

"Even death is fine in company." There is undoubtedly some truth in the Russian saying. But I don't think the presence of thousands of others made it any easier for the Jews and Communists driven out to be shot at Baby Yar... From early in the morning the courtyard at No. 24 was always full of people. Men, women and children, but mostly women. The very old and the very young. And no one said a thing, or else they spoke for some reason in whispers. The only guard in sight, however, stood by the door through the gate and with an affected severity enjoyed the spectacle of those who only the day before had been numbered among the "bosses." How different they looked now!

The line wound across the courtyard, bending round some other building, and then stretched out again towards its final destination, a small window in the wall. There information was given—exceptionally brief information. "Last night, for some reason," a stuttering, tearful voice would begin to explain, "they came to our apartment and arrested..." (a novice, evidently). "Surname, first name and patronymic," came the shouted response. Then the window slammed shut. After a minute or two it opened again. They only ever gave four replies: "Arrested and under investigation," "The investigation is continuing," "The investigation is completed: wait for an announcement," and "Apply to the inquiries office at the Military Tribunal."

They never answered any other questions. Once there was a

woman in front of me who replied, "Jasienski, Bruno Yakovlevich."
When she tried to ask something else about this well-known writer's
whereabouts they shouted, "You'll find out, you'll find out everything
later on!" And indeed we did. That woman, myself and the others
eventually ended up in other buildings of that accursed district and
there we learned something nearer the truth. The line at No. 24 was
only the beginning of a quest pursued through other courtyards and
at other similar hatches. No one ever informed us where our relatives
and friends were being held. To find out we had to travel from one
Moscow prison to another: Butyrki Central, Taganka Regional,
Lefortovo Military, the Moscow City prison at Matrosskaya Tishina
and the Women's Prison on Novinsky Boulevard. There we also stood
in long lines in order to hand over ten rubles, the only form of assis-
tance we were now allowed to give. With no indication whom it was
from, the ten rubles was impersonally transferred to the arrested individual's "account". At these hatches they either accepted the money
and the completed form (so he was there!), or answered: "No one of
that name here!" If we heard the latter reply, then we travelled to
the next prison on the other side of the city and tried to transfer the
money there. How happy people were when their ten rubles were accepted! He's here, right here, just behind these walls...

Those prison parcels, even the impersonal ten rubles, were very
important. How many parcels I handed in at the prisons of Moscow,
Stavropol and Georgievsk—and how many I received there! They
were a fine thread reaching out to the person who had vanished; if
they were accepted it meant that he or she was alive and there was
still hope of meeting again. How terrible, on the other hand, when
they handed back the form and the ten-ruble note and said, "No
longer listed here." And that was that. Where had he gone, and for
how long? They would not tell you, and Peshkova (who could find
out everything, and would also help you) was no longer at 24
Kuznetsky Street... Now you had to wait. You could go to the procurator's office and wait there, or sit at home for months on end or
even years before suddenly receiving a letter with the return address:
"P.O. Box No.... " More often people waited and waited, and never
heard a thing. No one informed them when prisoners died of torture
during interrogation, or in their cells or in the prison hospital. There
was no notification if they died in the prison trains or on the long and
terrible journeys between different camps. All those arrested were
swept off into oblivion and only twenty years later did the arrival of a
deceitful scrap of paper end the long silence. Not one word of truth
was written there, neither the date nor the cause of death, apart
from the admission of death itself.

How inexperienced we were then. How easy it was to cheat us,
and how easily we fell for such lies! Of all the replies that might be
given at the window at 24 Kuznetsky Street, the most terrible, of

course, was the last: "Apply to inquiries at the Military Tribunal." It
was not far away. You had only to cross Lubyanka Square and at the
very beginning of Nikolsky Street stood the small brick building of the
Supreme Court's Military Tribunal. (I think it's still there today.) There,
at a similar window, they gave a clear, direct and invariable answer:
"Ten years in remote camps without the right to correspondence."
This tribunal knew of no other sentence. That was the answer we received when we enquired about Oksana's father Gleb Boky and her
stepfather Ivan Moskvin. Though it seems extraordinary now, we actually drew comfort from this reply. Of course, ten years is a lot, we
argued, but a great deal can happen in that time: we can cope and
they may still sort things out. It's understandable why they can't
write letters. All the Old Bolsheviks, former People's Commissars and
Cheka men are being held in the same place and, for the time being,
will not be given the right to correspondence. But they'll be able to
write later. During the long evenings in our last home on Grenade
Alley we endlessly discussed where these camps might be, and how
the prisoners were being treated there—Lord knows what we didn't
say then! Such speculations reassured us and sometimes we even
tried the old intelligentsia pastime of divination. Opening a volume of
Blok's poetry we chose a certain line at random and saw in its words
an obscure answer to our hopes. Only once did we shiver with fear
when Oksana read aloud from those much-studied pages: "...And
only on high, by the Gates of Heaven did a child, versed in the
Mysteries, weep because no one would ever return."[2]

Not until many years later did I understand that Oksana had indeed been convinced of this: no one would ever return. Just as she
herself did not come back.

Yet there were other signs and omens from which we could have
divined what had happened. In one of his regular harangues about
enemies of the people Stalin demanded that vengeance against them
should take harsher forms. He could not understand, for instance,
why their belongings were not confiscated. Procurator-General
Vyshinsky immediately saw to it. A line was added to every death
sentence, "With confiscation of all his property." In the autumn and
winter of 1937 a great many strange shops opened in Moscow. I say
strange because even their signs—"Second-hand Bargains"—had been
hurriedly painted on cloth. They took over the premises of shops selling books, stationery and other goods. Each was filled with old furniture, worn carpets, second-hand or even new clothes, odd collections
of china, incomplete dinner services, antiques and paintings...

These were the leftovers from what the NKVD men had seized, or
simply stolen. Some of the State Security men had been given ready-
furnished apartments with all that they contained: furniture, books,
bed linen, clothes—everything including toothbrushes and the dried-
up pieces of soap in the washbasin. Others went to the warehouses

where all this booty had been collected and took their pick. Of course, it was all carefully allotted. The higher ranks got the best of everything: paintings, expensive carpets, antiques, well-bound books... Those of more humble standing contented themselves with ordinary cut glass instead of the Baccarat; they had the Russian Morozov china instead of the Meissen, and took more interest in dress material and expensive furcoats... The pieces that nobody wanted ended up in the shops selling "Second-hand Bargains."

In autumn 1937 I was walking past such a shop on Sretenka Street when I suddenly felt an urge to go in. As soon as I was through the door I saw our sofa, standing at the back of the shop... It was a long, awkward sofa covered in worn patterned leather with lions carved in ebony at each end. It used to stand in the dining room and countless times I had slept on it when I was still a visitor at Spiridonovka Street and had spent the night after a prolonged celebration or a conversation lasting into the early hours of the morning. Next to the sofa stood other pieces of furniture from my father-in-law Ivan Moskvin's study: the enormous desk, the high uncomfortable chairs and an antediluvian armchair. They were relics of some high-ranking Petersburg official's apartment which had passed on to Moskvin as secretary of the Central Committee's Northwest Bureau. Then, when he moved to Moscow, they had been sent there. Now this collection of unattractive furniture had finished its travels and reached its final resting place on a narrow street in Moscow, in a temporary shop for stolen goods.

Although I knew nothing at the time, I nevertheless understood that this was the end. In the official notifications of my father-in-law's death and rehabilitation various dates are given for his death, all of them false. Today I know that these shops were selling the belongings of those who were already dead. He, and others, were shot the same day, or at the very same hour, that they heard the words "...with confiscation of all his property." Those responsible did not just murder but pillaged as well. And like any murderers or robbers they performed these acts in the deepest secrecy: murder was disguised as "no right to correspondence," and robbery as the sale of "second-hand bargains." Almost half a century has since passed but their heirs and, perhaps, even the elderly robbers themselves, continue to live surrounded by those pictures and carpets and to eat off that china... Well, and let them! We must pay the full price for that long journey of understanding which began in the courtyard of 24 Kuznetsky Street...

EPILOGUE

Now the files are opened...

Finally I hold it in my hands. A thin brown file. My file. A faint trace of ink remains from the time that my infuriated interrogator struck the table and upset the inkwell. Now I know that his name was Lobanov. It all happened exactly 52 years and 7 months ago. Could I have imagined then that when Lobanov unhurriedly opened that new brown file I would still be alive half a century later, and leafing through the few pages it contains with a quaking heart? My life is there, and that of Oksana and Lena—the three of us who disappeared on 18 April 1938. And here is the record of what was, according to this file, my one and only interrogation. It is dated 25 April. So there was exactly a week between my arrest and this interrogation. During those seven days my only thoughts were of home and I was convinced that "home" still existed.

How did it begin, that week? When the doorbell rang piercingly in the night and I ran out into the corridor, I knew why it was ringing, and that they had come for me. It was the second time there had been such a ring at the door to that vast, overpopulated communal apartment. Today the building on the corner of Grenade Alley and Spiridonov Street is brightly painted and clean and it houses some exotic embassy, perhaps Ghana. To this day I cannot walk past calmly, without glancing up at the last two windows on the third floor where we used to live.

When the bell rang the first time the Bluecaps had not come for me but for the elderly and quiet actor from the long closed-down Semperante theater. Locking ourselves up in our two rooms we listened to the stamping of feet in the corridor, the subdued voices, the last receding steps up to the entrance of the apartment, and then the door opening and shutting... So when I opened the hall door and saw the Bluecaps and a pair of soldiers with rifles I already knew our time had come... Surname, first name, patronymic, hand over your passport! I handed them over, and myself as well. No longer the master but a temporary guest, I sat perched on the edge of a chair, watching how they pulled our clothes out of the drawers and gutted the bookshelves. Is there anything dubious there, I asked myself? Well, one miraculously preserved issue of *Novy Mir* carrying Pilnyak's "Tale of the Unextinguished Moon," a foreign edition of Chaliapin's memoirs *Mask and Soul*, and... One of the NKVD men gave a joyful exclamation and interrupted my reflections: "Comrade Captain! An anti-Soviet book! Pokrovsky's *World War!*" His superior cautiously took the discovered, seditious work. Of course, all the papers were then continually denouncing the "Pokrovsky School" of historians. The captain thought. He reflected...

I could not restrain myself. "Did you walk along Mokhovaya Street today?"

"Yes. Why?"

"Didn't you notice the sign on the University building?"

"Well, and what's written there?"

"The M.N. Pokrovsky Moscow State University."

That was my first lesson of many in our camps and prisons: never argue with the bosses and, most important of all, never correct them. The response was immediate: "Get packed!"

Oksana abandoned little Natasha and feverishly began to pack up a few belongings for me. No, not feverishly. It was a warm April night outside but she found the warmest, newest sweater, underwear, pyjamas, slippers and other trifles...

"That's quite enough! It won't take us long to get there. They'll keep him in for a little while and then release him."

But Oksana kept fretting and clinging to me and when I had said goodbye to everyone she ran out to me on the landing. From the way she then tore herself away from me I suddenly realized: she doesn't believe that we'll ever meet again. And she was right. We were saying goodbye for ever.

I was still incapable of understanding that, however, and my thoughts were still all of home. When they led me out of the ground entrance and to the car waiting a short way off, one thought was worrying me: what if they seal off one of our rooms and all four of us have to share the first, small room? The officer in charge was leading me.

"Please, the child is sick," I appealed to him. "Don't shut off the second room."

"What are you worrying about? We won't seal up the second room. Everything will be as before, I give you my word of honor!"

I should have known better than to believe a Cheka man's "word of honor." He drove me to the Lubyanka, returned to pick up Lena and then, a third time, came back for Oksana... One member of the family remained. But since she was fifteen months old she was not to be sent to the Inner Prison at the Lubyanka or to Butyrki but to a prison Infants Home. Natasha, however, escaped this fate. When they came for Oksana she said she would not leave the room until my mother had come and taken the child. She would break the window pane, wake up the whole street with her cries, and resist them but she would not leave otherwise. The NKVD men had no desire to cause an uproar at the depths of night in the middle of Moscow and the determination of this defenseless, sick twenty-two-year-old woman was so obvious that they ran out, phoned for permission, and then called my mother to come and take Natasha. Also for good.

They sealed up not one, but both rooms. The record of my interrogation stated that their total area was 29 square meters. But I knew nothing of this then. I was meanwhile being driven across Moscow to a familiar and accursed building and then processed: searched, deprived of buttons and laces, photographed, fingerprinted. Then I was led along the corridors and passageways to a door with a peep hole. With a clang that I can hear to this day the door opened and with difficulty I squeezed in past a small crowd of people. There were polished parquet floors in the cell, and four metal beds lined up in a row, covered with gray, distinctive prison blankets. Only one was occupied. A young man with a ginger stubble on his chin lay there, his hands folded behind his head. All the other beds were empty, although there were five or six people standing by the door. Elderly, clutching their falling trousers and the shirts or long johns doubling as bags and stuffed with their belongings, they stood motionless in front of the door, not exchanging so much as a word.

I lay down on a free bed next to the ginger-haired prisoner. He watched with interest as I undressed and took out my slippers.

"Why are you settling in, in that homely way? Are you really going to be here long?"

"For a long time, probably. But why do you ask?"

"You see that gang of idiots by the door? They've been standing like that for over two hours! They're all waiting for the door to open any minute, for an apology to be made and then to be allowed out. And here, at last, I've come across a sensible, normal person!"

My redhead neighbor, by contemporary standards, had already been in prison for a long while. Three months earlier he had been arrested in Kuibyshev where he worked as assistant to the new first secretary of the regional Party committee, the disgraced Pavel Postyshev. He and his boss had been picked up at the same time. My neighbor had already been through the first cycle of interrogations at the hands of the provincial thugs. Now he had been brought up to Moscow, for further "in-service training" as he put it: my first cellmate had not lost his sense of humor or irony.

It was from him that I first heard about the tortures. As soon as he mentioned them, I believed him implicitly. It is quite extraordinary, though. Throughout the previous terrible year we had turned over in our minds all the possible and impossible things that might happen to our arrested near ones. We had wracked our brains, trying to understand how the laughably improbable "confessions" of the accused at the show trials had been obtained. Here it was, the explanation, such a simple one that it had never occurred to either me or my friends. But how thoroughly our Soviet mentality had been drummed into us, if neither mind nor heart would countenance the idea.

Two days later I was taken with my things from the "kennel," as they called the part of the Inner Prison where those just arrested were kept, led out into the courtyard, squeezed into a green, gaily decorated van and driven off. It was dark inside and we had been tightly crammed into our separate compartments. We could not see one another and kept silent. The vehicle lurched along the already unfamiliar streets, then halted. We heard them opening the gates, we drove in, and the vehicle stopped. Awkwardly, stretching our cramped arms and legs, we clambered out of our attractive van. We were led up to a red-brick entrance and escorted into a vast hall, like a railway waiting room. Where were we? Among the questions in the very first prison form we had to fill in there, they asked, "How many times have you been in Butyrki?" So that was clear, we were at the famous Moscow prison.

Then... well, what happened then has been described by countless others. The stuffy, crowded cell, the doors singing out in the night as they opened to let people out for interrogation, and to let them in again. The constant and, for some reason, impatient expectation—when is it going to be my turn? Finally, the moment came, after your surname was announced, and you gave your "initials in full," when they told you "pack a few things" and led you out into a wide and pleasant corridor that did not at all recall a prison.

The first excursion into the prison. The warder walked ahead, tapping his key against the brass buckle of his belt. Occasionally he ordered, "Face to the wall" and we halted to let another prisoner pass. Then stairs to the upper floor where we halted outside heavy doors covered in leather and felt. The doors opened and we entered the deafening yells and noise of the "investigators' corridor" at Butyrki. I had never visited a slaughterhouse in my life but for some reason it struck me that this was what it should sound like: dull blows, cries of pain and the violent obscenities of the slaughterers... I was led to one of the numerous doors on the corridor, the guard knocked, and I was taken into a small room. Without speaking, they pointed to a stool by the door screwed to the floor. Opposite me sat me a young and very self-assured man who pulled a file out of the pile of new brown cardboard files standing on his desk, and began to fold it back so as to write on the papers there.

* * *

All this came back to me, 52 years and 7 months later, as I was sitting in a very different room: a comfortable office at the Lubyanka, behind a vast, empty polished table, rocking on a fashionable rotating armchair. No one hurried me here and the young man who had escorted me into the room sat silently in the corner, watching to make sure I observed the rules. I could read and even copy out what I wanted, but God forbid that I tear any little slip of paper from the "case file"!

There was, actually, nothing much to steal. The three "investigation files" on Oksana, Lena and myself were all here, in this slim cardboard cover. Even the "decree" which was the primary and main justification for arrest, interrogation, trial, hard labor or murder, was quite identical for each one of us.

At last I learnt the complete and quite official statement of my crime. I copied it out in full into the notebook I had prepared:

> Razgon, with the Boky sisters, has been actively spreading slanderous rumors about the leadership of the VKP(B) and is systematically carrying on an embittered counter-revolutionary agitation. Razgon asserts that both Moskvin and Boky are innocent. Discussing the film *Peter the Great* Razgon declared: "If things go much further we shall soon be hearing 'God Save the Tsar' again, in an appropriate new arrangement." Razgon has been spreading slanderous rumors about the arrests of Shvernik and Blyukher. During one of his regular drinking sessions with the sisters Boky, Razgon expressed sympathy for the enemies of the people and proposed a toast: "Let us drink to absent friends, who cannot share this toast with us." Wives of arrested persons are frequent visitors at the apartment, the wife of arrested NKVD employee Gopius and the wife of D. Osinsky who has also been arrested.
>
> Razgon must be arrested.
>
> Lieutenant of State Security Lobanov, commanding officer of section 10, 4th department of State Security.

Over this stand two signatures. To the left "Confirmed," Frinovsky; and to the right, "Agreed," Vyshinsky.

Amazing! It is all quite accurate. But why did they so clumsily disclose the only source from which they learned of my crime?

Sitting in that quiet office with its sealed windows, barely disturbed by the roar of traffic in Lubyanka Square below, I pondered this last question.

There was indeed only one possible source. Seated at the table where, very modestly, we celebrated my thirtieth birthday there was one other person apart from my two "accomplices in crime." She was a close friend, who shared a similar fate, and we were immeasurably sorry for her and tried to support her. Her husband had been arrested and by then, as we learned later, he had already been shot. She remained in a government apartment with three small children and no work. To save herself she was asked to perform a trifle, to inform on us.

Learning that had been my first shock when I was being interrogated. Many others followed. A few years later when I was allowed to write and to receive correspondence, and I began to get letters from my mother in the camp I learned that our former friend sometimes visited Ordynka Street, coming to play with Natasha and bringing her something sweet to eat... I wrote to my mother that I did not want her to visit the family home, or play with my three-year-old daughter. In her next letter my mother described the following scene, "'Tell me, why doesn't Lyova like you?' I asked.

'Why do you say he doesn't like me?'

'He doesn't want you to visit us and play with Natasha...' She burst into tears and as she was leaving said, 'Write to Lyova and tell him I am not the worst of them...'"

This was also true. Long before I was released my hatred, bitterness and vengeful feelings towards the person who had betrayed us all had passed. So much so, that against my rule of "hiding nothing" I shall not mention her name. Probably she is dead now, but there are children and grandchildren who bear the same surname. She was defenseless and naively supposed that she would escape all punishment if she informed on us. That criminal toast or the conversation about a film that Stalin liked were such trifles. They were quite sufficient to trap us, though. In a certain sense, that poor woman even saved me. I could have been charged with attempting to blow up the Kremlin. I would have signed the confession without inhibition and been rapidly shot...

But let us leave that unfortunate informer. What else was there in my file apart from the decree and its categorical conclusion, that I "must be arrested"? Nothing. Apart from the deposition of my interrogation on 25 April where the text repeats, word for word, what I have just quoted, and the decree of the Special Board on 21 June sentencing me to "five years in corrective labor camps for 'counterrevolutionary agitation,'" there is nothing else.

Yet that was not the only interrogation. In all I was taken out of the cell five or six times, I don't remember exactly how many now. There was my idiotic attempt to do a deal with my interrogators: I was not a counter-revolutionary and had not been carrying out agitation, I had not spread slanderous rumors but was a Communist and a very, very Soviet person. No trace of these other "interrogations" has remained in the investigation file. Nor has anything remained of those slips of paper that Lobanov showed me in order to bring my investigation to a decisive and rapid conclusion. These were brief notes that Oksana had sent to Lena and Lena, to Oksana.

"Yes!" said Lobanov, sprawling in his armchair, "We've got them both here. They're giving testimony and not being stubborn like you. Your wife and her sister are like little lambs. They gape at you, women who don't understand a thing. They are barely guilty, in fact neither you or they are guilty at all.

"Well, then. Now you will sign the deposition as it stands and admit you committed slander and were carrying out agitation. After that I promise you and give you my word of honor as a Communist and a Cheka man that your wife and sister-in-law will be immediately released. Of course, we can't let them stay in Moscow: I cannot promise that. They will be sent into internal exile. But they'll be free to move around there and my superiors have already chosen them a fine city, Kharkov. There are clinics there and insulin, and your wife will be able to get treatment. If you continue this idiotic stubbornness, though, I shall today order that your wife be deprived of insulin."

"But you'll kill her!"

"No, you'll kill her. We are simply doing our job. What's it to be?"

I immediately signed the solitary deposition for 25 April and would then have signed any paper of any content even one asserting that I had dug a tunnel between London and Bombay and was using it to transport explosives for blowing up the Kremlin. Yet they had not tortured me. Apart from the one traditional punch in the mouth and the most common obscenities, Lobanov had done nothing "of that kind" to me. Why did I believe the "word of honor of a Communist"? As far as I can remember now, I then still believed in Communism and a Communist's "word of honor." And it was also a chance, well, more of a hope, let's say. But that was enough for me.

Lieutenant Lobanov quickly finished off our three cases. For him they were trifling matters. I later learnt that comparable cases of "relatives" were termed "fragments" in the NKVD. As the more distant fragment I received five years; Oksana and Yelena, as closer members of that shattered family, were given eight years each. Yelena served her eight in Ustvymlag, then exile in Bashkiria. She waited until the rehabilitations of the late 1950s and managed to force them to issue certificates rehabilitating her father, mother, stepfather and sister. Soon after, she herself was dead. It was as if that was all she had stayed alive for.

Oksana was put into a transport of prisoners and deprived, of course, of the medicines without which she could not live. In October 1938 she died at the God-forsaken transit camp in Vogvozdino, without ever beginning the long march on foot into the Komi-Zyryansk forests. And thank God for that! That terrible reaction was the first to come to mind when, in spring 1939, I learned of her death. I repeated those words now when I held in my slightly trembling hands that brown cardboard file.

I was the only one left. As Boris Slutsky wrote, in a poem I have read to myself over and over again:

> ... And I must stand up and fall,
> And once again fall down,
> My time has not yet come.

* * *

My time has not yet come...

Because now I must sit here and attentively read through each and every paper in these, the most important files. I must understand not only the story of how one family perished but something that today is much more interesting and important for me. Now I shall read the most highly confidential documents and learn how the upper ranks of the Bolshevik elite were destroyed, those who created the Party, led the revolution and controlled this society.

Boky and Moskvin were indeed among those people. The fantasy of finding the answer was unreal and had no chance of coming true, yet for years it constantly haunted me and, probably, many others.

When it seemed to me that the time had at last come, I began to agitate for access to the holy of holies, to the most confidential archives of the KGB. I wanted to hold those bulging records marked "For Permanent Retention" in my hand, and learn and understand everything.

Now I had received those very files, from that same archive. My Virgil who led me through this quiet, almost uninhabited hell came in with an ordinary shopping bag. Probably he put his food allowance there or simply bread. Pulling three, slender, very ordinary office files from the crumpled grubby cloth bag, he handed them to me and sat down to watch.

I picked up the "case-file" of Gleb Boky.

Very rapidly I understood why Pirozhkov, the KGB deputy chairman, had given permission for me to see these and other files after only two to three months petitioning on my part. They contained no secrets. All those classifications, "Highly Confidential," and so on, meant nothing. One could not learn the answers from these files. They did, it is true, give some "food for thought." An experienced palaeontologist, it is well known, can recognize or imagine the skeleton of a dinosaur or some other extinct animal just from examining a single bone. I cannot claim to be an investigator of the same class. But I did learn a great deal. And even that which I did not find out became a form of knowledge.

For the most important fact about these files was what was missing, not what was there. The decree authorizing the arrests of Boky and Moskvin was signed by a certain Belsky, Commissar of State Security, second class, deputy to Yezhov. Who Belsky was, no one knows: another one of those nonentities with whom Yezhov surrounded himself. Yet he could not have taken the decision to arrest people of the rank of Boky and Moskvin by himself. So their names had first been discussed somewhere else and scanned by the eyes of he whose "fat fingers like plump worms"[1] slowly worked their way down the list, until he reached these familiar names. In fact he knew all the names inscribed there. Somewhere these lists exist, with notes and marks, and perhaps the accompanying resolutions. Yet they are not here, not in these files. They are stored elsewhere, as carefully as the deathless Kashchei of Russian folktale hid his life. Also preserved are the other small or large files where handwritten or typed slips of paper outline the scenario, or even spell out in full, how each victim was to be dealt with.

On 7 June 1937 Boky was summoned to Yezhov and did not return. His office was searched in the presence of Yezhov himself. They also searched his apartment, naturally. The decree and arrest warrant are dated not 7 but 16 June. There Deputy People's Commissar Belsky asserted, as an already proven fact, that Boky had been a member of a counter-revolutionary organization of Freemasons, the "United Laboring Fraternity," which was spying for England. Boky, furthermore, also ran a spiritualist club at which secret seances were held, "foretelling the future."

After these formal documents there follows the investigation file, consisting of no more than the records of two interrogations.

During the first the accused admitted that he had been a Freemason since 1909, becoming a member of the same lodge as Academician Oldenburg, the artist Roerich (throughout referred to as "the English spy Roerich") and the sculptor Merkulov. The lodge had continued an active existence since then and had spawned the "Great Fraternity of Asia," the activities of which read like a teenager's adventure story: the mysterious Ismaili sect, their ominous and legendary leader the Aga Khan, wandering dervish-spies... Only a week was needed to persuade Gleb Ivanovich to put his name, without hesitation, in his firm and clear handwriting to this schoolboy nonsense. What had happened during that week? Nothing, the investigation file would seem to say.

The cases of all the Boky family, Moskvin and Sofia Alexandrovna Moskvin-Boky were handled by the usual investigating team. A high-ranking official was in charge, and he rarely let his white gloves come in contact with the faces of his detainees. He was assisted, however, as always, by an experienced torturer with the lowly rank of lieutenant. In Belsky's case, the latter was a certain Ali Kutebarov, a Kazakh born in 1902. Kutebarov had never read, of course, the adventure stories on which intellectual giants like Belsky had evidently been brought up. His job was to beat the prisoners into agreeing to the fantasies of his superior.

However, the exotic story of Freemasons and Ismailis did not suit the main directors of these bloodthirsty entertainments. I have no doubt that the chief of them was Himself, for whom these scenarios provided his main form of relaxation. Boky was needed for more important things than the plot dreamed up by the failed *gymnasium* student Belsky.

In an article very flattering to myself ("A Freemason, and a Freemason's Son-in-law," *Literaturnaya Gazeta*, No. 52, 1990) Arkady Vaksberg wrote that Gleb Boky was in charge "not only of the special Solovki camp but of all the other Soviet concentration camps." This is a mistake. In all his long years of service in the OGPU and NKVD, Gleb Boky never had anything directly to do with the Main Administration for Camps, the Gulag, or with any other camps. His name became linked to the famous Solovki camp not only because the steamer which sailed between the mainland and the islands was named after him, but because it was he who thought up the idea of such a concentration camp.

Boky, however, belonged to quite a different generation of Cheka-men than Yagoda, Pauker, Molchanov, Gay and the others. The son of an old intelligentsia family, and well-educated, Boky knew music very well and loved it. In writing these words I do not want to apply even the lightest coat of whitewash to the picture of Gleb Boky. Neither education, family background nor even profession prevented the Cheka-men from being smeared from head to foot with innocent blood. Menzhinsky, the second head of the Soviet security forces, was a highly educated polyglot, a connoisseur of classical literature and had been trained as a researcher into the history of ballet. Boky was one of the leaders of the October coup d'etat and after the assassination of Uritsky he headed the Petrograd Cheka for several months. During that time he directed the "Red Terror," officially unleashed after the attempt on Lenin's life, until he was squeezed out by Zinoviev. Thereafter, from 1919 onwards, he headed the Special Section of the Eastern, and then the Turkestan, Front during the Civil War. There is no need to explain what such a post involved and it is impossible to estimate the number of innocent victims that lie on his conscience.

The idea of organizing a concentration camp for the intelligentsia on the Solovetsky archipelago was, it seems to me, part of the same policy behind the mass expulsion in 1922 of the most renowned thinkers from the country. The less famous names, who were quite capable of political opposition but not yet actively involved, were to be isolated from the rest of society. Quite specifically "isolated" since, unlike their Tsarist predecessors, there was not to be the faintest hint of hard labor or any other form of work for these exiles. Many memoirs of those first years on Solovki, for example by Academician Dmitry Likhachev, preserve a record of that extraordinary period. Those locked away on the island could live quite freely, marry and divorce, write poetry or novels, correspond with anyone they chose, and receive any amount of the most varied literature; they could even publish their own literary journal, which was openly on sale in state kiosks on the mainland. The only thing they were forbidden to do was to work, even to clear away the snow. Yet somebody had to clear the snow, and chop the firewood and provide many other necessary services in such a strange but large prison. So they began to transport criminal offenders to Solovki. In charge of them were placed people who were officially prisoners but suited to such work in character and biography. As can be easily appreciated, these were not young historians or learned philosophers but individuals who had been officers in the White or even the Red Army. The famous and brutal head of Solovki, Kurilko, had formerly been a White Army officer, and he was also one of those isolated on the island. Gradually the idiotic idyllic camp paradise was transformed into the most usual, and then a most unusual, camp hell. Boky visited Solovki for the last time in 1929 with Maxim Gorky. This was part of the extravagant spectacle put on to entice the famous writer back to Russia, and it made the Potyomkin villages erected during Catherine the Great's trip through Russia appear a naive and childish enterprise.

Boky, meanwhile, from 1921 until his death was the founder and director of a department that officially did not even form part of the OGPU organization, but was only "attached to" it. As far as I can judge, it was most like the American National Security Agency. Its job was to protect the secrets of the Soviet state and try to find out those of others. In the entire complex and vast Soviet intelligence and police apparatus, this department and its director were, perhaps, the most inaccesible of all. One of the first defectors, Besedovsky, who had been Soviet commercial attache in Paris, earned some of his keep by writing novels, and one of them was entirely devoted to Gleb Boky. It was entitled *The Code-Hunter*. Although I myself worked for his organization for two whole years I was very poorly informed of the functions of Boky's department. I do know, however, that it never arrested or interrogated anyone. Probably that was entrusted to other, more specialized departments. I saw my own first prisoner on 18 April 1938 in the Inner Prison.

I am writing this not to justify or tone down the portrait of my former father-in-law. Yet of all the possible and impossible figures in and around the center of power Boky was, through his job, the most informed and knowledgeable of all. It would have been impossible to conceal any secret from him. So it was more than stupid to present such a man with this schoolboy composition about Freemasons and Ismailis. The Chief Director consequently issued different instructions. This explains the record of a second interrogation in the file, dating from 15 August. This time it was not the great intellectual Belsky who conducted the cross-examination but his semi-literate torturer-assistant Ali Kutebarov.

Now the crimes recorded were far removed from amateurish Freemasonry. Boky confessed that he had always been a Trotskyist and that after the expulsion of Trotsky from the Soviet Union, he had continued to keep in constant and close contact with him. While Trotsky was in Europe, reads the testimony, he constantly corresponded with Boky through his emissaries and when he ended up in Mexico Boky installed a special radio-station at his dacha to keep in touch with Trotsky. Since the distance between them was now so great, they reached agreement with the Nazi intelligence service that the conspirators' messages would be received and relayed by them. Of course, the main aim of this conspiracy was to assassinate Stalin. The easiest way to achieve this was to send the whole Kremlin sky-high. There was someone in Boky's department who was always working on the idea of remote-control explosions using invisible rays. This was Zhenya Gopius and he was supposedly the one entrusted to carry out this crime. It would first have been necessary, naturally, to transfer a sizable quantity of explosives to the Kremlin but such details did not bother the authors of this childish fantasy. Boky had signed this second deposition, just like the first, at the bottom of each page in the same clear and steady hand.

This was all that was needed. Yet even for the ten-minute trials conducted by Ulrich such a show was insufficient. Therefore, in the minutes marking the "Conclusion of investigation" signed by Belsky on 15 November 1937 these Trotskyist-Masonic crimes were not entrusted to a court but handed over to the NKVD Special Troika. That same day the troika "sentenced" Gleb Boky to be shot and he was killed there and then, on 15 November.

In Ivan Moskvin's file, apart from the decree of his arrest as an accomplice of a Masonic espionage network, there were two records of interrogation. The first dated from immediately after his arrest. In it Moskvin denied all the fantastic accusations but also spoke words that indeed could only have belonged to him and were quickly entered into the record as a kind of confession. I copied out these brief sentences which could not have been imagined by either Belsky or Ali. "I felt, with a growing intensity, that all our life was trapped in a dense web of Party lies and falsehood. People, it seemed to me, lacked the necessary human dignity. I was oppressed by the thought that, numerous though the members of our society were, you only rarely met an individual who could by rights be called a real human being..."

The second deposition was quite different. It took up many pages, had been signed by Moskvin only three weeks later, on 4 July, and was written out in Kutebarov's clear tiny handwriting. Here was a confession that Moskvin had participated in a Right terrorist organization; here he compromised many of the leading figures in the Party (most by then, it is true, already arrested); here he admitted to anything, including being the organizer of a certain anti-Soviet, Right-Trotskyist organization. And, of course, he revealed in passing all the secrets of the mysterious Masonic circle and its members. Each page concluded with the very familiar signature of Ivan Moskvin.

In his case, however, he was not only taken before the Military Tribunal but on 27 November confessed his crimes before Ulrich and his two assessors in a trial that lasted the usual fifteen minutes. He was immediately sentenced to be shot and was executed very shortly after. All this took place in the Lefortovo military prison where both Boky and Moskvin were held. As a time-saving rationalization the executioners' troika, masquerading as a court, drove there from their own offices on Nikolsky Street. In a small office they sat in judgment on prisoners who, for the most part, were personally well known to Ulrich. The sentence, typed out before, was read out there, and the victim would immediately be dragged downstairs to have a bullet fired into the back of his head at point-blank range. After working for several hours, and dealing with twenty or thirty cases, the members of this "court" got into their cars and drove back to the waiting comforts of home—an enjoyable meal and a languid post-dinner doze.

* * *

Why did such men as Boky and Moskvin confess, willingly and comparatively quickly, to these quite horrendous and totally implausible crimes? If we can trust the investigation files, moreover, they did so during their first or, at most, their second interrogation. The puzzle of the "confessions" was hotly disputed earlier, during the show trials, when men known for their principle, courage and almost legendary bravery openly admitted the most slanderous falsehoods against themselves before the whole world. We could not understand it then and I doubt that it has become much more comprehensible today. For the answer remains just as much classified information as it was half a century ago. The present KGB has no wish to hand over these pages in its historical biography and allow them to be examined, despite all the liberal gestures which now enable close relatives to examine such highly secret files as I received.

As I have said, the most interesting and important thing in these investigation files is what is lacking, not what remains. Apart from the preliminary discussion and decision—who, when and how to kill—there is also no trace of the "management sessions" of the courts, as I believe they are officially called. I do not know what should take place at such meetings but it is obvious that the thugs and butchers who paraded around as the Military Tribunal of the Supreme Court then discussed and very rapidly decided the fate of those who still sat in their cells and did not know they were to be killed in an hour or two. The judges were able to work fast, moreover, because before them they had a list, typed out and signed by someone, that decided the lot of the "accused."

* * *

Over the years before my anonymous quiet KGB watcher pulled Boky and Moskvin's files out of his shopping bag I had repeatedly asked myself, did they confess? I knew them both well and was convinced that it had been impossible to break such people with threats and what are delicately referred to as "physical methods." Yet they cracked, it turns out, and unexpectedly rapidly, without any struggle. Why?

The fact that there are only one or at most two records of "cross-examination" in the majority of such files does not mean that these were the only times the individual was interrogated. The same people were called out, night after night, from our cell No 29 at Butyrki. Sometimes they did not come back for days on end and we knew they were being kept standing up, day and night without sleep, while one interrogator replaced another. Sometimes they would crawl back into the cell with battered faces and broken ribs. Sometimes they were carried in by the escort guards and tossed, like a rag, on the cell floor. In these "highly confidential" files all trace has been removed of what happened between one interrogation and the next. If, that is, they needed a second interrogation, as was the case with Boky. The evidence of torture was destroyed. Moreover, this involved techniques unknown not only to the feeble Middle Ages, but even such experts as the Gestapo.

* * *

The first task of the interrogators was to convince their prisoner that he was no longer a human being and anything could and would be done to him. The measures were suited to the individual. It would have been laughable, for instance, to threaten a Civil War hero like Muralov with an imitation execution. There was a quiet Jew in our cell, however, with a magnificent curly head of hair who had worked as a quality controller at the GUM department store. He studied at the Plekhanov Institute and during his student days wore a red peasant shirt, which led the wits to nickname him Terrorist. In 1938 some unfortunate former fellow student was being interrogated and told to name the terrorists he knew. Eventually, he replied that there was a student in his year who was called Terrorist because of his red shirt. Our "terrorist" came back quite unharmed from his interrogation but rather strange. He sat down on the bed boards, took a clump of his luxuriant curls in his hand and it came away as easily as if it had been glued to his skull. He repeated this several times and in a few minutes he sat before us with a completely bald shining head. When we rushed over to him he began to tell us how they had said they were about to shoot him and imitated pulling the trigger...

* * *

Their main task, however, was not so much to frighten as to humiliate the individual to the point where he realized that there was no limit to what they might do. There were torture chambers during the renowned reign of Ivan the Terrible, and later, when people were tortured and all the necessary instruments of justice, the tongs and pincers, were there. In those case, though, the "investigating department" was responsible and the clerks in charge conscientiously wrote down what methods of persuasion had been applied to the accused. They even noted when, from time to time, the victim "fell into a stupor," i.e., lost consciousness. In our famed socialist times nothing was recorded and the range of methods for destroying the individual were quite unlimited.

It did not end with physical tortures. For one thing, there were individuals, though they were rare, who were capable of resisting any physical torment. And then human beings are so physiologically contrived that once they reach a certain pain threshold they lose consciousness. Our torturers made use of much more effective methods: threats to the prisoner's family and, especially, his children. Not one of those unfortunates who were driven to comply by their tormentors at the Lubyanka or Lefortovo had any doubts that threats to do "something" to their children were quite real. Irrespective of the latter's age. The tiniest infants were handed over to special nurseries where they died almost instantly; older children were sent to special children's homes where they were first brutalized and then died, one after another. Those still older, were simply arrested and forced to pass through all the circles of hell.

How many people, and among them the most famous, agreed to everything, including participation in the farcical show trials, in the hopes of saving their child. They were given "a Communist's word of honor," allowed to have visits from the family, and sent faked letters. Just as Dostoevsky had written, for the Cheka men there was no God and therefore all was permitted.

I did not learn then and shall never know now how they forced Boky and Moskvin to sign these senseless confessions. It was not only fear for their families, it seems to me (Boky then had a year-old daughter, not to mention his other relatives). Neither of them, I believe, had any doubt what their fate would be: they knew enough about the system and the people who had organized it. They knew the people involved and had even, as in Yezhov's case, themselves promoted them. They knew they were to die and tried their utmost to speed that moment of release.

I do not feel rancour and disappointment, nor resentment: all I experience is the most usual and infinite pity. In an earlier chapter I attacked General Gorbatov for his proud assertion that while others had "confessed" he had never signed anything... Perhaps my language was intemperate but to this day I consider I was correct. No one has the right to accuse the victims of anything because, in so doing, they also justify their torturers.

* * *

The "case files" of Gleb Boky and Ivan Moskvin provided a minimal amount of information. Attached to them, however, were also the so-called rehabilitation files which contained all kinds of documents and papers examined both by the Central Committee's Party committee and by various figures in the Procurator's Office and the Supreme Court. Altogether, there were quite a few different documents, beginning with the admiring letters about Boky written by Stasova and Kalinin's wife and ending with the cross-examinations of various people who unanimously declared that Boky and Moskvin had been admirable and selfless individuals. Why the Party and state officials then went through such an elaborate rigmarole I do not know. Even the most uneducated person could see that the investigation files were falsified from start to finish: it had been a calculated murder and did not require any additional proof. But when you are well-paid, receive good food allowances and have your own chauffeur-driven car, it is not a strain to perform such meaningless tasks.

I did find something in these additional files, though, that should have satisfied my desires for revenge. Did Commissar Belsky and his personal torturer Kutebarov know that they themselves had no more than two years to live? In 1939 or 1940 they were being beaten by other young men and, perhaps, their former colleagues now did with them everything they had done to others. When Yezhov's turn came, and he was replaced by Beria, the latter removed and killed, after torture, all those who had come to power under his predecessor. Belsky and Kutebarov were shot on 5 June 1941.

* * *

It was in their files at the KGB that I at last found what had really happened to Sophia Alexandrovna. During my short family life in the apartment on Spiridonov Street she remained a joyful and radiant memory. I was sure that she had suffered the usual fate of a Member of the Family of Traitor, received eight years and been sent to the camp in Potma. There tens of thousands like her were gathered and held in isolation. Someone even told me they had seen her there, at the Yavaz station. I had no doubt whatsoever that she wouldn't survive and her weak heart would soon give way.

I took the last file out of the shopping bag. I could not tear my eyes away from Sophia Alexandrovna's prison photo. Her eyes wide with horror, she wore the summer dress in which they had taken her off to search the dacha at Volynskoe.

"Why take a coat?" the man in charge of the arrest, had said. "We'll be back here within the hour."

The first mention of her came in the letter Belsky sent to Yezhov, suggesting that Moskvin be arrested. Yezhov wrote his decision across the paper, "To Comrade Belsky: carry out the arrest," and signed it. And after his signature added the words, "and the wife too." I did not expect that Yezhov could make an exception for Sophia Alexandrovna, no matter how she had fussed about his health and treated him as a member of the family. I had been sure that she would suffer the fate of the other wives of "enemies of the people." Her first interrogation, indeed, was not conducted by Belsky and Kutebarov but a certain T. M. Dyakov, and the accusations were quite normal for such criminals, i.e., you could not help knowing of the misdeeds of your first and second husband. Three weeks later Kutebarov had driven Sophia Alexandrovna to admit she had concealed her husbands' misdeeds. A few days after that a standard form was added to the file in which she was accused of "concealment" and so came under the article dealing with Members of the Family of a Traitor. A Special Board or troika awaited her, and eight years in Potma.

This was the only indication that Yezhov had other plans for his former hospitable hostess. Sophia Alexandrovna was never taken anywhere else, however. A new cycle of interrogations, of which Kutebarov was now directly in charge, began. On 27 November 1937 his deposition closed the new case and the accusation and scenario were now quite different. Sophia Alexandrovna, it turned out, had intended to kill Yezhov himself. To this end she had recruited Dr. Badmayev as her accomplice. I knew Nikolai Badmayev very well. He was an intelligent, calm and educated Buryat, the nephew of the famous pre-revolutionary Badmayev, and followed in his uncle's footsteps: he treated the entire Kremlin court elite with his herbal remedies. Of course, he visited the apartment on Spiridonov Street and even gave me powders for some complaint (I used them to clean my canvas shoes). Sophia Alexandrovna had persuaded Badmayev to poison Yezhov who was also one of the fashionable doctor's patients. Badmayev retorted, supposedly, that he was an English spy and would not perform such assignments just like that. If Sophia Alexandrovna agreed to work for British intelligence, however... Of course, she agreed. Obviously, not at once.

* * *

When he was being interrogated in 1939, Belsky testified that after he had completed his investigation of Sophia Alexandrovna's "case," Yezhov summoned him and ordered him to obtain testimony from her that she had wanted to kill him. Belsky immediately entrusted this task to his experienced subordinate Kutebarov. Later, during his own interrogation, Kutebarov admitted that it had not been easy because his prisoner had resisted... But an expert knows the key to every case! On 27 November Kutebarov obtained the confession that she had been a spy and a terrorist. This was already quite a different matter. Now there awaited not the easy life in the women's camp but certain and immediate death. On 25 December the certificate confirming the end of the investigation was signed and on 27 February 1938 the charge sheet, signed by Belsky and Vyshinsky was drawn up. Finally, on 8 April 1938 Sophia Alexandrovna was driven from Butyrki, where she was being held, to that same building on Nikolsky Street where Ulrich ruled his malevolent kingdom, the Military Tribunal of the Supreme Court. She was tried not by Ulrich himself but his experienced assistants and on a quarter-page scrap of paper are recorded: the accusation (espionage and terrorism, Articles 58:6 and 58:8), the length of the trial (fifteen minutes), the accused's plea for clemency and the death sentence. Soon after, in a few minutes or maybe an hour, she was murdered, as a tiny slip of paper in her file confirms: "Sentence carried out 8 April 1938, record of shooting transferred for preservation in 1st special section of NKVD, vol. 3, sheet 142."

When Yelena returned from the camps, she began to inquire about her mother's fate. She already knew that her father and stepfather had been shot, and that her younger sister had died before even reaching the camps. She knew nothing about her mother. When she learned that Sophia Alexandrovna's case had come before the Military Tribunal she applied to them. It was August 1956. The Twentieth Party Congress at which Khrushchev made his "Secret Speech" had taken place and those of Stalin's victims who were still alive were beginning to return in straggling thin crowds from the camps. I found Yelena's application in her mother's file and the reply of 14 August 1956: "Inform Yelena Glebovna Boky that her mother was sentenced on 8 April 1938 by the Military Tribunal and died, while serving her sentence, on 12 September 1942." Signed lieutenant-general (jurisprudence) A. Cheptsov, chairman of the Military Tribunal of the Supreme Court.

I do not know if the wretched man who signed this deceitful, repulsive and lying document is still alive. There it is, with its secret classification, its crests and seals, and all the other decorations that should testify that this was the pronouncement of a major department in a great state, and not a gang of deceitful thugs. But, of course, Cheptsov was not alone.

And what are the numerous petty clerks who drew up these certificates with their falsified dates of death compared to the thousands, even many thousands, alive to this day who have always been precisely and unequivocally termed "butchers." A report issued by the Ministry of State Security in 1956, and never since officially refuted, stated that from 1 January 1935 to 22 June 1941 alone, 7 million people were shot. A million a year, in other words. During Alexander II's reign just over 60 political prisoners were hanged in Russia. That was hardly a large figure but the problem was different: there was only one executioner in the whole of the Empire, the famous prisoner Frolov. He was escorted from Butyrki prison in Moscow to the Shlusselberg prison in Petersburg, and to Odessa and Vilno everywhere that someone had to be killed "in accordance with the law."

However many executioners were needed to dispose of one million people each year? For they not only prepared and killed people but then they had to bury them in those fearful mass graves and plant over them the trees that were already waiting. Hundreds and thousands of people were involved. Yet, extraordinary to tell, not a single participant in any of these killings has been traced. On 12 April 1990 Procurator V. Zybtsev formally closed the criminal investigation into the mass shooting of 157 political prisoners at Oryol prison on 11 September 1941 (the victims included Kamenev's widow, Olga Okudzhava, Maria Spiridonova, Christian Rakovsky who was then sixty-eight and Professor Pletnyov, sixty-nine). "It proved impossible... to track down the participants in this operation or to locate the burial place of the condemned," he concluded. On 6 September Stalin gave the order, two days later Ulrich and his assistants rapidly passed "sentence" and a specially assembled team of executioners was sent out from Moscow. At the prison women sewed gags and forced them between the teeth of the condemned prisoners... Not one of them could be found. Well, perhaps it would be difficult to track down any of those women assistants, though for decades our heroic Chekamen and their successors have hunted and found, in apparently the most remote locations, those who served during the war in the German *sonderkommando*, helping the Nazis to shoot and bury their victims. Those criminals they found and ours... not a single one!

There was, incidentally, no need to search for the main culprits. They are quite well known. In his legal judgment, Procurator Zybtsev wrote, "Since the stated legal decision was based on a decree of the State Committee for Defense, at the time the highest authority in the state, the actions of Ulrich, Kandybin and Bukanov do not constitute a criminal act of any kind."

And the procurator decided to close the case. It merely remains unexplained why, after the war, when a German was arrested for having murdered old people and children and quite logically answered, "Ich bin soldat" (I was under orders), that this argument was not taken into consideration. The members of our troikas and the thousands of Soviet executioners could and perhaps did say exactly the same. To this day they remain nameless, because no one has hunted them down. When they did go through the pretense of locating them, it "proved impossible" to find them.

* * *

I am not a historian and I am not writing the history of such crimes. Or the story of those who then tortured and killed. Or that of those who today quite consciously conceal and protect them—no longer from any criminal court, it should be added, but from the judgment of history, time and conscience. For however much their successors may now pretend to be harmless lambs and assure their audiences, in theaters and on television, that they have changed, they remain the same... And, like the animals in the *Jungle Book*, when they meet their predecessors in the next world they will cry, in the flames of hell, "we are of one blood!" Each week the newspaper *Vechernyaya Moskva* publishes rows of tiny photographs of people killed 50-60 years ago, for no reason at all, yet I am not aware that any of the thousands who serve in that vast building on Lubyanka Square has gone insane, committed suicide, or publicly spoken out in tears of repentance, horror and mortal anguish... In Chekhov's story "A Fit" a student who goes to a brothel with his merry friends suddenly almost begins to lose his mind from the awareness that these unfortunate women are also people. Tormented, unfortunate people. Not one of his educated, clever and, probably, kind fellow students can understand what's wrong with him.

* * *

I must stop thinking of such things. I have long since stopped turning the pages of the file and they have lain next to me for more than an hour or two, growing cold with their own thoughts. My guardian is already beginning to cough suggestively and look at his watch. It's time to go. I have nothing more to do here. I hand over the files and they are negligently dropped again into the shopping bag. I go downstairs, along the empty corridors, past the sentries who do not even ask to see my papers, and step out into Lubyanka Square.

It's only 5 p.m. but it is already almost dark and a fine, quiet rain falls uninterruptedly. The building remains behind me and I stand on the pavement outside, wondering what to do next? How terrible that

I do not believe in God and cannot go into some quiet little church, stand in the warmth of the candles, gaze into the eyes of Christ on the Cross and say and do those things that make life easier to bear for the believer.

I stand there for a long time, so suspiciously long that one of the plainclothes men on duty at that old, terrible building positions himself not far away. Away to the left, in the distance, in front of the Polytechnical Museum, a wavering flame glimmers, almost lost in the fine drizzle. A candle on the Solovki Stone. Not long ago we commemorated this modest monument to the millions of victims, like my family.

Then it was no more than a stone, brought down from the White Sea. Now it has become more than a monument. A candle burns under a protective scrap of polythene, and beside it sit two apples and a branch of rowanberry. Damp flowers lie there on the stone. The words have already faded on the wreaths that stand in front. Someone lovingly bows down and places a small and carefully worked wooden cross on the pedestal and another leaves a page of verse. A dozen people stand around in silence. The remains of the mass which was served here at its opening have long faded away: it is now not a monument but a grave. The kind of familiar, long-prayed over grave that one can find in old, still functioning graveyards.

Like the others around me I take off my fur hat, and drops of rain or tears trickle down my face. I am eighty-two and here I stand, living through it all again, by the grave of those millions. And among them I hear the voices of Oksana and her mother... I can remember and recall them, each one. And if I remained alive, then it is my duty to do so.

My time has not yet come.

P.S. On Tuesday 8 November 1994 *Vechernyaya Moskva* carried its weekly page of photographs and names, and among them was that of Ivan Moskvin the Bolshevik. It is now known that he was buried at the Donskoi Monastery in Mass Grave No. 1.

Notes

Niyazov
1. Galich, "Hospital Gypsy Song."
2. Seventh class—the last year of required education at the time (age 14 approximately).
3. In 1942 German forces massacred all the inhabitants of the Belorussian village of Khatyn. (Not to be confused with Katyn in Russia, where in 1940, 23,500 Polish officers were murdered by the NKVD.)
4. From Dombrovsky's "Verses Written Upon Being Released" (Stikhi napisanno posle Osvobozhdeniia").

Ivan Moskvin
1. Orgburo and Orgraspred. Short for "organizational bureau" and "organized work allocation". The Orgburo was created together with the Politburo at the Eighth Party Congress in March 1919. The Politburo was created to enable the original five members to decide quickly on issues without resort to the whole Central Committee, and the Orgburo, also originally five members, was put in charge of personnel appointments. It oversaw the quick expansion of the Party bureaucracy and the introduction of special benefits.
2. In 1994 work began to restore them to their former splendor.

Military Men
1. Until 1940 the old officer titles were replaced by the term "commander" in the Red Army.
2. From Isaak Babel's story "My First Goose" in *Red Cavalry*.
3. St. George cavalier. The Order of St. George was established in Russia in 1769 to reward officers and generals for military accomplishments.
4. Renamed Stalingrad in the mid-1930s.
5. Pechorin is the hero of Lermontov's novel *Hero of Our Times*.
6. One of the exhibits in Peter the Great's Chamber of Curiousities in Petersburg, reputedly of impressive dimensions.

A Play with a Happy Ending
1. The quote is from the opening lines of Alexander Radishchev's *A Journey from Petersburg to Moscow*.

Roshchakovsky
1. Early seventeenth-century period of instability before the new Romanov dynasty restored order.
2. Nekrasov legacy—The writer and publisher Nikolai Nekrasov dedicated much of his work to the life of the Russian peasant and more than any writer of his time made his contemporaries aware of the peasants' sufferings.
3. Reference to the Black Hundreds, the anti-semitic movement tacitly supported by Nicholas II.
4. See Jailers chapter.
5. "Change of Landmarks" was an early 1920s response to the prophetic 1907 "Landmarks" collection.
6. The Grand Duke was assassinated by the SR Kalyayev in 1905.
7. From Eduard Bagritsky's "Till Eulenspiegel."

Boris and Gleb
1. Before the Revolution there was a Tsarist prison in the town of Ust-Vym at the confluence of the Vym and Vychegda rivers. In the early 1930s the Ustvymlag camp system, exclusively concerned with forestry work, began to spread throughout the Komi autonomous republic and by 1939 numbered 24 separate camps and numerous outposts with a total population vacillating

between 25 and 40,000.

2. "Frost, the Red-nosed," trans. by Alan Myers.

3. Prisoners who persistently refused to go out to work.

Strangers

1. Providing immunity against local police harassment, rather than a means to travel abroad.

2. This is not an exact quote but put in a Babelian way.

3. Characters in novels by the Polish writer Henryk Sienkiewicz.

4. France, 1987; New York, 1989.

Kostya Shulga

1. Since 1988 restored to the Orthodox Church and serving as the Russian Orthodox "Vatican."

2. Vasily Shkvarkin's comedy "Strange Child" [Chuzhoi rebenok].

3. Formally removed in the new 1993 Constitution.

4. Lev Slavin's play "Interventsiia."

5. In Russian, "zakonniki."

Jailers

1. The equivalent of a captain in the army.

2. Viy appears in a story by the same name in the collection *Mirgorod*.

3. The operetta *Silva* by Imre Kalman.

4. Razgon was writing about Peter Nikolayevich Lebedev (1866-1912), a gifted physicist who was hounded from the university.

Fear

1. Until the 1940s the Morozov and Shchukin collections of French art were kept in Moscow. Then the museum was closed and its holdings given to the Hermitage and other galleries.

2. From Pushkin's narrative poem *The Gypsies* (Tsygany).

3. The poem about Borgia is by Machiavelli.

4. In the story "Viy" in Nikolai Gogol's collection *Mirgorod*.

24 Kuznetsky Street

1. Daughter of Yefrem Berg, one of the defendants at the trial of the Socialist Revolutionaries in 1922.

2. From Blok's poem "A girl was singing in the choir in church" (Devushka pela v tserkovnom khore).

Epilogue

1. The reference to Stalin ("fat fingers like plump worms") is from Osip Mandelstam's poem no. 286, "We live without feeling the land beneath us" [My zhivem, pod soboiu ne chuia strany), written in November 1933. Mandelstam was first arrested in 1934.

BIOGRAPHICAL GLOSSARY

LIST OF ABBREVIATIONS

ChK or Cheka (Chrezvychainaia komissiia po bor'be so kontrrevoliutsiei, sobotazhem i spekuliatsiei) —All Russia Extraordinary Commission for struggle against counterrevolution, sabotage and speculation. Established in 1917.

GPU (Gosudarstvennoe politicheskoe upravlenie)—State Political Directorate (Secret Police)

GULAG (Glavnoe upravlenie lagerei)—Chief Administration of Corrective Labor Camps

KGB (Komitet gosudarstvennoi bezopasnosti)—State Security Committee

MGB (Ministerstvo gosudarstvennoi bezopasnosti)—Ministry of State Security

NKVD (Narodnyi komissariat vnutrennikh del)—People's Commissariat for Internal Affairs

OGPU (Ob''edinennoe gosudarstvennoe politicheskoe upravlenie)—Unified State Political Directorate

VKP(B) (Vsesoiuznaia Kommunisticheskaia partiia bol'shevikov)—All-Union Communist Party (Bolsheviks)

Note: from 1922-34 the political or secret police was known as the GPU or OGPU, rather than the original Cheka, and after 1934 as the NKVD, then the MVD and MGB, and from 1954 to 1991 as the KGB.

Alexander III (1845-1894). Emperor of Russia from 1881-94.

Alliluyeva, Nadezhda Sergeyevna (1901-1932). Party activist who married Stalin in 1919. Her suicide in 1932 was a great shock for him.

Anders, Vladislav (1892-1970). Polish general who was arrested in 1939 during the Russian invasion of Poland, then freed in 1941 in order to lead Polish forces fighting with the Western allies in the war against the Nazis. After the war he settled in England.

Andronikov, Irakly (Andronikashvili, 1908-1982). Soviet writer, literary critic.

Annensky, Innokenty (1856-1909). Poet, playwright, critic and translator of Euripides.

Artuzov, Artur (1891-1943). Head of NKVD Foreign Department. Arrested in 1939.

Babel, Isaak (1894-1940). Writer best-known for his short-story collections *The Odessa Tales* and *Red Cavalry*, about the war in Ukraine in 1920. Babel served in Budyonny's Cavalry Army in the Civil War and Polish campaign. Arrested in 1939, rehabilitated in 1956.

Bedny, Demyan (pseud. of Yefim Pridvorov, 1883-1945). Writer and Party member. One of the best known Communist propagandists during the Civil War period.

Berg-Razgon, Rika Yefremovna (1905-1991). Daughter of Yefrem Berg, a leading Right Social Revolutionary and second wife of Lev Razgon. Yefrem Berg was in and out of both Tsarist and Soviet prisons and his daughter followed him in order to send food parcels and provide other care. She was arrested in 1937 and met Lev in the camps. They married in 1946. Released in 1948, both were rearrested and sent to different camps. In 1954 Rika was released; Lev joined her a year later.

Beria, Lavrenty (1899-1953). Head of security police in Georgia before eventually replacing Yezhov as head of the NKVD in 1939. In 1941 he became a deputy prime minister of the USSR and in 1946 a member of the Politburo. In the struggle for power after Stalin's death he was arrested and executed.

Berman, Matvei (?-1937). Administrative head of the GULAG and also Chief of Construction of the White Sea Canal. Shot in 1937.

Bezymensky, Alexander (1898-1973). Poet and early Party activist who wrote propagandistic poems.

Bilibin, Ivan (1876-1942). Artist especially known for his illustrations of fairytales and a style which adapted motifs from Russian folk art.

Blok, Alexander (1880-1921). Leading Russian Symbolist poet, essayist and playwright. His epic poem *The Twelve* (1918) became famous as the first poetic response to the Revolution. Blok later became disillusioned with the revolutionary regime.

Blyukher, Marshal Vasily (1890-1938). Fought in WW1. He later commanded the army in the Far East. Arrested in 1938 as the Tukhachevsky military trials expanded and claimed more victims.

Boky, Gleb (1879-1937). Bolshevik, fought in the Revolution. Became head of the Petrograd Cheka. After 1921 worked in the OGPU and NKVD.

Boky, Oksana (1916-1938). Daughter of Sophia Boky and first wife of Lev Razgon. Died in transit to the camps.

Boky, Sophia Alexandrovna (1877-1938). Wife of Gleb Boky, and later married to Ivan Moskvin. Mother-in-law of Lev Razgon.

Boky, Yelena (1909-1957). Daughter of Gleb Boky and Sophia Boky-Moskvin and sister of Oksana.

Boussenard, Louis (1847-1910). French author of adventure tales and science fiction.

Brodsky, Isaak (1883-1939). Artist and illustrator.

Brodsky, Joseph (1940-1996). Russian poet from Leningrad who was arrested, exiled and in 1972 forced to emigrate to the West, where he became an internationally known figure for his poetry and prose. Brodsky won the Nobel Prize in 1987.

Bryullov, Karl (1799-1852). Russian artist who lived in Italy from 1823-35.

Budyonny, Semyon (1883-1973). Commander of the Mounted Cavalry which fought in Ukraine against Poland and other anti-Soviet forces. A hero of the Civil War, he later became a marshal of the USSR in 1935.

Bukharin, Nikolai (1888-1938). Communist theoretician of the "Right" faction of the Party who wanted to continue NEP and the struggle for a world socialist revolution. He was defeated by Stalin. Tried and executed in 1938 during the show trials, Bukharin was rehabilitated in 1988 under Gorbachev.

Bulganin, Nikolai (1895-1975). served in the OGPU. Protege of Kaganovich. He became chairman of the Council of People's Commissars of the Russian Republic and became a member of the Politburo in 1948. Colleague and rival of Khrushchev, Bulganin lost power in 1958.

Chaliapin, Fyodor (1873-1938). Opera singer who won international fame. At first sympathetic to the Bolshevik Revolution, he moved to the West in 1922.

Chapaev, Vasily (1887-1919). Hero of the Civil War.

Chaplin, Nikolai (1902-1938). Party leader in Leningrad in the 20s. Leader of Komsomol, purged in 1938.

Chekhov, Anton (1860-1904). Major dramatist and short-story writer.

Chirikov, Yevgeny (1864-1932). Russian novelist and playwright, at one time associated with the literary group Znanie. Emigrated in 1920.

Denikin, Anton (1872-1947). General of the White Volunteer Army which fought against the Bolsheviks in southern Russia during the Civil War.

Djugashvili, Yakov (1908-1945). Eldest son of Stalin, taken prisoner by the Germans.

Doller, Alexandre (1860-1893). Radical populist, exiled to Siberia. Father of Sophia Moskvin.

Dombrovsky, Yury (1909-1978). Novelist and short-story writer first exiled to Central Asia in 1932. Spent fifteen years in prisons, camps and exile. Author of *The Faculty of Useless Knowledge*.

Doroshevich, Vlas (1864-1922). Russian journalist and theater critic. Described the tsarist prison system in his book of essays *Sakhalin* (1903).

Dostoevsky, Fyodor (1821-81). Major novelist, short-story writer and journalist. Razgon refers to his novels *Crime and Punishment* and *The House of the Dead*, which describes the world of the prison camps where Dostoevsky had once spent four years for political crimes.

Dzhunkovsky, Vladimir Fyodorovich (1878-1938). Tsarist general and professional military man who became Deputy Minister of the Interior. Shot.

Frunze, Mikhail (1885-1925). Deputy Commissar of War. Died mysteriously during a routine medical operation. The strong suspicion that Stalin was behind his death is the barely-disguised theme of Pilynak's *Tale of the Unextinguished Moon.*

Gai, Dmitry (Gaik Bzhishkyan, 1887-1937). Military commander in the Civil war.

Gay, M. I. Worked in the NKVD. Shot in 1937.

Galich, Alexander (pseudonym of Alexander Ginzburg, 1918-1977). Poet and song-writer who became famous in the 1960s for his satirical and political songs. Expelled from the Writers' Union, he emigrated in 1974.

Gerasimov, Alexander (1881-1963). Artist. He did the portrait of Voroshilov mentioned here.

Gladkov, Fyodor (1883-1958). Novelist and short-story writer whose work was a model of Socialist Realism.

Gogol, Nikolai (1809-1852). Great nineteenth-century satirical writer, especially famous for his novel *Dead Souls* and the play *The Inspector General.*

Golovanov, Nikolai (1891-1953). Director, composer, and pianist who worked at the Bolshoi theater.

Gorbatov, Alexander (1891-1973). Military commander in World War II. Became a general in 1955.

Gorbunov, Ivan (1831-1895). Russian actor and writer.

Gorky, Maksim (pseudonym of Alexei Peshkov, 1868-1936). Influential writer, playwright, poet and critic who supported the Revolution and was considered the founder of socialist realism and Soviet literature.

Grashchenkov, Nikolai (1901-1965). Neurologist. Worked at the Institute of Experimental Medicine.

Gumilyov, Nikolai (1886-1921). Poet and critic associated with the Acmeist movement and co-founder of the journal *Apollon.* Shot in 1921 for conspiring against the Bolsheviks.

Gusev, Viktor (1909-44). Soviet playwright and poet.

John of Kronstadt (Ivan Ilich Sergeyev, 1829-1909). Russian Orthodox priest and ascetic who worked with the poor.

Kaganovich, Lazar (1893-1991). Longtime associate of Stalin. Became member of the Politburo in 1930. Under Stalin's administration he was in charge of heavy industry. Lost power under Khrushchev.

Kalyayev, Ivan (1877-1905). Social Revolutionary who assassinated the Grand Duke Sergei in 1905. He was executed.

Kalinin, Mikhail (1875-1946). Longtime Party activist. Became president of the Soviet Union in 1938.

Kamenev, Lev (1883-1937). Member of the Politburo, 1919-26. Defeated by Stalin in Party power struggles; defendant at Moscow show trial in August 1936. Condemned and shot. Rehabilitated in 1988.

Kaplan, Fanny (Feiga Roidman or Roidblat). A Socialist-Revolutionary and anarchist. She attempted to assassinate Lenin in 1918, and was executed.

Kassil, Lev (1905-1970). Writer who specialized in children's literature and worked for the magazine *Pioner. My Dear Boys,* referred to by Razgon, describes the lives of heroic children during World War II.

Khvostov, Alexander (1872-1918). Right wing politician who served for a time as Minister of the Interior under Nicholas II.

Khrushchev, Nikita (1894-1971). Party activist. After Stalin's death he emerged as the new leader. In 1956 in a famous speech at the Twentieth Party Congress, he denounced Stalin's policies. Became head of the government in 1958 and remained in power until 1964.

Kirov, Sergei (1886-1934). Bolshevik since 1904, he became Party boss in Leningrad in 1926. Member of Politburo and Secretary of the Central Committee, he had once sided with Stalin against Trotsky and Zinoviev. His assassination in 1934, when he was regarded as a critic of Stalin, is generally thought to mark the beginning of Stalin's purges.

Kleist, Heinrich von (1777-1811). Great German dramatist and novelist.

Kniga, Vasily, Major-General (1888-1961). Civil war hero.

Koltsov, Mikhail (1898-1942). Writer and journalist, who wrote many feuilletons for the newspaper *Pravda*.

Kon, Felix (1864-1941). Revolutionary activist. Sentenced to hard labor in 1884 for his political activites. Later joined the Communist party and actively supported the revolution.

Korchagina-Alexandrovskaya, Yekaterina (1874-1951). Famous Russian actress who first appeared on the stage in 1887.

Korneichuk, Nikolai (1882-1969). Wrote under the pen-name of Kornei Chukovsky. Writer, children's writer, critic, translator, editor.

Korolenko, Vladimir (1853-1921). Writer, critic, social activist. Was arrested and exiled for his political activities. Best known for his Siberian stories.

Korovin, Konstantin (1861-1939). Russian artist known for landscapes and stage decorations.

Korzhavin, Naum (pseudonym of Naum Mandel, 1925-). Poet acclaimed in the 1960s. He emigrated to the West in 1973.

Kosarev, Alexander (1903-39). Komsomol activist and leader. Was sent by Stalin to Leningrad to purge the Leningrad Komsomol after Zinoviev's defeat in December 1925. Became General Secretary of the Central Committee of the Komsomol in Moscow in 1929. Executed in 1939 when Stalin decided to purge most of the Komsomol Central Committee.

Kozhanov, Ivan (1897-1938). Naval officer. Became Admiral and Commander of the Black Sea Fleet. Arrested in 1937 during Stalin's purge of the Navy.

Kron, Alexander (1909-1983). Soviet writer and playwright.

Krupskaya, Nadezha (1869-1939). Party activist and wife of Lenin.

Kuibyshev, Valerian (1888-1935). Took part in 1905 revolution. Political leader in the Red Army during the Civil War. Part of the Left Communist faction of the Bolshevik Party, which was led by Bukharin. Some have seen his heart attack in 1935 as a covered-up murder on Stalin's orders, inasmuch as Kuibyshev was an obstacle to him at the time.

Kuzmin, Mikhail (1875-1936). Poet, prose writer, playwright and critic who was later associated with the Acmeist school.

Kuzmin, Nikolai (1890-19??). Graphic artist. Illustrator of literary works.

Kun, Bela (1886-1939?). Leader of the 1919 Communist Revolution in Hungary and member of the Third International. He was a victim of Stalin's purges, accused of "Trotskyism."

Kutyakov, Ivan (1897-1938). Deputy to Chapaev during the Civil War. After Chapaev's death he headed the division.

Lenin (Vladimir Ilych Ulyanov, 1870-1924). Founder of the Bolshevik Party and leader of the Revolution. First head of the Soviet state and formulator of the official Communist Marxist-Leninist ideology.

Lepeshinskaya, Olga (1871-1963). Political activist, biologist.

Leskov, Nikolai (1831-1895). Short-story writer, novelist, journalist.

Levitan, Isaak (1860-1900). Artist. Associated with the Peredvizhnik movement in Russian art.

Lisovsky, Nikolai. Red Army officer. Commander of the Central Asian military district until his arrest in 1937.

Litvinov, Maksim (real name Maks Vallakh, 1876-1951). Communist activist. Commissar of Foreign Affairs from 1930-39. Replaced by Molotov.

Lloyd George, David (1863-1945). British Prime Minister 1916-22.

Lysenko, Trofim (1898- 1976). Soviet biologist and agronomist. He became the highly controversial head of Communist biology under Stalin, and was Director of the

Institute of Genetics of the USSR Academy of Sciences from 1940 to 1965.

Malenkov, Georgy (1902-1988). Communist Party official who became a close associate of Stalin's in the 1930s. He was deeply involved in the party purges of the late 30s and in 1941 joined the Politburo. Malenkov continued to hold important posts until Stalin's death.

Malinovsky, Roman (??-1918). Agent provocateur who served from 1912-14 as Lenin's deputy in Russia and chairman of the Bolshevik Duma faction. Malinovsky regularly reported to the police on the Bolshevik Party's secrets, but at the same time helped publicize their program with his speeches in the Duma and his work on the newspaper *Pravda*. He was executed in 1918.

Malkov, Pavel (1887-1965). Commandant of the Kremlin in 1918 who was ordered to kill Fanny Kaplan. His memoirs were published in 1959.

Mandelstam, Osip (1891-1938). Major Russian poet and essayist. Member of the Poets' Guild and an early Acmeist. Arrested and exiled in 1934 because of his poem about Stalin. Arrested again in 1937. Died in a transit camp.

Markov, Nikolai (1866-?). One of the leaders of the "Union of the Russian People," the "Union of the Archangel Michael," and other extreme right organizations. Emigrated.

Marshak, Samuil (1887-1964). Poet, translator, children's writer. He organized the children's section of the Leningrad State Publishing House.

Martov, Julius (1873-1923). Revolutionary activist. Became a leader of the Mensheviks in 1903. Emigrated in 1920.

Masaryk, Tomas (1850-1937). Chief founder and first president of Czechoslovakia (in 1918) and a philosopher and sociologist.

Mayakovsky, Vladimir (1893-1930). Major poet and playwright who was associated with the Futurist school of writers and artists in the 1910s. After 1917 actively worked in the Left Front of Art, producing propagandistic pieces as well as his own more creative work. Committed suicide in 1930.

Milyukov, Pavel (1859-1943). Statesman and historian who helped form the Constitutional Democratic Party and served as foreign minister in the provisional government. Emigrated to Paris.

Molotov, Vyacheslav (1890-1986). Statesman and diplomat who was a major international spokesman for the Soviet Union during and after World War II. A long time revolutionary activist, he was a supporter of Stalin after Lenin's death and during the purges. He is also known for having negotiated the German-Soviet Nonaggression Pact (Molotov-Ribbentrop) in 1939.

Moskvin, Ivan Mikhailovich (1874-1946). Famous actor who began his stage career in 1896.

Moskvin, Ivan Mikhailovich (1874-1938). Member of Central Committee and head of Orgraspred. Father-in-law of Lev Razgon.

Muklevich, Romuald (1890-1938). A longtime Bolshevik who served both in the Soviet Army and Navy. After 1926 he played a leading role in modernizing the Soviet Navy. He was arrested in 1937.

Muralov, N. I. (1888-1937). Party activist and longtime Bolshevik. Arrested and tried in 1937.

Nezhdanova, Antonina (1873-1950). Singer who performed at the Bolshoi.

Nekrasov, Nikolai (1821-1878). Poet, writer, publisher. Known for sympathetic and "realistic" poems about rural conditions and the oppressed Russian peasantry.

Nemirovich-Danchenko, Vladimir (1858-1943). Theater director, playwright. Co-founder with Konstantin Stanislavsky of the Moscow Art Theater.

Nicholas I (1796-1855). Russian Emperor from 1825-55.

Nicholas II (1868-1918). The last Russian Emperor, who acceded to the throne in 1894 and was deposed by revolutionaries in 1917.

Nikolayev, Leonid (1904-1934). Young assassin who shot Kirov in 1934, an act which marked the beginning of Stalin's "Great Terror" policy.

Novikov-Priboi, Alexei (pseudonym of Alexei Novikov, 1877-1944). Writer who drew on his naval background for his fiction. His main work, the novel *Tsushima*, was widely read and won the Stalin prize.

Oleinikov, Nikolai (1898-1942?). Avant-garde poet known for his ironical verse. Arrested in 1937. Died in the camps.

Ordzhonikidze, Grigory (1886-1937). Party activist from Georgia who initially supported Stalin. Headed Commissariat for Heavy Industry and worked on the Five-Year Plan. Ordzhonikidze opposed Stalin's continuation of the purges and this conflict led to his suicide (or murder?) in January 1937.

Osinsky, Valerian (1887-1938). Party activist who belonged to the Left wing of the Communists, associated with Trotsky. Involved in the Bukharin trials, he was shot in 1938.

Ozerov, Nikolai (1887-1953). Tenor who sang with the Bolshoi from 1920-46.

Pauker, K. Revolutionary activist. Worked for the NKVD. Arrested in Yezhov's purge of the NKVD and shot in 1937.

Pavlov, Ivan (1849-1936). Physiologist famous for his work on conditioned reflexes. Won the Nobel Prize in 1903.

Pilnyak, Boris (pseudonym of Boris Vogau, 1894-1937). Major Soviet novelist and short-story writer. A dominant figure in Soviet literature in the early 1920s, he was known for his fragmentary, ornamental prose. Fell into political trouble in the late 20s. Arrested and shot in 1937.

Platten, Fritz (1883-1942). Swiss socialist. Leader of Social Democrats. Helped to negotiate Lenin's return trip from Zurich to Russia through Germany in 1917.

Pokrovsky, Mikhail (1868-1932). Soviet historian who reinterpreted Russian history.in the light of Marxist theory. He held a number of positions in government and academic institutions, but ideas were denounced by Stalin and he fell out of favor. He was rehabilitated in 1961.

Pushkin, Alexander (1799-1837). Considered the greatest Russian poet and a founder of the modern Russian literary language. *Eugene Onegin*, the novel in verse mentioned in Razgon's memoirs, is one of the masterpieces of Russian literature.

Radek, Karl (1885-1939). Communist activist and early leader of the Communist International. A supporter of Trotsky, he was expelled from the Party in 1927, later readmitted, but was arrested and tried in 1937 in the second show trial of the great purge.

Radishchev, Alexander (1749-1802). Writer, known for *A Journey from Petersburg to Moscow*, a critique of society which was considered politically subversive and for which Radishchev was sent into exile.

Radziwill. A famous aristocratic Polish family.

Rasputin (Novykh), Grigory (1872?-1916). Siberian peasant and mystic healer who was taken into the court of Empress Alexandra and Emperor Nicholas II and exerted enormous influence on the ruling circles during the last years of Romanov rule. He was murdered by a group of conservative conspirators.

Razgon, Israel (1898-1937). Cousin of Lev. Became military advisor to China in the 1920s. Shot in 1937.

Reisner, Larisa (1895-1926). Writer who also did political work at the front during the Civil War.

Repin, Ilya (1844-1930). Russian realist artist known for his historical genre paintings and portraits of historical figures.

Ribbentrop, Joachim von (1893-1946). German diplomat, foreign minister from 1933-45, and chief negotiator of the German-Soviet Non-aggression Pact of 1939, which enabled Hitler to attack Poland.

Rokossovsky, Konstantin (1896-1968). Polish-born Soviet marshal and war hero of World War II. He later became minister of defense of Poland, then deputy minister of defense of the USSR (1958-62).

Rudzutak, Yan (1887-1938). Party worker. Member of Politburo and Central Committee. Arrested in the purges in 1937.

Rykov, Alexei (1881-1938). Early Party activist who held various important posts after the revolution. Succeeded Lenin as Prime Minister. A political ally of Bukharin, he was tried along with him in 1938 and executed.

Saltykov-Shchedrin, Mikhail (1826-1889). Russia's great satirical writer, whose most famous work is *The Golovlyov Family.*

Schiller, Friedrich (1759-1805). German dramatist, poet and essayist, best known for his great historical dramas.

Shaposhnikov, Boris (1882-1945). Army commander, military strategist and Marshal of the Soviet Union. Served on the court which tried Tukhachevsky and other military leaders.

Shkvarkin,Vasily (1894-1968). A popular dramatist of the time. Shkvarkin was a pseudonym.

Shvernik, Nikolai (1888-1970). Bolshevik activist, fought in the revolution. Became Party secretary in the Urals. Promoted to the Politburo in 1939 along with Beria.

Sienkiewicz, Henryk (1846-1916). Polish novelist, short-story writer and journalist who won the Nobel Prize in 1905. Known especially for his historical novels.

Sikorski, Wladyslaw (1881-1943). Polish soldier and statesman who became the head of the Polish government in exile in London during World War II.

Slavin, Lev. (1896-1984). Novelist and playwright.

Slutsky, Boris (1919-1986). Soviet poet. He was a political officer in World War II. In the 1950s he won recognition for his poems about the war.

Speransky, Alexei (1887-1961). Pathologist. Member of Academy of Sciences.

Sobko, Vadim (1912-1981). Ukrainian novelist, short-story writer and playwright.

Solovyov, Vladmir (1853-1900). Russian poet, philosopher, teacher. He was an important influence on Russian symbolist literature and thought.

Solzhenitsyn, Alexander (1918-   ). Writer who became known throughout the world for his work about Soviet camps. He was first arrested in 1945, served for 8 years in a special prison, then was sent into exile until 1956. His *One Day in the Life of Ivan Denisovich*, set in Kazakhstan, brought him fame. But it was his 3-volume survey of the forced labor camps, *Arkhipelag GULag, 1918-1956,* which gave him international fame and led to his deportation to the West. Solzhenitsyn has now returned to Russia.

Somov, Konstantin (1869-1939). Russian artist from St. Petersburg who belonged to the group of artists associated with the *World of Art* magazine. Emigrated in 1923.

Stolypin, Pyotr (1862-1911). Conservative statesman who became Minister of the Interior in 1906. He carried out agrarian reforms but was also responsible for the arrest and persecution of his political opponents. He was shot in 1911 by the double agent Dmitry Bogrov.

Stalin, Joseph (Joseph Djugashvili) (1879-1953). Bolshevik from Georgia who became head of the Communist Party of the USSR after Lenin's death and ruled the Soviet Union as an absolute dictator from the late 1920s until his death.

Sverdlov, Iakov (1885-1919). Revolutionary. Party member from 1901. Chairman of the Russian Central Executive Committee of the RSFSR.

Tarle, Yevgeny (1875-1955). Russian historian, specialist in French history, author of essays on the French Revolution and the Napoleonic era.

Tolstoy, Alexei (1883-1945). Popular Soviet novelist, especially known for his historical novel *Peter the First* and a trilogy about the Revolution, *Road to Calvary.*

Tolstoy, Lev (1828-1910). Russian writer, known throughout the world for his major novels *War and Peace* and *Anna Karenina* and for his other short novels, stories and religious and philosophical writings.

Trotsky, Leon (Lev Bronstein, 1879-1940). Bolshevik theorist and activist who was a leader of the October 1917 Revolution and later Commissar of Foreign Affairs and War and also Stalin's chief rival. Trotsky successfully built up the Red Army during the Civil

War, but lost to Stalin in the power struggle that followed Lenin's death. Sent into exile where he continued to oppose Stalin until his assassination in Mexico.

Tsypin, Grigory (1899-1938). Head of Detgiz, publisher of children's books. Arrested in 1937.

Tukhachevsky, Mikhail (1893-1937). Soviet military leader who was executed along with other members of the Soviet High Command during the purges. Tukhachevsky had been a commander in the Civil War, a leader of the Russian offensive in the Russo-Polish War of 1919-20, deputy commissar for military and naval affairs. and a marshal of the USSR before his arrest.

Tupolev, Andrei (1888-1972). One of the Soviet Union's greatest aircraft desigers. Creator of the world's first supersonic passenger plane. Arrested in 1938 but released in 1943, he became a lieutenant general in the Soviet Army. He directed the design and construction of many types of military and passenger planes.

Tyutchev, Fyodor (1803-71). Russian poet who lived for many years in Germany and was influenced by German romanticism. Wrote lyrical and philosophical poems.

Vasilevsky, Alexander (1895-1977). Head of General Staff.

Voroshilov, Marshal Klementy (1881-1969). Red officer in Civil War. Member of Central Committee. Commissar of military and naval affairs.

Vyrubova, Anna (1884-1929?). Aide to Empress Alexandra from 1904, a go-between between the imperial family and Rasputin. Emigrated in 1920.

Vyshinsky, Andrei (1883-1954). Soviet statesman, diplomat, and lawyer who was the chief prosecutor in the purge trials in the 30s. He later became foreign minister (1949-53) and then representative to the United Nations.

Yagoda, Genrikh (1891-1938). Soviet chief of security police (NKVD) from 1934-36. He helped to organize the purges but became a victim himself in 1938 and was executed.

Yezhov, Nikolai (1894-1939?). Chief of the security police (NKVD) from 1936-38. Administered the purges during their worst period, which became known as the *Yezhovshchina*.

Yenukidze, Avel (1877-1937). Friend and political collaborator of Stalin.

Yudenich, Nikolai (1862-1933). Military commander who served in the imperial army, bacame a general in 1905 and commanded troops in the Caucasus during World War I. He left Russia when the Bolsheviks took power but returned to command White army forces during the Civil War. When his army lost he fled to France where he died in exile.

Zdrodovsky, Pavel (1890-1976). Epidemiologist. Arrested 1937.

Zhdanov, Andrei (1896-1948). Government figure and Party activist who was a close associate of Stalin. After World War II he carried out a restrictive, anti-Western cultural policy and attacked various figures, such as Shostakovich and Akhmatova, for art that was politically incorrect.

Zinoviev, Grigory (1883-1936). Bolshevik revolutionary who was an associate of Lenin before the revolution and became a central figure in the Party in the 1920s. After Lenin's death, he formed a coalition with Stalin and Kamenev against Trotsky, but was later pushed out of the Party power centers by Stalin. In 1935 he was arrested and sentenced to ten years imprisonment. The following year he was publicly tried, then shot; rehabilitated in 1988.